MW00527945

A Gallant Defense

A Gallant Defense

The Siege of Charleston, 1780

Carl P. Borick

University of South Carolina Press

Published in Columbia, South Carolina, by the
University of South Carolina Press

Manufactured in the United States of America

07 06 05 04 03 5 4 3 2

Library of Congress Cataloging-in-Publication Data

Borick, Carl P., 1966–
A gallant defense : the Siege of Charleston, 1780 / Carl P. Borick.
p. cm.
Includes bibliographical references and index.
ISBN 1-57003-487-7 (alk. paper)
1. Charleston (S.C.)—History—Siege, 1780. I. Title.
E241.C4 B67 2003
973.3'36—dc21 2002013378

In memory of the hundreds of American, British, and Hessian soldiers who lie in unmarked graves throughout the South Carolina lowcountry

CONTENTS

Illustrations

Maps

Figures *following page 160*

Preface

On the afternoon of 26 December 1779, from his post in the hills of eastern New Jersey, Brigadier General Anthony Wayne of the Continental line watched through his spyglass as an immense fleet of British ships cleared Sandy Hook and then disappeared below the horizon. Wayne counted 106 vessels in the fleet; it was one of the largest that the British had assembled in almost five years of war. Although he could only conjecture on the number of troops onboard, the transports of the fleet in actuality contained over seven thousand British and Hessian troops led by Lieutenant General Sir Henry Clinton, the commander in chief of British armies in America. While Wayne could not determine the size of the land force, nor could he know for sure who commanded them, one thing was certain: this armada was not embarking on a raid or small-scale operation. Clearly something more ominous was in store for the Americans. New York, from where the British fleet sailed, and New Jersey, from where Anthony Wayne observed their departure, had been the primary seat of war for the previous three and a half years. But the ships disappearing into the Atlantic signaled a sea change in British strategy, one that would embroil them in an attempt to suppress the rebellion in the south and that would eventually lead them to Yorktown and the loss of America.

The destination of the British force was Charleston, South Carolina. British military and political leaders asserted that the capture of Charles Town (the city did not become Charleston until its incorporation in 1783) would not only strike a blow at the rebels by occupying the most important city and port in the southern colonies, but would also provide a springboard from which they could subjugate the entire south. Underlying the commitment to this new southern strategy was the notion that multitudes of loyalists in the southern colonies would throw off the yoke their rebellious and tyrannical neighbors had imposed upon them and rush to the assistance of their liberators. British commanders anticipated that swarms of able-bodied loyalists would help them secure and maintain the peace for the Crown.

This work is about the British campaign against Charleston and the American response to that campaign. Traditionally, historians have referred to the siege of Charleston as a single event without recognizing that the British attempt to take Charleston and the army defending it was a campaign, one which consumed several months and ranged over fifty miles of the South Carolina lowcountry. It is a campaign that historians have underappreciated, often relegating it to a chapter or less in general accounts of the war in the south. Other than William Thomas Bulger's 1957 University of Michigan dissertation, no other thorough examination of the subject has ever been proffered. The siege of Charleston was one of the critical points in the military history of the American Revolution, and it deserves greater attention. Not only was it the longest formal siege of the American Revolution, but also it was the largest single British effort in South Carolina. Moreover, British operations against Charleston in 1780 launched their attempt to end the rebellion by subjugating the southern colonies, an effort which succeeded at the outset but which ultimately ended in disaster. A study of the Charleston campaign highlights the many difficulties that the Americans faced in attempting to survive as a new nation and that the British encountered in endeavoring to subdue a rebellion in the midst of a world war. The work demonstrates how interservice cooperation on the British side and political considerations on the American could negatively influence operations and make military success uncertain. Without question, the outcome of the campaign against Charleston was uncertain for both sides until its conclusion.

This work also examines the civilian cost, underscoring the hardships that the Charleston campaign imposed on the inhabitants of the South Carolina lowcountry. While both armies had an impact on civilians, British attitudes and actions toward them which emerged during the Charleston campaign served as a harbinger of things to come. The contradiction between the policies of British officers and the conduct of British soldiers and sailors toward civilians in the course of the campaign revealed a dichotomy that ultimately made it difficult for British military leaders to win over the people of the southern states. British behavior in the South Carolina lowcountry, and later the backcountry, gave them the character of an invading army, one to be resisted rather than welcomed. This persona was to have far-reaching consequences.

Much of the story of the campaign against Charleston is told through the words of the soldiers and civilians who experienced it. Accordingly, when quoting from original manuscript sources, I have retained the idiosyncratic capitalization and spelling of their letters and journals. Eighteenth-century prose often made use of a baseline dash where a comma, semicolon, period, or question mark was appropriate. In these cases I have employed the proper punctuation. Similarly, superscript letters have been made consistent with the rest of the text.

Acknowledgments

I am indebted to so many people for the completion of this work that it is impossible to list them all. I should begin with the staff of the Charleston Museum. If it were not for that institution and the wonderful employees there, I probably would not have been able to write this book. Brien Varnado, the museum's former assistant director, encouraged me on this project from day one. So many times when I became frustrated with research or writing, he was there to prod me to continue on. Although not a military historian, he showed enthusiasm and interest in the topic throughout our discussions of it. John Brumgardt, director of the Charleston Museum, also provided encouragement and vigorously promoted the manuscript to board members and museum patrons. I thank the Board of Trustees for their support of both the Charleston Museum and my book.

Sharon Bennett and Julia Logan of the Charleston Museum Archives helped me to locate endless documents, illustrations, and maps at other institutions. Other staff continuously asked how things were coming along. To have worked at the Charleston Museum, which is only a few hundred feet from where many of the major events of the siege took place, at the same time that I was composing the manuscript was inspiration in itself.

Lawrence F. Kohl at the University of Alabama was also influential in the publication of this book. He kindly read the first draft and offered many useful suggestions to improve it. He was an excellent mentor when I was in graduate school and is now a good friend.

I am equally indebted to other reviewers. Don Higginbotham, whose work I have always admired, also agreed to read the manuscript. His favorable opinion helped move the project along at a critical point. I must also thank the reviewers who read the manuscript for USC Press. Their suggestions and comments vastly enhanced it. In addition, I need to mention Robert Tinkler for his assistance in the process.

I owe a debt of gratitude to James Taylor and Peggy Clark of The Papers of Henry Laurens project at the University of South Carolina. Dr. Taylor allowed me to review volume fifteen of *The Papers of Henry Laurens* prior to its release; he also directed me to other unpublished Laurens documents.

The staffs of many institutions deserve thanks. Here in Charleston, the South Carolina Historical Society, Charleston Library Society, and Charleston County Public Library provided great resources and comfortable facilities for research. The collections of the Historical Society house several important manuscripts relating to the siege of Charleston, and staff there were very accommodating during my frequent visits. The Charleston Library Society, a true gem in the city, offered excellent primary and secondary sources. Charleston County Public Library's interlibrary loan department assiduously found every obscure work I was looking for, while personnel in the South Carolina Room and Periodicals department also rendered tremendous assistance.

Other people and institutions were instrumental along the way. The South Carolina Department of Archives and History is a first-rate place to do research, providing both original documents and a number of collections relating to the American Revolution on microfilm. Staff at the William L. Clements Library of the University of Michigan were very helpful, particularly John C. Harriman and Barbara DeWolfe. I must also thank all those who assisted me at the Boston Public Library, the Houghton Library at Harvard University, the Massachusetts Historical Society, New York Public Library, Morristown National Historical Park, the Rhode Island Historical Society, and the South Caroliniana Library at the University of South Carolina. Special thanks go to my good friend Matt Grubel at Morristown for helping me to gain perspective over the years through our many discussions of the military events of the American Revolution.

I am also grateful to those who assisted in the production process. Alexander Moore at USC Press expressed interest in my work early on and provided needed encouragement. Judy Burress was both timely and efficient in the production of the maps. She was also very patient with my many changes.

I wish to thank the following for permission to quote from previously published and documentary sources: the University of Georgia Press for passages from the Lachlan McIntosh Papers in the University of Georgia Library, edited by Lilla Mills Hawes; the University of Michigan Press for passages from *The Siege of Charleston with an Account of the Province of South Carolina,* by Bernhard A. Uhlendorf; and the South Caroliniana Library of the University of South Carolina for passages from six unpublished letters contained in the Henry W. Kendall Collection of the Papers of Henry Laurens.

Finally, I mention the person most responsible for the completion of this work: my wife Susan. She is more familiar with this work than anyone, having answered hundreds of questions from sentence structure to content. Her love inspired me to keep going and never give up. It is to her that I truly owe this book.

A Gallant Defense

Chapter One

Early Threats

The decision of the British high command to attack Charleston and shift their strategic focus in America to the southern colonies had its roots in the earlier operations of the conflict, specifically in the British failures. At the outset of the revolt, few on the British side anticipated that it would take long to subdue the rebels. But spirited resistance in the first year of the war, in the form of a blockade of the British army at Boston and a full-fledged invasion of Canada, convinced British commanders that they would have to make a substantial commitment of land and sea forces to end the rebellion.

After spending the first year of the war on the defensive, the British amassed an army of 32,000 men and a fleet of seventy-three warships for the campaign of 1776. Among these troops was a contingent of German mercenaries, or Hessians. The British ministry recognized that their peacetime military establishment was inadequate to both conduct offensive operations in America and protect their far-flung empire, so they contracted with several German principalities to provide soldiers to augment their forces.[1]

In operations around New York City in the late summer and fall of 1776, General William Howe's British and Hessian troops outfought and outmaneuvered General George Washington's inexperienced and inadequately trained army. Howe defeated the Americans in several battles, captured New York City, and forced Washington to retreat across New Jersey and into Pennsylvania. Although battlefield losses, desertions, and expiring enlistments in the course of the campaign reduced the number of troops serving with Washington, Howe failed to destroy the rebel army. While the British general established a series of scattered posts throughout New Jersey and went into winter quarters, Washington recrossed the Delaware River and attacked the

Hessian garrison at Trenton, New Jersey. He later defeated a British detachment posted at Princeton. These American victories compelled Howe to consolidate his troops in eastern New Jersey and around New York City to ensure their safety. More importantly, the survival of the rebels' military capacity meant the Revolution would continue.

In 1777, the British employed two armies against the Americans. General Howe directed his attention toward Washington's army and the capture of the rebel capital at Philadelphia, while General John Burgoyne marched down from Canada with the intention of driving to Albany. Burgoyne's plan called for Howe to send a force north from New York City to link up with him at Albany; another corps under Lieutenant Colonel Barry St. Leger advanced upon Albany from the west. The British ministry and commanders believed that the campaign to Albany would give them control of the Hudson River and allow them to isolate the populous and particularly rebellious and obstinate New England colonies from the rest.[2]

In operations around Philadelphia, Howe again enjoyed great success against the Americans. He defeated Washington at the battle of Brandywine on 11 September, and then outmaneuvered him to capture Philadelphia on 25 September, forcing the Continental Congress to flee the city. Washington's surprise attack on Howe's army at Germantown on 4 October resulted in another loss for the Americans. Although victorious in two major battles and in possession of the rebel capital, Howe again failed to destroy Washington's army. Nor did he send troops to assist Burgoyne. Unsupported by Howe, Burgoyne's army met with disaster in the wilderness of northern New York.

At the outset, Burgoyne's expedition achieved some success. In early July his army took possession of Fort Ticonderoga, considered one of the most secure fortresses in North America. As the summer progressed, however, his campaign unraveled. At the battle of Bennington on 16 August, American militia routed a detachment of Hessians and loyalists while Brigadier General Benedict Arnold turned back St. Leger's force that approached Albany from the west. Without assistance from the southward, and running low on provisions, Burgoyne fought two costly battles against the army of Major General Horatio Gates. Failing to dislodge the Americans, he retreated toward

Canada. Ultimately, Gates compelled Burgoyne and his army to surrender at Saratoga on 17 October. The Americans had gained their most important victory to date.

If the campaign of 1776 was a disappointment for the British, the campaign of 1777 was a disaster. Next to the loss of Burgoyne's army, Howe's capture of Philadelphia rang as a hollow victory. The rebel Congress merely fled the city and reestablished themselves at York, Pennsylvania. Moreover, Washington's army still existed as an effective military force. The window of opportunity to subdue the rebellion was closing for the British. The events of 1777 reached across an ocean and changed the course of the American Revolution.

The French, engaged in a global struggle for empire with the English since the end of the seventeenth century, had been keeping a keen eye on events in America since the commencement of hostilities. The rebellion in America presented them an opportunity to strike a blow at their longtime enemy. Almost from the beginning of the war, France secretly supplied the rebels with arms and other military necessities. After independence was declared in 1776, the Continental Congress sent a delegation to France to seek a formal alliance. The French leaders' reception of the American diplomats was initially cool, but news of the victory over Burgoyne's army, coupled with a spirit of revenge among the French, made the rebellious Americans' dream of an alliance a reality. Not only did France recognize the independence of the United States, but she also agreed to lend direct military assistance to the Americans. Under such circumstances, Great Britain had no choice but to declare war on her old adversary.[3]

The entrance of France into the conflict in 1778 drastically altered the nature of the war for the British. Now facing their chief European rival across the globe, the British ministry could no longer devote the scale of resources to the war in America as they had in 1776 and 1777. British interests in the West Indies, the Mediterranean, and India took precedence over events in the American theatre, which became something of a backwater in the global struggle. As Sir Henry Clinton later pointed out, when the ministry determined "that France had decidedly joined the Americans," they "relinquished all thoughts of reducing the rebellious colonies by force of arms, and to have determined to trust the decision of the quarrel to negotiation, that the collected strength of the realm might be more at liberty to act against this new enemy."[4]

The importance of the French fleet in this new phase of the war cannot be overemphasized. Previously, the Royal Navy held free reign in American waters. Control of the sea in the first three years of the war gave them superiority of mobility over the rebels. British transports, under the protection of warships, moved troops anywhere along the American coast with impunity, opposed only by privateers and the few ships of the Continental and state navies. The Royal Navy still possessed that mobility in the wake of the French alliance, but British generals and admirals recognized that major movements of the fleet required an absolute intelligence of the location of the French navy. They had to conduct operations along the coast with extreme caution due to the possibility that French ships might suddenly appear on the horizon. A major defeat to France might not only result in the loss of America, but could also injure Britain's standing in the European balance of power. The French navy's impact on events in America was almost immediate. Recognizing that their army in Philadelphia was vulnerable to a French fleet sailing up the Delaware River to trap them there, the British high command elected to evacuate the city and send the army back to its base at New York.[5]

Although France's entrance into the war drew British attention to other areas of the globe, the King and his ministry were still committed to subduing the rebels and restoring the colonies to their former allegiance. With military resources for operations in America stretched thin, the British ministry and military commanders sought other ways to end the rebellion. As an answer to their manpower shortage, the British, from 1778 on, came to rely increasingly on the loyalists.[6]

From the outset of the conflict in America, British military and political leaders believed that the rebellion was the creation of a few firebrands and that the majority of the population was still loyal to the King. They assumed that the rebellion only survived because the rebels, in seizing control of the colonial assemblies and in making frequent use of mob violence, had cowed those still loyal into submission. Meanwhile, the royal governors of Virginia, North Carolina, and South Carolina, and lesser royal officials, convinced British leaders that the loyalist presence was particularly strong in the southern colonies. Reports of numbers of loyalists in the south, coupled with the obstinacy that rebels in the northern states had shown in the first three years of the war, inspired the British to shift the focus of their operations to the southern colonies in 1778.[7]

The prospect of loyalist strength in America particularly impressed Lord George Germain. As Secretary of State for the American Colonies, or American Department, Germain was responsible for executing the decisions of the ministry and for communicating the wishes of king and cabinet to the commanders in America. In March 1778, Germain began to urge Sir Henry Clinton, who was to replace Howe as commander in chief of British land forces in America, to undertake an operation to the southward. "It is the King's intention that an attack should be made upon the Southern Colonies," he informed Clinton, "with a view to the conquest and possession of Georgia and South Carolina."[8]

Economic considerations also underlay the British decision to shift their strategic focus southward. In August 1777, the governors and lieutenant governors of South Carolina and Georgia addressed a memorial to Germain in which they stressed the economic importance of the southern colonies. According to the royal officials, destruction of the rebels' "trade in tobacco, rice, indigo, and deerskins" would deny them the means to resist. Sir Henry Clinton agreed; he later remarked that "the southern provinces . . . were alone capable of furnishing the means of purchasing the necessary supplies for the war, their staple produce being the only wealth the Americans had to carry to European markets." Lord George Germain also contended that the trade of the southern colonies "furnished the Congress with the chief means of purchasing supplies for carrying on the war." Royal officials persuaded British leaders that operations in the south would not only bring loyalists to the fore, but would also injure the northern colonies by cutting off the rebels' source of economic power. That British commanders overlooked the importance of northern grain and ports such as Boston and Philadelphia in the overall economic picture is an indication of how shortsighted they could be when presented with a solution that seemed to resolve their strategic dilemma.[9]

Sir Henry Clinton's only previous foray into the southern colonies had been far from successful. Clinton and Commodore Peter Parker led an expedition to the southward in the spring of 1776. Originally intending to support the loyalists of North Carolina, Clinton and Parker abandoned the idea when they discovered that a large force of North Carolina loyalists had gathered, but the rebels had soundly defeated and dispersed them in February at the battle of Moore's Creek Bridge. The British commanders then decided to move on to South Carolina. Clinton hoped to establish a base in South Carolina where loyalists of the province could seek refuge. He settled upon Sullivan's Island, a small sea island guarding the entrance to Charleston's harbor.[10]

South Carolinians had erected a fort of palmetto logs and sand at the southern tip of Sullivan's Island. The fort was unfinished at the time of the British assault, and Major General Charles Lee, whom the Continental Congress sent to oversee the defense of Charleston, called it a slaughter pen.[11] Clinton landed his troops on Long Island (now the Isle of Palms) on 16 June. The British plan entailed sending troops across Breach Inlet to the northern end of Sullivan's Island while the guns of Parker's ships hammered the fort from the sea. When the naval assault commenced on the morning of 28 June, the spongy palmetto logs of the fort's walls absorbed the shock of solid shot fired from British warships while the fort's guns inflicted serious damage on the attacking vessels. In the meantime, American troops posted on the northern end of Sullivan's Island and the depth of Breach Inlet prevented Clinton's soldiers from crossing over from Long Island. British losses were heavy: British sailors had to destroy the frigate *Actaeon,* which ran aground during the action, and Parker's crews suffered over 200 men killed and wounded; Commodore Parker was himself among the wounded. With their efforts thwarted, Clinton and Parker reembarked the troops and sailed for New York several weeks later. Charleston had survived its first attack by British land and naval forces.[12]

South Carolinians rejoiced in their victory over the British invaders, and patriotic fervor in the rebellious province soared. Indeed, they had repulsed a British fleet and army but British operations against

Sullivan's Island had been haphazard and mismanaged. This first southern expedition left the bitter taste of defeat with Henry Clinton and gave the people of South Carolina a sense of overconfidence in their ability to repel future incursions.[13]

Neither the defeat of the loyalists in North Carolina at Moore's Creek Bridge nor the repulse at Sullivan's Island dimmed British notions of loyalist strength in the southern colonies. If anything, the gathering of the North Carolinians demonstrated that southern loyalists possessed both the ability and will to organize and assist British forces. The disaster at Sullivan's Island was merely a military setback. While the defeat may have prevented South Carolina loyalists from coming forth, it did not destroy loyalist sentiment, and royal officials continued to assert that men in the southern provinces were ready to aid the British in the subjugation of the rebellion.[14]

In the fall of 1778, Clinton initiated the next phase of British operations in the south when he detached Lieutenant Colonel Archibald Campbell with 3,000 British and Hessian troops from New York to Georgia. Clinton instructed Campbell to "attempt the reduction of Georgia" and cooperate with Brigadier General Augustine Prevost who commanded British forces in East Florida.[15]

Campbell's troops attacked Savannah on 28 December 1778 and easily overwhelmed the outnumbered and unprepared Americans under Major General Robert Howe, the commander of the Southern Department. When General Prevost arrived shortly thereafter from East Florida, the British had over 4,000 men in Georgia. Prevost and Campbell commenced efforts to encourage the loyalists and bring the citizens of Georgia back into the fold. They issued proclamations which invited the people to assist in the suppression of the rebellion and promised the protection of the Crown to all who declared their loyalty.[16]

Campbell marched a body of troops up the Savannah River and captured Augusta on 31 January 1779. Although they suffered a setback when patriot militia under Colonel Andrew Pickens ambushed and routed a force of loyal North Carolina militia on their way to join the King's army, by the spring of 1779 the British had secured a foothold in the Georgia backcountry. It would be up to the new commander of the Southern Department to drive them from the state.[17]

On 3 January 1779, Major General Benjamin Lincoln took over command of the Southern Department from Robert Howe at Purysburg, South Carolina. As commander of the Southern Department, Lincoln was to oversee operations in Virginia, the Carolinas, and Georgia.[18] The Continental Congress selected Lincoln to replace Howe on 26 September 1778, but it had taken the Massachusetts general several months to get his affairs in order and then make the long overland trek to South Carolina. Lincoln possessed extensive military experience, especially in the areas of logistics, planning, and organization. He served in the French and Indian War as adjutant of the Third Suffolk regiment, and in that capacity was responsible for recruiting, training, and procurement for the regiment. He later helped the Massachusetts provincial government obtain supplies for the army that surrounded the British in Boston in 1775. Appointed a major general of Massachusetts militia in May 1776, he commanded that state's militia in the campaign around New York the following summer and fall. In the New York campaign, Lincoln gained the admiration of General Washington, who entertained "a very high opinion" of Lincoln's "judgement and abilities." The Continental Congress also appreciated his talents, inasmuch as they commissioned him a major general in the Continental army in February 1777. Because of Lincoln's influence with the Massachusetts militia, Washington sent him to upstate New York in the summer of 1777 to assist in the defense against Burgoyne's invasion. Along with Gates, Benedict Arnold, and Daniel Morgan, Lincoln was instrumental in stopping Burgoyne's army and forcing his surrender. Unfortunately for Lincoln, before the campaign against Burgoyne concluded he was seriously wounded in the right ankle by a British musket ball. General Gates lamented that Lincoln's wounding deprived him of one of his best officers. Army surgeons removed splintered pieces of bone from Lincoln's ankle, an operation which must have been excruciatingly painful for the New England general. The wound caused Lincoln to walk with a limp for the rest of his life. In terms of strategic insight, battlefield experience, and physical sacrifice, Lincoln had proven his mettle.[19]

The Continental Congress noted other qualities in Lincoln besides his valuable military experience. The southern command required a man with considerable patience and moral strength, who could lead and organize militia and cooperate diplomatically with southerners. Certainly, Lincoln had demonstrated these attributes but there was yet another reason for selecting Lincoln: in doing so the delegates hoped to tie southern interests to northern. According to a recent Lincoln biographer, this made Lincoln an ideal choice, since he was fiercely loyal to the concept of a United States and believed that a "breakup of the union would be a catastrophe." By placing a Massachusetts general in overall military command in the southern states, Congress followed a course similar to that taken in 1775 when they appointed George Washington, a Virginian, to lead the Continental army then comprised almost exclusively of New Englanders. Coincidentally, Lincoln assumed his new duties at the same time that the British were shifting their strategic focus to the southern provinces. By the time Lincoln reached Purysburg, British operations in the south were already underway.[20]

Lincoln's force at Purysburg numbered approximately 3,600 men, less than a third of which were Continentals. As in the north, American forces in the southern states were comprised of two different types: Continental army regulars and generally short-term and less-experienced militia. Brigadier General William Moultrie, Lincoln's second in command after Robert Howe's departure, stressed to the South Carolina authorities the importance of relying on Continental regulars rather than militia. He emphasized "the necessity of filling our [Continental] battalions" to Charles Pinckney, president of the South Carolina Senate. Moultrie later asserted to Pinckney that he saw "a large, severe, and serious piece of business" before them and that they "should have as many disciplined troops as possible" to face the British. Moultrie and other Continental army officers understood that the militia were a ready source of manpower in an emergency, but in general they could not stand up to British regulars on equal terms on the battlefield.[21]

Unreliable as they might be, patriot militia swelled the ranks of Lincoln's army after Pickens's defeat of the loyalists at Kettle Creek. By the beginning of April 1779, Lincoln had approximately 5,000 men in South Carolina, giving him enough of an advantage over the British army under Prevost to undertake offensive operations against them in Georgia. Lincoln planned to march up the north side of the Savannah River, cross over to Augusta, and threaten the British hold on the Georgia backcountry. Originally, he intended to leave 1,000 men each at Purysburg and Black Swamp to defend against a British incursion into South Carolina, but ultimately he opted to strengthen his Georgia force at the expense of these detachments. He left just over 1,200 men under General Moultrie at Black Swamp and Purysburg. Lincoln arrived at Augusta on 22 April and prepared to move into the Georgia backcountry. His strategic decisions during this campaign were to have far-reaching consequences not only in the coming months, but also for future operations against the British in South Carolina.[22]

Rather than engage Lincoln in the Georgia backcountry, Prevost, in a classic display of generalship, crossed the Savannah River at Purysburg and drove toward Charleston. Lincoln had planned for such a move, but in reducing the number of men left to guard the lower part of South Carolina he did not expect it. Each general was taking a serious gamble. Lincoln was going on the offensive and attempting to recover Georgia from the British, but he did so at the risk of leaving South Carolina exposed. Prevost was turning his back on the defense of Georgia in the hope that his incursion into South Carolina would draw Lincoln out of Georgia. Ultimately, Prevost raised the stakes by marching on the South Carolina capital. He pursued the larger payoff.

Prevost crossed the Savannah with an army of approximately 3,000 men on 29 April. Moultrie hurried off a letter to Lincoln informing him of the British movement then fell back with his troops toward Charleston. The Americans destroyed bridges over the rivers along their route to impede the British advance. Despite their efforts, on the day before he arrived at Charleston Moultrie was only four miles ahead of Prevost.[23]

While the Americans had been improving the defensive works before Charleston since March and had placed cannon on the lines, the city was ill-prepared psychologically for an attack. Upon reaching Charleston on 7 May, Moultrie found the town in chaos. He reported to Lincoln that "there is a strange consternation in town: people frightened out of their wits." Moultrie experienced this type of panic among his own soldiers. Many resided in the area through which the British were marching and they left the ranks to tend to their families and property. Still, with approximately 3,000 troops in Charleston (many militia had flocked to the city), Moultrie was confident that their numbers were sufficient to make a stand, especially since the men were entrenched behind fortifications. Moultrie also expected the assistance of Lincoln. Since leaving his camp at Black Swamp, he had written Lincoln several times apprising him of British movements and entreating him to return to South Carolina. Finally convinced of the seriousness of the British threat, Lincoln wrote Moultrie on 6 May that his army was on the way back to Charleston. Lincoln, however, was still almost a week's march away.[24]

Meanwhile, Prevost's advanced guard crossed the Ashley River and arrived before the town on 10 May. Moultrie believed that they could hold off the British until Lincoln arrived on the scene. Unfortunately, the fear that gripped the people of Charleston worked against him. In the predawn hours of 11 May, Governor John Rutledge sought out Moultrie as he was inspecting the lines and asked him whether they should seek a parley with the British. Rutledge had received accounts that the British force numbered between seven and eight thousand men and he suggested that the garrison was too weak to hold out against them. Despite Moultrie's arguments to the contrary concerning the size of the British army, the governor proposed that they send out a flag of truce to General Prevost to determine what terms he would grant to the soldiers and civilians of Charleston if the town surrendered. Reluctantly, Moultrie agreed to do so, but only if the governor's Privy Council consented. Moultrie preferred that they not send the flag in his name.[25]

Typically in eighteenth century warfare, when an attacking army surrounded a fort or fortified city, the garrison could ask for "terms" of surrender or capitulation from them. Rather than risk a storm by the attacking force or an extended siege in which both soldiers and civilians might be killed, the garrison surrendered themselves prisoners of war in hopes of receiving lenient treatment. If the defense of the besieged city or fort was lengthy or particularly heroic, or if the attacking force was hard-pressed to end the siege, they might obtain more favorable terms. For example, the besieging army might allow the garrison's soldiers to return to their homes or native country as prisoners of war on parole rather than physically detaining them.[26] Prisoners on parole gave their word that they would remain out of action until exchanged, thus avoiding the horrors of prison camps or prison ships.

Upon receiving the request for terms from the Charleston garrison, General Prevost informed them that he would regard as prisoners of war those "inhabitants" who did not choose to accept his "generous offers of peace and protection." By "peace and protection," Prevost meant that they must declare themselves loyal to the Crown. He reminded the garrison of the "horrors attending the event of a storm" and gave them four hours to respond. When Prevost's demands were received, Rutledge immediately met with the Privy Council, General Moultrie, and Moultrie's principal officers. Moultrie later related that Rutledge and the council discussed the prospect of "giving up the town amongst themselves." Moultrie, the Polish volunteer cavalryman Brigadier General Kasimir Pulaski, and Lieutenant Colonel John Laurens vehemently resisted this course of action. Moultrie represented to Rutledge that they had 3,180 men in the lines and that the best estimates of British strength were only 3,600. Any advantage the British possessed in numbers was offset by the fact that the Americans were protected by entrenchments. Not swayed, the governor and five of the eight members of the Privy Council decided to offer the following response to Prevost: "To propose a neutrality, during the war between Great-Britain and America, and the question, whether the state shall belong to Great Britain, or remain one of the United States . . . be determined by the treaty of peace between those two powers." Essentially, the executive of South Carolina and Privy Council were offering to keep South Carolina out of the war in exchange for the safety of Charleston and its garrison. That Moultrie and his officers were opposed to this proposal is an understatement. When Moultrie asked Lieutenant Colonel Laurens to deliver the message to the British, Laurens replied that he would do anything to serve his country, but he could not carry a message such as that. Ultimately, Moultrie had to order Lieutenant Colonel McIntosh and Lieutenant Colonel Roger Smith to convey it to Prevost.[27]

Ironically, Prevost's representative, his younger brother Lieutenant Colonel Marc Prevost, rejected the proposal, arguing that they were not authorized to act in a legislative capacity, only in a military one. The British officer again demanded that the garrison in arms surrender themselves prisoners of war. He further stated that their business was with General Moultrie as military commander and that they had nothing to do with the governor. When he received this message, General William Moultrie took charge. He announced to Rutledge and the Privy Council that he was "determined not to deliver [them] up prisoners of war," and added, "we will fight it out." Unknowingly, the British officers may have prevented the capture of the town and garrison by insisting that they treat only with General Moultrie. Moultrie informed the British that negotiations were at an end. They would defend the city.[28]

At daybreak on 13 May 1779, the citizens and soldiers of Charleston discovered that the British troops had stolen away in the night. Moultrie had called Prevost's bluff. Realizing that the arrival of Lincoln from Georgia would catch him between two armies, Prevost operated on borrowed time in his negotiations with the Charleston garrison. When he intercepted a letter from Lincoln to Moultrie confirming Lincoln's return, Prevost had no choice but to retreat. More than likely he thought his force insufficient to take the town, but he gambled in his dealings with the South Carolina authorities in the same way he gambled in crossing the Savannah and moving against Charleston. Thanks to Moultrie's assertiveness and leadership, Prevost finally folded before Charleston. He had not lost, however. In drawing Lincoln out of Georgia and foiling American efforts at reconquest of that province, Prevost's push toward Charleston had exactly the effect that he hoped it would.[29]

The actions of Rutledge and the Privy Council seem to indicate that South Carolina's allegiance to the new United States was uncertain. Only six men, Governor Rutledge and five members of the Privy Council, proposed the neutrality of South Carolina in exchange for the town. Although Rutledge represented the people of South Carolina, it was the people who really mattered. As Moultrie pointed out, "the citizens . . . knew nothing of what was going forward in the council: they all seemed firm, calm, and determined to stand to the lines and defend their country." Meanwhile, when *Rivington's Royal Gazette,* a loyalist newspaper published in New York, reported that Charleston had offered to capitulate in exchange for neutrality, *The Gazette of the State of South Carolina* countered that "THE PEOPLE *were entirely strangers to it, detesting the idea of a* NEUTRALITY; *and that, had a capitulation been offered, they would, nevertheless, have defended themselves to the last extremity, and finally, withdrawn with the Continental Troops*" (the *Gazette*'s italics). Even if Prevost had accepted the proposal, it is doubtful that backcountry South Carolinians would have honored such a truce. Prevost would have faced the same hornet's nest in the backcountry that other British officers later encountered. Rutledge believed he was acting in the best interest of the state, but most South Carolinians would have opposed the measure and continued to resist the British.[30]

Although Lincoln returned in time to rescue Charleston, his was a hollow victory. Not only had Prevost outfoxed him, forcing him to call off the Georgia operation, but soon after the British retreated Lincoln experienced the wrath of certain South Carolinians. Many Charlestonians criticized him for marching into Georgia with the main body of the southern army, leaving the city and surrounding area exposed and in "imminent danger." Dr. David Ramsay noted that there was "bitter exclamation against Congress and General Lincoln" due to the loss of property to the British army. "It appears, from the unkind declarations daily thrown out in your capital," Lincoln lamented to Moultrie, "that I have lost the confidence of the people . . . without which, I can render little service to the public." Several months earlier, Lincoln asked the Continental Congress for permission to resign, citing reasons of health. Congress granted his request, and when their answer was received in June on the heels of the recent fiasco, Lincoln was ready to follow through. In spite of being named as his temporary successor, Moultrie pleaded with Lincoln to stay and retain the command. Similarly, Governor Rutledge was adamant that Lincoln stay. Lincoln finally agreed to remain as commander of the Southern Department, but the events of the previous month were to have long-lasting effects. The next time Charleston was threatened Lincoln refused to abandon the city. Having always subordinated himself to civilian authority, he was acutely aware of public criticism and was inclined to modify his plans to conform to the will of the people. The British campaign against Charleston in the spring of 1779 had been a hard lesson in that conformity.[31]

Chapter Two

A "VERY ESSENTIAL BUSINESS" BEGINS

From his headquarters in New York City, Sir Henry Clinton expressed particular interest in events in the southern provinces in 1779. Prevost and Campbell's success in Georgia encouraged Clinton, but he realized that the British force was large enough only to hold Georgia and that Prevost's ability to undertake further offensive operations in South Carolina was limited. The British would require a more substantial army to make inroads in the south. The proceedings also inspired Lord George Germain. He wrote Clinton that "the feeble resistance Major General Prevost met with in his march and retreat through so great a part of South Carolina is an indisputable proof of the indisposition of the inhabitants to support the rebel government." Throughout 1778 and the first half of 1779, Germain continually pressed Clinton for a southern expedition, but Clinton vacillated. In Clinton's assessment, such a movement depended on two factors. First, he would not act until his army was adequately reinforced. He believed there were too few troops in America to defend the British bases at New York and Newport, Rhode Island, along with all of Canada, and simultaneously carry out offensive operations. Second, he wished to obtain definite information of the whereabouts and situation of the French fleet. The prospect of being immersed in operations along the coast and having a superior French fleet swoop down upon him frightened Clinton. Given his awareness of the outcry in London over Burgoyne's disastrous defeat, Clinton's hesitation was understandable. Yet, even in the absence of such retrospection, an examination of Sir Henry's character and personality demonstrates that the British commander would have proceeded with caution regardless of the circumstances.[1]

Henry Clinton was born into the aristocracy in 1730. His father, who rose to the rank of admiral in the Royal Navy, was the younger brother of the Earl of Lincoln. Ironically, Clinton spent several years of his boyhood in the American colonies. His father served in America from 1743 to 1751, and Admiral Clinton brought his family along with him to reside in New York. Following in the footsteps of his father, young Henry took up a military career but chose the army instead of the navy. He fought in Germany during the Seven Years' War, where he was wounded in battle, receiving a wound that, like Benjamin Lincoln's, caused him difficulty throughout his life. Clinton ascended steadily through the ranks of the British army, obtaining the rank of lieutenant general shortly after the outbreak of war in 1775.[2]

An examination of Sir Henry's conduct in the American Revolution sheds light on personality traits which help to define the man and the general. Clinton was a masterful planner, but he was often contentious in making his point about those plans to fellow officers. Quarrelsome to a fault, throughout his service in America he constantly feuded with both superior and subordinate officers. Still, Clinton's most overarching characteristic was his caution. As William Willcox explains, he "was obsessed by the need for avoiding a repulse." In the fall of 1777, Clinton attempted to assist Burgoyne when the latter's drive toward Albany faltered, but it was here that Clinton's caution was most overtly displayed. Anxious about leaving New York City weakly defended and uncertain whether his orders permitted a move up the Hudson, Clinton limited the scope of the operation to support Burgoyne. He escaped blame in the fiasco that followed, and his role in the affair did not prevent his appointment as commander in chief of British land forces in America in April 1778.[3]

When Clinton succeeded William Howe as commander in chief, he suffered the misfortune of doing so when the nature of the war on the North American continent was changing. With the American theater now a backwater in the larger global conflict with France, Clinton could not operate offensively as had Howe and Burgoyne. The British ministry not only provided him with fewer troops than General Howe, but they also from time to time ordered him to send reinforcements to other vulnerable posts such as the West Indies, Canada, or the Floridas. To undertake the type of expedition in the southern colonies that Lord Germain appealed for meant stretching all available resources.[4]

The need to strengthen other British posts delayed immediate follow-up to the success in Georgia. Having sent 5,000 men to the West Indies in mid-1778 and 2,000 men to Canada in 1779, Clinton had no choice but to act on the defensive until he could reacquire or replace those troops. In spite of manpower limitations and his cautious nature, Clinton was mindful of the wishes of Germain and the ministry concerning the southern provinces, and he looked for opportunities to operate in that direction. He understood "the great importance which [the] West Indies possessions were of to Great Britain," but lamented that the detachments from his army delayed the "carrying into execution a scheme" which he had considered for some time.[5]

Clinton's "scheme" consisted of an expedition against Charleston, South Carolina, which he believed they had to undertake to prevent the rebels from reconquering Georgia. In addition, the capture of Charleston would provide a springboard for major operations in the southern colonies. In reflecting upon the campaign, Clinton reiterated to Germain that in the south, "we have flattering hopes of assistance from the inhabitants held forth to us." He later noted: "Having in a manner pledged myself to administration [i.e. the ministry] for making the attempt, I could not now go from it without justly exposing myself to censure, as I had drawn the attention of government to this as an object of importance." Sir Henry had committed himself to a southern strategy.[6]

The city to which Sir Henry Clinton now directed his attention was the fourth largest in the American colonies at the outbreak of the Revolution, with a population of 12,000, half of whom were African American slaves. Although Charleston trailed Philadelphia, New York, and Boston in size, it rivaled those cities in terms of economic significance and was certainly the most important port in the southern colonies. The tonnage of vessels which passed through Charleston exceeded that of New York City. The city lay at the confluence of the Ashley and Cooper Rivers, the two rivers coming together to form Charleston's harbor. In the years before the Revolution, over 800 vessels cleared this harbor each year. Ships that called at Charleston sailed to and from England, Continental Europe, Africa, the West Indies, and the coastal cities of North America.[7]

While the British underestimated the economic capacity of the northern colonies in characterizing the southern colonies as the lifeblood of the rebellion, they were correct in affording respect to the economic strength of South Carolina. Colonial South Carolina possessed the highest per capita income and wealth of any of the colonies, and may have had the highest economic growth rate in the world at the time of the Revolution. South Carolina's staple crops, rice and indigo, ranked third and fifth respectively in value among colonial exports and many South Carolinians amassed great fortunes in the export of these crops.[8]

South Carolina's prosperity came primarily from the lowcountry, the lower coastal plain which had been the original area of settlement and where rice could be most easily produced. Charleston was the center of power in this region. Lowcountry planters who grew rice and indigo and merchants who arranged for the export of these commodities dominated the economic and political life of Charleston, and thus South Carolina. Wealthy planters and merchants such as Henry Laurens, Henry Middleton, Thomas Lynch, Christopher Gadsden, William Henry Drayton, Rawlins Lowndes, and Charles Cotesworth Pinckney controlled the Commons, South Carolina's colonial assembly, and they continued to lead the colony as it hurtled toward rebellion. Although the emerging districts of the South Carolina backcountry gained greater representation in the wake of the Regulator Movement of the 1760s, lowcountry leaders still held sway on the eve of the Revolution.[9]

The affluence of South Carolina's leading men was evident in the city of Charleston. A French visitor in 1777 noted houses "of brick, or well-constructed of wood" that were "pleasing to the eye." An English traveler who visited Charleston in 1774 was impressed that "many of the Genteeler sort" in town kept "handsome four wheeled carriages," and some of them had gone so far "as to have Carriages, Horses, Coachmen and all, imported from England." A Hessian officer who served in South Carolina remarked that the wealth of the elite "can clearly be seen in their beautiful and splendid furniture and home decorations." He marveled that a "house is seldom entered in which the furniture is not of mahogany and where there is much silver service."[10]

Visitors to Charleston also admired the city's wide and straight streets that ran at right angles to one another, although the Hessian officer complained that most were unpaved. The "new" Anglican church at the corner of Broad and Meeting Streets, St. Michael's, awed them. Dominating Charleston's skyline, the large white steeple served as a navigational point for sailors entering the city and would play an important role in the upcoming British campaign against Charleston. On the opposite corner of Broad and Meeting stood the State House, "a large, handsome, substantial building" where the elected assemblies of South Carolina met. On the Cooper River end of Broad Street, town leaders erected the impressive Customs House, or Exchange, shortly before the war. The rest of the city comprised innumerable houses, stores, gardens, and open spaces.[11]

The merchants and planters could not have succeeded economically, and thus politically, without the artisans, white laborers, and African American slaves who also inhabited Charleston. Collectively, the diverse population had weathered two British threats to the city. Unlike inhabitants of Charleston's sister cities to the north, Philadelphia, New York and Boston, they had not suffered the burden of British occupation. But with Clinton now focusing his energies on Charleston, the city would be threatened again.

An opportunity for Clinton's expedition to Charleston finally arose when 3,800 reinforcements from England arrived in New York in August and September of 1779. Fearing they were vulnerable to an attack by the French, Clinton also ordered the commander of the British garrison at Newport, Rhode Island, to evacuate that post and bring his troops to New York, which gave Clinton another 4,000 men. The same circumstances that forced the evacuation of Newport, however, demonstrated that the British no longer controlled the tempo of military events in North America. Although reinforced, Clinton's other major concern became very real. In late September, Admiral Marriot Arbuthnot informed him that a French fleet had left the West Indies bound for the Georgia coast, and the crew of a British privateer, which arrived at New York on 8 October, confirmed this intelligence.[12]

Admiral Count Charles-Hector Theodat d'Estaing, the commander of this fleet, sailed from the West Indies with 33 warships and 4,000 troops, arriving off the Georgia coast in early September. Faced with such opposition, especially the vast French naval force, Clinton postponed operations in the southern provinces. He contended that the presence of the French fleet confined his "thoughts . . . to the security of such of his Majesty's American possessions as were immediately near [them]." The cautious Clinton did not believe he possessed sufficient strength to attack the French or make any other offensive moves while they were on the American station.[13]

Meanwhile, d'Estaing cooperated with Lincoln's southern army in a joint operation against the British base at Savannah. After threatening Charleston in May, General Prevost retreated south through the sea islands along the coast and eventually consolidated the bulk of his force at Savannah.

The combined French and American operations against Savannah were disastrous for the new allies. Admiral d'Estaing demanded the surrender of the British garrison before Lincoln even arrived with his own army, gallingly doing so in the name of France only. The French commander gave Prevost twenty-four hours to consider his ultimatum, which provided time for 1,000 British soldiers to steal into Savannah from Beaufort. Reinforced and in command of 3,200 men, Prevost rejected d'Estaing's overture. The French and Americans then lay siege to the town. Just two weeks into the siege, d'Estaing and his subordinate admirals grew restless and the French commander insisted that the armies storm the British defenses. The attack took place on 9 October and was repulsed with heavy losses.[14] Convinced that Prevost would not yield, d'Estaing reembarked his troops on 20 October and departed for the West Indies leaving Lincoln no choice but to return to South Carolina.[15]

Confirmation of the successful British defense reached Clinton on 19 November. Upon receipt of this intelligence, he began to make preparations for an expedition to Charleston. An attack on a coastal city such as Charleston would require the close cooperation of the British army and navy. With a divided command structure, friendly cooperation between the two branches was not guaranteed. Commanders of British land and naval forces in America were completely independent of one another. Both received orders from the ministry but neither outranked the other when they campaigned together. This arrangement complicated collaborative efforts for even the friendliest of army and navy officers, but when a quarrelsome personality such as Sir Henry Clinton was involved, joint operations became particularly troublesome. Clinton had difficulty enough getting along with fellow officers of his own service; relations with naval commanders could be even more contentious. As William Willcox points out of Clinton: "No one else pulled in harness with him for long and kept his good opinion."[16]

In February 1779, the British Admiralty appointed Admiral Marriot Arbuthnot to the top command in North American waters. Arbuthnot, whom Clinton would later refer to as an "old woman," was almost seventy years old at the time. Unlike Clinton, he probably possessed no aristocratic pedigree and his military career developed slowly. He still held only a captain's rank at the outbreak of the war. Somehow gaining the favor of the Earl of Sandwich who headed the British Admiralty and who was consequently responsible for making naval appointments, Arbuthnot received the post of navy commissioner at the Halifax Dockyard in 1775. With the threat of war with France looming, the Admiralty increased the number of flag officers in January 1778 and promoted Arbuthnot to admiral. His service as navy commissioner at Halifax familiarized Arbuthnot with affairs in America, and this service was probably instrumental in the decision of the Earl of Sandwich to appoint him Commander in Chief of His Majesty's Ships and Vessels in North America.[17]

Given Clinton and Arbuthnot's dissimilar personal backgrounds and Clinton's quarrelsome disposition, one might presuppose the nature of their association, but Arbuthnot's own quirky personality exacerbated relations between the two. In examining the relationship between Clinton and Arbuthnot, William Willcox notes that Arbuthnot "was a pompous weathercock, well-meaning, perhaps, and given at times to odd outbursts of friendliness, but never predictable." He was also stubborn, slow to take responsibility, and quick to take alarm. Willcox calls the ministry's decision to pair Arbuthnot with Clinton "folly" given what they knew of Sir Henry's temperament.[18]

Still, the two commanders would have to work together if the Charleston operation was to succeed. The expedition, the largest the British had undertaken in America since the fall of 1777, required tremendous logistical efforts from both services. The fleet that would sail from New York consisted of over 100 ships, including 90 transports to carry the army and its apparatus to the south. In addition to soldiers and their accoutrements, the vessels conveyed camp equipment such as tents and bedding, clothing, horses, entrenching tools, artillery pieces, gunpowder, and food stores. To protect the transports from French warships and American privateers, Admiral Arbuthnot commanded five ships of the line, one fifty gun ship, two forty-four gun ships, four frigates, and two sloops.[19]

For the southern operation, Sir Henry Clinton amassed a force of 8,708 men, which rivaled in size that of Burgoyne for the 1777 campaign. Clinton later maintained, however, that the army he took to Charleston was at least sixteen thousand men less than what General Howe had at his disposal. That the ministry could find enough soldiers for Clinton to attack Charleston and protect the base at New York was an impressive feat considering they had committed so many troops to other theaters by the end of 1779.[20]

The soldiers who embarked for Charleston exhibited great diversity both in function and derivation. They included British infantry, cavalry, and artillery, Hessian infantry, and provincial loyalist units. The regular British infantry consisted of the 7th, 23rd, 33rd, 63rd, and 64th regiments of foot, a detachment of the 71st regiment, two battalions of light infantry, and two battalions of grenadiers.[21] In addition, a squadron of the 17th light dragoons and Lord Cathcart's Legion, consisting of a mixed force of infantry and cavalry, accompanied the expedition. The Hessian, or German, troops included the Regiment von Huyn, four grenadier battalions, and 250 jaegers. The jaegers were the German version of British light infantry. Armed with rifles rather than muskets, they were responsible for scouting, picket duty, and skirmishing and were to play a key role in operations against Charleston. The loyalist units consisted of the New York Volunteers and American Volunteers. Finally, a detachment of the Royal Artillery also sailed with Clinton. Experienced artillerymen would prove invaluable if the rebels made a vigorous defense of the city.[22]

On 16 December, British, Hessian, and loyalist troops began boarding transports in the East River. Severe winter weather hampered the already arduous process of loading men, supplies, and equipment on the ships and getting them underway. Hessian Major General Johann Christoph von Huyn recorded that the fleet was supposed to depart on 19 December, but "very cold weather and rough water" prevented all vessels from reaching the embarkation point until 21 December. The weather was so harsh that one transport, the *Pan,* was destroyed when ice floes pushed by the incoming Atlantic tide drove the ship into the rocky shoreline of Long Island. Ice damaged six other transports so badly that they were unable to make the voyage. The transfer of men and equipment from the damaged ships to other vessels further delayed the fleet's departure. The soldiers and sailors were experiencing only the beginning of what would be one of the worst winters of the eighteenth century. The winter brought numerous snowstorms to the northern states and temperatures so cold that New York Harbor froze over so completely that the British could drag cannon across the ice from Staten Island to New York. Meanwhile, violent gales raged in the Atlantic, wreaking havoc on the British convoy as it sailed southward.[23]

The complex personalities of Clinton and Arbuthnot clashed before the British fleet cleared the coast of New York. Initially, Clinton planned to strike Charleston first then undertake operations in the Chesapeake once the reduction of South Carolina was underway. Since the beginning of the war, British leaders theorized that the rebel army drew much of its strength in men and supplies from Virginia. As a result, they repeatedly considered expeditions against the Chesapeake region. The French incursion into American waters had already delayed the move against South Carolina, and when Clinton received intelligence that several French warships were wintering in the Chesapeake, he put off going there. Admiral Arbuthnot, on the other hand, welcomed the news, perceiving it as an opportunity to strike a blow at their enemy. With his timetable for the expedition already upset, Clinton was apprehensive about Arbuthnot's desire to engage the French. From the warship *Romulus,* anchored off New York, he cautioned Arbuthnot that "no secondary object should make us deviate from the purpose for which we sail." He expressed his "anxiety to get to the Southward" and reminded the admiral that the ministry expected them to proceed with the plan against South Carolina. Finally, he asserted that a move against the French ships in the Chesapeake "could not justify any interruption in the very essential business we have undertaken." Clinton ultimately convinced Arbuthnot to eschew the endeavor into the Chesapeake, but their divergence of opinion was a portent of things to come.[24]

On the morning of 26 December 1779, Admiral Arbuthnot gave the signal to weigh anchor and the British fleet finally left the coast of New York, bound for the rendezvous point at Savannah. It was not a moment too soon for Clinton who maintained that "had we not taken [. . .] advantage of the favorable wind which offered on the 26th of December, it is more than probable the expedition would have been totally frustrated, as a most violent snowstorm came on the next day." While the British avoided the snowstorm that hit New York, they were unable to escape winter gales at sea. Captain Johann Ewald of the Hessian jaegers recorded that as they sailed southeast on 27 December "a very severe storm arose which continued until the 30th." Another storm "combined with rain, hail, and snow" buffeted the fleet between 1 and 6 January. They then received a short respite until 9 January when another tempest blew up. A week later, turbulent weather wracked the fleet again. Captain Johann Hinrichs of the jaegers chronicled that of thirty-six days that his transport, the *Apollo,* was at sea, on fifteen of them they experienced stormy conditions. He noted sourly that the men could not enjoy "a moment of sleep because of the fearful rolling and noise" in the cabins of the ships.[25]

Besides unsettling soldiers, the storms were terribly destructive to the ships and their cargo. Powerful winds scattered the fleet, causing ships to lose contact with one another and blowing many vessels off course. The frightful weather conditions pushed one transport carrying a detachment of Hessians so far off course that it sailed to England, and drove another, which carried one of the army's vital engineers, all the way to the Bahamas.[26]

Gale force winds dismasted many vessels while other ships developed serious leaks; still others were lost completely to the weather. According to Clinton, hardly a day passed on the voyage that was not marked by the foundering of one of the transports. The most serious loss was the ordnance ship *Russia Merchant,* which carried much of the heavy artillery and ammunition. British sailors could not recover the ordnance stores and equipment, so necessary for operations against fortifications, from the sinking craft.[27]

Foul weather also affected the state of provisions onboard the transports. At least two ships lost their entire supply of rum, a loss which the men would keenly recognize. More seriously, much of the fleet sailed into the Gulf Stream, which pushed the vessels further eastward and southward than British captains intended, lengthening the time spent at sea and causing many ships to run dangerously short of provisions before they reached Savannah. According to loyalist Charles Stedman, the voyage to Savannah ordinarily took ten days, but due to the "tempestuous weather" it took them five weeks to reach the Georgia coast. The destruction of seven transports by ice in New York harbor exacerbated provision shortages since many vessels had to bring on additional men over and above what they were supplied for. By 20 January, the agent of the *Margery* curtailed the daily allowance of water to three pints for each man onboard. One British naval captain complained that the presence of large numbers of rats on the ships intensified the dissipation of provisions, especially the stores of bread.[28]

Shortage of provisions also contributed to the loss of the army's horses. As supplies of water and forage for the animals ran out during the extended journey, the British could do little else but throw the horses overboard. Rough seas killed some of the animals onboard the vessels while others perished in the holds of sinking ships. In the course of the voyage, the army lost almost all of the horses belonging to the cavalry, the quartermaster department, and commissary department, which would affect the British severely once they began to move cannon and other heavy stores on land.[29]

In spite of the weather difficulties, most British ships safely reached the rendezvous point at Tybee Island off the mouth of the Savannah River by the beginning of February. On 1 February, Captain Peter Russell, who served on Clinton's staff, reported that only twelve of the expedition's vessels were still missing. From the anchorage at Tybee Island, Clinton sent ashore approximately 2,500 men under the command of Brigadier General James Paterson. Paterson was to make a diversionary march toward Augusta to keep the men of the back-country settlements in Georgia and South Carolina from reinforcing Charleston. Meanwhile, he disembarked the cavalrymen of Lord Cathcart's Legion and the 17th light dragoons to collect horses to replace those lost at sea.[30] The remainder of the British force prepared to move against Charleston. Clinton wished to convey his troops from Savannah to Charleston in boats along the sea islands on the South Carolina coast, which would keep them from going to sea again and would avoid a long overland march, but his officers convinced him to let the Royal Navy's transports carry them.[31]

Clinton preferred to land his army on one of the sea islands south of Charleston. He ruled out the area above the city due to shallow waters there and the proximity to rebel fortifications and batteries. No doubt his experience in operations around Sullivan's Island in 1776 influenced this decision. Once ashore, Clinton intended to move troops overland via the sea islands and then up the Ashley River, making use of the navy's smaller vessels to transport his men across and along the various waterways. Once the navy had taken them over the Ashley, Clinton's soldiers would lay siege lines across the peninsula formed by the Ashley and Cooper Rivers and shut in the town from the landside. Meanwhile, Admiral Arbuthnot and the Royal Navy would attack Charleston from the seaward side, a responsibility fraught with difficulties. Not only would Arbuthnot's ships have to cross the large sandbank protecting the harbor entrance, but British captains would also have to fight their way past Fort Moultrie which had so devastatingly halted their ships in 1776.[32]

The many rivers which ran through the South Carolina lowcountry and emptied into the Atlantic offered the British a distinct advantage in their operations. Coastal inlets provided the Royal Navy's ships a safe anchorage from which to disembark troops and gave British officers a ready transportation network upon which they could ferry cannon and other heavy equipment inland. Going northward from Savannah, the primary options available to Clinton and Arbuthnot were the North Edisto River emptying into the Atlantic between Simmons Island (now Seabrook Island) and Tuckers Island, and the Stono River, separating Johns Island and James Island.

With regard to the landing place, the two commanders again differed in opinion. Arbuthnot wished to sail the transports into the Stono while Clinton preferred the North Edisto. The Stono, Clinton surmised, lay too close to Charleston and would be more heavily defended by the rebels than the North Edisto. Clinton also expected that sailing into the North Edisto would keep the troops at sea for less time, a weighty consideration after the voyage they had just been through. He was desirous to get the men ashore since water and provisions on many transports were running low. By 5 February, two transports, the *Diana* carrying 220 men and the *Silver Eel* carrying 307, had completely exhausted their supplies of beef and bread. Others had only enough on hand for three or four days. The issue was settled when Arbuthnot assigned one of his subordinate officers, Captain George Keith Elphinstone, the task of overseeing the landing. Elphinstone, who was familiar with the coastal waters and sea islands of South Carolina, agreed with Clinton that the troops should disembark in the North Edisto anchorage.[33]

Elphinstone was also to be responsible for ferrying the British army and its supplies to Charleston. Ultimately, it was to be a wise choice. Clinton, at first anxious that Arbuthnot as commander of the expedition's naval forces was not going to oversee the landing, soon gained tremendous respect for Elphinstone's abilities. Moreover, he found it much easier to deal with Elphinstone than with Arbuthnot.[34]

Setting sail on the morning of 9 February, the fleet entered the North Edisto around noon on 11 February. Captain Ewald noted that the mouth of the river was wide enough for only two ships to pass through at the same time, but inside this natural entrance the surrounding sea islands formed a circular basin large enough for one hundred vessels to ride at anchor. Captain Elphinstone guided the flotilla through the narrow portal and into the harborage without incident, the ships coming to anchor off Simmons Island near the mouth of Bohicket Creek. The commissaries issued four days' provisions to the troops, and in the evening the crews of the transports lowered flat boats into the water to take men ashore.[35]

The British light infantry and grenadiers under the command of Major General Alexander Leslie were to be first ashore. These elite troops, accustomed to difficult assignments, were to immediately secure a position on land and reconnoiter the surrounding area for any sign of the enemy. The Hessian grenadiers led by Major General Heinrich von Kospoth were to be next ashore, followed by the jaegers and British 33rd regiment under the command of Lieutenant Colonel James Webster. The British 7th and 23rd regiments under Lieutenant Colonel Sir Alured Clarke were to succeed them. Finally, the 63rd, 64th, and Hessian regiment von Huyn under the command of Major General Johann Christoph von Huyn were to land.[36]

The foul weather which plagued the expedition since it embarked at New York continued to hamper British efforts. At ten o'clock on the night of 11 February, the British light infantry and grenadiers went ashore in the face of a strong wind, which soon developed into a gale with heavy rain. General Clinton accompanied the first debarkation, and as Captain Peter Russell noted, he spent the night "under a Tree in the Rain." Cautious and contentious he certainly was, but it does honor to the character of Sir Henry Clinton that he shared the hardships of his men. Clinton's second in command, Lieutenant General Charles Earl Cornwallis, also came ashore. Even if the weather had not been stormy, the light infantry and grenadiers would have encountered no opposition, for there were no American forces on Simmons Island. Captain Ewald remarked that they did not find a single man of the American army in this area, and he mused that "no one, either in the countryside or in the army, had believed that any person would think of landing in this area and marching towards Charlestown from this side."[37]

On the morning of 12 February, the weather calmed enough for the rest of the troops to land. As they were coming ashore, the light infantry and grenadiers advanced across Simmons Island toward Johns Island. By evening, they crossed Bohicket Creek and encamped on Johns Island on the road leading to James Island and the mainland.[38] The remainder of the troops encamped on Simmons Island.[39]

In selecting Simmons Island, Clinton chose an isolated location distant enough from Charleston and the rebel army to ensure a secure landing, but such a place also meant that the troops had to traverse demanding terrain. Captain Hinrichs of the jaegers complained that the day's march to headquarters took them "through a wilderness of deep sand, marshland, and impenetrable woods where human feet had never trod!" "What a land to wage war in!" he ranted in his journal. The men sometimes waded through waist-deep water while marching through creeks and marsh. When on dry land, they had to cut their way through brush and undergrowth with axes and bayonets. Ensign Hartung of the Huyn regiment recorded that his unit trudged several miles "in a morass . . . where the men had to walk in single file, in order not to sink in." British grenadiers preceded Hartung's detachment and at one point Hartung and his fellow Hessians lost sight of them. When they heard firing in their front, the Hessians sent ahead patrols to investigate but soon discovered that it was from British grenadiers, who were firing their muskets in hopes of locating other British troops. In spite of the intricacies of the terrain, the British and Hessians were ashore and advancing toward their objective.[40]

The British forces were now seven weeks from their departure at New York. The stormy voyage southward had been arduous and close to disastrous. They lost ships, horses, artillery, and other much needed supplies along the way. Conditions obliged the commissaries to cut the provisions of the men onboard the ships, and many transports nearly ran out of food altogether. But now, no longer subject to the whim of Atlantic winter gales, Clinton's troops were back on land. Spending a night in the rain without cover, traversing marshes, and cutting through undergrowth were not so difficult after what they had experienced. Clinton and the British army had established a foothold on South Carolina soil and again controlled their own destiny. They could now proceed on their own terms with the "very essential business." Approximately twenty miles to the north lay their objective, Charleston. It did not take South Carolinians long to recognize that the enemy was at hand.

Chapter Three

Reaction North and South

On the afternoon of 11 February 1780, Major General Benjamin Lincoln sent a hurried note to the governor's council informing them that a British fleet was off the coast of Charleston and that, to the misfortune of the town, the wind was "fair for them to come in." Lincoln had no way of knowing that the British were merely preparing to disembark troops in the North Edisto rather than attack the city without delay. Although they had anticipated a renewed British offensive in the southern states for several months, the city was caught off guard by the sudden appearance of enemy ships immediately off their coast. Earlier that day, Lincoln wrote the council notifying them that he had just received information that a fleet of over 150 ships with 8,000 men led by Sir Henry Clinton himself had recently reached Savannah. Lincoln, his army, and the people of Charleston were unprepared for such a hasty arrival of British forces in the environs of the city.[1]

One month earlier, Lincoln had gained his first intelligence that a large British fleet had departed New York apparently bound for the southern states. He wrote John Mathews, a South Carolina delegate to the Continental Congress, that on 10 January a transport laden with troops was spotted off Charleston Bar evidently enroute to Savannah. In response to rumors of a British fleet in the area, Lincoln ordered that two frigates immediately proceed to sea, cruise between Cape Romain and St. Augustine, and attempt to discover the whereabouts of the enemy. The crews of the frigates did in fact "discover" a few ships off Port Royal, South Carolina, and many others off Tybee Island at Savannah. On their return, the American vessels captured two British sloops and brought them into Charleston. Meanwhile, the tender *Eagle* decoyed a British brig into Charleston harbor. From men on the three captured vessels, Lincoln learned that they were part of a fleet with troops onboard "in very great force" that left New York at the end of December bound for Georgia.[2]

To ascertain British movements once they disembarked at Savannah, Lincoln ordered Colonel Daniel Horry to "constantly keep a party of horse patrolling the Country near the river Savannah." On 6 February, Horry reported to Lincoln that the British troops and ships which sailed from New York had arrived at Tybee. If Clinton moved his army overland from Georgia, Lincoln would have at least a week, and probably more, to prepare for the enemy's approach.[3] The recognition that British ships were immediately off the coast shattered this illusion however.[4]

By eight o'clock on the evening of 11 February, Lincoln's advanced scouts reported that fifty British ships had anchored in the North Edisto that afternoon. By the next day, Lincoln and his officers received intelligence that the enemy had pushed their way onto Johns Island. Word of the British presence spread quickly, causing panic among the people. Two days after the landing, Mrs. Ann Manigault of Charleston recorded in her journal that "we are much afraid of the British, who are on Johns Island." Lincoln informed the Continental Congress that many Charlestonians expected the enemy to appear before the town soon. Many citizens fled the city to escape the British terror. On 15 February, Mrs. Manigault noted: "People go out of Town very fast." The refugees included her granddaughter and her friend Miss Wragg. The march of Prevost's army through the lowcountry in the previous year awed Mrs. Manigault and those that fled. Their fear was justified. In the course of their incursion, Prevost's troops plundered and burned dozens of plantations, and killed or drove off great numbers of livestock. The successful British defense of Savannah also convinced South Carolinians of their military strength. People abandoned their homes rather than risk the consequences of such force. When Gabriel Manigault arrived in Charleston during the second week of February he "found every thing in confusion, accounts having been just received of the landing of the British army, under the command of Sir Henry Clinton, on Johns Island."[5]

In spite of confusion among the citizenry, a renewal of British operations against South Carolina was not entirely unexpected. In the wake of Prevost's thrust against Charleston and the repulse at Savannah, Americans both north and south feared for the safety of the state. With the war a stalemate in the north and Georgia all but secured, South Carolina was the next logical step for the British. At the end of 1779, John Matthews, writing from the Continental Congress in Philadelphia, informed Governor Rutledge that the British intended to send a reinforcement from New York to the southern states; Rutledge himself was convinced that "another Attempt will be made on this Town." On 4 February, a week before the British landed in the North Edisto, Charleston's *The South-Carolina and American General Gazette* reported that a British fleet consisting of ninety-four vessels with eight thousand men on board "under the command of Sir Henry Clinton or Lord Cornwallis" left New York the previous December bound for the southward. Five days later, *The Gazette of the State of South Carolina* published a similar account. Just as General Lincoln had, the newspapers obtained this intelligence from the crews of the captured British ships. On 5 February, Henry Laurens wrote his friend Nathaniel Peabody "we are here preparing for the reception of a menaced attack by a very formidable force from New York & Georgia." Given the speed with which Mrs. Manigault and others learned of the British landing, the information provided in the newspapers must have disseminated rapidly. The stories generated little concern at first. Accounts of a fleet at sea with an as yet unknown destination were one thing, but positive confirmation of a British army on a neighboring sea island was another matter entirely. That certainly was cause for panic.[6]

Recognizing the impending danger in the months before the British appeared, Lincoln and the South Carolinians were able to take precautions for the likely onslaught. South Carolina was not alone in preparing for this exigency, however. While historians have dwelled upon the parochialism and self-interest of the several states during the Revolution, the members of the Confederation were actually quite willing to furnish assistance to their sister states when their resources permitted them to do so.[7] Revolutionary leaders realized, as Benjamin Franklin intimated long before the war broke out, that they must hang together or they would surely hang separately. Throughout the war, the Continental Congress called on militia from various states to respond to British threats in neighboring states. New England militia were instrumental in the defeat of Burgoyne in New York in 1777, while North and South Carolina militia units flocked to Georgia in reaction to the British presence there in 1778 and 1779. States also supported each other with provisions, weapons, and other military supplies, although these came more slowly and they did not have the immediate impact of an armed military force.

As early as November 1779, members of the Continental Congress conjectured that the British intended to redouble their efforts in the south in the near future. In the wake of the Savannah disaster, General Lincoln wrote Congress imploring them to send additional aid southward. Lincoln suggested that the repulse at Savannah would not only secure Georgia for the British, but would lead to a renewed offensive against South Carolina and probably "the total loss" of the state. Recognizing "the present distressed situation . . . of South Carolina and Georgia," the Continental Congress promised "to use every means in their power, to prevent if possible, the loss of those states." For Congress, "every means in their power" translated to ships, supplies, and men for the Southern Department.[8]

On 10 November 1779, they ordered three Continental frigates stationed at Boston to sail "immediately" for Charleston, instructing their captains to place themselves under General Lincoln's command until otherwise informed. The ships that ultimately sailed were the frigates *Providence, Boston,* and *Queen of France* and the sloop of war *Ranger.* The sending of three frigates to South Carolina exemplified the seriousness with which the Continental Congress took the threat to Charleston. Frigates, three-masted vessels which carried their usual complement of twenty-four to forty cannon on a single deck, were the largest vessels available to the fledgling Continental navy. While they were no match for the sixty-plus gun ships of the line of the Royal Navy, the allocation of three of them to the Southern Department was a major gamble for Congress. The next day, the delegates ordered John Mitchell, the deputy quartermaster general at Philadelphia, to procure a ship to transport gunpowder, entrenching tools, camp kettles, artillery supplies, bayonets, musket flints, and other military supplies requested by Lincoln to South Carolina. Mitchell procured the schooner *Dove* to make the voyage.[9]

Because the Royal Navy remained a threat to American shipping even after France's entrance into the war, the captain of the *Dove* could not simply embark from Philadelphia and sail directly to Charleston. While the Royal Navy possessed too few ships to maintain a close blockade in American waters, they did have enough to patrol entrances to bays and harbors along the coast, giving their cruisers opportunity to capture inbound and outbound vessels. The entrances to Delaware and Chesapeake Bays were favorite hunting grounds for British captains and were therefore especially dangerous. Rather than risk losing valuable military supplies to British forays, American quartermasters transported the *Dove*'s cargo partly by land and partly by water, a long and expensive journey. Movement by horse- or oxen-drawn wagons not only slowed conveyance of stores, but also made it more expensive, since agents had to hire out animals and wagons along the way. Ultimately, the distance involved and the Royal Navy's presence along the coast made it difficult for the Continental Congress to supply southern states from the north. Throughout the war, supplies going from north to south often took months to reach their destination.[10]

With regard to reinforcements for the Southern Department, the Continental Congress sought General Washington's assistance. On 11 November, they directed Washington to order North Carolina troops attached to his army to reinforce General Lincoln without delay. The North Carolina Continentals had performed hard service with the main army since the campaign of 1777. Initially consisting of ten regiments, battlefield casualties, sickness, and desertion reduced the North Carolinians remaining with Washington to just two regiments. Washington complied with the request to send the North Carolinians, but with some reluctance, since their departure diminished the numbers he had available to keep the British in check around New York. Upon being briefed more fully on the desperate situation in the southern states, however, he not only firmly agreed with the decision, but offered to further reinforce General Lincoln. This briefing came not from Congress but from Lieutenant Colonel John Laurens. Lincoln sent Lieutenant Colonel Laurens to see Washington personally to report on the effort against Savannah and the abject state of the southern command. Earlier in the war, Laurens served as aide-de-camp on Washington's staff, a position of considerable trust, so his word carried much weight with the commander in chief.[11]

Arriving at Washington's headquarters in late November, Laurens outlined in detail the deplorable state of the Southern Department. He reported to Washington that their Continental forces had decreased substantially and they could place little dependence on the militia in the southern states. He also revealed that the Southern Department lacked cavalry, which were useful in putting down Tory insurrections and "securing the Country from the incursions of the Enemy's Cavalry." After conferring with his former aide, Washington observed that South Carolina and Georgia were in a "more defenceless condition than [he] had ever apprehended."[12]

The report of Laurens coupled with intelligence from spies that the British were preparing to make a "considerable embarkation of troops" from New York convinced Washington of the necessity of detaching additional men from the main army to South Carolina. He immediately recommended to Congress sending the entire Virginia line to the Southern Department. While the North Carolinians that marched on 23 November numbered only 828 officers and enlisted men, the Virginia Continental troops comprised over 2,500 men. With just over 18,000 soldiers in the army around New York, the departure of the Virginians was a significant reduction in Washington's force. Washington also ordered Baylor's Light Dragoons to join General Lincoln. This unit, under the command of Lieutenant Colonel William Washington, a distant cousin of the commander in chief, consisted of 125 cavalrymen. Washington recognized that his army would have to continue to operate on the defensive, but considering the "disagreeable consequences" that would result if the enemy overran South Carolina and Georgia, he asserted that "it may be adviseable to hazard a good deal here for their security."[13]

Washington's decision to part with the Virginia line demonstrates strikingly his willingness to subordinate his interests to the interests of the whole, weakening his army to reinforce a separate theater of operations. Dedicated to the success of the Revolution for the states united as a nation, he had the strategic insight to understand that the war was now going to be won or lost in the southern states. Although he would never personally command troops in the field south of the James River in Virginia, Washington's influence extended to the other southern states in the form of his readiness to make sacrifices for them.

As with transportation of supplies, movement of troops over great distances was no easy task. Washington hoped that the Virginia troops would travel by sea because "fatigue, sickness and desertion" would reduce their numbers in an overland march. He was especially apprehensive about their passage through Virginia, where men would face great temptation to return home. Ultimately the same fear of British cruisers, which hindered the conveyance of supplies by water, kept the soldiers on land. Both the North Carolina and Virginia troops would proceed to South Carolina on foot—a journey that normally took several months. The North Carolinians marched from New Windsor, New York on 23 November 1779 but did not reach Charleston until 3 March 1780. The last of the Virginians left Morristown, New Jersey, on 12 December and did not reach Charleston until 7 April.[14]

A march from New York or New Jersey to the southern states imposed months of hardship on soldiers and civilians alike. The troops had to tramp hundreds of miles on poor roads, wade through innumerable streams and rivers, sleep in tents in all kinds of weather, and often settle for substandard rations. The army's commissaries were responsible for obtaining provisions along the route, but by late 1779 the depreciation of the Continental Currency made procurement of supplies challenging. The Continental Congress issued so much of this paper money to finance the war that it lost much of its initial value and consequently its purchasing power. As a result, commissaries often resorted to impressment, which meant that the army appropriated what they needed by force. Officers distributed warrants or promises to pay for the goods at a later date, but generally the "supplier" had little choice but to turn over what the commissaries requested. Needless to say, impressment was not very popular with the people. Civilians that the army encountered faced not only the prospect of impressment, but the vagaries of the soldiers themselves. Soldiers often stole food from the local populace or destroyed their property. Throughout the war, Washington repeatedly threatened enlisted men with severe penalties for destroying fences of local farmers. It was much easier for a soldier to remove fence rails from a fence for firewood than it was to cut down trees.[15]

In spite of the hardships Continental troops could inflict on the civilian populace along their route of march, General Lincoln greatly required the reinforcements. Manpower was Lincoln's foremost problem in preparing to defend Charleston and Lieutenant Colonel Laurens had not understated the Southern Department's dire need for soldiers. At the end of January, Lincoln informed Congress that he had only 1,400 Continental infantry and cavalry fit for duty along with approximately 1,000 North Carolina militia, but he lamented that "this is our whole force, & more we may not soon expect." Moreover, his men badly lacked military necessities. Lincoln found it difficult to obtain clothing and shoes for the infantry, and the cavalrymen were short of horses, saddles, bridles, and swords.[16]

Lincoln's infantry was comprised primarily of South Carolina Continentals augmented by two small detachments of Virginia Continentals and one of North Carolinians. As with the North Carolinians serving with Washington, the number of men serving in the South Carolina line had ebbed significantly in the previous three years. In 1777, the six South Carolina Continental regiments consisted of 2,400 men, but attrition reduced them to less than 800 by 1780. Lincoln asked the South Carolina Assembly for 2,000 men for the campaign of 1780, but the raising of such a force was doubtful. The previous year General Moultrie had lectured members of the Assembly on the dangers of relying on militia for the defense of their state and urged them to take steps to complete the Continental regiments to their full complement; the Assembly responded with an ordinance to fill up the Continental battalions. According to the ordinance, men were to enlist for sixteen months and were to receive a cash bounty at the time of enlistment in addition to their regular pay as soldiers. Despite this effort, Governor Rutledge reported to the House of Representatives on 26 January 1780 that "no recruits have been procured for the Continental regiments." Meanwhile, recognizing that there was little prospect that South Carolina, like the other states, could completely fill her allotted regiments, the Continental Congress resolved that South Carolina's five infantry regiments be consolidated into three. As a result, men from the 5th and 6th South Carolina subsequently transferred into the 1st and 2nd regiments. The 4th South Carolina maintained its separate organization as an artillery regiment. With the condition of the South Carolina Continental regiments being what it was and the success of future recruiting uncertain, news that the North Carolina and Virginia Continental troops were marching to reinforce him could only have mollified Lincoln.[17]

Even as their Continental troops were marching from Washington's army to the Southern Department, Lincoln called upon the states of North Carolina and Virginia for further assistance. Lincoln wrote Governor Richard Caswell of North Carolina that he expected a British push against South Carolina "much sooner than the reinforcements ordered from the Main Army can arrive," and he entreated Caswell to send all the troops that the North Carolina legislature had authorized to Charleston "with the greatest dispatch." He later instructed Caswell that they should furnish their militia with shoes, stockings, and shirts, since the supplies of clothing in Charleston were only adequate for the men on hand. Lincoln also reminded Caswell of the need for North Carolina to complete her Continental battalions. To Thomas Jefferson, now serving as Virginia's governor, Lincoln requested that Virginia provide clothing for the Continental troops as they passed through the state on their way to join the southern army. He lamented to the Virginia governor that "blankets, shoes and shirts are now exceedingly wanted here."[18]

To consolidate his force around Charleston, Lincoln ordered his two Virginia Continental detachments, commanded by Colonels Richard Parker and William Heth, to return from Augusta. Parker's and Heth's men had been serving in the Southern Department since the previous year, and Lincoln posted them at Augusta to respond to any British moves up the Savannah River. Directing a battalion of Georgia and South Carolina militia to take their place at Augusta, Lincoln requested that the Virginians "march w[ith] all possible dispatch" to Sheldon. These troops gave Lincoln approximately 350 additional rank and file with which to defend Charleston.[19]

Lincoln also anticipated the support of the South Carolina militia in the coming campaign, although in what numbers he was desperately uncertain. He could count on the immediate cooperation of the Charleston Regiment of Militia comprising approximately 600 men and the Charleston Battalion of Artillery, which would give him an additional 270.[20] But the assistance of other South Carolina militia regiments was suspect. In a letter to the Continental Congress, Lincoln predicted that few militia from the South Carolina backcountry would come to Charleston in the event of a siege of the city. He expected that the British, by "stimulating" the loyalists and Indians in the backcountry, would force the militia to stay and defend their homes. Other officers held a more dim view of the loyalty of some of the state's militiamen. On 11 February, Colonel Daniel Horry asserted to Lincoln that the militia of Port Royal were "bad people" and had quit their post. He presumed that "none of them" would join his detachment. Fortunately for General Lincoln, Governor Caswell ordered on North Carolina militia reinforcements. By 10 February, a body of 1,248 of them, under the command of General Alexander Lillington, arrived in Charleston.[21]

With militia support uncertain, Lincoln looked for other ways to supplement his force. Acting on the advice of the Continental Congress, he urged Governor Rutledge and the South Carolina Assembly to arm a number of black battalions to serve with the army. "From our own inconsiderable force," Lincoln wrote Rutledge, "the little prospect of an early reinforcement from the North, the strength of the enemy, and the evidence we have that the reduction of this State is their object [I am induced] to request that our deficiencies may be in part supplied by arming some Blacks agreeable to the repeated recommendations of Congress." African American soldiers performed admirably with Continental units in the northern states, and some South Carolinians such as John and Henry Laurens strongly favored the measure. Despite the imminent danger of a British attack against their state, most South Carolinians, however, were unwilling to entrust their slaves with weapons and the Assembly refused to follow up on the proposal. The ratio of blacks to whites, especially in the lowcountry, was too great and the possibility of slave insurrections too ominous to justify such a step. Furthermore, the enlistment of blacks into the army could also result in large property losses for slave owners whose bondsmen might be killed or maimed in service. Lincoln was at first angry at the response of the Assembly, but he then tempered his appeal. Rather than arming blacks, he suggested that they act with the artillery and assist in fatigue duties. Basically fatigue duty translated to hard labor, but it certainly did not require the issuance of muskets to slaves.[22]

Lincoln's concern for manpower and the overall defensive posture of Charleston had deepened since he was determined to hold the city. His decision to make a stand at Charleston was based on several factors. Although the Continental Congress had not directly ordered him to defend the city, he believed that their spirited efforts to support him with ships, men, and materials implied their desire for him to do so. Lincoln also theorized that his small army could do little against a much larger British force in open country and that he would have to abandon substantial military property in the event of an evacuation. Posting his army behind fortifications would increase their effective strength in relation to the British and would allow them to safeguard the city, the supplies within, and the Continental shipping. While these appear to be compelling reasons, Lincoln's experience in the prior year cannot be overlooked in the final analysis. The harsh criticism that many South Carolinians heaped upon Lincoln for marching into Georgia and leaving Charleston exposed in the spring of 1779 profoundly affected him. Believing the people had lost confidence in his abilities, he came close to resigning command of the Southern Department. Like Washington, Lincoln was willing to yield to the civil authorities when necessary. Unfortunately, this moderation interfered at times with his ability to command effectively. The opinions of local authorities and the memory of the stinging reproach of 1779 no doubt also influenced Benjamin Lincoln's decision to defend Charleston in 1780.[23]

Determined to hold South Carolina's capital, Lincoln also tended to the city's fixed defenses, especially those which sheltered it from attack via the neck. The line of fortifications, which extended from the Ashley River to the Cooper River on the outskirts of Charleston, had originally been laid out in the 1750s under the direction of a French engineer, William Gerard de Brahm. Charlestonians attempted to strengthen them in the spring of 1779 in response to Prevost's threat to the town, but further work was now required. The lines began on a stretch of ground bordering a tidal creek of the Ashley River just east of present day Smith Street in Charleston. From there, they ran just south of present day Vanderhorst Street, crossed King Street onto present day Marion Square, passed over Meeting Street, continued approximately along Charlotte Street, and turning on a sharp angle northward, finally reached to Town Creek in the vicinity of present day Chapel Street. A redoubt constructed of masonry and tabby, known as the hornwork, lay across King Street and was the focal point of the defenses. Engineers also established batteries on Coming's Point facing James Island and on the southern side of Charleston facing the harbor.[24]

The condition of the defensive works thoroughly displeased Lincoln. In December 1779, he reported to the Continental Congress that Charleston "is uncovered by works, and we have no expectation that it will soon be in a better state." His prediction was not inaccurate. Two months later, on the day that British ships sailed into the North Edisto, Lincoln wrote to Washington. "The works here are by no means completed," he said, and added: "It has not been in my power to effect this most desirable purpose."[25]

Lincoln's two French engineers, Colonel Jean Baptiste Joseph, the Chevalier de Laumoy, and Lieutenant Colonel Louis Antoine Jean Baptiste, the Chevalier de Cambray-Digny, set about the task of improving Charleston's fortifications. Uncertainty as to where the British would direct their attack coupled with a lack of men made this a challenging assignment. "[Since]we don't know wich [*sic*] Side of the Town is most in danger, wich the enemy mean to attack . . . ," Laumoy explained to Lincoln, "we must extend our cares to all [sides] as much as possible, to be very near equally strong every where at the same time." Laumoy oversaw the construction of batteries, parapets, and ditches on all sides of the city, but he informed Lincoln: "It is Sorrowful to me to think that I will not be able to do more for the Security of this most momentous place . . . with the means I have." Laumoy estimated that he would need at least 1,600 slaves to make the works tenable in a week's time.[26]

Raising the number of laborers that Laumoy petitioned for would not be easy. At the end of January, Lincoln requested of Governor Rutledge to "order 1,500 Negroes to assemble in the vicinity of this town with the necessary tools for throwing up lines immediately." The House of Representatives approved the measure, but the Senate was slower to respond. They wished to consider other means of procuring laborers to strengthen Charleston's defenses. Lincoln also repeatedly reminded Rutledge of the need for a corps of "Black Volunteers" to assist the army. In spite of the reluctance of Rutledge and members of the Senate, ultimately hundreds of African Americans toiled on the defensive lines of Charleston. They risked their lives, sometimes under British fire, to preserve the capital of their masters.[27]

The chain of fortifications and batteries ringing the city that Laumoy and the unfortunate African Americans labored to complete comprised only a portion of the city's defenses. While works on the peninsula protected Charleston from the landward side, Fort Moultrie secured it from seaborne attacks. The South Carolinians had since completed and strengthened Fort Moultrie, which so vigorously resisted British attack in June 1776. The fort, situated on the southwest end of Sullivan's Island, commanded the entranceway to Charleston harbor just below Sullivan's Island. Ships sailing into the harbor had to navigate their way down a relatively narrow channel between Sullivan's Island and the Middle Ground, a large shoal on which Fort Sumter later stood. The waters south of the Middle Ground were too shallow for vessels to traverse safely. Enemy ships endeavoring to break into the harbor had to pass directly under the guns of Fort Moultrie. The fort's designers laid it out as a square with bastions at each corner. The soldiers and slaves who built the fort constructed each wall by piling palmetto logs one on top of the other in two rows sixteen feet apart. They then filled in the space between the two rows with sand. This unique construction served the fort well during the British attack in 1776. The sponginess of the palmetto wood coupled with the abundance of sand between the rows of logs swallowed up British cannon balls fired into the ramparts, preventing major damage to the yet unfinished fort.[28]

Although Fort Moultrie bristled with forty cannon, Colonel Charles Cotesworth Pinckney, the fort's commander, complained to Lincoln that he was short of both men and ammunition. Pinckney reported that the fort needed round shot, grapeshot, and canister shot for its cannon and affirmed that he would require 1,215 soldiers to man the walls, artillery, and outlying defensive works protecting the fort. He had only 200. Colonel Pinckney hoped to receive half the number needed, but he recognized Lincoln's shortage of manpower and the uncertainty of reinforcements. "If half cannot be obtained," he gallantly asserted, "I shall make the best defense in my power with the number that may be allowed me." While Fort Moultrie lacked men and ammunition, Fort Johnson on James Island, which covered the southwest side of the harbor, was completely out of commission; the patriots had blown up the fort the previous year to keep it from falling into British hands during Prevost's incursion into the lowcountry. Even if the fort were intact, Lincoln did not possess sufficient troops to properly garrison it.[29]

While their man-made defenses were not as strong as desired, Lincoln and the Charlestonians were also relying on the city's natural defenses to stave off the British threat. Lincoln asserted that Charleston's "natural strength" made it more defensible than any other port on the American coast, while a French officer noted that the city was "stronger because of its location than because of its fortifications." Although the Ashley and Cooper Rivers allowed a waterborne enemy access to the Charleston peninsula, the peninsula itself was surrounded by mud flats and marsh at low tide, making it difficult for an enemy to land troops there. Numerous tidal creeks, which were a great impediment to an army moving on foot, also cut into the peninsula at various points. Likewise, the sea islands, which the British had to cross to reach Charleston, were a maze of tidal creeks, marsh, and swamps. To further hinder British movements along lowcountry waterways, the Assembly ordered that all boats lying within two miles of the sea coast, forty miles to the north and forty miles to the south of Charleston, be brought into town to keep them from the British. Still, the most significant natural obstacle protecting Charleston was the Bar, a large sandbank lying just outside the harbor entrance. The Bar ran several miles from north to south, extending from Sullivan's Island down to Lighthouse Island. Since the water over the Bar was so shallow (only three to four feet of water covered it in some places), ships could only cross it by sailing through one of six channels. The main channel, known as the Ship Channel, lay at the southern end of the Bar and was just over twenty feet deep at high tide and at low tide only twelve feet deep. Lincoln intended to use a combination of the Bar's natural protection, his shipping, and the guns of Fort Moultrie to keep the British navy out of the harbor.[30]

As to shipping, Lincoln believed he was adequately supported. He informed Congress that the arrival of the Continental frigates they had ordered to the Southern Department was "an event which gives great satisfaction to the people here." The addition of the three frigates from Boston gave Lincoln six frigates, the sloop of war *Ranger,* and numerous smaller vessels with which to defend Charleston harbor. The frigates consisted of *Bricole* of forty-four guns, *Providence* bearing thirty-two guns, *Boston* also of thirty-two guns, *Queen of France* with twenty-eight guns, and *L'Aventure* and *Truite,* each bearing twenty-six guns. He could also count on *Ranger* with twenty guns and two brigs, *General Lincoln* and *Notre Dame,* carrying twenty and sixteen guns respectively. Commodore Abraham Whipple commanded the naval forces. Lincoln was so confident in his naval strength that he wrote Washington that they were devoting most of their defensive preparations "to the land-side of the Town." He boldly asserted that the ships "will cover the harbour and preserve it from insult."[31]

Fully aware of its strategic significance, Lincoln insisted that the Continental ships make a stand at the Bar to prohibit British ships from gaining access to the town. He contended that if they could keep the Royal Navy out of the harbor, the British would only be able to assault Charleston from the landside, thereby increasing the defenders' chances of success. Moreover, with the harbor remaining open to American shipping, the patriots could still bring supplies in by sea. Lincoln hoped to forestall a British crossing by stationing his warships inside the Bar to safeguard the channels which traversed it. Even if the British made it over the Bar, Lincoln expected that, with the guns of Fort Moultrie acting in concert with the American ships, they could still block them from entering the harbor. Whether Commodore Whipple and his captains could put this plan into execution remained to be seen.[32]

Although Lincoln was short of both troops and supplies, the natural and man-made defenses of the city presented a significant obstacle for the British. For both the British army and navy, Charleston would not be an easy target to approach or attack. Severe winter weather had already hampered their expedition. Sir Henry Clinton and Admiral Marriot Arbuthnot would now face the formidable defenses and terrain of Charleston.

In Charleston, notice that British troops were on nearby sea islands and the appearance of the first British ships off the Bar meant that the time for preparation was coming to a close for soldier and civilian alike. The South Carolina Assembly immediately adjourned when they received word from General Lincoln of the British landing. They would not convene again for almost two years. In one of their last acts prior to adjournment, the Assembly granted to Governor John Rutledge the "power to do everything necessary for the publick good, except the taking away the life of a citizen without a legal trial." As governor, Rutledge commanded the state's militia forces and he promptly took steps to bring them into the field. Lincoln insisted to Rutledge that the Continentals "have the fullest assurance" of support "by the people of the Country," and he requested that Rutledge call out 2,000 men "from the Country" to assist them. Rutledge would convey control of the militia to General Lincoln once they joined his army.[33]

Meanwhile, Lincoln prepared the troops already under his command for action. He ordered all officers of the army to immediately join their regiments and to compile "exact returns" of arms and accoutrements needed to properly equip their soldiers. The orders dictated that once the men were properly accoutered, the officers were to inspect the troops' arms on a daily basis to ensure that they were always fit for duty. The general officers assigned alarm posts to all units in Charleston to which they were to repair in the event of an attack, and the army's artillerymen readied their pieces for battle.[34]

Commodore Whipple also endeavored to ensure that he had sufficient men to serve on board the ships and defend the harbor. On 13 February, he declared to Governor Rutledge that it was "essentially necessary that every sailor in [Charleston] be actually imployed in service by land or water." The Commodore maintained that no excuses should be allowed for those who attempted to avoid performing duty. Rutledge agreed and issued a warrant that empowered Whipple "to cause all the Seamen in and about [Charleston], and on board of the Private Vessels in port, to be apprehended, and secured, in order to be imployed in the most Effectual Manner for defence of this Harbour." Wielding powers that the Assembly had granted him and demonstrating how seriously he took his responsibility to defend Charleston, Rutledge also authorized Whipple "to cause any suspected Houses to be searched, and (if necessary,) broke open, to find Seamen who may be concealed." Rutledge asked Lincoln to aid Whipple "with a sufficient number of Continental Troops" so that the warrant could be put into effect. Whether a mariner intended to serve in the navy or not, he was going to assist in the defense of Charleston.[35]

The flurry of military activity in and around Charleston soon affected those civilians who had not fled the city. Whipple's authorization to break into homes to find reluctant and wayward sailors certainly threatened any citizen "suspected" of hiding a seaman, but there were more apparent effects on inhabitants who remained. Lincoln ordered the army's drummers to beat tattoo at half past nine each evening, which was the signal "for every one to repair to their respective homes." No person was to be in the streets after that time and anyone who disobeyed this order was subject to arrest. Sentries were to commit to the main guard any soldiers who were out after tattoo without a pass. Meanwhile, Lincoln expressed to Governor Rutledge his hope that "all the inhabitants" of Charleston would be "induced personally to give every assistance in fortifying ye. Town." Charleston was quickly taking on the character of a garrison town.[36]

The eighteenth century has often been referred to as an age of limited war in which armies fought limited engagements for limited objectives, and unlike the twentieth century, civilian populations were not heavily involved. For the most part that was true, but when military operations moved close to populated areas as in sieges of cities or towns, civilians did become involved. Already, as the two armies prepared to face one another, civilians were experiencing the impact of war. Many in Charleston panicked and fled at the first word of the British landing, while those that stayed no longer enjoyed freedom of movement in their own city and were being called upon to assist in its defense. In the countryside around Charleston, especially south and west of the city, plantation owners and farmers would soon feel the wrath of a British army in search of supplies and forage. For those civilians, touched by the demands of two armies, war was not limited.

In early January, General Lincoln had written a prescient letter to the Continental Congress in which he asserted that he no longer had any doubt that the British would soon make a move against South Carolina. Of the South Carolinians, he asserted their "idea of perfect security will now be lost." With curfews imposed and soldiers patrolling their streets, with their governor authorizing soldiers to break into homes, with their slaves working on the fortifications of the town, with British warships cruising off the Bar, and with an entire British army on the neighboring islands, that "perfect security" was surely fading.[37]

Chapter Four

The British on the Sea Islands

Sir Henry Clinton's decision to disembark in the North Edisto River ensured that the navy would have a sheltered anchorage and the troops would get ashore unopposed, but the landing on Simmons Island left his army twenty miles from Charleston. The nature of the lowcountry terrain, laced with rivers, creeks, marsh, and swamps, heralded a difficult journey for the British. Still, their advance could not be hindered enough for Lincoln and the Americans. Lacking sufficient troops to oppose the British army west of the Ashley, Lincoln's forces could harass the British as they pushed forward but could not stop them. This circumstance was to have unfortunate results for inhabitants south and west of the city.

Although Sir Henry Clinton and his army were free of the transports, their ultimate success remained inextricably linked to that of the navy. The reduction of Charleston would have to be a joint effort by British land and sea forces. The failure of either to achieve its objective would more than likely result in the failure of the entire operation. If Clinton's army cut off Charleston from the mainland by laying siege lines across Charleston neck, the effort would be of no avail if rebel ships could still sail up the Ashley and Cooper Rivers or enter and leave the harbor at will. Supplies would continue to flow into the city and an avenue would remain open for Lincoln's army to escape if necessary. Likewise, British naval control of the harbor offered no advantage if Lincoln's army possessed the ability to retreat inland to a more secure position.

In the watery expanse of the South Carolina lowcountry, British army operations were tied even more directly to the navy in terms of transport and supply. While no longer confined to transports, Clinton's troops depended on the seamen of the Royal Navy to move them along and across the numerous waterways that lay before Charleston. Meanwhile, provision ships, or victuallers, stationed in the North Edisto, continued to feed the soldiers. When the army moved inland, the navy's flatboats and galleys carried their supplies up the various creeks and rivers.[1]

In the days after they came ashore, British troops fanned out across Johns Island and found no sign of the rebels. On Johns Island, Clinton's initial focus became the post at Stono Ferry on the upper Stono, the principal crossing to the mainland from Johns Island. On 14 February, Clinton ordered the 33rd regiment and Hessian jaegers to move toward the ferry. Captain Johann Ewald of the jaegers reported that the Americans "had stationed a strong corps in the vicinity of Stono Ferry" and that they seemed "determined to contest [their] crossing of the river." Along the march, the jaegers captured a young slave boy, whom they hoped would guide them since they had no maps of the area. According to Ewald, "this boy spoke such a poor dialect that he was extremely hard to understand."[2] Their difficulty in communicating with him almost brought them to disaster. As the Hessian advance guard neared Stono Ferry, the youth directed them to a causeway made of logs and stone, which, after crossing a swamp on the south bank of the Stono, led directly to the crossing at the ferry. The British and Hessians reached the end of the causeway to discover that they were within firing distance of American cavalry and infantry fortified on high ground on the opposite bank. Captain Hinrichs admitted later that it gave him a "shudder" to think of their situation on the causeway where the Americans could have cut the detachment to pieces. They had run headlong into the enemy with little or no room to maneuver. Their only option was to fall back on the pathway as quickly as they could. Meanwhile, the Americans on the north bank of the Stono were equally surprised to encounter an enemy force and made no effort to fire on the British and Hessian troops on the causeway across the river. Captain Ewald could scarcely believe that the Americans did not attack them.[3]

The Americans at Stono Ferry were most likely a detachment from Colonel Daniel Horry's command, which Lincoln had recalled from Sheldon on the Saltketcher River. Horry resolved "to discover the Enemy's movements" and "give them all the annoyance and check" in his power. He too was unfamiliar with "this part of the Country" however, and he experienced difficulty in procuring proper guides. The Americans' surprise at the sudden approach of the enemy was no doubt a result of their unfamiliarity with the terrain around the ferry and a lack of men. Although the two sides exchanged no shots, American and British forces had made their first contact of the campaign.[4]

The following day, General Clinton himself reconnoitered Stono Ferry and other potential crossing sites on the Stono. The Stono River describes an arc from Wadmalaw Creek on the western side of Johns Island around the northern end of the island and then down to Stono Inlet where it meets the Atlantic. If this arc is viewed as a clock face, Stono Ferry approximates ten o'clock, Fenwick's plantation two o'clock, Mathew's Ferry three o'clock, and Chisholm's plantation and ferry four o'clock. In planning their next move, the British had several alternatives as to where to pass the river. They could force their way across Stono Ferry or march farther downstream and cross at Fenwick's, Mathew's, or Chisholm's. The American detachment posted at

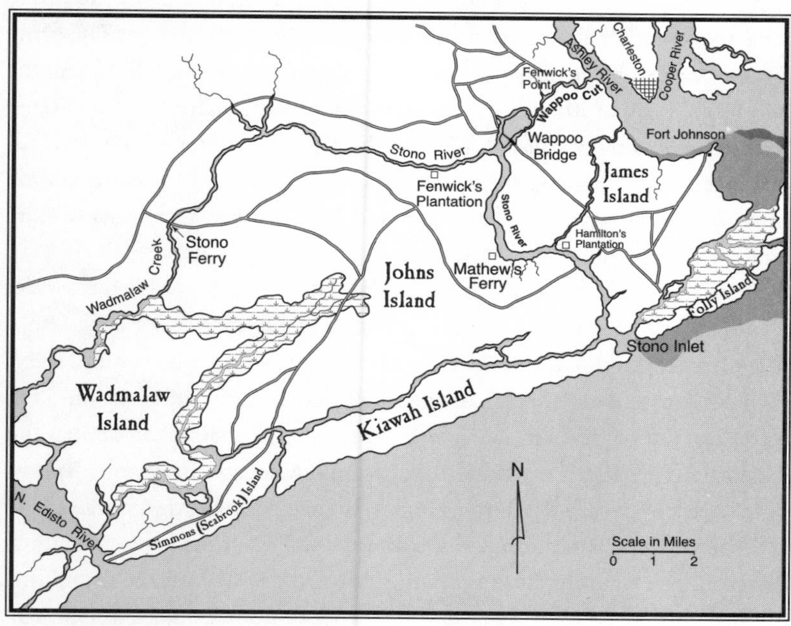

Sea Islands South and West of Charleston

Stono Ferry was too small to cover the entire river, and if the British crossed farther downstream toward James Island they could cut them off. Lincoln elected not to oppose a British crossing at Stono Ferry since the few men he had there "could not be supported by the main Body of our Troops, nor a large one detached without risquing an attack from James Island while Our Troops were absent." So in the early morning hours of 16 February, the Americans abandoned their works at the ferry.[5]

Even though the Americans had withdrawn from Stono Ferry, a crossing of the river was still a difficult task for the British. The Americans most certainly destroyed the crossing apparatus at the ferries, forcing the British to find their own boats to make a passage over the river. The South Carolina Assembly's orders that all boats within two miles of the seacoast be confiscated and brought to Charleston apparently had great effect. The British had to rely on the few American boats they found and several small craft of their own, which soldiers and sailors floated up Bohicket Creek and dragged overland across Johns Island. Physically landing troops on the north side of the Stono also presented problems. One of Clinton's officers observed: "The army labour under great difficulty in going in and out of Flat Boats as the Country is full of Marshes." The men often waded through waist-deep water in traversing these marshes. The British also faced the possibility that Americans might be waiting in ambush on the opposite bank, making the slow debarkation through the marshy terrain even more challenging.[6]

Nevertheless, the British light infantry successfully crossed the river on the morning of 16 February and took post at Stono Ferry. Other units joined them later in the day. Although the capture of Stono Ferry provided the British access to the mainland, Clinton did not intend to pass the rest of the army over the river there. The British commander would have taken a great gamble in conveying his entire force inland and leaving the supply ships behind. He wished instead to move closer to Charleston via James Island, which would keep the army in contact with the fleet, rather than marching toward the city on the mainland. Clinton proposed to make a feint toward Dorchester on the upper Ashley River, but he preferred a crossing point much lower on the river and nearer to Charleston.[7]

Communication with the fleet and the means of supply would be vastly improved if the Royal Navy were to push transports into the lower Stono. After the seizure of Stono Ferry, Captain Elphinstone provisioned the British troops on Johns Island by dispatching boats from the North Edisto up through Wadmalaw Creek to the Stono. It was difficult to provide for the entire army using these small craft however, and the portage was subject to the whim of the tide. Clinton urged Elphinstone to conduct the transports from the North Edisto to Stono Inlet at the mouth of the Stono. He explained to Elphinstone that his troops could prevent the rebels from sending ships down Wappoo Cut to attack them. The naval officer responded that he did not think it safe to bring the vessels in until he could "get some thing of force to protect" him. On 19 February, Elphinstone's men sailed two schooners, each armed with a twenty-four pound cannon, and a flat boat armed with a twelve pound cannon into the Stono to cover the transports. When Clinton ordered the light infantry to march farther down the river to Mathew's Ferry, the distance that ships would have to proceed upriver to link up with British troops was reduced, further ensuring their safety. By 20 February, Elphinstone was able to get the transports into the river. The vessels sailed to Mathew's Ferry where their crews could now debark supplies directly to the army. With the navy in the Stono, the British not only enhanced communication between their land and sea forces, but they made themselves masters of Johns Island and the Stono River.[8]

Despite Clinton's concerns, the British secured their hold on Johns Island with little or no resistance from Lincoln's army. Since receiving word that the British had arrived in the North Edisto River, General Lincoln kept the bulk of his army on the Charleston side of the Ashley River to protect the city rather than attempting to engage the British on Johns Island. Shortly after the British landing, Lincoln called a council of war of his officers to discuss their situation. He asked the assembled officers whether they thought it "expedient" to "go out to Meet the Enemy, and attack them," as he felt that they "may have opportunity on their March to Town." With the exception of Colonel François Malmedy, a French cavalry officer, everyone agreed that they should not attack. Lincoln and his officers recognized that they did not have enough troops to defend the city and move against the British on

Johns Island. Venturing out against Clinton and leaving Charleston unprotected might invite a British descent from James Island or by sea against Fort Moultrie. No doubt the experience of leaving Charleston practically defenseless in the spring of 1779 influenced Lincoln. "If this Town should be attacked, as now threatened," he wrote to Washington, "I know my duty will call me to defend it as long as opposition can be of any avail." He would concentrate the bulk of his force in Charleston.[9]

In planning his mode of conduct, Lincoln gathered all the intelligence he could of the British forces. He detached Colonel Malmedy with thirty cavalrymen to "the country around Edisto . . . to reconnoitre the enemy, and discover if possible their intentions." Meanwhile, Peter Timothy, a Charleston printer and dedicated Whig, volunteered to take post in the steeple of St. Michael's Church and report on enemy land and sea movements. From his post, Timothy obtained an excellent view of the Royal Navy's actions off the Bar, and he could see the smoke of British campfires on Johns Island, which indicated the location of their encampments. Based on Timothy's observations and information from his cavalry patrols, Lincoln began to piece together "the enemy's situation and intentions."[10]

Perceiving little reason to expect "a substantial force" overland from Savannah, Lincoln recalled Colonel Daniel Horry's detachment from their post at Sheldon on 15 February. Lincoln instructed Horry to "cause all the Cattle, Hogs, Horses and indeed every article which shall either nourish the enemy, or facilitate their movements, to be removed" as his troops fell back toward Charleston. He cautioned Horry, however, that he did "not mean the provisions of any distressed family" who were unable to evacuate. Horry was to join General Moultrie at Bacon's Bridge, the main bridge over the Ashley River on the narrower upper Ashley, near present day Summerville. Lincoln assumed that the American campaign to destroy or carry off all boats in the area had been successful and that the British, in lacking boats, would march from Stono Ferry to Bacon's Bridge where they would cross the Ashley. He ordered Moultrie to erect a redoubt at Bacon's Bridge to defend it against such a move. In addition, he repeated the instructions given to Horry, directing Moultrie to remove all livestock, carriages, boats, and "indeed every thing which may comfort the enemy." Lincoln requested that Moultrie keep his cavalry west of the Ashley River "as near the [British] as possible," noting that the cavalrymen should "hang on their flanks" and "Harrass the Enemy on their March as occasion offered."[11]

Although outnumbered in total combat troops, Lincoln possessed a decided advantage in cavalry. His army included at least 379 cavalrymen of all ranks, while Clinton's force that landed on Simmons Island had no cavalry at all. Loss of the horses on the stormy voyage southward deprived Clinton of a key element of his army. He would be without that key element until the cavalrymen, who were collecting horses in the Beaufort area, rejoined him with new mounts. Cavalry acted as the eyes and ears for an eighteenth-century army, especially important when operating in unfamiliar territory. When patrolling in front of the main body, they provided information on the presence and location of the enemy, available forage, and terrain and topography.[12]

Lincoln's cavalry performed a crucial service in reconnoitering the British force, hindering their foraging and scouting parties, and delaying them at critical points along their march. The British, lacking cavalry of their own, encountered great difficulty in gathering intelligence about Lincoln's army, since the American horse patrols prevented their foot soldiers from advancing far from the main body. Meanwhile, American cavalry could move in close to obtain information and then quickly ride away when pressed by British fire. Colonel Horry reported to Lincoln that he intended to "always . . . have One party in and near their Neighborhood." Lincoln suspected that the British lost most of their dragoon horses on the voyage southward, and he recognized the advantage that this presented them. He wrote Congress that none of their cavalry "yet have appeared, and our Horse keep their parties from strolling and plundering the inhabitants." Horry continually sent out parties under the command of Majors John Jameson, Hezekiah Maham, and Paul Vernier to observe and harass the British as they advanced. These cavalry officers were extremely effective in harrying the British troops.[13]

The British soon learned how dangerous it was to send out small parties to reconnoiter or collect forage when American cavalry detachments were in the area. On 18 February, cavalry under the command of Major Jameson captured three British soldiers of the 23rd Regiment. On 22 February, an American horse patrol commanded by Major Maham captured an officer and eight privates who were attempting to retrieve a grindstone for grinding grain from a farm just north of Stono Ferry. Two days later, dragoons under Major Vernier ambushed a British foraging party that was returning to Stono Ferry after collecting livestock. The British troops, distracted by the herd of animals they had taken, were not marching in any organized formation and many had not even loaded their muskets. Vernier's horsemen waited until the British party reached a narrow stretch of road with marsh and heavy brush on both sides and then charged. The cavalrymen made short work of the British soldiers with their heavy sabers and lances. The American dragoons would have cut the detachment to pieces if the jaegers had not rushed to their rescue. The jaegers drove off Vernier's cavalrymen with rifle fire, but Captain Hinrichs reported that the British suffered six men wounded in the action. The successes that American cavalry attained in picking off British patrols prompted Francis Marion to assert that "the Cavalry keep the Enemy in so Close they dont show their Nose."[14]

Although American cavalry patrols were effective in delaying and harassing enemy troops, their small numbers in comparison to the British army could not prevent the inevitable British advance. In addition to being numerically inferior, American cavalrymen still lacked adequate supplies. The horsemen were short of swords, cartridge boxes, saddles, and even clothing. Most critically, they were in want of ammunition. At the end of February, Major Vernier's cavalrymen had only four rounds of ammunition per man.[15]

Lincoln hoped that his force could delay the British until they were adequately reinforced and resupplied. Although he had received word that Virginia and North Carolina Continentals were marching to the Southern Department, Lincoln realized it would take them several months to reach him. In the meantime, he expected North and South Carolina militia to join his army. Assistance from the militia would be critical if he was going to be able to defend Charleston. Governor Caswell of North Carolina promised 2,000 militia and 1,500 drafts for the North Carolina Continental regiments, but of these, only 1,248 militia had arrived at Charleston. As for the South Carolina militia, Governor Rutledge attempted to satisfy Lincoln's request for 2,000 men, but South Carolinians were slow to respond to Rutledge's call to arms after the British landing.[16]

Two factors influenced the low turnout of South Carolina's militia. Locally, many men who would serve in the militia were busily employed in securing their families and livestock, especially south and west of Charleston. Lincoln wrote Governor Caswell that they had received "little succour" from the South Carolina militia, and he explained that "the southern parts of [South Carolina] are invaded by the enemy, and threatened [with] being plundered by the Tories[,] which keeps ye. militia in that quarter at home under a pretense at least of guarding their families, and securing their property." Colonel Horry asserted that many militia were traveling on the roads, but they did not appear "to have any intention to Collect at any One place." A fear as great as that of the British army, however, kept most of the militia from marching to Charleston: the fear of smallpox. Unfortunately for Lincoln, smallpox had broken out in Charleston the previous November and rumors permeated the countryside that it was still present in the city. In an age of relatively primitive medical practices, smallpox probably generated more dread among eighteenth-century Americans than any other epidemic disease. If one did not die from it, they would surely face disfigurement from the numerous pockmarks that the illness left on the skin. William Moultrie commented that the militia "dreaded that disorder more than the enemy." A Hessian officer remarked that "the people of this country, just as in Germany, fear [smallpox] as much as the black plague." David Ramsay, a Charleston physician who served in the South Carolina Assembly, was also well aware of people's fear of the disease. He understood that this fear "discouraged many from reporting to the defense of the capital."[17]

The failure of the South Carolina militia to turn out in great numbers disturbed General Lincoln. He found it "unreasonable" that they wished to avoid marching to Charleston because of rumors of smallpox, especially since "the safety of the town" depended "upon their coming to its assistance." He complained to Moultrie that the North

Carolina militia had arrived with no such apprehensions. To ease the South Carolinians' fears, Lincoln publicized that no trace of the disease could be found in the city. His general orders for 1 March 1780 read: "The strictest search having been made yesterday by the commissioners, surgeons, and several officers of the Army, the General is happy to inform the Garrison that the smallpox is nowhere in Charlestown." In a letter to a South Carolina militia colonel, Governor Rutledge also asserted that "the small pox is not in town." He agreed with General Lincoln, however, that even if it were present in Charleston "the circumstance" was not a valid "excuse for the militia not coming down when ordered." According to Doctor Ramsay, when the militia still did not respond, Rutledge threatened to confiscate their property if they did not perform their duty. Still, they were slow to answer the call. Ramsay asserted that "no more country militia could be brought into the town, and very few could be persuaded to embody in the country." Lincoln's prospects for a large reinforcement from the South Carolina militia were indeed gloomy. He made the following prediction to Governor Caswell: "If we expect any considerable force" from South Carolina "we shall probably be disappointed."[18]

In some areas of South Carolina, men refused to turn out for militia duty because of their aversion to the patriot cause. While Lincoln understood that the inhabitants of "the upper parts" of South Carolina "are obliged to supply a very considerable force" for protection against Indian attacks, he asserted to Governor Caswell that "near the centre of ye. State the people in general are disaffected, and the friendly are insufficient to restrain ye. unfriendly." After the British landing, William Skirving, a South Carolina militia colonel, informed General Moultrie that only one out of four companies lying on the frontiers of his district would join the regiment. The rest, he learned, "are in Arms against us."[19]

Without the militia reinforcements he hoped for, Lincoln continued on the defensive. Keeping the bulk of his troops on the Charleston side of the Ashley River essentially forced Lincoln to concede the region west of the Ashley to the British. This strategy had unfortunate effects on the area's inhabitants, leaving them vulnerable to the advancing British army. Consistently, historians have portrayed military events only as a clash between opposing armies while they have overlooked or underemphasized an often tragic third element: the civilians who by no choice of their own were caught in the middle of those events. The British campaign against Charleston was to have a profound impact on the citizens of the South Carolina lowcountry. Yet contrary to popular belief, the injury and devastation British soldiers and sailors wreaked on civilians were not due to any overt policy of destruction on the part of their leaders. In fact, most British officers attempted to treat leniently Americans not in arms against them. It made little sense to antagonize those who did not resist British rule. Conflict between the British military apparatus and the civilian populace was bound to occur, however, due to the British need for supplies and the simple nature of military operations and those who conducted them.

British troops on Johns Island relied primarily on Admiral Arbuthnot's transports to fulfill their supply needs, but shortly after landing Clinton established facilities for collection of captured rebel property. On 13 February, he appointed three officers, Major James Moncrief, Major George Hay, and C. S. Stone, each a commissary of captures. Clinton's instructions to Moncrief and Hay, and the manner in which foraging parties ultimately carried out those instructions, demonstrate the inconsistency between British policy regarding civilians and British actions toward them.[20]

Clinton was among a group of British officers who intended to impose as little burden as possible on the civilian populace in the collection of supplies. Clinton deplored the depredations that the soldiery often committed against civilians, and in one instance he even ordered that the body of a British cavalryman killed while plundering be hung from a gibbet as a warning to others. In proposed regulations on discipline drafted in 1779, Major John André, Clinton's deputy adjutant, asserted that no one could "justify the plunder of Household Furniture, the Stripping or insulting Inhabitants on the Supposition of their being Rebels; With the Soldier this is the Apology and not the principle." André himself had "seen soldiers loaded with household utensils" they had taken "for the wanton pleasure of spoil" and witnessed these same men throw the looted items away an hour afterward. He claimed that in many cases the victims were "a harmless peasant, a decrepit Father of a Family, a Widow or some other person as little an Object for Severity." In the regulations, André decried that such actions by the troops brought about no public or private good, and increased the possibility that people would view them as enemies. Sir Henry Clinton certainly agreed with the assessment of his deputy adjutant general.[21]

Although he lamented soldiers' mistreatment of civilians, Clinton made no provision in his instructions to the commissaries of captures to prevent it. The instructions declared that since "Sundry persons in Actual Rebellion and bearing Arms against His Majesty . . . have deserted their Habitations and Plantations leaving thereon Stocks of Cattle[,] Horses[,] Forage[,] Rice[,] Corn and other Articles," the commissaries of captures were to take into their custody these articles and "all such Valuable Property as shall be found belonging to any person in Rebellion and faithfully preserve the same" for the army's use. Here Clinton employed the same "Apology" of the private soldiers in presuming that any individuals or families who fled their homes were rebels. In making that assumption, he branded all abandoned homes or plantations as rebel property. He ignored the possibility that many who were lukewarm supporters of the rebellion or who were even neutral had taken flight out of fear of British depredations. Clinton's own policy ran contradictory to his deputy adjutant's proposed regulations on plundering.[22]

Even when he issued orders to respect civilians' welfare, Clinton could not personally supervise the numerous foraging details that now ranged throughout the South Carolina lowcountry, sent out daily to "hunt up Negroes and livestock" for the use of the army. Most of these detachments were comprised of a captain or lieutenant and fifty to one hundred men whose thoughts and actions were far removed from the commanders at headquarters. These men physically collected enemy property. Captain Ewald provides an indication of how the inhabitants received them: "The country people . . . hated us from the bottom of their hearts because we carried off" their belongings.[23]

Plundering and destruction came not only from the army, but also from the navy. On 5 February, Admiral Arbuthnot issued a memorandum declaring that any naval crews "detected in . . . plundering the Country people" would be "delivered up to the Provost Marshal of the

Army, to be punished in so exemplary [a] manner as will sufficiently deter them from a repetition of the like atrocious practice." Despite these warnings, Captain Peter Russell affirmed that British sailors went ashore on Edisto Island and "plundered wantonly and indiscriminately." From Wadmalaw Island, William Carson complained about the situation: "There has not been a day nor a plantation on the island, since my arrival without being molested by Seamen." Edisto inhabitants protested to Captain Russell that sailors had "shot down" their cattle and hogs, leaving them dead on the ground. Russell, fearing the incident would induce civilians to move their livestock out of reach of the army, reported it to headquarters. Officers there informed him that General Clinton "was not desirous of granting Protections to the Inhabitants" until they gave more definite evidence of their loyalty to Britain. It is no wonder that Clinton assumed that all abandoned plantations were rebel property. No one was present to make an assertion of loyalty to the Crown. While he may have reflected upon John André's concern for "the harmless peasant, the decrepit father of a family [and the] widow," Clinton took few steps to ensure the security of these individuals other than to demand their unyielding loyalty to Britain, and when the foraging parties arrived at their homes, these civilians suffered.[24]

With Johns Island secured, the British army's next objective would be a crossing to James Island, which would put them in sight of the city. Fortunately for Lincoln and the Americans, the British, even though they were moving closer to Charleston, were still in no position to attack the city. Clinton grew impatient with the progress. Unaware of Lincoln's difficulties in persuading the South Carolina militia to come to his support, the British commander feared that the delays were presenting "the rebels . . . time to collect in great force in the back country." Clinton and his officers also recognized that their languid pace gave the Americans an opportunity to strengthen their fortifications, which in turn would lengthen the time and scope of operations needed to reduce the city.[25]

Several factors hindered British progress. First and foremost, severe winter weather, which had plagued the British expedition since the outset, continued to disconcert them. A hurricane-like storm forestalled

Clinton's intention to cross over to James Island on 21 February. "The late violent weather has prevented our landing on James Island," he told Arbuthnot three days later. High winds and heavy rains accompanying the storm also prohibited the navy's vessels from bringing supplies up the Stono to the army. Captain Russell asserted that the wind "blows such a Hurricane that a Boat can scarce live in the open sea." The tempest drove out to sea over twenty British transports arriving in a convoy and blew ashore two others posted in the North Edisto. Aware of the advantage the weather afforded them, General Moultrie reported to Lincoln that the heavy rains made it difficult if not impossible for the British to move their supplies and equipment.[26]

Losses suffered on the voyage southward also hampered British activities. Several ships containing articles crucial for siege operations were lost at sea. When the ordnance ship *Russia Merchant* foundered and sank en route to Georgia she took with her much of the artillery and artillery shot, while the *Defiance* had on board critical entrenching tools when she went down off Tybee Island. Operations against a fortified city could certainly not proceed unless these items were replaced.[27]

To remedy the deficiencies, Clinton wrote the commanders of the British posts at St. Augustine, the Bahamas, and the West Indies entreating them to send what artillery and stores they could spare. He also asked Admiral Arbuthnot to furnish artillery pieces from his warships to replace those on the *Russia Merchant.* Arbuthnot willingly turned over the cannon, although Clinton believed that he had been somewhat ungenerous in his donation. Privately he complained that he requested two hundred rounds per gun, but Arbuthnot only forwarded one hundred per gun. In addition, Clinton was annoyed that Arbuthnot promised him all the guns that his sailors saved from the wreck of the *Defiance,* but they were never received. Still, the navy's artillery and ammunition along with replacement entrenching tools which arrived on 3 March made good Clinton's more serious losses.[28]

On 24 February, the weather cleared enough for British troops to cross to James Island. The light infantry embarked in boats at Fenwick's plantation on Johns Island and landed on James Island just below Wappoo Cut. The grenadiers, meanwhile, disembarked at

Hamilton's plantation.[29] Captain Elphinstone's gunboats covered the flatboats that carried the soldiers over the river. Clinton was pleased with the "zealous and animated exertions" of Elphinstone, especially in the manner in which he moved the army and its provisions along and across the waterways of the lowcountry. "[It is] impossible to say how much we are obliged to you for your exertions," Clinton praised the naval captain. "To them we owe everything, from them we shall expect everything."[30]

The eastern shore of James Island afforded Sir Henry his first view of Charleston since 1776. Although possession of James Island put the British in sight of the city, it was to be only a stepping stone and staging area for the ultimate move to the Charleston peninsula. As on Johns Island, they encountered little resistance from the Americans. The rebels destroyed the bridge over Wappoo Cut that led to the mainland, but Lincoln posted no troops on James Island. American cavalry remained north of the Wappoo to harass the British as they had around Stono Ferry. The British light infantry and grenadiers took up a position where the Wappoo bridge had stood on the western end of the cut near its confluence with the Stono.[31]

Over the next several days, other British and Hessian units crossed over from Johns Island. The Hessian grenadiers marched to their assigned post at the abandoned Fort Johnson. Upon reaching this site, they found little left of the works to provide them cover. Under direction from Governor Rutledge, on 15 February Commodore Whipple ordered two of his captains with their marines "to level, destroy and totally demolish the remains of Fort Johnston." The Hessians soon learned their close proximity to Charleston put them in immediate danger. Fort Johnson itself was out of range from artillery fire from the town, but American frigates stationed in the harbor could bombard the position with relative ease. After Lincoln determined that the British had moved to Fort Johnson, he recommended to Whipple that he "annoy" the enemy troops there if it could be done without too much risk. On 28 February, Whipple requested the captain of the *L'Aventure* to "fall down" near Fort Johnson and "fire upon the enemy or their encampment." The ensuing cannon fire from the American vessel killed two Hessian grenadiers and a British soldier. In response to the naval attack, Clinton rode out to Fort Johnson and instructed General Kospoth "to retire into the woods with his brigade, so that he should not be exposed to the cannonading."[32]

Despite the threat from American shipping, lack of opposition on the island proper gave the British and Hessians free reign on James Island. By 1 March, Captain Ewald claimed that they were "now masters of James Island." In control of both banks of the lower Stono, the British sailed the remaining transports from the North Edisto into the Stono. The upper reaches of the river were now of little use to them, so Clinton ordered the troops at Stono Ferry to destroy and abandon the works there. With the exception of a detachment left behind to protect the Johns Island bank of the Stono, the entire army moved to James Island. On James Island, the light infantry continued in their advanced position at Wappoo Bridge while other British and Hessian regiments encamped across the island.[33]

Covered by the light infantry, British working parties rebuilt the wrecked bridge over the Wappoo so that troops could cross to the mainland. On 4 March, Clinton informed Arbuthnot that they had completed repairs to the bridge and that they would "soon proceed to further operations on the other side of it." For the next week, Clinton's men unloaded transports that had sailed into the Stono and established supply depots on James Island. Finally, at four o'clock in the morning of 10 March, Lord Cornwallis led the light infantry, British grenadiers, Hessian jaegers, and 7th, 23rd,and 33rd regiments across the Wappoo.[34]

Before the army could move further up the west bank of the Ashley River, Clinton wished to secure their right flank from attacks from American shipping. The rebel navy's bombardment of the Hessians at Fort Johnson underscored this threat. To protect the flank exposed to the river from American warships, Clinton ordered Cornwallis's detachment to establish a battery at Fenwick's Point on the north side of Wappoo Cut (present day Albemarle Point). On the morning of 11 March, British soldiers burned down a house on Fenwick's Point to provide a clear field of fire for cannon. That evening after dark, Major Moncrief of the British engineers traced out a battery, and by the morning of 12 March, working parties completed the fortification with five embrasures for cannon to fire through. British troops immediately put to use the guns Arbuthnot had sent ashore, rolling three thirty-two pound cannon and two twenty-four pound cannon, along with a howitzer, into place in the battery. This was no small feat; twenty-four pounders and thirty-two pounders generally weighed over two tons each. The twenty-four and thirty-two pound designations represented the weight of a single solid shot cannon ball that the artillery piece fired.[35]

Charlestonians awoke on the morning of 12 March to see the first British gun pointed at their city since the appearance of Clinton's army. At 1,900 yards, British cannon fire could easily reach the city, but it was the American shipping which was the battery's primary target. Before the morning was out, the battery on Fenwick's Point received its first test as the American galleys *Lee* and *Bretigny* sailed up the Ashley River and fired upon it. The galleys' attack had little effect, however, and Peter Timothy observed that it "was wasting ammunition." Gabriel Manigault, who also viewed the action from Charleston, reported that the battery's brass thirty-two pounders returned fire and drove off the American ships. Later that morning, Captain William Sisk, commanding the brig *Notre Dame,* by a mistake of orders anchored his vessel directly opposite Fenwick's Point, and as John Laurens related, "the Enemy fired several well directed shot at her." The cannonballs tore through *Notre Dame*'s rigging, but her crew quickly brought the vessel back down the river before the British could damage her any further. The battery's heavy ordnance dissuaded any American vessels from approaching it. A cannon firing twenty-four pound solid shot "was capable of piercing the thickest timbers of any wooden warship up to a range of 600 yards." Charlestonians later found two thirty-two pound cannonballs in the city, making it evident that the battery could bombard them. One landed in the marsh between Coming's Point and the hospital while the other landed near the Sugar House.[36]

The British later strengthened the position on Fenwick's Point by constructing another battery just beyond the first but further up the Ashley. Working parties muscled additional cannon into the batteries and erected a redoubt between the two to protect them from land assault. Mounting six thirty-two pound cannon in one battery and three smaller pieces in the other, the fortifications on Fenwick's Point represented an effective deterrent to American shipping. With this formidable position, Captain Russell asserted that "the mouth of the [Wappoo] Creek was effectually cleared of Gallies and other armed Vessels." Lincoln recognized that the Fenwick batteries were "at too great a distance to annoy our works." But he conceded that their cannon "will prevent our ships lying in Ashley River, which would interrupt their passage" if the enemy conducted boats into the Ashley via Wappoo Cut. The batteries at Fenwick's Point opened the way for just such a move up the Ashley.[37]

For the citizens of Charleston, the British threat was now unmistakable. Mrs. Ann Manigault found the "people very much distressed" over the presence of the enemy on James Island. Some, using a spyglass, may have caught a glimpse of Hessian grenadiers with their rich blue uniforms and tall mitered caps at Fort Johnson before American frigates had driven them further inland, but the batteries at Fenwick's Point were plainly visible to all on the western side of the city. The cannonballs that landed in town during the action of 12 March provided evidence that shots from the Fenwick batteries could reach them. Captain Hinrichs of the jaegers noted that "the inhabitants were moving from their houses on this side of the city to the eastern side" due to their fear that the Fenwick batteries would fire "hot shot"—cannonballs heated in fires to such a temperature that they ignited any flammable materials on which they landed—into their midst. While General Clinton considered it "absurd, impolitic and inhuman" to burn cities and towns, the people of Charleston could not know that. For all they knew, Sir Henry Clinton and his minions were going to use every effort to destroy the South Carolina capital.[38]

If General Lincoln wished to assuage Charlestonians' fears by attacking the British west of the Ashley, his numbers prevented him from doing so. By 12 March, Lincoln had under his command approximately 4,300 men. Of these, perhaps one quarter were unfit for duty due to illness or lack of clothing or arms. Lincoln's troops included two Virginia Continental battalions numbering 362 men, three South Carolina Continental infantry regiments with approximately 660 men, and the North Carolina brigade of Continentals of approximately 760 men.

The North Carolinians arrived in Charleston only on 3 March after their grueling march from Washington's army. Five companies from the 3rd North Carolina were already serving with Lincoln. Even with the addition of the North Carolina brigade, Lincoln lamented to Washington that "we were before and are now much too weak." With regard to cavalry, on 23 February General Moultrie informed Lincoln that he had 379 cavalrymen under his command at Bacon's Bridge, but constant skirmishing with the British and desertions reduced this figure somewhat. Lincoln's force also included 387 artillerymen from the Charleston Battalion of Artillery, the 4th South Carolina regiment, and the North Carolina Continental artillery. Of militia, 1,248 North Carolina militia reached the city in February, but the South Carolina militia still only trickled in. Lincoln could count 437 men from the Charleston Brigade of Militia, but very few men had materialized from districts outside Charleston. From Bacon's Bridge, Francis Marion reported on 5 March that "only 22 malitia has yet joined us." Monthly returns for Lincoln's army at the end of February show that only 66 men had come in from neighboring Berkeley County. Fears of a smallpox outbreak in town and belief that the British or Indians would threaten their home districts were still keeping the militia from marching to Charleston. Lincoln reported to Washington in early March that only 200 of the "Country Militia of this State" had come in to his army.[39]

Of the troops in his army, Lincoln could only regard the Continental infantry, the cavalry, and the artillerymen as seasoned veterans. If he were to attack the British, veteran troops would be of utmost importance. Offensive operations in eighteenth-century warfare dictated that armies maintain discipline along the march and in tight formations on the battlefield. The notion that yeoman farmers fighting from behind stone walls and trees were responsible for winning the American Revolution is a myth. Most of the war's major battles occurred out in the open just as they had in Europe throughout the eighteenth century. Because the primary infantry weapon, the smoothbore musket, was inaccurate except at close ranges, commanders employed massed formations of men against one another. Soldiers lined up shoulder to shoulder and faced their enemy generally without cover. They had to be able to move quickly in these formations onto and across the battlefield. To expose untrained raw militia to this type of warfare invited disaster. Lincoln would require a preponderance of veterans to engage the British outside of his fortifications. This he did not have.

Against Lincoln's army, Sir Henry Clinton could bring to bear a force of at least 6,700 men.[40] Although new recruits joined the regiments from time to time, British and Hessian units consisted primarily of seasoned regulars. Among Clinton's army were 1,200 light infantry and 925 grenadiers, the elite troops of the British army. Lincoln's veterans, the Continental infantry, artillery, and cavalry and the Charleston artillerymen, numbering only 2,548 altogether, scarcely exceeded the British elite corps. Given the disparity in numbers between the British and American armies, especially with regard to veterans, Lincoln could not afford to take the offensive.[41]

The loss of his second in command, General Moultrie, also hampered Lincoln. Moultrie came down with a severe illness at the end of February and was unable to carry out his duties for several weeks. As a native of the lowcountry and South Carolina's ranking Continental officer, Moultrie would be indispensable to any offensive operations against the British. The army also still needed critical supplies, especially ammunition. Major Vernier's cavalrymen were down to four rounds per man while Marion's infantry at Bacon's Bridge had only twenty-five rounds per man, well short of the standard complement for Continental infantry of forty rounds per man. Meanwhile, the advance guard at Bacon's Bridge lacked an adequate supply of rum. When they established the daily ration at the beginning of the war, officers of the Continental army and members of the Continental Congress recognized the beneficial effects that a daily allowance of spirits could have on the army's morale. Congress determined that one gill of spirits (approximately four ounces) should be issued to the men each day. The deficiency of spirits could negatively affect morale when the army was in short supply of that article. Even Francis Marion, who supposedly imbibed little if at all, complained to Lincoln that his men were "entirely out of rum." Whether it was the shortage of rum or other circumstances, on 15 March Major Jameson indicated to Lincoln that discord prevailed among certain of his troopers. He warned that "some of the first regiment intended to desert the first opportunity" that they got.

A few apparently succeeded. On 16 March, two deserters from the post at Bacon's Bridge went over to the British. Outnumbered, poorly supplied, and with a potential morale problem on his hands, Lincoln was in no position to cross the Ashley in force to attack the British.[42]

While Lincoln lacked the manpower and resources to attack Clinton, Clinton on the other hand was unable to push beyond his position just north of the Wappoo, even after his troops established the battery at Fenwick's Point. Throughout the advance across Johns Island and then James Island, Clinton's soldiers remained dependent on the Royal Navy for supplies and for transport. Coordination between army and navy now reached a critical point. Any further movement by Clinton's force rested directly on the actions of Admiral Arbuthnot and his warships.

After escorting British transports to the mouth of the North Edisto on 11 February, Admiral Arbuthnot sailed north with his warships to threaten Charleston from the seaward side. By 13 February, from his post in the steeple of St. Michael's Church, Peter Timothy reported the sighting of "a 60 or 70 gun ship" from Arbuthnot's fleet approaching Charleston from the southeast. The vessel that Timothy spotted was a British ship of the line. Ships of the line generally carried a complement of either sixty-four or seventy-four guns and were the backbone of the Royal Navy. Arbuthnot left New York with five ships of the line: *Europe, Russell, Defiance, Raisonable,* and *Robust. Defiance* ran aground on a sand bar off Tybee Island and was later destroyed by a storm. The remaining four ships of the line, a fifty gun ship, two forty-fours, and four frigates successfully navigated the tempestuous voyage to southern waters, and Arbuthnot would now employ their might against Charleston. Anchoring his ships off Charleston Bar, Arbuthnot contemplated how he would get his ships past it and into the harbor, which promised to be no easy task. Once he accomplished this, however, his warships could prevent American vessels from entering or leaving the harbor, effectively cutting off Charleston from the Atlantic.[43]

As for the army, Clinton asserted "more serious operation could not go on until . . . the Admiral could pass a naval force into the harbor." Clinton could advance no further because he required direct assistance from Arbuthnot in the form of artillery, ammunition, boats, and sailors to man them. The likelihood that they would have to lay siege to Charleston made additional artillery and ammunition particularly important. Furthermore, the navy would have to convey troops and their equipment across the Ashley.[44]

Convinced of Lincoln's determination to hold Charleston, Clinton recognized that he also needed reinforcements. Besides soldiers for conducting siege operations on Charleston neck, he would require men to maintain the line of communication between his army on the neck and the British fleet via James Island and the Stono River. Accordingly, Clinton ordered Brigadier General James Paterson, whom he had sent from Savannah to make a feint toward Augusta, to join the main army with his troops. Paterson's corps would take several weeks to march to Charleston. Meanwhile, the seamen, boats, and additional ordnance Clinton coveted would not come until Arbuthnot pushed his ships over the Bar. Sir Henry would be unable to influence when or if that would occur. Privately critical of Arbuthnot's decisions since the outset of the expedition, Clinton maintained a friendly tone in their correspondence. Given his attitude toward the admiral, it must have been difficult to keep up such geniality. The success of Clinton and the British army, however, was now contingent on Arbuthnot's success, and Sir Henry would now have to wait for the admiral.[45]

Chapter Five

That Infernal Bar

Although the Americans offered little resistance to the steady progression of the British army across Johns and then James Island, Lincoln was still counting on probably his most important defensive asset to impede further British operations: Charleston Bar. The topography of the South Carolina lowcountry had already tested the British army, but now it was the turn of the British navy to contend with its idiosyncrasies. A nuisance for mariners putting in at Charleston in peacetime, in wartime the Bar stood like a bulwark across the front of the harbor. With only a few narrow and extremely shallow passageways across it, British captains would have to display exemplary seamanship to clear the Bar. Meanwhile, Lincoln intended to use all his naval resources to make a crossing even more dangerous and demanding for them. Unfortunately, Lincoln's expectations with regard to naval matters were frustrated. Through Commodore Abraham Whipple, the captains of the ships, and Charleston's harbor pilots, he soon discovered that defense of the Bar would be more difficult than he anticipated. Moreover, while the Continental Congress expressly instructed Commodore Whipple to put himself under the orders of General Lincoln, Lincoln soon learned that he and the commodore held greatly diverging opinions on how best to utilize their warships.

Keenly aware of the strategic importance of Charleston Bar, Benjamin Lincoln had every intention of making it his first line of defense. Although Fort Moultrie was the chief fortification of Charleston on the seaward side, Lincoln viewed the seaward defenses in a larger context. For Lincoln, Fort Moultrie represented the inner defense line while the Bar acted as the outer line. Just as a parapet in a land fortification, the American commander needed to man the Bar to prevent the enemy from passing it. Unlike a land fortification, the defenders sheltered behind its mass were to be not men but ships.

Lincoln believed he had the requisite number of vessels to defend the city from the seaward side. In addition to the Continental ships, the South Carolina state navy contributed three vessels of over twenty guns to Lincoln's fleet. The South Carolinians obtained *Bricole, Truite,* and *L'Aventure* from the French squadron that assisted in the attack on Savannah, and these ships were now posted at Charleston. Although *Bricole,* with forty-four guns, carried the largest complement of armament of any of the American ships stationed at Charleston, the French originally built her as a transport and therefore she was not designed to withstand the punishment of a close naval bombardment. The same was true of the twenty-six gun *Truite,* also a converted transport. Per instructions of Governor Rutledge, Commodore Whipple was to take command of the South Carolina shipping. The combined strength of

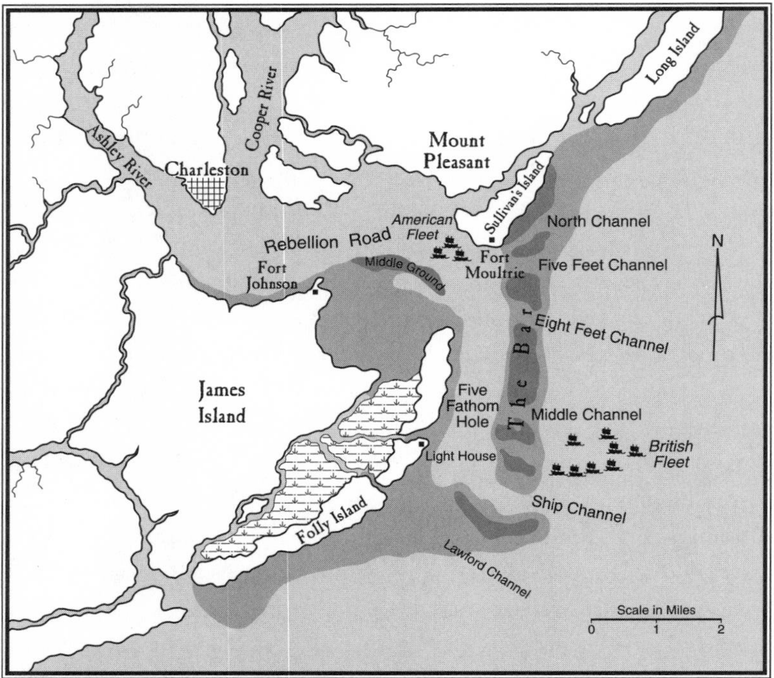

Charleston Bar and Harbor

the Continental and South Carolina vessels afforded Lincoln and Whipple an adequate naval force with which to defend the Bar and harbor.[1]

As early as 18 January, Lincoln determined to defend Charleston harbor from a British sea attack by making a stand at the Bar. He desired the navy to station ships inside the Bar with broadsides to the Ship Channel, the primary crossing point at the southeastern end of the Bar, which would allow them to cross the "T" of the British ships as they worked their way up the channel. When Charleston harbor pilots reported that such a station might not be feasible, Lincoln ordered Whipple to look into the matter immediately. On 30 January, he instructed Whipple to have his captains and "the best pilots you can obtain" sound "the internal part of the bar." He also directed him to ascertain whether ships could lie "in such a manner as to command the passage and leave the Station if it should become necessary." To encourage the commodore to fulfill his responsibilities, Lincoln reminded him that the Continental Congress had sent the "frigates under your command as a protection to this part of the United States."[2]

Whipple and his captains proceeded to gather intelligence on the dynamics of the Bar. After reviewing the situation with the harbor pilots, the captains reported that a station near the Bar was impractical for their frigates, explaining that ships drew too much water lying there and risked running aground. They also offered an opinion as to the practicability of a station in Five Fathom Hole, further up the Bar off the southern end of present day Morris Island. Going under the assumption that the British would cross with an easterly wind and flood tide, the captains asserted that under such conditions there would be such a swell in Five Fathom Hole as to render it impossible for a ship to anchor with broadsides to oncoming British ships. They also maintained that the flood tide would give attacking British ships an opportunity to reach Fort Moultrie before them, cutting them off from Charleston harbor. The British warships would then easily destroy or capture the American vessels.[3]

Their representations did not dissuade Lincoln however. On the day after receiving word that the British were off the coast, he wrote Whipple further expressing his desire to defend the Bar. Lincoln conceded that "it may be difficult, if not impossible" for ships to lie with their broadsides to the Ship Channel and that some vessels might be lost by taking station in or near Five Fathom Hole. Still, he believed it worth the risk if they could stop the British from getting into the harbor. Citing the "evils" that would occur if the enemy succeeded, Lincoln insisted that the attempt to defend the Bar "ought to be made, and that the measure thereby can be justified." He declared that "the safety of this Town lyes in reducing the enemy's attempt on it to a land attack." Lacking the strength to repel both a land and sea attack, Lincoln understood that Charleston's best chance of survival lay in thwarting British naval operations. If the Royal Navy passed the Bar, Lincoln foresaw them pushing past Fort Moultrie and driving the American vessels into the Ashley and Cooper Rivers. If that transpired, Charleston would be at the mercy of British warships. Given these circumstances, Lincoln requested Whipple to "as soon as possible station the Providence, Boston, Bricolle, and Truite with such Gallies as in your opinion may be serviceable near the bar, so as best to command the entrance of it." Moreover, he desired that Whipple leave his flagship, *Providence,* and come ashore to direct the movements of all ships in the harbor.[4]

Prodded by Lincoln, Whipple ordered Captains Samuel Tucker and Thomas Simpson to take *Providence, Boston,* and *Ranger* down to the Bar and moor them so as to defend it, but the same hurricane-like storm which harried the British foiled their efforts. When the weather cleared on 24 February, Whipple issued the same instructions to Captain Hoysted Hacker, his second in command, but Hacker and the other captains were apparently slow to take up the position. Lincoln discerned the navy's reluctance to station their ships near the Bar. Exasperated, he ordered "the Sea officers with the Pilots to make critical examination into the matter and report" back to him. Eager to obtain "a just and impartial representation" of the situation, Lincoln himself spent "two days in a boat" reconnoitering and sounding the Bar. From his own "observations" Lincoln found that there were in fact unexpected "difficulties" in anchoring the frigates near the Bar, but he was not ready to give up just yet.[5]

On 26 February, Lincoln asserted to Whipple that Congress sent him to Charleston "to cover the bar of this Harbour, a measure highly necessary" and therefore an attempt to defend it "should be made but on the fullest evidence of its impracticability." He asked Whipple several pointed questions concerning the naval situation of the Bar. Specifically, he wished to know the depth of the stretch of water between the Ship Channel and Five Fathom Hole, the distance between those two points, and "whether in that distance there is any place where your ships can anchor in a suitable depth of water" to cover the Bar. Lincoln was losing hope that Whipple would take up such a position, however. After pursuing this information, he also requested that the commodore suggest a station where his ships might lie so as to defend the town "if you cannot anchor so as to cover the Bar." Whipple once again consulted his captains and harbor pilots. After providing detailed answers to Lincoln's inquiries, none of which supported a station near the Bar, Whipple indicated to Lincoln that it was the opinion of he and his officers that "the ships can do the most effectual service for the defence and security of the Town" by acting in conjunction with Fort Moultrie. Interestingly, in his letter to Lincoln he conceded that there was a position "off the North breaker head, where the ships can be anchored to moor them, that they may swing in safety." According to a letter that Whipple had written earlier to one of his captains, the "North breaker head" was fairly close to the entrance of the Bar. Such a station would have allowed the American ships to fire on the British as they sailed up the channel inside the Bar toward Charleston just as Lincoln desired. Given this information, it appears that Whipple had not been completely forthcoming with Lincoln concerning the circumstances of the Bar. A month had frittered away in this discourse between the two officers, and it seems that Whipple never had any intention of placing his ships so as to defend the Bar.[6]

The experience nettled Benjamin Lincoln, and he now faced the loss of Charleston's most important defensive obstacle. Lincoln understood the strategic significance of Charleston Bar to the point of accepting the loss of some of his ships in defense of it. That he did not entirely trust the opinions of Whipple and the naval officers is evident in his continued insistence that they find a station to defend the Bar and in his personal reconnoitering of the Bar for two days. Still, Lincoln did not coerce Whipple into following his orders, even after Whipple admitted that American ships could anchor inside the Bar after all.

Other than instructing him to choose a position which "best answer[s] the purposes of your being sent here, and the views of Congress," Lincoln did not pressure the commodore. As the commander of all Continental forces in the Southern Department, he surely had authority to remove Whipple. On ordering Commodore Whipple and the frigates to Charleston, the Continental Congress resolved that the ships were "to be under the direction of the commanding officer for the time being in the Southern department, until farther orders." Lincoln did not remove him, however. As a major general in the Continental army, he may have felt that it was not his place to remove an officer in the Continental navy. To consult the Continental Congress on the matter could take months of correspondence, and with the British army and navy at their doorstep, time was of the essence. Lincoln may have also feared that Whipple's removal might provoke a backlash among the other naval officers who then might refuse to honor his commands. Whipple's answer to Lincoln's inquiries was signed by his three immediate subordinates: Captains Hoysted Hacker, Samuel Tucker, and Thomas Simpson. Obviously the naval officers concurred in the manner in which they should employ their ships. Any change in commander of naval forces would not guarantee a change in strategy.[7]

To Whipple's credit, the Continental Congress entrusted him with three of the eight Continental frigates then in existence.[8] For a captain to lose his ship was serious enough, but to risk the loss of a third of the Continental navy's frigates was quite another. By taking station near Fort Moultrie as he desired, the guns of the fort could cover his ships. Conversely, if he moored them in Five Fathom Hole or even further down the Bar as Lincoln wished, they would have no supporting fire and would face the British ships alone. Whipple and his captains rejected as impracticable the idea of protecting the ships with floating batteries or shore batteries on the sea islands since the naval crews could not evacuate their garrisons in the event of a retreat. Whipple had not reached his decision alone; his answers to Lincoln's inquiries were signed not only by his captains, but also by five harbor pilots.[9] Whipple had been ashore from 20 February until 26 February, but his captains were on the scene and they had direct knowledge of nautical conditions inside the Bar. Still, as ranking Continental naval officer in the Southern Department the ultimate decision rested with Whipple, and he demonstrated a very limited strategic view in his unwillingness to risk misfortune for the greater good. The fear of losing his frigates prevented Whipple from following Lincoln's recommendation to make every effort to defend the Bar. In ignoring his commander's wishes, he would soon see the folly of affording the British such an opportunity.[10]

With Arbuthnot's ships cruising before the Bar, the Americans could clearly see what they were up against. From his post in St. Michael's steeple, Peter Timothy made daily reports to Lincoln on the movements of British ships. On 16 February, he watched as "3 of the British Men of War . . . paraded before the Harbour," and in the afternoon of 18 February, he noted that an enemy frigate appeared "in full view of the Town as if challenging our ships to go out, or bidding them Defiance." Timothy discerned that the presence of the British warships off the Bar effectively blockaded the harbor. Lieutenant Colonel John Laurens, now serving as a marine on board *Providence,* plainly observed their crews "making dispositions for passing the bar." The Royal Navy's arrival before Charleston came in the midst of Lincoln and Whipple's correspondence over the defense of the Bar, and the "full view" of British warships probably contributed to Whipple's apprehension for the safety of his own vessels.[11]

Although he failed to cover the Bar as Lincoln wished, Whipple had previously suggested and put into effect several other measures to hinder the British navy's progress. On 13 February, he recommended to Governor Rutledge that they destroy "the Beacon and lighthouse" to prevent the British from using these markers to navigate their ships past the Bar. Rutledge agreed and ordered it done "as soon as possible." The Americans also "blackened" St. Michael's Church to make it less discernible to British navigators. Traditionally, mariners used the great white steeple as a landmark when piloting their way into Charleston harbor. In addition, the Americans removed all the buoys denoting the main channel over the Bar, and on 28 February Lincoln requested Whipple to send the brigs *General Lincoln* and *Notre Dame* down to the Bar to prevent the enemy from laying new buoys. Recognizing the consequence of this assignment, Whipple appointed Captain Hacker to oversee it and he later augmented the force with the galleys *Lee* and *Revenge*.[12]

American actions soon compelled Clinton and Arbuthnot to take countermeasures. To prevent American shipping from harassing them while they sounded the channel and denoted a passage with new buoys, Clinton sent the 71st regiment with two cannon to Lighthouse Island to cover the lower end of the Bar. Later, a British galley and schooner sailed into the channel to protect the buoys. These efforts kept American vessels at bay. Although Whipple reported to Lincoln on 9 March that the force he "sent down is sufficient to prevent their sounding or buoying the bar," the following day Lieutenant Colonel Laurens observed that the British had "found means to establish a large white buoy on the bar."[13]

Persistent foul weather prevented Admiral Arbuthnot from attempting a crossing until conditions improved. With his warships riding in the open sea off Charleston Bar, the delays made Arbuthnot anxious. Like Whipple, he too was concerned with the loss of his ships. To Clinton, he asserted that "the season advances in which it will be the utmost hazard for the ships to remain on the coast." The "hazard" was that a superior French fleet would sail into American waters, a fear which plagued British sea captains operating on the American station from the time France entered the conflict until the end of the war. Arbuthnot worried that England's longtime enemy would make "a sudden appearance" and thwart their efforts. "Every moment increases my apprehensions of the French once more snatching the opportunity of rescuing Charles Town from us," he had earlier declared. With many of his heavy guns transferred ashore and his captains concentrating on the passage of the Bar, Arbuthnot's small fleet was in no position to face a French naval attack. Only a crossing of the Bar and a subsequent culmination of operations against Charleston would completely quell Arbuthnot's uneasiness. In the meantime, he sent a message to Admiral Sir Peter Parker at the British base at Barbados informing Parker to notify him of French naval movements in the West Indies.[14]

Arbuthnot planned to send only his smaller warships over the Bar, the larger ships of the line being of too much draft and too great a value to hazard in the passage. A large vessel risked running aground in the Ship Channel, which was only twenty feet deep at high tide. Having already lost *Defiance* to a sand bar off Savannah, the admiral did not wish to chance it. The ships of the line would remain outside the Bar while *Renown* of fifty guns, *Roebuck* and *Romulus,* each of forty-four, and four frigates, *Richmond, Raleigh, Blonde,* and *Virginia,* attempted the crossing. Arbuthnot transferred from his flagship *Europe* to the *Roebuck,* and in this vessel he would endeavor to pass the Bar.[15]

Although fifty and forty-four gun ships drafted less than ships of the line, their crews still had to remove much of their guns and stores for the vessels to clear the channel. Arbuthnot's sailors had already sent some of their cannon to Clinton's army on James Island, but they now transferred others, along with casks of water and other heavy stores, into transports. Once the warships successfully crossed the Bar, the lesser-drafting transports would follow and the mariners would load stores and guns aboard the warships again. This lightening of the warships put them in a dangerous position. Lincoln suggested to Whipple that he might attack the British vessels after they cleared the Bar but before their crews brought the guns back aboard. Whipple's undertaking such an attack was doubtful, but other dangers existed for the British naval captains. According to Johann Ewald, the removal of the guns threw off the ships' "normal balance," making them too buoyant and increasing the possibility that a severe storm could blow them out to sea. The precariousness of their situation contributed to Arbuthnot's uneasiness. Aboard *Roebuck,* he lamented to Clinton on 16 March: "It is not easy to describe my situation." He bemoaned that he had been "eight days riding in the open sea without guns, provisions, & c. and in one word [was] a wreck." The admiral yearned for the favorable wind and flood tide which would allow them to attempt the Bar.[16]

In spite of his worries, the American decision to retire from the Bar was a fortunate circumstance for Arbuthnot. Had Whipple taken station in Five Fathom Hole or further down the Bar as Lincoln suggested, the British ships would have outgunned him but the American vessels would still have had the advantage of position. Only the South Carolina navy's *Bricole* matched the British *Roebuck* and *Romulus* in firepower, and no American ship equaled the fifty gun *Renown,* but a position astride the channel inside the Bar with broadsides to the Ship Channel would have allowed the American ships to present half their guns at the advancing British. The British ships, on the other hand, with few guns in their bows would have been able to return only limited fire. Avoiding such a prospect surely pleased Arbuthnot.

By early March, Commodore Whipple had anchored the small American fleet under the guns of Fort Moultrie "within point blank shot of the fort." Lying on the Charleston side of Fort Moultrie in a stretch of water known as Rebellion Road, Whipple's ships formed a line of battle between the fort and the Middle Ground. From this line of battle, they and the guns of Fort Moultrie could rake the narrow channel between Sullivan's Island and the Middle Ground with artillery fire as the British attempted to pass it. The vessels could also prevent the British from landing troops to attack Fort Moultrie.[17]

Under Lincoln's orders, Whipple's captains and crews labored on a chain of obstructions that they endeavored to lay across the channel in front of Rebellion Road to block the entrance to British ships. The foundation of this barrier was to consist of unusable ships, which sailors would sink in the channel. They would then lash spars, chains, and cables between the masts to complete the boom between the sunken vessels. Any British attempt to remove the obstruction would be done under the guns of Fort Moultrie and the American warships. On 11 March, Whipple and his captains sent Lincoln and Rutledge a request for materials needed to complete the boom; their application included two large anchors, twenty-four small anchors, twenty-four hundred feet of cable, eighteen hundred feet of chains, and twelve "Craft or Boats." Lincoln also pressed the navy to prepare fire ships, consisting of aged vessels loaded with combustibles which they would set ablaze and drive at enemy ships to set them afire. Although the Americans conceded the Bar crossing to the British, Lincoln was confident that these new defensive measures would impede the Royal Navy's attempt to pass Fort Moultrie. The fire ships in particular encouraged him. He asserted that with them "there is so great a prospect of success nothing I think should divert us." The South Carolinians even offered some "large public vessels" for this purpose. The commodore was soon to disappoint Lincoln again however.[18]

On 16 March, Lincoln wrote Whipple and expressed his hope that "the chain across the channel in front of your ships" was near completion. Aware of Lincoln's concerns, Whipple reported that "at present the wind blows so hard, the boats cannot work." He also contended that he would require three more vessels of approximately seventy tons each to conclude the undertaking. Acquisition of materials for the project presented a problem for Whipple and his captains. Captain Thomas Simpson complained on 12 March that he obtained anchors and cable only "with much trouble." After Whipple called upon two captains of the South Carolina state navy, David Lockwood and James Pyne, to assist him, Simpson apparently gathered what was needed. A sufficiency of materials did not guarantee success, however, and in light of his previous experience with his naval officers, Lincoln probably conjectured as much. Whipple ultimately determined that the channel was too deep and too wide and the tide too strong to finish the chain. Lieutenant Colonel Laurens asserted that "the unconquerable elements" foiled "the greatest exertions" of the naval officers to lay the boom. As to fire ships, Whipple ordered two of his captains to "use their utmost efforts to collect materials" for them, but the navy never completed the fire ships. Whipple again failed to carry out Lincoln's orders, and time was now running out. The spring flood tide would arrive on 20 March. By 19 March, General Moultrie, keenly aware of Charleston's tides, expected the British to attempt the Bar "tomorrow or next day." His prediction was to prove accurate.[19]

The spring flood tide did not guarantee the Royal Navy success. They also required favorable weather and a fair wind. The persistent foul weather was the Americans' last hope to keep the British outside the Bar. With a hard rain on 18 and 19 March, fortune seemed to be smiling on Charleston. General McIntosh recorded on 19 March that "the Enemy's Ships off the Barr disapeared being Stormy last Night," but when the storms dissipated that afternoon, the British ships were right back at their station. The day of 20 March dawned clear and cool with a brisk northeasterly wind, and Arbuthnot finally had the conditions he had waited for. For sixteen days, his ships had been riding in the open sea at the mercy of the weather. At approximately seven that morning, Arbuthnot, in the *Roebuck,* gave the signal to weigh anchor and led *Richmond, Romulus, Blonde, Raleigh, Perseus,* two transports, and several smaller vessels through the Ship Channel and across the Bar. *Virginia* and *Renown* crossed later in the day. The British ships made the passage without incident and sailed safely into Five Fathom Hole where General Lincoln had hoped the Americans would make a stand.[20]

Although British ships had traversed the Ship Channel, Commodore Whipple had one last chance to oppose them at the Bar. Shortly after they came through, Captain Charles Crawley of the South Carolina state navy proposed to Whipple that he order the galleys down to the Bar to attack them before they brought their cannon back aboard. Whipple put the question of whether they should make such an attempt to seven of his captains. Only Crawley, who commanded one of the galleys which would participate in the venture, voted "to go." The other six captains voted "not to go."[21] From the Ship Channel to Fort Moultrie, nothing stood in the way of the Royal Navy.[22]

The crossing of the British vessels greatly alarmed Whipple and his captains. They had not anticipated that the British could get a ship as large as the fifty gun *Renown* over the Bar. Even with the assistance of Fort Moultrie's forty cannon, the Royal Navy would outgun them 286 to 248.[23] According to Lieutenant Colonel Laurens, American naval officers feared that enemy warships could, "with a leading wind and tide pass the fire of Fort Moultrie[,] break through our line of battle, and then come to immediately having our ships between them and the fort." Their guns could then cut the Americans ships to pieces. Meanwhile, the maneuver would neutralize Fort Moultrie since fire from the fort risked hitting friendly ships between it and the British ships.[24]

Immediately after the British passed the Bar, Lincoln sent a hurried note to Whipple inquiring whether he thought the partially completed obstruction across the channel in front of Fort Moultrie was "sufficient to check the progress of the enemy's ships." He also wished to know whether Whipple's ships could still safely act in conjunction with Fort Moultrie, and if not, did he recommend moving them to a new station. Lincoln gave Whipple entirely too much leeway in the manner in which he phrased his questions, opening himself up for a negative response from the commodore. Whipple had already shown that he was unwilling to risk ships to British fire, and with even larger than anticipated British vessels now across the Bar, he was not going to alter that position.[25]

Responding to Lincoln's inquiries, the naval officers unanimously agreed that "the present or even any obstructions we can throw in the way of the enemy will be insufficient to check such heavy ships as the enemy now have in the harbour." They also declared that Fort Moultrie's guns could no longer protect them and that they ought to change their station as soon as possible. In a weak attempt to justify his earlier argument for a position near Fort Moultrie, Whipple maintained that "when we recommended this as a suitable station, it was at a time when the enemy's force off the Bar, did not exceed half what they now have in the harbour." The commodore also claimed that he and the captains made the decision "when we had every assurance that a ship larger than fifty guns could not be got over the bar." When South Carolinian John Lewis Gervais heard this explanation he acidly observed that "it is a little surprising that we should have been in possession of the Country a Century & at this day only know that a Vessel of such a draft of water could come in." John Laurens also found it perplexing that Charleston's pilots miscalculated the ease with which a large warship could cross the Bar, asserting that the difficulties in passing it had been "greatly exaggerated." Gervais and Laurens hinted strongly that certain seamen erred grievously in their efforts to safeguard the harbor.[26]

Lincoln now faced the collapse of his planned naval defense. Recognizing that Whipple would not stand and fight, he had little choice but to order the American ships closer to town. At noon on 20 March, he instructed Whipple to "take up the several Cables and Anchors you have put across the channel . . . [and] leave your present station as soon as possible." On the afternoon of the following day, the six American frigates and sloop of war *Ranger* left Rebellion Road and returned to Charleston. Their anchorage in the Cooper River emancipated them from any possible action with British warships in the harbor. As General Moultrie pointed out, "Commodore Whipple did not choose to risk an engagement with the British fleet." As a result, the Royal Navy passed the city's chief natural defensive obstacle with relative ease, and now only Fort Moultrie stood between them and Charleston itself. Charlestonians pinned their hopes on a repeat of June 1776 when Fort Moultrie had fought off Parker's fleet alone.[27]

With his ships bottled up in the Cooper River, Whipple could no longer disappoint Lincoln. He could no longer plead for a change of station, because there was no alternate station for the American warships. There would be no more excuses. If matters were not so perilous, the end of Whipple's wavering probably would have come as a relief to Lincoln. Charleston *was* now in serious peril, however. The experience with Commodore Whipple and the manner in which he utilized the small American fleet had exasperated Lincoln. With militia reinforcements only trickling in, Lincoln recognized that their best chance lay in the most effectual employment of the naval force. Commodore Whipple, on the other hand, was too concerned with the preservation of individual ships to have such strategic insight, and he failed in his duty completely.

Despite the risks involved, Lincoln's decision to defend the Bar was the correct one. Given Admiral Arbuthnot's innate caution and his anxiety over the possible appearance of a French fleet, a stubborn defense of the interior of the Bar might have caused him to rethink the undertaking. It may have even prompted him to withdraw, leaving the Americans free access to the sea. By stopping the Royal Navy at the Bar, Lincoln hoped that Charleston would have to face a land attack only. But Lincoln had even underestimated the importance of the Bar crossing to Clinton's army and the degree to which they depended upon the navy. For British operations against Charleston to succeed, the army and navy had to attack the city from both landward and seaward sides, and maintain communications as they did so. By passing the Bar, Arbuthnot was in effect covering the rear of Clinton's army. If the navy failed to get into the harbor, Clinton's army would be exposed to an attack from the rear via James Island assuming that Clinton was still willing to proceed up the Ashley River. But without Arbuthnot's support, the overly cautious Clinton would not have dared to make such a move. An advance up the Ashley would have been an extremely difficult endeavor indeed without the navy's boats and sailors to transport the army. Had a stout defense of the Bar forced Arbuthnot to withdraw, Clinton would have also had to retire. Dependent on British transports for provisions, the army's troops would have to evacuate aboard those vessels or retreat overland to Savannah if Arbuthnot decided he had risked enough. This set of circumstances does not seem so farfetched when one considers the British experience in the attack on Sullivan's Island in 1776. Although the fort on Sullivan's Island had severely punished Parker's flotilla, Clinton's army still remained intact on Long Island. Parker did not see fit to renew the attack on the fort, however, and without the navy Clinton could do nothing. Consequently, the entire British force departed South Carolina just a few weeks later. Now almost four years later, Lincoln's hoped-for defense of Charleston Bar had not come to fruition, and Fort Moultrie would certainly meet with another test from the Royal Navy. John Lewis Gervais asserted that if the British attempted Fort Moultrie, he had "no doubt" that the fort would "make a Valiant defence."[28]

The Americans had yielded the Bar to the British, and not only was Charleston cut off by sea, but Admiral Arbuthnot could now extend resources to the army. Clinton expressed the anxiety that he felt previous to the crossing of the Bar when he wrote Arbuthnot shortly afterward "joy to you sir[,] to myself and to us all upon your passage of that infernal Bar." While Clinton supposed that the admiral was primarily responsible for the delay in crossing the "infernal Bar," he was satisfied that Arbuthnot would now furnish him with men and boats to transport his troops. He wrote a close friend that his army could now obtain the Royal Navy's assistance and that they would move in a few days. Sir Henry Clinton and his army were ready to resume their advance toward Charleston.[29]

Chapter Six

The Defenders of Charleston

While awaiting the outcome of British efforts to cross Charleston Bar, Lincoln and the Americans addressed the city's defenses. Rather than risk his army in battle against a superior British force west of the Ashley River, Lincoln resigned himself to securing the city from behind its entrenchments. Almost two months had passed since Charleston's soldiers and civilians first learned of the British expedition against the state; that span of time provided Lincoln the opportunity to prepare his army and to improve the defensive lines on the outskirts of town. In the words of one British officer, their delays afforded the Americans "an opportunity to perfect their fortifications" and "gave them confidence to hazard their lives and fortunes upon the event of a siege."[1]

Since the British landing on Simmons Island in early February, Lincoln and his officers had taken extensive steps to prepare the troops for action. Properly arming and equipping them was a priority. Lincoln ordered that all soldiers be provided with fifty rounds of ammunition per man, and officers were to ensure that each man was furnished with a bayonet for his musket. Bearing out the weapon's critical nature, Lincoln expressly decreed that any soldier misusing his bayonet would receive ten lashes without benefit of a court-martial. To make certain that each man was properly armed and judiciously attending to his weapons, Lincoln directed that "officers commanding Reg[imen]ts will daily have their arms and accoutrements inspected, that they may always be ready for action."[2]

Lincoln also endeavored to keep his army intact. Desertion plagued the Continental army throughout the Revolution and was a problem which American generals could never eradicate. Officers were particularly sensitive to desertion when action with the British was imminent. Not only did desertions weaken the army in the face of the enemy, but also in many cases runaways would go over to the British and provide information to them. British officers had already reported the arrival of several American deserters to their army.

To reduce the risk of desertion, Lincoln ordered sergeants to call the rolls every morning and every evening, and he insisted that all officers be present for the roll calls. Per general orders, no soldier was "to be absent . . . from his barracks" after the evening roll call "under any pretense whatsoever." Meanwhile, Governor Rutledge suggested to Lincoln the necessity of placing an officer on the lines "to keep an account of all white men going out of town." This measure was intended to stop deserters and keep spies from reporting to the British. Despite these precautions, men continued to desert. General orders of 9 March reported that a court-martial had found George McCartey of the 3rd North Carolina guilty of desertion and sentenced him to receive "100 lashes on his bare back with switches." The officers of the court, however, recognized their need for manpower at such a critical hour and remitted McCartey's sentence.[3]

Although Lincoln did not attack the British army as it advanced across the sea islands, his troops were far from idle. Lincoln sent Francis Marion with 200 light infantry to Bacon's Bridge while the 1st South Carolina regiment manned Fort Moultrie. A smaller command of 175 to 190 men detailed from other regiments protected the landing at Ashley Ferry. Lincoln designated the remaining Continentals and militia the task of strengthening the city's fortifications. African American slaves labored alongside them in bolstering Charleston's defenses. At Fort Moultrie, John Laurens noted that the garrison and "a number of Negroes are employed in improving that post." Lincoln assigned Continental infantry and artillery and the Charleston Battalion of Artillery to the lines on Charleston neck where he anticipated the most severe fighting would occur. The militia he posted to the works and batteries facing the harbor. Units were responsible for improving and constructing the fortifications at their allotted positions.[4]

In early February, Lincoln ordered one-third of the troops to parade every morning at eight o'clock to perform fatigue duty. He warned the officers "to be careful that men do not idle away their time." Lincoln not assigned to other duties, and on 21 February, he directed the entire army, with the exception of those already appointed other responsibilities, to turn out for fatigue duty. As to the militia, Lincoln was all too familiar with their generally unsoldier-like conduct and he reminded them that they were repairing the fortifications not only for the safety of the town, but also for their own safety.[5]

Lincoln rode the lines for several hours each day to encourage the men and inspect their progress. Archibald Gamble, one of his engineers, deposed that Lincoln paid attention "to the Construction of every work necessary for the Defense" of Charleston. He maintained that Lincoln "always was one of the first at and last from the Works[,] giving directions to the Overseers and encouraging the Labourers." James Cannon remembered that Lincoln was "on horse back from 5 in the morning until 8 or 9 at night pushing on the Works." The commander of the Southern Department even toiled along with the soldiers. Cannon declared that he often submitted "to the common duties of [the] fatigue Men" so that he could "set an Example of Emulation that none might think it beneath him to give his Assistance." Just as Henry Clinton slept in the rain alongside his men, Benjamin Lincoln demonstrated to his men that he was willing to share in their hardships.[6]

Who were these men with whom Lincoln shared the hardships of defending Charleston? What motivated them to labor for hours each day on the batteries and redoubts of Charleston and ultimately face the prospect of British cannon, muskets, and bayonets? While the militia augmented their numbers, the men of the Virginia, North Carolina, and South Carolina Continental regiments bore the brunt of the duty in the Southern Department in 1780, but who were these men and why did they fight? A review of the muster rolls and payrolls of the South Carolina Continental regiments in 1779 and 1780 produces a long list of English, Scots-Irish, and Irish names, but reveals little about those individuals. Payrolls do demonstrate that a large proportion of them could neither read nor write, the soldiers having denoted the receipt of their pay with an "X" rather than a signature. Court-martial records indicate that some of them were a rough lot. In addition to simple disobedience of orders, their crimes ranged from stealing from their fellow soldiers to drunkenness to bullying civilians. Walter J. Fraser has argued that there were an inordinate number of courts-martial among the South Carolina Continentals. According to Fraser, approximately fifty percent of the rank and file of the South Carolina troops had some charges brought against them by court-martial boards at one time or another. The number and frequency of these courts-martial among the South Carolinians is strong evidence that their ranks contained many insubordinate and recalcitrant individuals, but it offers little insight into those who obeyed orders and treated their fellow soldiers and civilians with respect.[7]

The life of a soldier, whatever his personal character, was quite hard. Soldiers went months without receiving the six and two-thirds dollars per month prescribed by the Continental Congress, and more seriously, they often did not receive the full daily food ration established by Congress. On many occasions men went without food for an entire day. On campaign, the army sometimes marched ten to twenty miles a day, often in the heat of a Carolina summer. It is little wonder that soldiers risked court-martial and sold their issued woolen regimental coats. In camp, they were subject to such dread diseases as smallpox, the bloody flux (dysentery), and various fevers. Finally, they faced the prospect of maiming or death on the battlefield, or even worse, days or weeks of suffering in a hospital before death relieved them of their misery. Nor were these difficult circumstances temporary. Typically, men in the South Carolina Continental regiments enlisted for sixteen months, but some enlisted for the duration of the war. Given such conditions, one can understand why men deserted. But what of the men who did not?

A lively debate has emerged in recent scholarship over the motivation of men who fought in the American Revolution. Most historians examining the social composition of the Continental army agree that after 1777 most recruits were uneducated and from the lower economic strata of the population. Edward Papenfuse and Gregory Stiverson analyzed property holdings of recruits for Maryland's Continental regiments and found that by and large they were of meager means. John R. Sellers also concludes that the common soldier of the Revolution was either "small-propertied or propertyless." Going a step further, historians Mark Lender and James Martin have argued that men who joined the Continental army, being primarily of meager means, were motivated by their economic station to join up. Martin and Lender contend that men enlisted in the Continental army to take advantage of land bounties offered by Congress and the states to entice men to join the ranks. They assert that "financial inducements" were "of paramount importance" to the recruit who had "little or nothing in life." An examination of the South Carolina line adds weight to their argument. South Carolina instituted a land bounty in its quest for men, and Walter Fraser has pointed out that South Carolina regiments were made up of "reluctant, unpropertied, and vagrant recruits." Given South Carolina's booming prewar economy, which was weighted so heavily on ownership of land and slaves, a quest for land and a corresponding stake in society as a motivation for these men has some merit.[8]

Charles Royster disputes the notion that economics was the primary motivating factor for those who served in the Continental army. Royster does not view poverty and belief in revolutionary ideals as mutually exclusive, and suggests that statistical studies of soldiers' poverty fail to prove that self interest was a key motivating factor among the men. He points to the incredible hardship and disease that soldiers had to face as being a deterrent to those with purely economic motives. Claiming that desertion was easy for soldiers, Royster's response is that something greater than economic self-interest motivated soldiers and kept them with the army: a love of country and belief in revolutionary ideals.[9]

While Royster's point that preenlistment poverty did not necessarily rule out revolutionary idealism is valid, he fails to make a convincing argument that love of country motivated the Continental soldier. It is difficult to accept that a relatively uneducated class of people on the bottom rung of the economic ladder would be flushed with revolutionary idealism. Certainly, as Fraser has shown, the dichotomy between the wealth and property of officers and the penury of soldiers in South Carolina regiments would prompt the soldiers to direct their efforts toward an overthrow of their own social system rather than toward British oppressors. South Carolina at one point resorted to a vagrancy act to raise troops, and later the state offered cash bounties of five hundred dollars at enlistment and two thousand dollars at the end of service, along with one hundred acres of land, to lure recruits. The necessity of offering such generous enticements suggests that revolutionary principles alone fell short in persuading South Carolinians to join the Continental army.[10]

Still, as has often been the case in American history, the lower strata of society contributed a significant number of men to the military establishment. While these men may not always have had at heart the revolutionary ideals espoused by America's political leaders, they were the backbone of the Continental army, and their service allowed those ideals ultimately to come to fruition. Unruly and insubordinate they certainly sometimes were, but the Revolution could not have succeeded without them. With men such as these, Benjamin Lincoln would attempt to hold Charleston.

To ensure that their ragtag army would be ready for the imminent British approach, Lincoln and his officers established a series of alarm posts and signals in the event the enemy made a sudden descent upon the city. Captain Richard Bohun Baker of the 2nd South Carolina remarked that the garrison was "Apprehensive of a Surprise" and took "the Greatest precaution to prevent it." General orders for 12 February instructed the men that "in case of an alarm, the several corps will instantly assemble, on their alarm posts, and there wait for orders." Lincoln directed Commodore Whipple "to send a row guard into the mouth of Wappoo cut" to warn the town if the British moved by water against them via the Wappoo. Lincoln recommended that artillerymen fire a number of cannon at intervals from different locations to signal the garrison to turn out. Meanwhile, the Americans posted sentries or pickets outside the Charleston lines to detect any British movement toward the city from the neck.[11]

Officers commanding pickets issued specific instructions to their men on how to deal with unfamiliar individuals entering camp and for alerting the garrison in case of attack. Orders required soldiers on picket duty to be posted within shouting distance of one another and every quarter of an hour throughout the night to call out "All is Well" beginning with the sentry at the hornwork and going around by the right of the lines. This system ensured that sentries could determine if one of their comrades had been overtaken, had left his post, or had fallen asleep. Falling asleep on picket duty was the unfortunate fate of Private Joseph Robinson of the Virginia Continentals. A court-martial found Robinson guilty of "sleeping on his post as a sentry" and sentenced him to fifty lashes. So serious did General Lincoln consider this offense that he insisted that Robinson's sentence be carried out while on the same day he remitted the sentence of one hundred lashes for another soldier found guilty of desertion. In general orders, Lincoln stressed "the alarming consequences which may result from a Centinel sleeping on his post, at a time when the utmost vigilance and alertness are required." Having attentive sentries on duty would be crucial if the British made a surprise attack on their lines. Later, when the British army was before the town, Lincoln directed that sentries on the lines "be relieved every half hour in the night."[12]

As for the daylight hours, Lincoln utilized the commanding vantage point of the steeple of St. Michael's by posting Peter Timothy there to report on British activities. By the end of March, when the British advanced closer to Charleston, Lincoln incorporated St. Michael's into the night watch as well. He ordered men to ring the church's bells every quarter of an hour, which was the signal for sentries to call out to one another. Not only did this obviate their need to estimate the time, but the ringing bells also helped them to stay awake. Lincoln also instructed the field officers of the day to visit the pickets during the night to check on the men.[13]

While sleeping sentries might fail to alert the garrison in the event of an attack, Lincoln also worried that numerous false alarms could make soldiers inattentive to the alarm for an actual emergency. Accordingly, he ardently took steps to prevent their occurrence. Aware that his own troops would be the most likely culprits, Lincoln issued orders that "the unsoldierlike and dangerous practice of firing in the Vicinity of the Camp or lines is strictly forbid." To emphasize the seriousness of this dictum, Lincoln instructed officers to read it directly to their men. He also decreed that artillerymen fire no cannon from either the batteries or ships in the harbor "without previous Notice being given at Head Quarters, except in case of the Approach of the Enemy." Any loaded muskets or cannon that had to be cleared of their charges were to be fired only at times appointed by headquarters. Finally, in what may seem as one of his more extreme and grisly measures, Lincoln issued orders for two detachments of one hundred men each "to patrol the several streets & alleys in the town, & kill all the dogs they shall find." The soldiers were to "destroy them in any way whatever, saving that of shooting." Lincoln wished to ensure that no noise, whether it was from a weapon or an animal, inadvertently alarmed the garrison. Although a grim measure, Lincoln was enabling his sentries to do their duty without distraction so that they might protect their fellow soldiers and the citizens of Charleston.[14]

The approach of the British army forced Lincoln to take other harsh measures to protect the garrison. In early March, he ordered that Hamilton Ballendine be put to death for attempting to leave the garrison and provide information to the British. As a warning to others, the condemned man was hanged in plain view outside the Charleston lines. The execution was clearly visible to the British on James Island; "A Man [was] hanged at Charles Town to day," Captain Russell noted, "in Sight of our Lines." That information from Charleston was reaching the British on James Island is evident in that a British officer could almost identify Ballendine by name just a few days later, remarking that the hanged man was one "Valentine."[15]

Leaks of information from Charleston presented a real problem for its defense. In an intelligence report compiled on 10 March, John André, the British deputy adjutant general, was able to give General Clinton a detailed account of the troops in Charleston and of its fortifications. Unfortunately for Lincoln, the screen of pickets ringing the city could not completely stop flow of traffic from the city, nor could they prevent desertions from American cavalry serving west of the Ashley. Although the American cavalry screen prevented British infantry from reconnoitering the American army, the information of deserters and spies filled the void to a certain extent for the British.[16]

As preparations for Charleston's defense progressed, morale rose among soldiers and civilians alike. Lincoln asserted to the Continental Congress that the arrival of Brigadier General James Hogun with the North Carolina brigade gave "great spirit to the Town, and confidence to the Army." Likewise, he reported to Washington that with work on their fortifications "constantly going on . . . matters every day grow better." "The people," he told his commander in chief, "are recovering their spirits, and have now high expectations." Thomas Pinckney agreed, writing his sister that the entire garrison was in "high Spirits," while another officer noted that "the army and citizens . . . have no doubt of their being able to defend the city, and make Sir Henry again give up the thought of taking it." Captain Richard Bohun Baker informed his wife, who had already fled Charleston, that "the Lines may be now said in a Great Measure to be Impregnable." Dr. David Ramsay also believed the town "strong," but as a precaution he sent three thousand dollars to his friend Benjamin Rush in Philadelphia for safekeeping just in case Charleston fell.[17]

General Moultrie asserted that the garrison was in high spirits because of the expected arrival of the Virginia line and hopes of assistance from a Spanish fleet. Virginia troops were indeed on the march to Charleston, but support from the Spanish was more doubtful. In early February, Lincoln sent Lieutenant Colonel Jean Baptiste, Chevalier de Ternant on a mission to Havana to seek naval assistance from the Spanish governor there. Spain joined her Bourbon ally France in the war against Great Britain in 1779, but she had yet to recognize American independence. Accordingly, authorities at Havana rejected Lincoln's plea for help. At the end of March, Ternant returned to Charleston with the disappointing response, which confirmed that the Americans would be on their own.[18]

On 26 March, Lincoln ordered General Moultrie to return to Charleston from Bacon's Bridge, and appointed him "to direct the Disposition of the Artillery of the different Batteries & works in & about the Town." Having resigned himself to a siege, Lincoln wanted his most able general to oversee its artillery and fortifications. If they were to stop the British, it was going to be at the gates of Charleston and nowhere else. American cavalry remained in the field to harass the British, but the delays they imposed on them would be only temporary. In Charleston, Lincoln and his army endeavored to complete the works and wait for the enemy. Once the Royal Navy crossed the Bar, they would not have to wait long. On 18 March, Brigadier General Isaac Huger reported to Lincoln that two British deserters had come into the camp at Bacon's Bridge. The deserters, Huger noted, were apprehensive that the Americans would detain them in Charleston. Huger attributed this apprehension to their suppositions that the British army would soon make a move toward the city. He had assumed correctly. The British were coming.[19]

Chapter Seven

Across the Ashley

Once Admiral Arbuthnot led his ships across Charleston Bar, the momentum of action returned to Sir Henry Clinton and the British army. The advance guard had pushed over Wappoo Cut to the mainland and British troops had established batteries on Fenwick's Point, but the bulk of Clinton's army remained on James Island. With Arbuthnot now able to send him boats and sailors and with General Paterson on the march from Savannah with reinforcements, Clinton prepared to cross his army over the Ashley River to Charleston neck. Lincoln, meanwhile, still had too few troops to oppose the British west of the Ashley or to prevent them from crossing the Ashley. Accordingly, he and his officers decided to consolidate the bulk of their force in Charleston. Unaware of Lincoln's serious shortage of manpower, Clinton expected the Americans to vigorously contest his passage of the river.

Clinton would again rely greatly on the British navy in the advance to Charleston. Sir Henry anxiously awaited the return of Captain Elphinstone to direct the army's movements by water. "You are of so much consequence to us that we cannot stir without your assistance," he remarked to him. Upon Arbuthnot's request, Elphinstone had rejoined the fleet to assist in getting the warships over the Bar, and with that accomplished, he was to serve with the land forces once more. On 22 March, Clinton instructed Elphinstone to bring the 71st regiment and all the boats "our good friend the Admiral can spare" when he came back to the army. Arbuthnot accompanied Elphinstone to Clinton's headquarters on James Island to confer with Sir Henry. Clinton informed them that he intended to march the army overland to the designated crossing point on the Ashley River while the navy's sailors conveyed flatboats through Wappoo Cut and then up the

Ashley to meet them. Arbuthnot promised to send him seventy-five flatboats and crews to man them for the purpose. With Paterson's troops and reinforcements expected from New York, Clinton would have enough men both to move against Charleston and to secure his position on James Island. They would proceed once Paterson arrived.[1]

On the day of the conference with Arbuthnot, Clinton ordered a body of light troops into St. Andrews Parish west of the Ashley River to "facilitate the junction" with Paterson's corps, which was approaching Charleston from Georgia. Paterson's troops, comprised largely of loyalist units, included the American Volunteers, New York Volunteers, Royal North Carolina Volunteers, and South Carolina Royalists. Joining them from Beaufort were Lieutenant Colonel Banastre Tarleton and the Legion.[2]

Tarleton had gone to Beaufort to obtain mounts for his cavalrymen to replace those lost on the voyage southward. Meanwhile, Lincoln ordered Lieutenant Colonel William Washington, who had only recently arrived from the north with his cavalry regiment, to screen and harass the advance of Paterson's force as it approached Charleston. Washington reported that "the Enemy loose no [. . .] time In collecting all the Horses they can in order to mount Dragoons," and he lamented that there were "[m]any fine horses" in the area, which he expected would fall into their hands if not removed. Tarleton, however, complained that the quality of the horses they had taken was "inferior to those embarked at New York." Even so, these mounted cavalry were a welcome addition to Clinton's army, allowing them to counter incursions from the American cavalry and obtain information about the American force.[3]

In their march toward Charleston, Paterson's corps met with some opposition from the South Carolina militia, particularly from the Colleton County militia who harassed them as they neared the Saltketcher River. Lieutenant Colonel Washington reported that the militia were busy felling trees across the roads leading to Saltketcher Ferry, while Colonel James Ladson's men destroyed all the boats at the ferry. In spite of the efforts of the militia, Paterson's troops pressed on. On 18 March, a detachment of eighty militia posted on the north side of the Saltketcher exchanged shots with a company of the British Legion, which had arrived on the other side of the river. Taking for granted that the British were going to cross there, the militia were unaware that Paterson's light infantry and the remainder of the Legion had traversed the river farther down. They then moved up the river and fell in upon the American rear. The results were fatal for the militiamen. The British troops made a bayonet charge in which a captain and sixteen privates of the militia were killed. The attackers suffered only four men wounded. While they had valiantly attempted to keep the enemy from crossing the river, the militia, like the American cavalry in front of Clinton's army, were too few to stop the British advance.[4]

When they crossed Rantowles Creek on 26 March, Paterson's troops were within fifteen miles of the advanced elements of Clinton's army. Clinton, Lord Cornwallis, and General Leslie rode out to meet General Paterson that day. Clinton now had the reinforcements he had been waiting for, and with the return of the 71st regiment on 24 March, he was ready to proceed against Charleston.[5]

Captain Ewald of the jaegers also accompanied Clinton when he rode out to meet Paterson, and he was struck by the large number of "Negroes, horses, and cattle which [Paterson's troops] had collected in the countryside." The advance of this force overland from Georgia placed an additional burden on the people of South Carolina. Along the march, Paterson sent a detachment under Major Patrick Ferguson to destroy rebel property and gather livestock for the use of the army. These men drove off all the horned cattle, horses, mules, sheep, and fowl that they could from the various farms and plantations. They also commandeered rebels' slaves and employed them to drive confiscated livestock back to the army. Lieutenant Anthony Allaire asserted that on the march from Georgia the army lived "on the fat of the land, the soldiers every side of us roasting turkeys, fowls, pigs, etc., every night in great plenty." Allaire rejoiced that men smashed furniture and broke windows in accomplishing their mission. The fact that Paterson's army was comprised primarily of loyalists may account for the great satisfaction his soldiers seemed to derive from laying waste rebel goods. The attitudes and actions of the loyalists in Paterson's corps were a harbinger of the bitter internecine civil war that would characterize the fighting in South Carolina throughout the rest of the war.[6]

Meanwhile, Clinton's army continued to plunder lowcountry farms and plantations as they waited for reinforcements and for the navy to cross the Bar. On James Island alone, British foraging parties confiscated 187 bushels of corn from various farms, and on the march to Fenwick's Point the army's advance units seized fifty-two head of beef cattle and one ton of straw. By 22 March, records of the commissaries of captures revealed that the army had commandeered 120 horses and 42 oxen, and by the end of March, there were 230 head of cattle "in the Pen at Pinkney's Plantation." The actual number captured was most likely greater since the troops consumed cattle on a daily basis and the returns showed only live animals. The British destroyed all that they did not put to use. The cattle fed the army while the corn subsisted captured livestock; horses were used to mount officers and dragoons while oxen pulled the army's wagons. Unfortunately for the defenders of Charleston, the flourishing farms and plantations of the South Carolina lowcountry produced more crops and livestock than they could remove. Falling into British hands, the lowcountry's generous yield provided a significant addition to the invaders' provisions and forage.[7]

Returns of British commissaries disclose the quantity of property the British obtained, but the numbers on the returns fail to show the often terrifying impact that their foraging parties had upon the civilians involved. On one foraging expedition, Captain Ewald and his jaegers came upon a plantation "from which all the people had fled except an aged woman." Fearing what the Hessians might do to her, Ewald noted that the woman "trembled and begged forbearance for her life." Likewise, with her husband in Charleston, Mrs. Rawlins Lowndes acknowledged being "often alarmed & sometimes a good deal frightened" by British plundering parties. No physical harm came to these women, but they, like many other women throughout the lowcountry whose husbands and sons were fighting with the Americans, faced the marauding British alone.[8]

Yet even those civilians who had no attachment to the rebellion were subject to British forays. Mrs. Keir, a James Island widow, maintained that she had "no Relations at all in arms against Government" and held that she "never had any thing to do with the present Disturbances." In spite of her opposition to the rebellion, a party of British soldiers had "stripped" her of some of her property, and she feared greatly that it would happen again. Her friend Richard Lorentz wrote to British headquarters on her behalf and informed them that Mrs. Keir was "very much afraid she will lose all she has got." Similarly, William Giekie had no fondness for the rebel cause, but he had also refused to act as a pilot when requested to do so by the British navy. "My plantation a few miles from town [was] destroyed and laid waist [*sic*]," he later complained to Sir Henry Clinton. Already, Clinton had asserted that he "was not desirous of granting Protections to the Inhabitants" until they showed "their attachment to Government." Obviously, if civilians did not immediately express their allegiance or directly assist the British, they could expect destruction of their property. Sir Henry's policy permitted the British rank and file to plunder friend and foe alike. As a result, the widow Mrs. Keir and others like her suffered.[9]

British depredations affected another group of noncombatants in addition to the women who stayed behind: the African American slaves. Paterson's soldiers forced captured slaves to drive livestock, while the jaegers compelled an African American youth to lead them to Stono Ferry shortly after the British landing. By 17 March, the British commissaries of captures reported that they had 317 "Negroes" in their service. This return probably included only the African Americans actually performing specific tasks. On 4 March, Major John André requested 500 blankets and 500 hats "for Clothing negroes," which suggests that the number with the army was much greater. African Americans with the British included men and women whom foraging parties seized from "rebel" plantations and a large number who willingly ran away from their masters in hopes of finding freedom under the protection of the British army. Slaves deserted rebel and loyalist plantations alike. The loyalist William Carson bemoaned that one of his slaves was acting as "a footman to Mrs. Folly[,] Lady of Mr. Folly[,] one of the Band of the 63rd reg[imen]t." He tried to recover the man but soon found that "Mrs. Folly [could not] part with him." Two of his other slaves were "equally employed about the [British] camp."[10]

Slaves who left their masters and attached themselves to the British army often did so in response to Clinton's Philipsburg Proclamation, which he had issued the previous summer. The proclamation promised "full security" to African Americans who deserted the rebels and came over to the British. In putting forth this edict, Clinton hoped to undermine southerners' ability to resist by depriving them of their primary labor source.[11]

So many slaves eventually deserted to the British that both Clinton and Cornwallis agreed that they were a burden to the army. Cornwallis found the presence of large numbers of runaway slaves "very troublesome to us," and Clinton later instructed him to "make such arrangements as will discourage their joining us." While African Americans were useful additions to their workforce, the British faced the prospect of feeding, clothing, and housing them, not to mention dealing with irate loyalists from whom many slaves had run off. The multitudes of African Americans who came over to the British ultimately compelled Clinton to formulate more specific policies for handling them.[12]

While the British endeavored to provide them with food and clothing, former slaves soon discovered that life with the British army could be as difficult as it was with their previous masters. Many African Americans, such as those of William Carson, were employed as servants to officers or enlisted men. The British assigned most, however, more arduous duty. Although their foraging details had accumulated a number of horses and oxen, the British still had too few to move their cannon and heavy stores overland. They soon delegated this laborious task to the bondsmen. Some drove cattle to the army or collected provisions while others toiled on British fortifications. That many African Americans found conditions with the British no better than on the plantations is suggested by their attempts to flee the British. Charles Morris, deputy purveyor in the British army hospital, complained that "no Dependance" could be placed on the African Americans since "many have taken the first opportunity of Deserting from their Duty." Sir John McNamara Hays added that African Americans sent onshore to gather supplies for the transports ran off once they reached the shore. The slaves were caught in the middle of the conflict, and for many the choice of participation was not theirs to make. Whether laboring on the American defense line or British redoubts and batteries,

African Americans endured the same dangers as their white military counterparts but without possessing the same degree of freedom. They may be the most tragic civilian casualties of the operations around Charleston.[13]

Paterson's arrival and the promise of flatboats from the navy allowed Sir Henry Clinton to make final preparations for a crossing of the Ashley. His troops still had to advance cautiously because of the continued presence of American cavalry. On the day that Paterson's force crossed Rantowles Creek, Lieutenant Colonel Washington cut off and captured two officers and seven cavalrymen in the immediate environs of the British army. British dragoons pursued Washington's cavalry, catching up with them near Governor Rutledge's plantation on the Stono River where a smart skirmish ensued. Mounted on superior horses, the American cavalrymen wheeled on their opponents and drove them back. Cavalrymen, wielding heavy sabers to slash the upper bodies of their enemies, inflicted serious wounds on the heads, necks, shoulders, and arms of their opponents. Lieutenant Anthony Allaire reported that a British sergeant suffered just such a wound in the skirmish, being hit in the face with a broadsword. Several other dragoons in the British Legion were also wounded. After driving off the enemy cavalry, the Americans withdrew to safety without suffering any casualties themselves. Captain Ewald surmised that Washington's detachment might have easily captured all the British general officers that day as they returned from their meeting with General Paterson without escort along a heavily wooded road.[14]

After reconnoitering the Ashley River, Clinton ultimately resolved to cross the army at Drayton Hall. Located thirteen miles from Charleston, the former home of the late William Henry Drayton was far enough from the main American position to avoid a surprise attack from Lincoln's troops. When Captain Evans of the Royal Navy arrived with seventy-five flatboats from the fleet on 26 March, the army was ready to move. On 28 March, the 7th, 23rd, and 71st regiments, British grenadiers, Hessian grenadiers, and British cavalry marched to Drayton Hall. The light infantry, jaegers, and 33rd regiment had encamped there several days earlier. The 63rd and 64th regiments with the bulk of Paterson's force remained west of the Ashley to secure communications between the army on Charleston neck and the Royal Navy.[15]

The British tried to conceal Captain Evans's flatboats in Wappoo Cut, but they were plainly visible to the Americans in Charleston. On the afternoon of 27 March, Peter Timothy counted over thirty, which had come through the cut, "skulking in the marsh." Late in the afternoon, Timothy witnessed a great deal of activity among British soldiers and sailors along the Wappoo, and he presumed that they were preparing to move the boats up the Ashley. Under cover of darkness with oars wrapped to muffle the sounds of the rowing, sailors did convey the craft up the Ashley to Lining's Creek where five days earlier British engineers had constructed a redoubt to cover them once they came into the creek.[16] The movement of the boats to Lining's Creek and the redoubt there suggested to Lincoln and his officers that the enemy intended to cross the river from that point and land at Gibbes's plantation, approximately two miles from the American lines and just north of the present-day site of the Citadel. On the night of 28 March, however, British sailors conducted the boats from Lining's Creek to Drayton Hall where they arrived at three in the morning.[17]

No rest awaited the seamen of the Royal Navy at Drayton Hall, since Clinton intended to cross the Ashley River to Charleston neck that morning. At dawn on 29 March, the light infantry, jaegers, and first battalion of British grenadiers boarded the flatboats, and the sailors rowed them across the river. A second division consisting of the remaining British grenadiers and the Hessian grenadiers followed them. Finally, a third division consisting of the 7th, 33rd, and 71st regiments made the passage. Armed galleys covered the crossing from the river, while the British Legion and 23rd regiment screened the embarking troops from land. The Americans offered little resistance to the troops that landed at Fuller's plantation on the opposite bank. Skirmishers fired scattered shots at the British and then fell back. Captain Ewald, who was with the first division, conjectured that these few cavalrymen and riflemen were "observing rather than hindering us."[18]

Lincoln had not opposed the British crossing for the same reason he had not attacked them west of the Ashley; he had too few troops. "We have to lament that, from the want of Men, we are denied the advantages of opposing them with any considerable force in crossing this river," he informed the Continental Congress several days earlier. Fearing the British would make an attempt on the city in their absence, Lincoln was reluctant to dispatch a large body of troops outside the fortifications of Charleston. He was so determined to hold the city that he was willing to risk keeping the bulk of the army of the Southern Department within it. Lincoln did, however, take steps to harass the British on the neck as they advanced toward him. On the day of the crossing, he ordered the formation of a light infantry battalion, comprised of the light companies of the 2nd and 3rd South Carolina and the light companies from the North Carolina brigade, to be commanded by Lieutenant Colonel John Laurens. Although consisting of only 200 men, these were the best of Lincoln's Continental troops. Laurens's light infantry were to take post outside the city's defenses "to watch the motions of the Enemy and prevent too sudden an approach."[19]

Completing the crossing by three in the afternoon of 29 March, the British army advanced down the road from Dorchester toward Charleston.[20] By nine that evening, the light infantry reached the Quarter House, a tavern just six miles from the city. The remainder of the army encamped between the Quarter House and Bellinger's House, approximately three miles to the rear. While they had encountered little resistance from the rebels, the British troops expected more serious action at any moment. The jaegers and light infantry had marched seven miles since they landed and only experienced a few scattered shots. The next day's march would not be so uneventful.[21]

On the morning of 30 March, the British army broke camp and proceeded down the road toward Charleston. Clinton, Cornwallis, and General Leslie accompanied the jaegers in the vanguard. The British light infantry was close behind, followed by the rest of the corps. Meanwhile, Lieutenant Colonel Laurens had posted the bulk of his soldiers in a small redoubt, or fleche, one mile outside of the city; approximately two and one-half miles from Charleston, a party of American riflemen set up an ambush in a stretch of woods along the main road leading into town.[22] Around noon, when the British column approached them, the marksmen opened fire on the jaegers and general officers.

Lord Caithness, an aide to Clinton, was "shot thro the Body" by this opening volley. The jaegers immediately returned fire and the British light infantry moved up to support them. The superior number of British troops forced Laurens's men back down the road toward Charleston, but they fired as they retreated, resulting in a running firefight. According to Captain Russell, "the Enemy immediately fell back but kept up a considerable fire from behind the Trees." The skirmishing continued for half an hour until the Americans withdrew out of range. In addition to Lord Caithness, one of the jaegers had also been wounded.[23]

Laurens's riflemen eventually joined the rest of the American light infantry in the safety of the fleche. When Laurens and his second in command, Major Edward Hyrne, advanced from the work to reconnoiter, they soon found themselves in a predicament similar to that of the British officers earlier in the day. A party of jaegers had moved up the road toward the American position using the trees alongside the road as cover. Without warning, they opened fire on the American officers. One of their rifle shots wounded Major Hyrne through the cheek, knocking him from his horse.[24] Lieutenant Colonel Laurens drove off Hyrne's horse to prevent it from falling into the enemy's hands, and bravely helped his stricken fellow officer to safety. Although he failed to mention it, Laurens no doubt accomplished this task under a hail of rifle fire from the Hessians.[25]

At the first appearance of the British that day, Laurens sent a request to General Lincoln for "a couple of field pieces" to allow them to keep the enemy at bay. Shortly after retiring to the advanced work with the injured Hyrne, however, Laurens received word that Lincoln wished to avoid a serious engagement and he wanted Laurens to withdraw. As the Americans fell back, parties of jaegers and British light infantry endeavored to move up on their flanks, and Laurens's riflemen exchanged shots with them before retreating with the rest of the troops. Believing they had driven the rebels from the fleche, the jaegers took possession of the now empty work. Evidently by some mistake of orders, the field pieces, which Laurens had requested earlier in the day, arrived late in the afternoon along with a reinforcement of men. Consequently, Laurens decided to counterattack the British. After forming his men, he ordered a bayonet charge on the enemy troops posted in the recently evacuated fleche. Captain Ewald maintained that the Americans attacked them "with considerable violence" and bayoneted three of the jaegers. Overwhelmed, the Hessians quickly gave way. Laurens's men found one of the jaegers dead in the redoubt with Major Hyrne's hat in his hand. Hyrne left the hat behind after he was wounded and the German had evidently taken it as a prize.[26]

Shortly thereafter, the British light infantry came up to support the jaegers and together they forced Laurens's men from the redoubt, driving them back toward the American lines. Clinton forbade his troops from pursuing the rebels any further because he feared that they were trying to lure them within range of Charleston's guns. The British, meanwhile, wheeled up field pieces of their own and a short artillery duel brought an end to the action. Gabriel Manigault asserted that "the engagement continued until evening when the Americans retired, after having several times forced their opponents to give way." Darkness found Laurens and the light infantry safely within the lines of Charleston. Proud of his men, he summed up the day's action as "a frolicking skirmish for our young soldiers." He had reason to be proud; his men held their own against the elite troops of the British army, the light infantry and jaegers. While General Moultrie and other superior officers believed Laurens to be somewhat rash in his quests for glory, some admired his bravery. With regard to Laurens's role in the day's skirmishing, Peter Timothy remarked approvingly: "I observed him all Day every where."[27]

While not the first engagement since the British arrived in the lowcountry, it was the first the two sides had fought within sight of Charleston. One American officer noted that the action occurred "in view of . . . many ladies" who had apparently witnessed it from the lines of Charleston. Unsure of its importance, he argued that the battle for the advanced redoubt was "a mere point of honor, without advantage!"[28]

Both sides overestimated the losses of their enemy, and casualties were relatively light, as would be expected given the limited scope of the engagement. For the Americans, Major Hyrne survived his wound but Captain Joseph Bowman of the North Carolina Continentals was killed by cannon fire late in the engagement. The Americans also had seven privates wounded. British officers reported two jaegers wounded and one killed, which would account for the three jaegers that Ewald claims were bayoneted in the redoubt. These figures do not include the British officer and jaeger who were wounded in the skirmishing earlier in the day.[29]

That evening the British camped in and around Gibbes's plantation where Lincoln had anticipated they would cross the Ashley. Clinton had indeed intended to use Gibbes's plantation not as an initial crossing point, but as a staging area on Charleston neck. The post shortened the British line of communication, mitigating the need to move stores farther up the Ashley to make the crossing where they would be exposed to attacks from American cavalry. The British now moved artillery and stores up the Ashley to Lining's Landing where flatboats carried them over to Gibbes's. "We proceeded immediately to pass our Stores & Tools from [Lining's] Landing to Gibbs' Landing," Lieutenant Wilson of the engineers noted. From his post high above the city, Peter Timothy watched the next day as boats loaded with men, tools, tents, and casks crossed the river. The crossing of the boats was "so incessant the whole Day, [that] it was impossible" for him to count them all. With these men and implements, Sir Henry and his army would lay siege to Charleston.[30]

The garrison of Charleston now had the British army encamped within two miles of the gates of the city. Advanced British pickets were so close that they could hear sentries on the lines calling to each other in the night. They could also hear dogs barking in the city, but that presumably came to an end when Lincoln's orders for the destruction of the city's dogs went into effect. Although the British were within earshot, there was no reason for the Americans to panic. Most of the garrison's Continental troops had faced the British before and so had many of the militia. Meanwhile, the Virginia Continental troops were on the march and only a short distance away. By 26 March, the Virginians were already on the Peedee River. As for the people of Charleston, had not Prevost been just as close to the city less than a year before? Had not Fort Moultrie, in a yet unfinished state, driven off a British fleet in 1776, forcing an entire British army to withdraw?

Threats from the British army and navy were nothing new for the capital of South Carolina. They would deal with this one as they had the others. David Ramsay had once said of South Carolinians that they could often be "very remiss" in their long-term planning, but he asserted that they were "very active at the approach of danger." Six weeks after landing on Simmons Island, danger was now at their door. The stage was set for the siege of Charleston to begin.[31]

Chapter Eight

Siege Warfare

While the popular conception of military action during the American Revolution is one of armies clashing upon open fields or of small parties skirmishing in the countryside, siege warfare also comprised much of the fighting during the war. Sieges took place in varying degrees in almost every year of the Revolution. The Americans' lack of military experience early in the war did not prevent them from besieging British strongholds. Washington's army surrounded Boston during the winter of 1775–76 and kept the British within its confines, while General Richard Montgomery besieged the British fort at St. Johns, and Benedict Arnold laid siege to Quebec. In the campaigns of 1777, the British used siege tactics to wrest Fort Ticonderoga from the Americans and to reduce the forts on the Delaware River, which protected the southern approaches to Philadelphia. The Americans and French attempted to besiege the British post at Newport, Rhode Island, in August 1778 while their joint effort against Savannah in 1779 ended disastrously. As with major land battles of the Revolution, traditional European methods dictated the tactics employed in siege warfare. An understanding of the science and intricacies of eighteenth-century siege warfare is central to an understanding of British operations against Charleston in 1780.

The methodology of siege warfare used by all combatants in the Revolution had emerged in the previous century. Sebastien le Prestre de Vauban, chief engineer to Louis XIV, modified the European system of capturing fortresses, formulating an "exact scheme" for the attacking army's approaches. His ideas were to be a mainstay of siege warfare for two centuries. Prior to the introduction of Vauban's system, European armies laying siege to enemy fortresses constructed meandering trenches, which had no standardization to them and which often did not protect the soldiers of the attacking army. Vauban's system utilized transverse support trenches and approach trenches to propel the attacker toward the fortifications of the enemy garrison with some degree of security for the besieging army's soldiers.[1]

The transverse support trenches Vauban devised were known as parallels, because the besieger constructed them essentially parallel to the lines or works of the enemy. The attacking army sequentially dug three or four parallels, one in front of the other, which in turn moved them ever closer to the enemy fortress. The attacker placed cannon in batteries along the length of each parallel to batter the opponent and his works. When they had completed the first parallel anywhere from 600 to 1,000 yards from the enemy lines, the attacking army pushed forward approach trenches from the front of it. Approach trenches were referred to as saps, or zigzags, because they generally wound forward in a zigzag pattern to protect the men digging them and the men posted in them. An approach trench aimed directly at the enemy fortress allowed the defenders to fire right down the trench, but the zigzag trench came in at an angle, giving the attacking soldiers a modicum of security against enemy fire. In general, the besieging army did not build approach trenches as sturdily as parallels since they were primarily intended as a means of movement rather than as a place from which to cannonade the enemy. When the saps reached a point approximately 300 to 500 yards from the opponent's lines, working parties opened a second parallel. As cannon from the first and second parallels battered the city or fortress, the besiegers began new approach trenches from the second parallel, constructing a third parallel at the heads of these trenches. If enough space existed between the third parallel and the enemy lines, a fourth parallel might be utilized, but three was more typical. In some cases, the attacking army pushed saps from the third parallel, not as an avenue to a fourth parallel but as a way to breach the enemy defenses or as a point to launch an assault from if that became necessary.[2]

Customarily, the two sides remained in contact throughout the siege. Before commencing siege operations, the commander of an attacking army often gave the defenders notice of his intention to take the town by summoning the garrison to surrender. Once the siege was underway and the besieger's guns had sufficiently battered the town or fortress, that commander would again give them an opportunity to surrender. Depending upon the condition of the two armies, the officers of the besieged garrison might even propose the terms of capitulation. If the defenders continued to hold out, even after withstanding bombardment by heavy cannon at close range, the attacker might have to resort to a direct assault on the enemy works. Generally, most fortresses capitulated before a storm became necessary, but if an attacking army's supplies ran low or if an enemy relief column was marching to assist the garrison, the commanding general of the besieging army might have no choice but to assail the fortifications. Because of French impatience at the siege of Savannah in 1779, Admiral Count d'Estaing and General Lincoln imprudently assaulted the British works, which ultimately brought an end to their operations.[3]

While the system of parallels and approach trenches conveyed the attacking army toward the enemy, the attacker's artillery was the means by which he reduced the enemy's fortifications. The besieging army used their cannon to destroy the defender's gun emplacements, dismount artillery pieces, knock down ramparts, and kill or wound enemy soldiers. Meanwhile, the defender retaliated with his own guns, subjecting the besieger's working parties to continual fire as they dug parallels and approach trenches.[4]

The artillery of the era consisted of smooth-bore muzzle loading pieces made of iron or brass. There were three principal types of artillery utilized in the Revolution: field guns, howitzers, and mortars. British and American forces employed all three during the siege of Charleston.

Field guns, the most common, were generally mounted on large-wheeled carriages and were fired at a low angle. Field guns varied in size from three pounds up to forty-two pounds, the weight designation referring to the weight of the solid shot that they fired. With regard to the weight of the piece itself, a thirty-two pounder, the largest type used on land during the siege of Charleston, weighed between 4,200 and 5,800 pounds, depending on the length and whether it was iron or brass. Even a three pounder weighed as much as 250 pounds. Given the weight of these field pieces, it is easy to see why the British army's lack of horses put a strain on their ability to move cannon overland. Howitzers were similar to field guns but with much shorter and stockier barrels. Unlike guns, howitzers could be fired at either a low or high angle. Mortars were very short artillery pieces, similar in concept to the modern mortar in that they fired at a high angle, generally forty-five degrees. Mounted in wooden beds rather than on carriages, mortars lacked mobility and were used almost exclusively in garrison or siege batteries. Howitzers and mortars were designated by the caliber of their barrel, measured in inches. Thus, a thirteen inch mortar typically fired a projectile with a diameter just under thirteen inches. Mortars and howitzers were certainly as cumbersome as field guns. A brass howitzer with a caliber of four and two-fifths inches weighed approximately three hundred pounds, an eight inch brass mortar weighed over four hundred pounds, and an iron one almost double that.[5]

Guns, howitzers, and mortars also varied as to range and the type of projectile fired. Solid shot, grapeshot, canister shot, and shells constituted the major types of projectiles. Guns and howitzers fired solid shot, grape, and canister, while mortars fired only shells. Solid shot was simply an iron ball, which could be employed against enemy fortifications or personnel. Grape and canister were primarily anti-personnel weapons. Grapeshot consisted of a cylindrical net of cloth or leather filled with iron balls, each approximately two inches in diameter. When fired from a howitzer or field gun, the covering of the grapeshot came apart scattering the balls in a shotgun effect against the enemy. Canister shot comprised a small metal container, or one similar to that of grapeshot, filled with musket balls, which, like grape, scattered among the enemy when fired from the artillery piece. Mortar shells consisted of spherical iron balls that were hollow on the inside. The shell had a single fuse hole through which an artillerist filled it with gunpowder, then plugged the hole with a conical wooden fuse. A small opening cut down the length of the fuse was then filled with a slower burning powder. When the mortar was fired, the exploding charge of the mortar lit the fuse, which burned down in flight, then set off the gunpowder inside when the shell reached the enemy. Artillerymen varied the time until ignition by changing the length of the fuse.[6]

With regard to range, iron pieces could fire projectiles greater distances, but they also had a greater tendency to burst, thus endangering the lives of their crews. Artillerymen altered the distance a mortar shell traveled by modifying the angle of the mortar or by increasing or decreasing the powder charge in the mortar. A thirteen inch brass mortar could hurl shells 1,300 yards, while an iron one could throw them 2,700 yards; the smaller five and one-half inch brass mortar could send them 1,000 yards. The range of field guns and howitzers was comparable to that of mortars. The range of brass guns varied between 1,200 and 1,900 yards depending on the size of the piece, while an iron thirty-two pounder could propel a shot 2,900 yards. Howitzers could fire a projectile between 1,300 and 2,000 yards. Whatever the type of piece, any siege begun within 1,000 yards of an enemy's fortifications, as was the siege of Charleston, was well within range of the artillery of the day. Accuracy and effectiveness at that distance was another matter entirely. Artillerists aimed field guns and howitzers by moving the carriage of the piece from left to right or by slightly raising or lowering the barrel. Gun crews could only aim their cannon as far as they could see, however, and the direction and intensity of the wind often had a severe impact on the flight of projectiles. The simple laws of physics also adversely affected artillery fire. For all smoothbore weapons, velocity of the projectile dropped off rapidly as range increased, thus reducing its "hitting power." For instance, shot fired from an eighteen pound gun traveled at 1,600 feet per second when leaving the muzzle, but when it reached 1,500 yards, it had a velocity of only 523 feet per second. To be truly effective against fortifications, armies had to fire solid shot within 1,000 yards of the target.[7]

The artillerymen who fired the pieces practiced a specialized and often dangerous science. On the battlefield, a full gun crew for a six pounder consisted of fourteen or fifteen men, but siege and garrison artillery pieces required only eight or nine men, since the piece did not have to be moved from point to point as on the battlefield. A veteran crew could fire thirty rounds in an hour. To fire the piece, one member of the squad loaded the cartridge, consisting of the projectile with an attached cloth or flannel bag of gunpowder, into the muzzle. Using a rammer, another artilleryman pushed the cartridge to the base of the barrel. Another crew member pierced the cloth or flannel of the cartridge with a needle-like instrument through the vent, a small hole at the base of the barrel. Still another man filled the vent with powder or with a special tube containing powder. When the powder in the vent was then ignited, it burned down to the powder in the cartridge and set off the piece. Artillery officers instructed their men to keep their mouths open to avoid having their eardrums blown out when the cannon was fired.[8]

Although artillerymen often fought from behind fortifications, their duty may have been more hazardous than that of infantrymen on the battlefield. In addition to enemy fire, artillerymen also confronted the inherent danger of their own pieces. After the cannon was fired, the crew thoroughly sponged out the barrel to extinguish any remaining sparks or embers from the previous charge that might ignite the new cartridge as the men loaded it into the piece. One member of the gun crew dipped a sponge mounted on the end of a barrel-length staff in a bucket of water and then swabbed out the inside of the cannon. At the same time, another artilleryman put his thumb over the vent to create a vacuum effect as the piece was sponged. If not done properly, the results could be quite deadly. On 13 April, Captain Russell reported that one British artilleryman was killed and another wounded "by one of our Guns in consequence of carelessness in not stopping the Vent." Such incidents were fairly common among both American and British artillerymen. The following day, Lieutenant Colonel John Faucheraud Grimké of the South Carolina line noted that two men in the South Carolina artillery were killed "by a twelve pounder accidentally going off while they were loading her," and on the same day, "a similar Accident" killed one man and wounded another in the militia artillery. An improperly sponged barrel or open vent was certainly the cause in both cases. Accidents such as these occurred more frequently during sieges because men who normally served in the infantry were called upon to perform service on the lines with the artillery. Unaccustomed to the handling of artillery pieces, they often suffered death or serious injury as a result. Both British and American artillerymen faced a daunting task in carrying on the science of siege warfare.[9]

Using Vauban's tactics and a train of siege artillery, Sir Henry Clinton and the British army would have to overcome the American fortifications and the army manning them if they were to take Charleston. In Clinton's words, the American defenses "were by no means contemptible." The tabby and masonry hornwork, a defensive work with two bastions in its front connected by a curtain, was the heart of the American defenses, and throughout the siege Lincoln used it as his command post.[10] The hornwork lay across King Street and guarded the entrance to the city. Its gate, located in the center of the curtain, was covered by a lunette standing just to the front of it. The two bastions of the hornwork jutted forward to allow the defenders to enfilade any enemy soldiers who approached them. A ditch also surrounded the work. In front of the hornwork, the Americans had constructed a line of redoubts, redans, and batteries, all of which were connected by a parapet so that a continuous wall existed between the Ashley and Cooper Rivers. This constituted the main defense line of Charleston. Two redoubts, one on the Ashley River side and one on the Cooper River side, anchored the flanks of this line. The redoubt on the Cooper River side was advanced slightly for reasons explained below. According to Captain Ewald, the Americans built the walls of the redoubts on the flanks with palmetto trees, the wood of which had in 1776 withstood the bombardment at Sullivan's Island so well.[11]

In front of the parapet of the main defense line, the defenders dug a ditch five to six feet deep and eight to twelve feet across. The ditch, a typical feature of defensive works of the era, made it more difficult for soldiers of an attacking force to scale the parapet, since it essentially raised the height which they had to climb to get over it. Meanwhile, the defending soldiers, covered by the parapet, could pour fire down upon them as they attempted to scramble out of the ditch and up the wall. The ditch before the American parapet was double-palisaded, or double-picketed, meaning British soldiers would have to fight through two rows of pointed wooden stakes set close together and driven into the ground at the bottom of the ditch.[12]

The Americans placed two lines of abatis in front of the double-palisaded ditch. Defenders could prepare an abatis, a precursor to modern barbed wire, in several ways. The easiest method was to fell a number of trees so that the tops of the felled trees pointed toward the enemy. The crossed and entangled branches of the trees would then ensnare attacking troops as they advanced. Another method was to construct a cheval de frise (or chevaux de frise), which consisted of a large beam several feet in length with sharpened stakes along its expanse at ninety degree angles to one another. Viewed from the side, the cheval de frise took the shape of an "X" but from the front it presented a series of continuous wooden spears to an approaching foe. At Charleston, the Americans seem to have employed a combination of these frame structures and felled trees to construct the abatis. Whether an abatis or palisade, enemy troops could not easily climb over or through these obstructions, and they would have to clear them away before they could even get to the ditch or parapet.[13]

In front of the abatis, the Americans constructed a wet ditch, or canal, by digging a trench between two tidal creeks on the Ashley and Cooper River sides of the Charleston peninsula. The canal was eighteen feet across and six to eight feet deep. The Americans controlled the depth of it by means of sluices on the Cooper River side. They had pushed forward the redoubt on the right side of the lines to cover the canal and sluices. Meanwhile, in front of the parapet on the Ashley River side, they erected a detached work, known as the advanced redoubt, or half moon battery, which defended the canal from the left. Dr. Ramsay explained that "the lines were made particularly strong on the right and left, and so constructed as to rake the wet ditch, in almost its whole extent." With regard to the British approach toward Charleston, the canal was an extremely effective defensive measure, since the British first had to cross it before making any effort against the remaining works. Finally, the Americans dug several pits, which John Laurens termed "wolf-traps," between the canal and the earthworks to break up the line of march leading toward Charleston. The Americans had fashioned a very potent defense in depth. If British troops were to assault the town, they would first have to cross the canal, struggle through two rows of abatis, avoid falling into deep holes, plunge into a ditch, climb over or cut through two palisade walls, and then climb up a steep parapet. All would be done under a hail of fire from enemy muskets and artillery.[14]

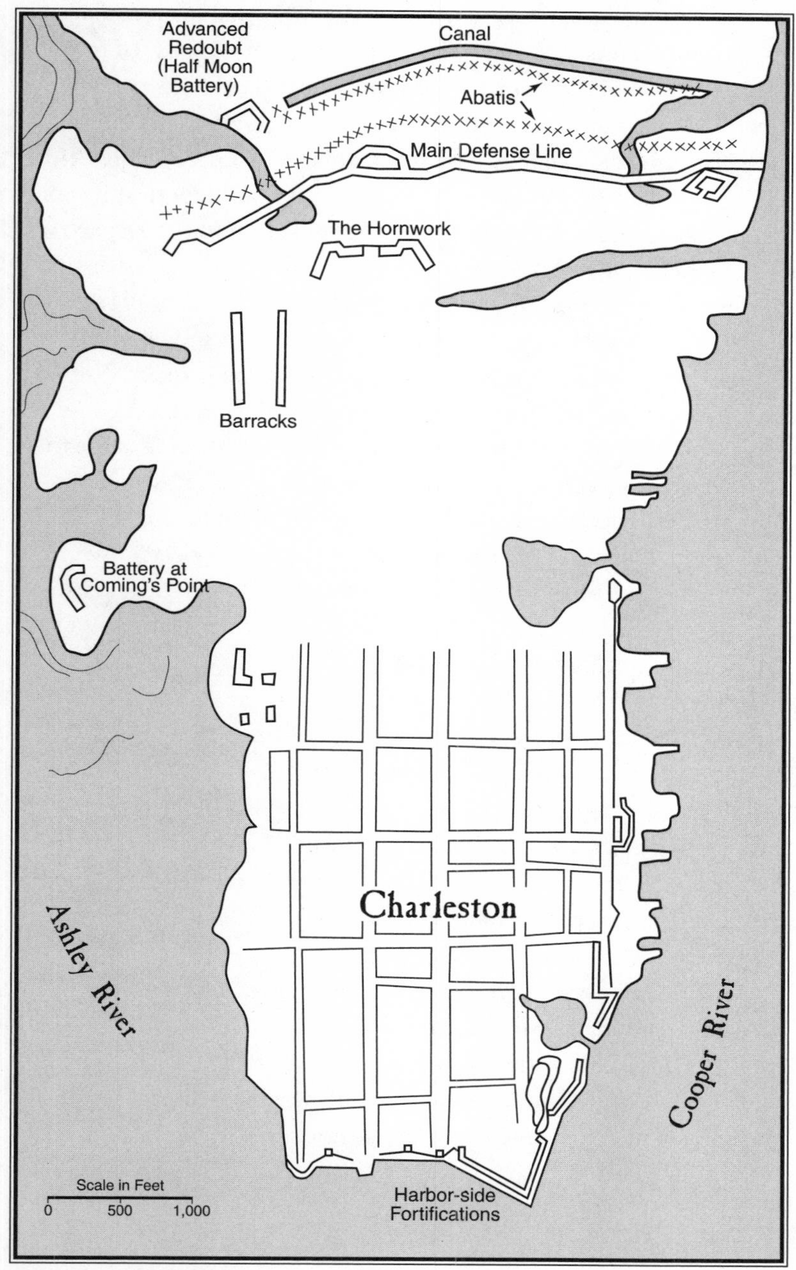
Advanced
Redoubt
(Half Moon
Battery)
Canal
Abatis
Main Defense Line
The Hornwork
Barracks
Battery at
Coming's Point
Charleston
Ashley River
Cooper River
Scale in Feet
0
500
1,000
Harbor-side
Fortifications

American Defenses

The area between the British camp and American fortifications was level ground interspersed at various points by tidal creeks fed from the Ashley and Cooper Rivers. Under Lincoln's orders, the Americans cut down the trees and undergrowth on the neck and destroyed all the houses to reduce the amount of cover available to the attacking British. Civilian authorities had provided Lincoln with an imperfect response in this matter. As early as November 1779, the Southern Department commander had represented to Governor Rutledge "the necessity of cutting and removing the standing wood between the lines of the Town and the outer work near Strickland's as it would be a cover to the enemy in case of a siege." Upon Lincoln's second request, Rutledge agreed that it should be done, but he wrote Lincoln that he and the Privy Council hoped that the army would limit the clearing of the trees. The Americans ultimately removed enough of the obstructions for Captain Hinrichs to remark that a large plain lay before the British with "every house razed and every tree and shrub chopped down." Little remained to screen their advance toward the potent defenses of Charleston. They would have to rely on their own siegeworks to shelter the men from cannon and small arms fire.[15]

In the days following the British crossing of the Ashley, Lieutenant Colonel Grimké represented that "the Garrison [was] employed in mounting Cannon [and] throwing up Traverses"—walls built behind and perpendicular to the parapet to give additional protection to the men. With pick and shovel, soldiers on the lines, assisted by the African American slaves that the army could commandeer, worked "spiritedly" to strengthen the parapet and drag cannon into place in the several batteries.[16]

General Moultrie oversaw the final disposition of artillery in the batteries. Having commanded the American forces at Sullivan's Island in 1776, Moultrie was a veteran both in the management of artillery and in defending against it. He was also familiar with the reactions of men to cannon fire. He confided to a friend that "this sort of fighting" created "a great deal of noise," but there was "little danger" from it. The Americans employed over 200 artillery pieces throughout the various fortifications of the city. When completed, the batteries facing Charleston neck bristled with seventy-nine field guns, a howitzer, and several mortars. As to shot and shell, John Wells Jr. informed Henry Laurens that the town possessed an "abundance of ammunition." He noted that if that became scarce, the garrison could fire the British shot that fell upon the town back at them.[17]

While the garrison was adequately furnished with artillery, manpower still presented a problem. Despite urgent calls by General Lincoln and threats from Governor Rutledge, hoped-for support from the South Carolina militia failed to materialize. Lincoln later speculated that only 300 militiamen from the South Carolina backcountry participated in the defense of Charleston. Meanwhile, the enlistments of many of the North Carolina militia expired on 24 March, and they marched for home. In informing Governor Caswell of their departure, Lincoln asserted that "they could not, few excepted, be prevailed on to continue longer." The enlistments of the remainder, saving approximately one hundred men, were to expire on 6 April. Lincoln theorized that they too would leave his army. Even the immediate presence of the British did not influence them to stay. Their behavior was fairly typical of any of the state militias in the American Revolution. The men were civilians engaged for a fixed and generally short period of time, and they returned to their homes when their terms of service expired. Neither General Lincoln nor General Hogun, the commander of the North Carolina Continentals, nor even General Washington for that matter, could have compelled them to stay.[18]

As to Continental reinforcements, Lincoln had received word that the Virginia Continental troops would soon reach Charleston, but he was disappointed to learn that Brigadier General William Woodford had only 737 men fit for action in his brigade and Brigadier General Charles Scott was coming without any troops at all. Lincoln was exasperated that Scott's troops remained behind in Virginia: "For they are not yet clothed." He wrote Woodford, entreating him to "move with every possible dispatch to this place." Lincoln asserted to the Virginia brigadier that "there never has been a time since the commencement of the war, when reinforcement was of the like importance." The defense of Charleston would rest on the troops currently under Lincoln's command and the men of the Virginia brigade. Once the

Virginians reached the city, Lincoln would have approximately 4,500 Continentals and militia under his command.[19]

Lincoln posted most of the militia in batteries along the waterfront and put them under the command of Brigadier General Lachlan McIntosh of Georgia. He distributed the artillery brigade, commanded by Colonel Barnard Beekman, among the batteries on the neck. The 2nd and 3rd South Carolina regiments were brigaded with the two Virginia Continental detachments already in camp. Colonel Richard Parker, a Virginian, led this brigade, which occupied the left of the lines. General Hogun's North Carolina brigade held the right. The light infantry under Lieutenant Colonel Laurens remained as a reserve, and the 1st South Carolina under Colonel Charles Cotesworth Pinckney continued to garrison Fort Moultrie.[20]

Up to this point, Charleston's defenders had only engaged the British on a limited scale, but now, six weeks after landing on the South Carolina coast, Sir Henry Clinton and his army lay before them. Although Clinton had to wait one more day until his men had transported enough entrenching tools across the Ashley to begin constructing parallels, no other delays immediately confronted him. For the Americans, the waiting, as well as the time for preparation, had come to an end.[21]

Chapter Nine

Breaking Ground: The Siege Begins

Under cover of darkness on the evening of 1 April 1780, 3,000 men marched from the British camp at Gibbes's plantation and advanced toward Charleston. The force consisted of 1,500 laborers and an equal number of men to guard them against an attack from the garrison. The detachment proceeded to the site that Major James Moncrief, Clinton's chief engineer, had chosen to begin the siegeworks, and the men designated as laborers commenced construction of three redoubts 800 to 1,000 yards from the Charleston lines. The working parties carried with them mantelets—wooden blinds six feet high and twelve to sixteen feet long that soldiers shoveled earth against to form the front wall of each redoubt. An officer of the Graf Grenadier Battalion noted that "the work went quickly" due to the sandiness of the soil. The covering infantry stood ready to defend against a sally from Charleston, but throughout the night the garrison remained quiet. Sir Henry Clinton was amazed that in one night his troops "compleated 3 Redoubts and a communication without a single shot" being fired at them.[1]

British engineers designated the completed redoubts Numbers Three, Four, and Five. In all, Major Moncrief's plan called for six fortifications in the first parallel. Facing the American lines, the redoubt known as Number Three lay to the right of the Charles Town Road (now upper King Street) while Numbers Four and Five lay on the left of the road.[2] British workmen modified a trench, which the Americans had neglected to fill in, into a line of communication connecting the three works. The redoubts, together with the communications trench, constituted the nucleus of the British first parallel.[3]

The following morning, Samuel Baldwin, an inhabitant of the city, declared: "We were surprised . . . at the sight of the works thrown up by our neighbors during the night." Lincoln's troops had yet to even finish transferring their artillery into the batteries. One British officer noted that the Americans had a "good many" embrasures opened in their fortifications, but he detected few cannon in them. From the British redoubts, Captain Russell heard the grunts of the Americans moving the ponderous ordnance into position. By afternoon, they had positioned enough guns to fire between thirty and forty shots at the enemy. Peter Timothy noted that "our shot" scored several hits on the mantelets in front of the British redoubts, but the artillery fire inflicted little or no damage on their works. Moreover, British light infantry posted on the lines reported no casualties from the desultory American firing.[4]

The remaining British troops were employed throughout the day in bringing stores and artillery across the Ashley to Gibbes's plantation, and in constructing wooden platforms on which to place cannon in their own batteries. African American laborers hauled British cannon, munitions, and provisions from Gibbes's to the lines. From St. Michael's, Peter Timothy noted that the intercourse between the enemy posts on the Ashley was "incessant and considerable." He watched as boats crossed "without interruption . . . loaded with Men and women, some with Hurdles, others with Tents, and others with empty casks." With their activities in full view of the American lines, the British would have to perform further work on the first parallel after dark, especially since the garrison now had several operational batteries.[5]

After dark on 2 April, British working parties developed further the fortifications of the emerging first parallel. They thickened the parapets of the first three redoubts and began construction of another, Number One, on the Ashley River facing Charleston. Clinton wished to also fortify rising ground on their left, which bordered Town Creek. He concluded that this elevation, which the Americans called Hampstead Hill, was the key to taking the city.[6] Expecting the rebels to steadfastly defend this commanding position, he wrote: "It may cost to get it but when in possession of it we take the town." Deferring to Moncrief's judgment, Clinton acceded to the completion of the redoubt on the right first.[7]

By 3 April, the Americans had moved the bulk of their artillery into the batteries allowing them to offer more serious resistance. Throughout the day on 3 April, their field guns, howitzers, and mortars spat deadly projectiles at the new British works. The cannon fire produced much noise and smoke, but again did little damage to the British fortifications. "Our cannon have been pretty constantly playing on the Enemy since they broke ground," Major William Croghan of the Virginia Continentals observed, "yet they seem to proceed with their works." Captain Russell marveled that "the Rebels fired near 300 Shot and 30 small Shells, but did no manner of Injury," while Captain Peebles recorded that British grenadiers manning the parallel suffered no casualties.[8]

The British could not respond to the American fire since they had no functional batteries in the parallel, the construction of which required much time and effort. Once British working parties completed and strengthened the parapet of the first parallel, they could then drag wooden platforms, which supported the cannon and prevented them from sinking into the earth, into place at the respective battery sites. For mortar batteries, the men built heavy frames of durable wood to absorb the shock of the mortar when it was fired. After installing frames and platforms, the working parties cut embrasures into the parapet for cannon to fire through. The placement of cannon into the battery was probably the most labor-intensive task of all. Lacking adequate horses, British soldiers and seamen and African American slaves hauled them overland from Gibbes's Landing to the lines. Even if they had sufficient horses and oxen to bring artillery to the batteries, the men still had to move the often several ton pieces into position themselves. Finally, they had to transport and stockpile ammunition and stores needed to fire the guns. With their working parties still strengthening and securing the first parallel, it would be several days before the British could answer the shots from Charleston.

When American firing subsided after dark on 3 April, British laborers returned to their duties. During the night, they directed their efforts toward Clinton's desired fortification on Hampstead Hill, which, coupled with the work thrown up close to the Ashley River the previous night, extended the British works from river to river across the peninsula. Lying 400 to 500 yards from the American redoubt on the Cooper River, Clinton anticipated that the battery on Hampstead Hill would "have a great tendency to ruin the defences on the Enemys Right." Although the new fortification, which the British designated Number Six, pleased Clinton, the nature of the battery's construction alarmed him. The engineers had fashioned only a two face work with one side to Charleston and the other side to the Cooper River, making it difficult to defend if the garrison sallied out to seize it, as Clinton expected they would. In anticipation of a sortie, Clinton posted a detachment of 100 jaegers to the battery.[9]

The following morning, the new British battery on Hampstead Hill immediately drew the attention of the garrison. Initially, only two American guns were in position to fire on it, but American artillerymen soon dragged three more up to support the first two. These five cannon furiously bombarded the new work. Meanwhile, the sloop of war *Ranger* sailed up Town Creek to threaten the east face of the British fortification. *Ranger* carried aboard Major Matthew Clarkson, one of Lincoln's aides-de-camp, who was to ascertain the strength of the position. Upon Clarkson's report "depended the propriety of a sally" against it. The attack was to begin as soon as *Ranger*'s captain, Thomas Simpson, issued the prearranged signal.[10]

Captain Simpson maneuvered *Ranger* into Town Creek, and from there the vessel's guns hammered the left flank and rear of the British fortification, raining destruction down upon the men inside. "For over an hour we had to endure heavy cannon fire," decried Captain Ewald, commanding the jaegers. Still, Lieutenant Wilson of the British engineers, exuding more than a hint of pride, asserted that "no Loss from the Enemy's fire" was sustained "on the Battery." Men outside the work did not fare so well; one British soldier was killed and another was wounded as they tried to make their way to Number Six after daylight. In response to the bombardment, the British moved a howitzer and a twenty-four pounder onto a point further up Town Creek and fired on the American warship. One shot hit *Ranger* in the bow, and although the force of the shot was not sufficient to pass through her hull, it did lodge in her side. In the face of this threat, Captain Simpson ordered the vessel to fall back down the river. Alerted to the danger posed by American shipping, British engineers had closed the rear of the battery on Hampstead Hill as Clinton desired. From the deck of *Ranger,* Major Clarkson discovered this modification, and when he reported to Lincoln that the work was now enclosed, Lincoln dispensed with plans to assault it.[11]

On the night of 5 April, British working parties began construction of Number Two, the final planned work in the first parallel. Clinton wished to see his men complete the parallel so that they could begin digging approaches toward a second parallel. He wrote Arbuthnot that he hoped to "bring such a force in artillery against them as . . . will make a serious impression." Clinton's desire to bring his artillery against the town was not soon to be realized, however. His men finished the trenches and fortifications of the first parallel by 7 April, but they required more time to conclude construction of the batteries along the line. Meanwhile, American batteries cannonaded the British troops throughout each day and night. Peter Timothy maintained that their firing "prevented [the British from] working on the Hampsted [*sic*] Battery," while Lieutenant Colonel Grimké noted that the mortars and cannon of the garrison continually annoyed the enemy's works.[12]

While American bombardments had inflicted only minor damage on the British fortifications, the continuous daily cannonade from Charleston took its toll on their workmen, especially since they were unable to return fire. On the night of 4 April, John Lewis Gervais reported that American batteries "Fired a great deal all night & threw Several Shells at the Ennemys Works." The following day, the diarist of the Graf Grenadier Battalion wearily recorded that "from seven o'clock yesterday morning until seven o'clock today the enemy fired 573 heavy cannonballs at us." No doubt the thud of cannonballs striking earthworks in the darkness and the hissing of fuses of as yet unexploded shells must have unnerved British working parties as they labored through the night.[13]

To raise the spirits of the men and distract the Americans, Clinton ordered the battery at Fenwick's Point and the galleys stationed in Wappoo Cut to fire upon Charleston. After dark on 5 April, the four galleys and the Fenwick's battery opened up on the city, directing their fire principally against the town itself rather than the American lines. Although stray shots from Fenwick's Point had landed in Charleston previously, this was the first time the British intentionally bombarded the city, and the cannonballs whistling through the night air caused a great stir among the people. Captain Ewald, who had reconnoitered close to the American lines to determine the effect of the firing, heard a "terrible clamor" arise among the inhabitants of Charleston and "the loud wailing of female voices" in the city dismayed him.[14]

The terror in the voices of these women was justified, as twenty-four and thirty-two pound shot hit several houses in town, one striking as far as Mr. Elfe's house on Queen Street. British gun crews would have been particularly pleased to know that two shots slammed into Governor Rutledge's house. The governor was appalled at "the insulting Manner in which the Enemy's Gallies have fired, with Impunity, on the Town." In addition to frightening civilians, British firing also wounded a soldier of the 3rd South Carolina posted at Coming's Point. The Fenwick's battery and galleys cannonaded the town again the following night with more deadly effect. The galley *Scourge* alone fired eighty-five times and James Duncan, the galley's lieutenant, bragged that "every shot of them [went] into the town." Peter Timothy related that one shot "killed Morrow, a Carpenter at the Old Sail in King Street." John Lewis Gervais added that the man was struck "just as he was going out of his house" by one of "at least 200 shot" fired by the British that night. Five other cannonballs hit Mr. Ferguson's house and outbuildings while two went through General McIntosh's quarters, in the rear of Ferguson's, killing two of McIntosh's horses in the yard.[15]

For the British, the bombardment appeared to produce the desired effect. Captain Russell related that the American batteries "were pretty quiet" the morning after the first night's cannonade, while Clinton claimed that "our firing from Fenwicks and galleys had eased the workmen much." Although the cannonade shocked the city's inhabitants, it affected the soldiers on the lines little. The lull from their guns was due more to a lack of powder and shot in the batteries than it was to British fire from across the Ashley. American officers commanding the batteries spent the morning of 6 April replenishing these articles, as general orders of the previous day had instructed them to do. The orders required officers to complete batteries with 100 rounds per gun and an equivalent amount of powder. By four o'clock that afternoon, the Americans again began firing on the British.[16]

Although Clinton claimed that the cannonade from Fenwick's Point "eased the workmen much," that morale on the British side was nowhere near exuberant is evidenced in the amount of squabbles, disagreements, and mistrust that manifested itself among the British officers and men in the early stages of the siege. Whether due to constant American artillery fire, recurring delays in operations, or the general anxiety of laying siege to the city, there seems to have been an inordinate amount of bickering among the British forces, from the commander in chief on down to the rank and file. Without question, the quixotic Clinton seriously disapproved of Admiral Arbuthnot's conduct, and he privately criticized him. In his journal, Clinton confided that his troops had constructed "a parallel of 2 miles in 3 days" while the admiral "harps upon delays." He enumerated in great detail the manner in which he believed Arbuthnot had retarded their progress from the time the army and fleet had departed New York to the present moment. It was not only Arbuthnot that rankled Sir Henry, but also his second in command, Lord Cornwallis.[17]

Suspicion and dislike between Clinton and Cornwallis went back as far as 1776, and five years later their feud would contribute to the climactic crisis at Yorktown.[18] Tensions between the two officers, which ultimately poisoned their relationship, began to fester seriously during the Charleston campaign. The underlying issue in their downward-spiraling association was Clinton's desire to resign from command in America. Clinton had asked Lord George Germain for permission to resign the previous year, and he was still awaiting Germain's reply at the time operations against Charleston commenced. Cornwallis, the second ranking officer in America, held a dormant commission to replace Clinton if he resigned, was killed, or became incapacitated. Cornwallis apparently feared that if the attempt against Charleston were a failure and Clinton's resignation were accepted, the stigma of the failure would attach to his tenure as commander in America. As a result, Cornwallis informed his commander that he had given "too much" to Cornwallis's opinion and "had consulted him too considerably." In the future, he wished "not to be consulted as he was afraid of responsibility." According to Clinton, Cornwallis pulled him aside somewhat informally while they were in the process of reconnoitering the Ashley River to make these assertions.[19]

Whatever the timing and gist of their conversation, Cornwallis set the stage for a poor relationship with his commander, who soon became displeased with anything his subordinate did. To Cornwallis's credit, his appointment as commander in chief in America was a real possibility, and he did not want to bear the blame for a deteriorating situation before he had even taken command. But he had served with Clinton since the beginning of the war, and, most certainly aware of his contentious personality, he probably could have broached the subject more tactfully. Clinton realized that it was not a time "for altercation," but he asserted that he could "never be cordial with such a man." Although Clinton received word from London during the course of the siege that his resignation had not been accepted, relations between the two officers remained cool.[20]

Squabbles also arose among officers of lower rank, and declining morale affected the enlisted men. Clinton noticed "great disputes" between the chiefs of artillery and engineers, while British sailors, whom Arbuthnot sent ashore to assist the army with the siege, quarreled with the same men they came to assist. The sailors were unhappy serving under officers of the artillery rather than their own officers, so Clinton ordered the working parties to construct a new battery solely for them. Meanwhile, the Hessian grenadiers believed themselves slighted by their duty assignments. When, one evening early in the siege, the detachment sent to protect the men in the trenches consisted entirely of British grenadiers, John André recorded that "the Hessians at large felt themselves hurt at not giving a proportion of the covering party." Some of them in turn complained to André, who as deputy adjutant general issued orders and duty assignments to the various corps. Major André admitted that grievances such as those of the Hessian grenadiers gave him "much anxiety," but the grumbling of soldiers who disliked laboring throughout the night on the works utterly exasperated him. "For 7 weeks I have been one of 500 who did not sleep one night in two," André protested, while during the same period the soldiers worked in the day and slept at night. André was losing his patience with such complaints.[21]

Other British and Hessian soldiers were completely discontented with their conditions. Some expressed their dissatisfaction with their feet. On 4 and 5 April, three British soldiers and two Hessians deserted to the Americans. One British soldier was so desirous to free himself from the shackles of the King's army that he "paddled himself over [to Charleston] on a plank from James Island." Given the strained relations between British officers and the tenuous state of morale among the troops, it is remarkable that they were able to push forward their operations against Charleston as well as they did. In the midst of it all, Major André noted that the enemy "lay under their Works contently."[22]

Morale indeed remained high among the Americans in the early days of the siege. Shortly after the British crossed the Ashley, Thomas Pinckney informed his sister that the garrison was "very well prepared to receive" the enemy, and that "Matters are getting fast into the best Order." Not only had Lincoln bolstered the city's fortifications and prepared the men to face the enemy, but the commissaries had endeavored to supply the garrison with food. Dr. Ramsay believed enough provisions were on hand to last them six months, but he was far too optimistic. Peter Timothy commented that British sailors manning the galleys were feasting on mutton, "while we can't get beef." Even so, the confidence and placidity of the American soldiers extended to some civilians as well. "The women walk out from town to the lines, with all the composure imaginable, to see us cannonade the enemy," General Moultrie marveled.[23]

The garrison of Charleston received a great boost to morale on 7 April, when the Virginia Continentals sent by General Washington finally arrived to reinforce them.[24] Embarking that morning onboard schooners and brigs at Addison's Ferry on the Wando River, by two o'clock in the afternoon Brigadier General William Woodford and his men were landing at Gadsden's Wharf. Once all were ashore, they marched directly to the lines. As the Virginians came up to the lines, their comrades saluted them with three cheers and a firing of thirteen cannons, one for each of the independent states. The artillerymen fired the cannons in the manner of a *feu-de-joie* or "fire of joy," which was a running fire of musketry or cannons produced when the weapons were fired in succession. Meanwhile, church bells pealed throughout the city welcoming them.[25]

The arrival of the over seven hundred veteran Virginians, whose regiments had participated in all the major campaigns of the war and who now took up positions on the lines on either side of the hornwork, brought great joy to soldier and civilian alike. John Wells thought the Virginians looked the part of professional soldiers, asserting that they "wear the appearance of, what they are in reality, Hardy Veterans." Many Charlestonians had questioned whether they would ever reach the city. Moses Young remarked that the presence of the Virginia troops "made an amazing alteration in the countenances of the Citizens who had almost despaired of their arrival." Although pleased at the reinforcement, some inhabitants were still anxious about remaining in the town. Later in the afternoon when the vessels which had brought the Virginia Continentals to Charleston sailed back up the Cooper River, they carried away many civilians who wished to evacuate. For those who stayed behind, especially the officers and men of the army, the reinforcement was a welcome relief.[26]

The British had not failed to notice the arrival of the Virginia troops. Captain Ewald grumbled that they sailed down the Cooper and into the city "right before our eyes." Throughout the afternoon, the besiegers heard the sounds of celebration emanating from Charleston. Ensign Hartung recorded that the Americans "cheered in the town and cannonaded us very sharply towards evening, and showed their courage by means of a constant pealing of bells." Those who had experienced sieges before would have recognized that reinforcements to an army ensconced behind fortifications were worth twice as much as troops in the open field, which made the jubilant resonation even more galling. That evening, American artillerymen extended the festivities to their enemy by saluting them with "a continuous cannon and mortar fire." Unfortunately for Lincoln and the garrison of Charleston, the joy in the city and boost to morale were to last just over twenty-four hours. By evening of the next day, the British would have overcome another obstacle, making the situation of Charleston even more dire.[27]

The withdrawal of Commodore Whipple's fleet into the Cooper River after Admiral Arbuthnot and his warships crossed Charleston Bar set the stage for the next phase of British naval operations. Bottled up in the harbor, American ships could take no real offensive action against the British forces. Lincoln now intended to use the fleet to keep the Royal Navy out of the Cooper River and prevent them from making a junction with Clinton via that river. If British ships pushed past Fort Moultrie, made their way into the Cooper, and then destroyed the remaining American ships, the British army and navy would completely surround Charleston. The Americans had to forestall such an event to keep open their line of communication and their link to the South Carolina backcountry.

Lincoln employed two courses of action to keep the Royal Navy from the Cooper in the event Fort Moultrie's guns failed to stop them. First, American ships were to take a station in the Cooper from which they could fire at any British ships trying to come into it. Whipple had to stand and fight now, since there was no other place to which he could fall back. A movement farther up the Cooper or into the Wando would remove his vessels completely from the theater of action and would produce no positive result whatsoever. The second stratagem was to block the channel between Charleston and Shutes Folly, a large sand bar at the mouth of the Cooper between Charleston and Mount Pleasant.[28] Lincoln and Whipple were more successful in obstructing this channel than the one between Fort Moultrie and the Middle Ground, the effect of the tides evidently not being as pronounced.[29]

Ironically, some of the same ships that were to have defended the Bar and operated with Fort Moultrie came to greater use at the bottom of the channel between Charleston and Shutes Folly. The Americans sunk *Bricole, Queen of France, Truite,* two brigs, and several smaller vessels in a row across the channel. From the Exchange building at the end of Broad Street to Shutes Folly they constructed a boom of cables, chains, and spars, held in place by the sunken hulks. Together, the boom and scuttled vessels formed an impassable barrier that prevented British ships from getting into the Cooper between Charleston and Shutes Folly; the narrower and shallower Hog Island channel between Shutes Folly and Mount Pleasant still remained open, however. Armed vessels stood guard behind the boom to thwart British attempts to destroy it. Lieutenant Colonel Laurens lamented that they could have completed the obstruction without sacrificing so many ships, but the sacrifice of these vessels was of little consequence, since the American fleet lacked any real room to maneuver and the naval officers seemed disinclined to attack the Royal Navy. Moreover, as converted transports, *Bricole* and *Truite* could not withstand a close naval bombardment, while Commodore Whipple had previously reported that *Queen of France* was "found so defective in her Hulls as renders her unfit to proceed on a cruise without considerable repairs." The scuttling of these vessels also brought a welcome reinforcement of men and guns to the Charleston garrison. Lincoln assigned the approximately 1,100 seamen and 150 pieces of artillery from the sunken ships to the fortifications ringing the city, the addition of which, as Laurens informed his father, "have made our batteries very formidable." *Providence, Boston, L'Aventure,* and *Ranger,* having been spared the ignominious fate of being scuttled, remained in the Cooper River behind the boom.[30]

Over in Fort Moultrie on Sullivan's Island, Colonel Charles Cotesworth Pinckney's vastly understrength 1st South Carolina and a small battalion of country militia were now the only defenders standing between the British fleet and the city. Colonel Pinckney had barely enough troops to man the fort's cannons. Still, Charlestonians counted on a repeat of the already legendary performance of Fort Moultrie in 1776. But the circumstances four years earlier had been somewhat different. In 1776, the British thrust was not directed against Charleston, but against the fort itself. Commodore Peter Parker's warships had spent an entire day trying to pound the fort on Sullivan's Island into submission, and the anchored British vessels had made easy targets for American artillerymen. Admiral Arbuthnot, on the other hand, wished only to get his ships past Fort Moultrie and into the harbor. His vessels would be exposed to the fort's fire for only as long as it would take to sail by the fort and out of range of its guns, probably only a few minutes with a favorable wind and tide. Once they cleared Fort Moultrie they could take station at Fort Johnson, a safe distance from Moultrie's cannon.

Since crossing the Bar on 20 March, the British warships lay in Five Fathom Hole. Arbuthnot would again have to wait for a flood tide before making the attempt to pass Fort Moultrie. He also wished to ascertain whether the Americans had successfully obstructed the channel between Sullivan's Island and the Middle Ground. Any ship that ran aground or got hung up on an underwater obstruction would at the very least be severely damaged, and at worst be destroyed, by Fort Moultrie's guns.[31]

Anxious for the Royal Navy to enter the harbor, the impatient Clinton privately questioned Arbuthnot's apparent dilatory conduct. In his correspondence with Arbuthnot, Clinton remained genial and expressed confidence in the naval chief's abilities. On 4 April, veiling his impatience only slightly, he wrote Arbuthnot of the army's progress on the lines and inquired of "what hopes" there were of passing Fort Moultrie. Arbuthnot reassured the British general that he would make the attempt the "first favorable opportunity." That opportunity came just a few days later.[32]

The morning of 8 April was overcast and rainy with a light breeze. As the day progressed, the southeast wind stiffened until it became "as fair a wind as can blow." Arbuthnot now had the conditions he required. At half past three in the afternoon, he gave the signal to weigh anchor, and nine warships and three transports moved slowly up the channel toward Fort Moultrie. As they approached Sullivan's Island around four o'clock, the fort's guns opened upon them. Arbuthnot, in the forty-four gun *Roebuck,* would attempt the passage first. *Roebuck* turned into the channel between Sullivan's Island and the Middle Ground and plunged ahead, coming within 800 yards of the fort, well within effective range of its guns. Solid shot whizzed through the air as *Roebuck* returned fire. All of Fort Moultrie's seaward guns were trained on the British vessel, but by half past four Peter Timothy asserted that "the Admiral has received & returned the Fire of Fort Moultrie and passed it without any apparent Damage."[33]

Inspired by *Roebuck*'s example, the other captains turned their vessels into the channel one after the other. Fort Moultrie's guns blazed away at them as they passed, and heavy smoke from the firing of so many cannon quickly enveloped both fort and ships. Lieutenant Oben of *Richmond,* the next ship after *Roebuck* to make the attempt, recorded that "Fort Moultrie fired briskly upon us." Pinckney's gunners had now found the range and their shot pummeled *Richmond.* Oben reported that the fort's guns shot away her foretop mast and delivered several cannonballs into her hull "which dismounted a gun." The lieutenant also noted that the crew suffered "2 Men & 1 Boy killed & 3 wounded" from the salvos. Still, *Richmond* struggled onward and soon joined *Roebuck* under the safety of Fort Johnson. Next came the forty-four gun *Romulus,* which received "a pretty smart Fire" but escaped without serious damage. The frigates *Blonde, Virginia,* and *Raleigh* followed. Although Lieutenant Waudby of *Raleigh* asserted that "we rec[eive]d many shot in our hull & rigging," these ships also made the passage successfully. The fifty gun *Renown,* the last of the large warships to go through, like the others encountered "a severe fire" as she crossed in front of the fort. Finally, it was the turn of the sloop of war *Sandwich,* a schooner, and the three transports. One transport ran aground and quickly drew fire from the fort. Her crew abandoned the ship and British sailors returned later that night to burn the vessel to prevent her from falling into American hands.[34]

By half past five that evening, Peter Timothy noted that with the exception of the transport "every ship ha[d] now come to Anchor." In just ninety minutes, British seamen sailed eleven of the twelve ships in their flotilla past Fort Moultrie's forty guns. Even Timothy had to admit that "they really make a most noble Appearance, and I could not help admiring the Regularity and Intrepidity with which they approached, engaged, and passed Fort Moultrie." Although *Richmond* lost her foretop mast and sailors had to destroy the transport, the other vessels sustained only minor damage to their masts, rigging, and hulls—a small price to pay for the successful entrance into the harbor. The sailors onboard the ships were not so lucky, having suffered to Moultrie's guns twenty-seven men killed and wounded. It was the largest loss for the British on a single day since operations against Charleston commenced. Colonel Pinckney reported no losses inside the fort.[35]

On shore, all attention was focused on the action in the harbor. Men stood upon the parapets in an attempt to better view the proceedings.

A Hessian officer estimated that there were nearly 6,000 men from the garrison standing atop Charleston's fortifications "who wanted the pleasure of seeing the ships blown out of the water." Smoke from the cannons, the distance, and overcast weather soon obscured the combat from their sight however. Ensign Hartung of the Hessians recorded that "neither the ships nor Sullivan's Island could be seen for some time owing to the smoke." But British and American soldiers clearly heard the intense boom of the cannonade. According to Captain Ewald, the roar of the fort's cannon "resembled a terrible thunderstorm."[36]

Once all British ships successfully reached Fort Johnson, American guns on the lines fell silent. Both Ewald and Hinrichs conjectured that the Royal Navy's passing of Fort Moultrie had so demoralized the garrison that they consequently did not fire. That night, Peter Timothy still maintained that "We are all in high Spirits," but the day's events must have disheartened the garrison's soldiers and civilians. The diarist of the Graf Grenadier Battalion noted that after the second British warship passed the fort "a great many small vessels were seen on the Cooper River, heading inland" from Charleston. The Hessian went on to assert that they "had revenge for yesterday's cheering." The British ships resting safely near Fort Johnson were plainly visible to those who had cheered the day before. No other British warship had forcibly entered the harbor since 1775.[37]

Sir Henry Clinton was obviously pleased with Arbuthnot's success, which had the immediate effect of making it easier for the two commanders to communicate. When Arbuthnot came ashore on the evening of 9 April to meet with Sir Henry, Clinton "congratulated him most cordially" on his entrance into the harbor. The officers conferred on operations over the next two days.[38]

Securing control of the Cooper River was a priority for Clinton. Until this was accomplished, Lincoln could still use it as an avenue for supplies and reinforcements to flow into the garrison or as a route of escape. Arbuthnot informed Clinton that he would assume responsibility for maintaining the communication on James Island. This overture allowed Clinton to move more men across the Ashley to his army on the neck, which in turn provided an opportunity to detach a force from the neck across the Cooper River. Sir Henry intended to push "a Considerable Corps" over the Cooper River, but the army alone could not secure the river. He expected Arbuthnot to send ships into it via the Hog Island channel on the north side of Shutes Folly. The admiral agreed to do so, but insisted that Clinton post troops on Mount Pleasant to cover the vessels as they made the passage. The two officers finally resolved that the navy would sound the channel and determine the feasibility of conducting ships through it. Meanwhile, Clinton would send a body of troops across the Cooper. He noted confidently that "the Admiral left me with [the] intention of examining what could be done by the hog Is[land] channel." Although he probably suspected that his difficulties with Arbuthnot were far from over, Sir Henry had no idea that the most frustrating episodes still lay ahead.[39]

Clinton and Arbuthnot also decided to summon the garrison even though British working parties had yet to complete the batteries in the first parallel. By 10 April, they had only mounted guns in the batteries of two fortifications. Because they lacked draft animals, Captain Ewald pointed out that "all the pieces and ammunition, and practically everything required for the siege, must be brought from the landing place up to the destination points by the sailors and Negroes, all of which takes up considerable time." The swampy low-lying terrain, which was even wetter than usual due to recent heavy rains, made it especially difficult for men to transport heavy cannon overland, and pieces became easily mired in the mud. John Laurens thought that the enemy's slow progress in completing their works inspired "a State of hope" among the garrison.[40]

Despite the admonitions of Major Moncrief to wait until they had completed more batteries, Clinton and Arbuthnot ordered Major André and Sir Andrew Hamond of the Royal Navy to draw up the summons. Major William Crosby, one of Clinton's aides-de-camp, carried the message into Charleston late in the afternoon of 10 April.[41]

The summons read:

> Sir Henry Clinton K. B. General and Commander in Chief of His Majesty's forces in the Colonies lying on the Atlantic from Nova Scotia to [Florida] and Vice Admiral Arbuthnot[,] Commander in

Chief of his Majesty's Ships in North America[,] regretting the effusion of Blood and distress which must now commence[,] deem it conformant to humanity to warn the Town and Garrison of Charlestown of the havock and devastation with which they are threatened from the formidable force surrounding them by Sea and Land.[42]

An alternative is offered at this hour of saving their Lives and Property contained in the Town or of abiding by the fatal consequences of a cannonade and Storm.

Should the place in a fallacious Security or its Commander in a wanton indifference to the fate of its Inhabitants delay a Surrender or should the public Stores or Shipping be destroyed[,] the resentment of an exasperated Soldier may intervene[,] but the same mild and compassionate Offer can never be renewed. The respective Commanders who hereby summon the Town do not apprehend so rash a [path] as farther resistance will be taken, but rather that the Gates will be opened and themselves received with a degree of Confidence which will forebode further reconciliations.[43]

The document's wording was standard for an eighteenth-century summons. The commander, or commanders, of the attacking army often expressed regret at "the further effusion of blood" for both armies. The besieger appealed to the opposing commander's humanity and his desire to preserve the lives of the garrison's soldiers and civilians. More ominously, the typical summons usually included a veiled threat of what might happen to the garrison if they continued to hold out and the besieger had to storm the city or fortress. At the siege of Savannah, Admiral d'Estaing reminded General Prevost that he held Prevost "answerable [. . .] for every Event and Misfortune attending a Defence," while in June 1781 General Nathanael Greene informed the commander of the fort at Ninety Six that he would have to answer "for the consequences of a vain resistance or destruction of Stores." In medieval times, and even as late as the Thirty Years War, besieging armies, which had finally persevered after lengthy sieges, routinely sacked fallen cities causing untold misery to the inhabitants. Gentlemen commanders excused themselves of any culpability in this event, especially if they had asked their opponent to surrender honorably at an earlier point in the siege. Officers of the besieging army extended no guarantee that they could control their "exasperated" soldiers after several weeks or months of continuous brutal warfare when the garrison had refused the civil offer of terms. But the defenders, by giving themselves up, had the opportunity to avoid such unpleasantness. This, General Lincoln and the Charleston garrison were not prepared to do.[44]

Lincoln's answer, delivered that night, was short and to the point. "Gentlemen," he responded, "I received your Summons of this date. Sixty days have passed since it has been known that your Intentions against this Town were hostile in which time has been afforded to abandon it, but Duty and Inclination point to the propriety of supporting it to the last extremity." Lincoln had remained in Charleston to defend it and this he was now determined to do. At ten o'clock, British soldiers in the trenches became aware of the garrison's desire to fight on "by means of their guns," which proceeded to cannonade them throughout the night.[45]

The summons rejected, Clinton and Arbuthnot proceeded with operations against the town. Over the next two days, working parties redoubled their efforts to complete the batteries in the first parallel. Accordingly, Captain Ewald related that they "hauled ammunition day and night to the small magazines in the trenches." American batteries continued to bombard them as they worked. Although Captain Russell reported on 12 April that they had suffered only twelve casualties since the Americans began cannonading them, British and Hessian soldiers working on the fortifications could not ignore the unremitting artillery fire.[46] Even Clinton was not immune to the danger. Captain Archibald Robertson noted that an enemy shell burst "very near Sir Henry and suite" during one of his visits to the trenches. In spite of the rebel fire, Moncrief promised Clinton that the magazines for the batteries would be ready by 13 April. Although all were not complete by that date, the British were able to mount seventeen twenty-four pound cannon, two twelve pounders, three eight inch howitzers, and nine mortars of various sizes in three of seven batteries.[47]

On the morning of 13 April, General Lincoln convened a council of war of his senior officers at his headquarters marquee near the lines.

Lincoln described to the assembled officers a very gloomy situation, detailing for them the critical state of the troops, provisions, stores, and artillery. Moreover, he informed them that he had little hope that any further "succour of Consequence" would reach the city. The engineers, he related, conjectured that their fortifications could hold out but a few days. After presenting this information, Lincoln asked the officers to consider "the Propriety of evacuating the Garrison." General McIntosh immediately welcomed the idea, exclaiming that they should not lose "an hour longer in attempting to get the Continental Troops at Least out" while the Cooper River was still open to them. McIntosh argued persuasively that "the Salvation not only of this State but some other" depended on the survival of the Continentals. The Georgian believed that most of the officers present agreed with him. Lincoln entreated the officers to "consider maturely of the expediency & practicability of such a Measure" before their next meeting. At that moment around ten A.M., a tremendous roar of cannon fire from the lines interrupted the council. The British batteries on the neck had finally opened on the city, and the meeting immediately adjourned as the officers hurried to their posts.[48]

The firing from the Fenwick's batteries and the galleys in the Ashley had been nothing compared to the opening of the British batteries on the neck. British artillery crews poured cannon and mortar fire upon the lines and the city from ten that morning until midnight, with only brief intermissions. Never before in its history had Charleston experienced such a terrific bombardment. The Fenwick's battery also joined in, contributing to the terror in the town. As Major William Croghan explained, "the balls flew thro' the streets, & spent their fury on the houses; & those who were walking or visiting in the town, as was usual during the former quiet, now flew to their cellars, & others to the works, as the places of greatest safety." When the British cannonade began, American batteries returned fire, which must have produced a remarkable thundering on the lines and in the city.[49]

The British had recently received a reinforcement of artillerymen who handled their guns quite expertly. Captain Ewald maintained that the first thirty shots from their batteries scored several direct hits on the American lines. According to Captain Hinrichs, the battery at Number

Two was so effective that it silenced the guns in the American redoubt closest to the Ashley River. Meanwhile, the battery on Hampstead Hill propelled hot shot into the city, which set ablaze several houses in the Ansonborough district. British sailors onboard the ships in the harbor rejoiced as they observed part of the town in flames. Clinton was not amused, however, and he ordered the battery to cease firing on the city immediately, asserting that it was "absurd, impolitick, and inhuman to burn a town you mean to occupy."[50]

The garrison was granted a reprieve when the firing finally stopped around midnight. It had been a dreadful day for Charleston. Lieutenant Colonel Grimké reported that British artillery killed two soldiers of the North Carolina brigade, severely damaged one of the embrasures on the lines, completely destroyed a twenty-six pounder, and dismounted an eighteen pounder. Tragically, Grimké also noted that some women and children had been "killed in Town." Two houses burned down completely while others were severely damaged. In throwing cannon fire into the city, the British operations in South Carolina were bringing warfare directly to the civilian populace.[51]

The day's exchange of artillery fire did not come without a price for the British and Hessians, who suffered at least seven men killed or wounded. Despite the larger number of casualties in their ranks, it is interesting to note the apparent superiority of the British gunners' fire over that of the Americans. The Americans had fired continuously at the British lines for ten days, but, as several British officers related, their shot caused no serious damage to their works. Captain Russell conjectured that the rebels had fired "above 4000 Shot and Shells" at them since the opening of the trenches, with very little effect. In contrast to the erratic American fire, the British, firing from just three batteries, destroyed two American guns and an embrasure in only one day. Certainly, the recent arrival of members of the Royal Artillery helped the British, but the Americans also had many experienced artillerists on their side. Another possibility for the inconsistent American fire was the recent loss of Captain Joseph Gilbank, a skilled artilleryman who specialized in making fuses for shells. An accidental explosion of an American shell had taken his life several days earlier. Whatever the cause of the British superiority, that superiority did not bode well for the defenders of Charleston. The British gunners' fire would become even more effective as they advanced toward a second parallel.[52]

General Lincoln recognized the perilous situation of the garrison. Although he suggested the possibility of evacuation to his officers in the council of war, Lincoln himself was reluctant to abandon Charleston to the depredations of the British army before his own army had made a determined stand. With matters becoming more critical each passing day, Lincoln and his officers persuaded Governor Rutledge and several members of the Privy Council to leave the city. The American commander enumerated to Rutledge the arguments in favor of his departure. "Hereby you would keep alive the Civil authority[,] give confidence to the people, and throw in the necessary succours and supplies to the Garrison," he pointed out to the governor. By urging Rutledge to retreat to the backcountry, Lincoln was attempting "to preserve the Executive Authority" of South Carolina in the event Charleston succumbed to the British. If the capital fell, Rutledge alone would represent the people of South Carolina. Moreover, Lincoln hoped that the governor would urge the backcountry militia to come to Charleston's assistance. Christopher Gadsden, as lieutenant governor, and five members of the council remained behind as the chief civilian officials.[53]

Departing Charleston at the same time as Rutledge and his entourage were a number of invalids, whom Lincoln ordered to be moved to a safe location in the country. Among them was Lieutenant Colonel Francis Marion, who had suffered what would eventually be considered a very fortuitous injury. Ironically, Marion had not incurred the injury in the line of duty, but during a party at the home of Captain Alexander McQueen on 19 March. Following dinner, Captain McQueen locked all the doors and began to propose a series of toasts. Marion, who was not a heavy drinker, excused himself by dropping out one of the windows. When he landed, he came down awkwardly on his foot, either breaking a bone or severely spraining it. With the malady still not healed by the beginning of April, Lincoln requested him to join the other invalids in evacuating the garrison.[54]

Rutledge and his party retired from the city by boat around noon on 13 April, just a few hours after the British bombardment began.

Crossing the Cooper River in the midst of the cannonade, Rutledge and his companions witnessed from the river a scene of carnage as had never been seen before in Charleston. Smoke, fire, and thunderous explosions belched forth from heavy cannon on both sides, and artillery fire rained down upon the city's houses, wounding and killing civilians. John Lewis Gervais, one of the evacuees, plainly observed two houses in Ansonborough in flames as they left the town. Earlier in the day, he had heard that a child and its nurse had been killed in the same district. Like never before, warfare had come to the people of Charleston. With British warships riding at anchor in the harbor and British troops on Charleston neck cannonading them, Charlestonians were sharing the ravages of war that their fellow citizens in New York, Philadelphia, and Savannah had experienced previously. Those cities had all fallen to the British. As the smoke from the city's fires faded in the distance, Rutledge, Gervais, and the other men could only hope that Charleston's fate would be different.[55]

Chapter Ten

The Cooper River Communication

Although Clinton's army had constructed a line of entrenchments across Charleston neck and Arbuthnot's ships had blockaded the harbor, the ease with which Governor Rutledge and his attendants departed Charleston clearly demonstrated that the British were far from surrounding the city completely. In the days following the Royal Navy's entrance into the harbor, British officers and soldiers watched as numerous civilians fled the town via the Cooper River. As long as the Americans maintained control of the Cooper and kept the region east of it free of British troops, a path remained open for reinforcements and supplies destined for the city. Equally important, command of the river ensured that an avenue of escape was available if they deemed evacuation necessary. Conversely, if the British became masters of the Cooper, Charleston was surely doomed. As the siege progressed on Charleston neck, General Lincoln endeavored to keep open his line of communication over the Cooper River. Sir Henry Clinton, meanwhile, attempted to wrest control of the river away from the Americans. As they had throughout the campaign, both generals encountered obstacles in this struggle. But the stakes for Lincoln and the garrison of Charleston were becoming more momentous. Actions taken along the Cooper River would determine the fate of the city and the army within.

For Benjamin Lincoln, freedom of access along the Wando-Cooper River corridor was of paramount importance. Troops and supplies from the back parts of South Carolina would most likely move down the Santee River first and then south to Charleston via the Wando and Cooper Rivers. Any reinforcements from North Carolina would cross the Santee at Lenud's Ferry and reach Charleston by the same route. Unfortunately for Lincoln, he had to defend against a likely crossing of British land forces over the Cooper and the equally probable entrance of British warships into the river. Already he employed the bulk of his army in the defense of Charleston itself and had few troops to spare for operations along the Cooper. One crucial body of troops he had not brought into the garrison was his cavalry, which had skillfully screened and slowed British movements west of the Ashley. Lincoln intended to rely primarily on the cavalry and a series of fortifications along the Cooper and Wando Rivers to keep open the communication with the backcountry. Meanwhile, he hoped that the boom between the Exchange and Shutes Folly, along with the warships stationed behind it, would bar the Royal Navy from the river.

Beginning in early April, Lincoln pushed forward efforts to protect the communication along the Cooper River. He sent Colonel François Marquis de Malmedy and 200 North Carolina militia to "secure the several passes on the Cooper River" and to establish a defensive work at Cainhoy on the north side of the Wando River, "a strong commanding Ground" nine miles from Charleston. The work at Cainhoy was to serve as a depot for stores destined for the garrison. Colonel Louis Antoine Jean Baptiste, Chevalier de Cambray, one of Lincoln's engineers, reconnoitered Cainhoy and found it "very favorable" for the purpose. Lincoln also instructed Malmedy to fortify Lampriers Point, or Hobcaw, a small nub of land which jutted into the Cooper just below its confluence with the Wando. The posts at Cainhoy and Lampriers Point would secure the water passage from Charleston up the Cooper River and on to the upper reaches of the Wando.[1] Lincoln was so convinced of the necessity of properly defending Lampriers Point that on 11 April he ordered his officers to transfer six eighteen pound cannon from Fort Moultrie to the new redoubt there. Lincoln could undertake this measure now that British ships had run past the fort. The fortification on Lampriers Point, armed with eighteen pound cannon, would deter British ships from entering the Wando, and the work soon became the focal point of the American defense of the Cooper.[2]

While Lincoln provided the new work at Lampriers with artillery, the allocation of manpower and shipping to it presented a more challenging task. The insufficiency of men, which prevented Lincoln from opposing the British crossing of the Ashley River, now made defense of the Cooper River also problematic. Malmedy wrote Lincoln that it was his opinion and also that of the "inhabitants" east of the river that there were "a great number of landings to be kept" along it. He hinted at the difficulty of covering all of them with the troops then available. Lincoln hoped that Governor Rutledge could help alleviate the shortage of men. He urged Rutledge to "take quarters in the Country near Cainhoy" and "call forth the strength" of the country. Lincoln reminded the governor that he could not man the new works "from our present force in town."[3]

As to shipping, Colonel Malmedy maintained that without "vessels of force" in the mouth of the Wando, "the communication from Wandoo & Cooper river with the town, cannot Exist." He proposed that Lincoln send *Ranger* and *L'Aventure,* along with some galleys, to the entrance of the Wando to further secure it. Lincoln did not wish to transfer these vessels from the defense of the lower Cooper, but he did order that the polacre *Zephyr,* carrying eighteen guns and a crew of thirty-six, should "guard the mouth of Wando and Cooper rivers." He also directed Malmedy to collect all the armed vessels that he could find along the Wando and move them down river for the same purpose.[4]

To alleviate Malmedy's lack of men and to expedite construction of his fortifications, Lincoln ordered Colonel Pinckney to send African American slaves from Fort Moultrie to Lampriers Point to assist in the completion of the works there. The arrival of Woodford's brigade along with a few North Carolina militiamen who had trickled in allowed Lincoln also to provide Malmedy some reinforcement of foot soldiers. Besides fortifying Cainhoy and Lampriers Point, Malmedy also collected provisions for the garrison, securing the stores further up the Cooper River. The French officer could not foresee that control of the upper Cooper was soon to become very tenuous for the Americans, however.[5]

While Malmedy endeavored to strengthen the American position east of the Cooper River from Lampriers Point to Cainhoy, Lincoln's cavalry guarded the upper reaches of the river. Under Lincoln's orders,

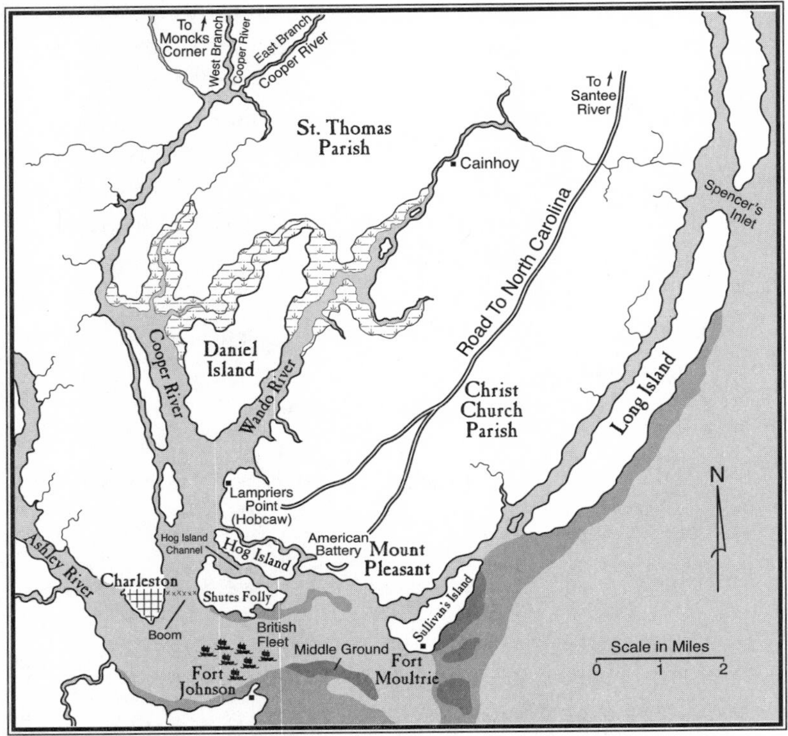

Region East of the Cooper

Brigadier General Isaac Huger posted the cavalry, which consisted of Washington's, Horry's, Bland's, and Pulaski's horse, and a small detachment of militia to Biggin's Bridge on the west branch of the Cooper River near Moncks Corner. At Biggin's Bridge, Huger's horsemen covered the right flank of the Cooper and could defend against a British attempt to cross along its shallower and narrower upper reaches. Meanwhile, their mobility allowed them to keep in contact with friendly forces lower down the river or oppose enemy crossings elsewhere.[6]

Clinton recognized the need to deal with the American cavalry before undertaking any serious operation east of the river. He resolved to send Lieutenant Colonel James Webster with 1,500 men across the

Cooper to fall in upon the rebels' communication, narrow their avenues of escape, capture or destroy supplies, and drive off their remaining corps in the country. Webster was to march with his own 33rd regiment, the 64th regiment, the Legion infantry, and the North Carolina Volunteers to Strawberry Ferry on the west branch of the Cooper. Meanwhile, Lieutenant Colonel Tarleton advanced with the Legion cavalry, a detachment of the 17th Light Dragoons, and the American Volunteers toward Biggin's Bridge, where Clinton hoped they would find and surprise the American light horse. Once reunited with the cavalry, Webster was to move toward Cainhoy and the forks of the upper Wando, dispatching troops from there across the Wando into the north end of Christ Church Parish. These measures would give the British forces a strong foothold east of the Cooper and hinder any escape attempt by the Charleston garrison.[7]

Webster's detachment represented only one arm of a pincers movement, which Clinton envisioned would give them control of the Cooper. While Webster's corps would cross the upper reaches of the Cooper and fall down upon the Wando basin and east bank of the Cooper, Clinton expected that Admiral Arbuthnot would force his way into the Cooper from the harbor. He issued instructions to Webster to cooperate with the British ships when they entered the river. When these two pincers met, Charleston would be completely cut off. As with the passing of the Bar and of Fort Moultrie, Arbuthnot's failure to act quickly again frustrated Clinton. Seeing "little probability" of Arbuthnot making a move into the Cooper, Clinton relied on Webster to establish himself east of the river and fall in upon the rebel communication.[8]

By 13 April, Webster and Tarleton had taken post at Middleton's plantation in Goose Creek and were ready to move toward the Cooper River. Although Tarleton's dragoons had replaced the mounts lost on the voyage from New York with horses obtained on Port Royal Island and along the march to Charleston, the quality of their horses was still inferior to that of the Americans. With inferior mounts, British cavalrymen would find it quite difficult to best the Americans in an even contest. Accordingly, Tarleton would have to rely on the element of surprise to defeat them, and this he endeavored to undertake. At ten o'clock on the night of 13 April, Tarleton set out with his horsemen and Ferguson's American Volunteers on the eighteen mile march to Biggin's Bridge.[9]

At Biggin's Bridge, the primary crossing point on the west branch of the Cooper, General Huger had approximately 400 cavalry and militia under his command.[10] The militia, which had only recently joined him, were wretchedly armed, however. He wrote Lincoln that forty of them from North Carolina arrived on 12 April with muskets but no ammunition, and two other companies came in with no arms at all. Huger complained that they were of "no use" to him without proper equipment. He posted the poorly armed militiamen out of the way on the eastern end of the bridge around Biggin's Church while his cavalry guarded the road from Goose Creek on the western end of the bridge. Other than the militia, Huger had few foot soldiers to support his dragoons which prevented him from seeking out the enemy. He called his situation "rather disagreeable" inasmuch as the enemy cavalry "never move without a large detachment of infantry."[11]

On the march to Moncks Corner, Tarleton's advance guard captured an African American slave, who was carrying a letter from Huger to Lincoln. Unfortunately for the Americans, from the contents of the letter and from the captured man Tarleton ascertained the disposition of the American cavalry and militia at Biggin's Bridge. His men pushed on toward Moncks Corner, covering the eighteen miles in just over five hours. In the early morning hours of 14 April, they approached the American position undetected, and Tarleton prepared his troopers for the attack.[12]

Huger had posted only a single patrol of horsemen on the road leading to Goose Creek to raise the alarm in the event of an attack. Swamps covered this road on either side, so Tarleton's men would have to advance straight down it into the American camp. Silently approaching the patrol, Tarleton instructed his cavalrymen to charge them and drive them back into the main body. According to Tarleton, his men followed this order "with the greatest promptitude and success." Catching them completely by surprise, the British horsemen, drawn sabers held aloft, forced them back and flew into the bivouac behind them. At once chaos ensued among Huger's men. The sound of British cavalry horses thundering into the camp roused the unprepared Americans, but by then it was too late. Under deadly blows from the heavy sabers of British dragoons, they bolted for their horses or tried to flee to the woods. Sabers thudded sickeningly into heads and shoulders, while men shrieked in agony and fear. The cries of whinnying horses and wounded men resounded in the early morning darkness. Brigadier General Huger, Major John Jameson, and several other officers made their way into the swamps on foot while some men were able to get away on horseback. To Tarleton's chagrin, he noted that Lieutenant Colonel Washington "was Prisoner but afterwards thro' the Darkness of the Morn escaped on foot." Others were not so lucky. Major Vernier, who had performed so nobly against the British west of the Ashley, suffered several grievous wounds in defending himself, including a severe saber blow behind the ear. Appealing for quarter from his attackers, he was struck again by British swords. A loyalist officer who saw Vernier reported that he was "mangled in the most shocking manner." Having completely routed the American cavalry, Tarleton ordered the Legion infantry to attack the militia around Biggin's Church. Major Cochrane led the assault with fixed bayonets and easily drove them off. In just a few minutes, Tarleton's cavalry and infantry had all but wiped out the American force at Biggin's Bridge.[13]

The Americans suffered fifteen men killed and eighteen wounded in the attack. Including the eighteen wounded, the British captured sixty-three officers and enlisted men. Tragically, Major Vernier survived for several hours only to be "frequently insulted by the privates" of the Legion "in his last moments." The British also seized over forty wagons loaded with ammunition, horse equipage, food, and clothing. Even more damaging to the Americans, on the following morning Tarleton distributed ninety-eight new dragoon horses to his officers and men. Not only had the Americans lost their superior mounts, but British cavalrymen were now riding them. Clinton contended that the capture of these horses allowed the British dragoons to be better mounted than when they left New York. Among the abandoned American baggage, Tarleton's troops discovered the correspondence between Generals Lincoln and Huger, which disclosed to the British Lincoln's intentions with regard to defending the communication along the Cooper River.

In inflicting these heavy losses on the Americans, Tarleton had only two men wounded.[14]

The American cavalry's crushing defeat at Biggin's Bridge was an unmitigated disaster for the American cause and for the security of Charleston. Scattered throughout the countryside and divested of a large number of their horses, the cavalry could no longer oppose the British in an organized fashion. Two weeks after the defeat, John Lewis Gervais related from Georgetown that many "Light horse" were expected to come there "to refit for they are not yet in a Condition to face the Ennemy." In addition to their horses, Gervais noted that the cavalrymen lost "Saddles[,] pistols & Swords" at Biggin's Bridge—in effect, everything that a dragoon needed to take the field.[15]

Covered by Tarleton's now well-mounted horsemen, Webster's force could cross the Cooper River without interference and operate east of the river virtually unopposed by cavalry. When word of the disaster reached Lincoln on 16 April, he knew full well the serious implications of the defeat. He recognized that the British now had an open door into St. Thomas Parish, lying between the Cooper and Wando, and Christ Church Parish, lying between the Wando and the sea islands. With a limited number of troops to defend the Cooper River communication, Lincoln realized that they could not hold Cainhoy or fortify a position at Scot's Ferry as he had hoped given the size of Webster's detachment. Consequently, he ordered the infantry east of the Cooper to retreat to the defensive work at Lampriers Point. By scattering the enemy cavalry, which had protected the right flank of the American defense line along the Cooper, the British now rolled up that line. With one stroke, they secured access to the entire region between the upper reaches of the Cooper and the upper reaches of the Wando, and now had an inroad to the complete investiture of Charleston.[16]

Given the grave consequences, one must question how American cavalry officers could have allowed such a defeat to occur. According to Tarleton, his men succeeded because they completely surprised the Americans who were unable to recover "from the confusion attending an unexpected attack." Tarleton noted that his troops encountered only one "grand guard" outside the American camp, and he asserted that General Huger failed to send out patrols along the road leading to

Biggin's Bridge. As a result, British cavalry charged into the American position undetected. Lieutenant Colonel Washington refused to acknowledge that the attack was a surprise, however. For two months, the American cavalry had operated in close proximity to the British, making it seem curious that their enemy could have caught them flat-footed. One week earlier, John Laurens related that Tarleton had tried to assail them in their position at Goose Creek, but General Huger "was on his guard and eluded the maneuvre by retiring." The account of Lieutenant Allaire adds weight to Washington's assertion that the Americans were not caught unaware. Allaire, a loyalist, contended that the Americans were under marching orders and were in the process of breaking camp, "which alone prevented their being all taken completely by surprise." While the Americans may not have been surprised, they were certainly soundly defeated.[17]

Much of the credit for the British victory belongs to Lieutenant Colonel Tarleton. Tarleton's audacity in planning and executing a night attack on the American position and the speed and ferocity with which his men carried it out go a long way toward explaining British success at Biggin's Bridge. Generally in a night attack, darkness contributes to the defenders' confusion. Meanwhile, with the information obtained from the captured slave, Tarleton's cavalrymen had the advantage of knowing something about the disposition of the American cavalry. The Americans had no such information with regard to their foe, and the swiftness with which the British cavalry fell upon them gave them little time to ascertain much of anything. British horsemen charged into their midst before they could even respond to the alarm. The lightning attack became a trademark tactic of Banastre Tarleton throughout his career in the south. The speed and relentlessness of his attacks, coupled with the same viciousness that had been shown Major Vernier, produced a general fear and hatred of Tarleton among southern patriots. Feared and hated he might have been, but as he demonstrated at Biggin's Bridge his tactics could be brutally effective.

In laying open the country east of the Cooper to Webster's detachment, the defeat of the American cavalry also exposed the inhabitants of that region to British foraging parties and their depredations. Sir

Henry Clinton instructed Webster to determine if he could "subsist himself in the Country"—which meant from the area's farms and plantations. No longer threatened by American cavalry, British foraging details fanned out across St. Thomas Parish. John Lewis Gervais noted to Henry Laurens that "in some places the Ennemy have behaved very well . . . in others very Ill." As they had west of the Ashley, the British plundered where "there was nobody at home," but Gervais reported that they also pillaged in spite of the inhabitants being at home. At the Widow Broughton's, British soldiers "plundered every thing belonging to her," and at Henry Laurens's Mepkin plantation, the marauders "broke open every trunk & carried off every thing they could carry without a Cart." From William Roddick, Laurens's Mepkin overseer, they took "what little Money he had[,] his Watch, Shirts[,] Stockings [. . .] & even the Shoes from his Wife's feet." The men who robbed this woman of her shoes ostensibly did so for the pure cruelty of it. It was this kind of soldier whom Major André observed would steal household goods from civilians "for the wanton pleasure of Spoil and which they have thrown aside an hour afterwards." Thirty miles away and conducting a siege of a well-fortified city, Sir Henry could do little about the conduct of these men.[18]

Women whose husbands served with the American army seem to have borne the lion's share of suffering. According to Gervais, a British foraging party took "every thing" from Mrs. Butler, whose husband was a major in the South Carolina militia.[19] Another group of soldiers accosted Mrs. Mary Motte, wife of Colonel Isaac Motte, even going so far as to seize the clothes of her children. Holding a baby in her lap, Mrs. Motte begged them not to take the clothes, but the soldiers responded that they wished they had the baby's father for "they [would] rip his damn[e]d rebel heart out." With her children endangered, her husband insulted, and herself facing the British alone, the experience must have terrified Mary Motte. Mrs. Motte was luckier than other women who were physically abused by British soldiers.[20]

On the night of 14 April, two dragoons of the British Legion forcibly entered Fair Lawn, the home of Lady Colleton, with drawn swords. One of them, Henry McDonagh, accused Ms. Colleton of harboring rebels, and finding no enemy soldiers there he attacked the poor woman with his sword, severely cutting her hand. He then tried to sexually assault her but her "Shrieks & Struggles" prevented him "from accomplishing his Designs." After stealing a "jug of Rum," the two men left the terrified woman. Mrs. Ann Fayssoux then had the misfortune to encounter them. Ms. Fayssoux later declared to Lieutenant Colonel Tarleton that McDonagh "made a Similar attack upon her Person." In addition to abusing her "most sorely with his Sword," he "almost strangled her." He then sexually assaulted her. Tragically, Ms. Fayssoux begged the man "to take her Life & not to violate her Person." The brute did not heed her cries, however. Two other women witnessed the attack and confirmed that McDonagh was the culprit. Tarleton and Major Patrick Ferguson were very sympathetic to the plight of these women. Tarleton sent a surgeon, an officer, and twelve men to Mrs. Fayssoux's home to protect and assist her, and he had McDonagh arrested and confined.[21]

Tarleton, whose sympathy for these women is in sharp contrast to the unattractive picture that many historians have painted of him, suggested to Clinton's deputy adjutant general that McDonagh be hanged for his cruel offenses. Major Ferguson wanted the two dragoons put to death immediately, but Lieutenant Colonel Webster followed proper military channels and sent McDonagh back to headquarters to be court-martialed. Over a month later, he was still confined in the British provost awaiting trial. Charles Stedman contended that the guilty dragoon was eventually flogged for his offenses.[22]

While such violent acts against the civilian populace appalled British officers and they in no way condoned them, they continued to send out foraging parties to gather supplies. When foraging parties were in the field, officers at headquarters or in camp could do little to prevent abuse of civilians. Meanwhile, gangs of soldiers wandered the countryside and attempted to pass themselves off as sanctioned foraging details. One such group of soldiers stopped at Rawlins Lowndes's Crowfield plantation and insisted to his wife that they had explicit orders to plunder. But Sarah Lowndes was a brave woman, and she challenged them, asserting that she "was convinced they had no such orders." She later explained to her husband that she told them that "they should have nothing from me but what I gave them willingly."

Fortunately for Mrs. Lowndes, the soldiers departed peaceably after taking "breakfast & a plenty of Drink."[23]

Officers could confine and court-martial men for plundering or abusing civilians (at one point six of nineteen men confined in the British provost were confined for just such offenses), but they could not stop these practices completely. The fact that many of the men involved in foraging details east of the Cooper were from loyalist units probably contributed to their mistreatment of civilians. Many of them no doubt had families whom the rebels had affronted in the same manner. Sadly, the nature of war in any age, especially a civil war as the American Revolution in the south would eventually become, often brings out the worst in those men whose responsibility it is to use force against others. As in the lowcountry of South Carolina in 1780, the aged, meek, and defenseless have frequently suffered as a result.[24]

Plundering of civilians was one of the tragic consequences of the defeat of the American cavalry and Lincoln's decision to consolidate his army within the confines of Charleston. Lacking enough troops to cover the countryside, especially after the defeat at Biggin's Bridge, Lincoln was unable to protect those remaining there. Ironically, many Charlestonians fled the city to escape just such horrors of war. They now found themselves at the mercy of the enemy in the countryside.

When Sir Henry Clinton learned of the defeat of the American cavalry he was unmistakably pleased that Webster could now threaten the rebel communication by land. Although he wrote in his journal that the event "will make the Admiral not going into Cooper of less consequence," Clinton apparently did not truly believe that. In the same letter in which he informed Arbuthnot of Tarleton's success, he implored the admiral to notify him if he thought he could maneuver through the Hog Island channel. He declared to Arbuthnot: "I am yet Sir in the same anxious Expectation, I before expressed, to know, if you believe the Hog Island Passage will be practicable." By 19 April, Clinton confided to his journal that Webster's force "cannot act with vigor" unless the admiral "can come into the Cooper." The complete investiture of Charleston would be quite difficult without the cooperation of Admiral Arbuthnot and his warships.[25]

Since their meeting on the day after British ships passed Fort Moultrie, Clinton and Arbuthnot haggled over the Royal Navy's entrance into the Cooper River. Arbuthnot's statements at first indicated that his vessels would make the attempt. He asserted to Clinton that he would "move Heaven & Earth to accomplish the passage into the Cooper." The admiral assured Clinton that he would reconnoiter the Hog Island channel and inform him whether his ships could get through it. The two commanders resolved that if necessary they would occupy Mount Pleasant to cover the ships as they went through the channel. Although they appeared to be in agreement on the issue of landing troops at Mount Pleasant, ultimately it was on this issue that Clinton and Arbuthnot eventually disagreed most.[26]

Hints of Arbuthnot's reluctance to force his way into the Cooper River surfaced just two days after the commanders' 9 April meeting. To begin with, the American fortification at Lampriers Point alarmed him. He asserted to Clinton that the work "will be of greatest danger" to the frigates he intended to send into the Cooper. On 13 April, he wrote Clinton, worried that he had observed "the distinguishing lights of an encampment" the previous two nights in the environs of Lampriers Point. To assuage the admiral's fears, Clinton responded, saying: "From observation here we have no reason to suppose the Enemy are busying themselves defensively at Hobcaw." He assured Arbuthnot that the detachment he was sending across the Cooper would secure any point "for the protection of the Shipping." Fully aware that Webster had not yet crossed the river, Clinton attempted to soothe his naval counterpart's misgivings in any way that he could. The following day, he certified to Arbuthnot that rebel posts on the opposite bank of the Cooper would not "prevent the fleets getting in to the Cooper."[27]

Clinton's reassurances meant little, however, when Arbuthnot learned that American field pieces posted at Mount Pleasant had fired on one of his officers who was sounding the Hog Island channel. Sir Andrew Hamond explained to Captain Elphinstone the difficulty of sounding this channel, the entrance of which was "within musquet shot of the shore." He noted that when British boats approached it the Americans brought cannon down to Haddrell's Point on Mount Pleasant to drive them off. Meanwhile, warships providing cover for sounding vessels had to do so "within gun shot" of Fort Moultrie. Still, Arbuthnot maintained that ships could approach near enough to Mount Pleasant to secure the landing of troops.[28]

Whether in response to Clinton's prodding or by his own volition, on 15 April Arbuthnot informed Clinton that "the Troops and Armed Vessels are now nearly ready to attempt the passage of the Cooper." The following day, he asserted to Clinton that "Every effort will be made to pass the Frigates and armed vessels into the Cooper," but he again expressed concern over the American fortification at Lampriers Point. Encouraged by the news, Sir Henry responded that he was "exceeding glad to find . . . that you are determined to attempt the passage." By 18 April, he was hopeful that Arbuthnot would do so "the first fair wind." Again wishing to ease his fears regarding the American work at Lampriers Point, Clinton suggested that if Webster succeeded at Cainhoy, the rebels would abandon Lampriers altogether.[29]

Clinton was purely speculating about Webster, since he did not know exactly where the lieutenant colonel was and had not heard from him since 16 April. Although reports of increased activity on the Wando and Cooper Rivers implied that Webster's force was safe, and Cornwallis maintained that it would take Lincoln's entire army to "injure" him, dearth of news from him increasingly concerned Clinton. On 18 April, he wrote Webster "not having heard from you since you passed the Cooper . . . I am a little anxious." The same day, he ordered Lieutenant Colonel Nisbet Balfour to march with the 23rd regiment to Biggin's Bridge to attempt to make contact with him. Although reinforcements from New York arrived off Charleston on 18 April, the loss of Webster's corps would represent a severe blow to the British effort against the city. The possibility that the rebels had surprised and defeated the detachment somewhere east of the Cooper was surely in the back of Sir Henry's mind.[30]

Meanwhile, Clinton fretted about the navy's passage into the Cooper. On 20 April, Arbuthnot sent Sir Andrew Hamond ashore to discuss "my idea of our naval co-operation with your Excellency in future." When they met, Clinton informed Hamond that he did not anticipate serious operation for British ships once they entered the Cooper and that he only wanted to establish communication with his troops east of the river. His having been out of touch with Webster since 16 April obviously reinforced this desire. Clinton pledged that if necessary he would order Webster to Mount Pleasant to cover the navy's entrance into the Cooper or to Lampriers Point to cooperate with Arbuthnot's marines in an assault on the American position there. He pointed out, however, that he could provide no support "on the other Side of the water" until he heard from Webster. Meanwhile, Hamond reiterated Arbuthnot's intention to pass into the Cooper River the following day or the day after; but just as Commodore Whipple had repeatedly disappointed Lincoln, so Arbuthnot frustrated Clinton. The root of this frustration lay in the misunderstanding over operations at Mount Pleasant.[31]

On the morning of 22 April, Arbuthnot notified Clinton that "if the Rebels took post with heavy cannon at Mount Pleasant, they would greatly annoy" his ships lying under Fort Johnson. Consequently, he desired Clinton to detach troops to Mount Pleasant. This information dumbfounded Clinton. Increasingly upset by Arbuthnot's reluctance to pass into the Cooper, he responded that he had not previously "heard any Apprehensions of Annoyance . . . from Mount Pleasant in your present station." He argued that the distance between Mount Pleasant and Fort Johnson was too great for cannons positioned at the former "to be an Annoyance to the Fleet." Without Webster's assistance, Clinton insisted that it would take at least 1,000 men to seize Mount Pleasant. Sir Henry's assertions failed to persuade the admiral and American actions further congealed his stance.[32]

In the course of the day on 22 April, Captain Charles Hudson onboard *Richmond* noted that the Americans were "Constructing Works" on Mount Pleasant within cannon shot of the stations of *Raleigh* and *Blonde*. The new battery at Haddrell's Point was situated so as to command the entrance to the Hog Island channel.[33] Hudson forwarded this information to Arbuthnot, who immediately recognized the danger that the guns of the work would pose to his ships when they attempted to wind their way through the narrow passage. Arbuthnot hastily represented to Clinton that this battery "renders it impracticable to enter the Cooper, unless you will land a Force under cover of our Guns to protect us in the execution of this measure." The admiral also reported to the already anxiety-ridden Clinton that "the whole Rebel naval Force are prepared to move . . . with a view to transport their Garrison up the Cooper." He speculated that the rebels might even attempt an evacuation that very evening. As irascible as Clinton could be, one can certainly understand his frustration with the naval chief. So concerned was Arbuthnot with the safety of his own vessels that he overlooked the possibility that the entire American army was about to escape. All the two commanders had worked toward for over two months might soon dissolve before their eyes while Arbuthnot droned on about landing troops at Mount Pleasant. That the American army might still exist to fight another day against the British army on some inland battlefield mattered little to him. His ships would remain intact. Although reports of an American evacuation proved untrue, Arbuthnot's concern for his ships to the detriment of the greater objective mirrors strikingly the views of Commodore Whipple in the course of his failure to defend the Bar and entrance to Charleston harbor.[34]

The news of Arbuthnot's refusal to move into the Cooper obviously infuriated Clinton. Meanwhile, Clinton's letter arguing against a landing on Mount Pleasant surprised Arbuthnot. He responded that since their 9 April meeting he had impressed upon Clinton the need to send troops to the other side of the Cooper to allow him to pass ships into it. He asserted that "should the Rebels have Batteries on that side, no ships could lay in Cooper River with any security," and warranted that "every letter I have written since that time intimates the same idea." In concluding, Arbuthnot confirmed what Sir Henry already knew: that the American work at Mount Pleasant "prevents me from sending the armed Vessels I intended through the Hog Island Channel."[35]

The admiral had presented Sir Henry with a choice: either detach troops to Mount Pleasant or complete the encirclement of the city and its garrison on his own. With the prospect of an escape by the American army before him, coupled with the increasing probability that Arbuthnot would not enter the Cooper River, Clinton pursued other measures to complete the investiture of Charleston. On 18 April, reinforcements from New York, consisting of the 42nd regiment, the Queen's Rangers, Prince of Wales regiment, Volunteers of Ireland, and Hessian Regiment von Dittfurth, sailed into the Stono River. The arrival of these troops, numbering 2,566 men, afforded Sir Henry the opportunity to strengthen the corps east of the Cooper while maintaining the size of his force besieging the city. Clinton confidently asserted:

"Let me only pass two Regiments to Webster and I defy Lincoln's ingenuity to escape." He eventually sent twice that number, ordering the Volunteers of Ireland, New York Volunteers, and South Carolina Royalists to join the 23rd regiment in a move to the east side of the Cooper. Clinton's anxiety concerning Webster finally abated on 23 April, with word that he and his troops were safely encamped at Cainhoy.[36]

Clinton also appointed a new commander east of the Cooper, Lord Cornwallis. Although the relationship between the two officers remained strained, Cornwallis as second in command was the natural choice to lead such a sizeable detachment, which now numbered approximately 2,300 men. Other considerations may have also influenced Sir Henry's choice. After Cornwallis informed Clinton that he did not wish to be consulted so liberally on operations, John André suggested to Clinton that the earl could eventually "be detached to a greater distance." Clinton later related to a friend that whenever Cornwallis was around him "there are symptoms I do not like." In sending Cornwallis across the Cooper, Sir Henry may simply have been attempting to get "His Lordship" out of his hair. Given his ill-feeling toward his subordinate, sending him across the Cooper made sense merely for Clinton's own peace of mind.[37]

While Clinton now relied on Cornwallis and the detachment east of the Cooper to cut off the escape route from Charleston, he did not relinquish altogether the hope that Arbuthnot's ships would pass into the Cooper. He instructed Cornwallis to move toward the American positions at Lampriers Point and Mount Pleasant, reminding him that the admiral most likely would not stir until they captured those posts. Believing Lampriers Point strongly defended, he warned Cornwallis not to attempt an attack there "at any Considerable risk." As to Mount Pleasant, he suggested that Webster dispatch troops in that direction to determine the feasibility of taking it. Meanwhile, Clinton continued to cajole Arbuthnot, writing him on 23 April: "I should rejoice on every account to see a Naval force in the Cooper." Try as he might, Clinton was unable to free himself from the mutually dependent relationship with his naval chief.[38]

Clinton's obsession with the Royal Navy's entrance into the Cooper demonstrates how uneasy he was about a potential escape by Lincoln and the garrison. His fear was entirely justified. He had ever maintained that his true objective was Lincoln's army and not the city itself. Clinton believed that the fall of Charleston would bring about the defeat of both Carolinas, but the capture of the city would mean little if Lincoln slipped into the countryside and there provided a rallying point for the populations of the two states. Such a turn of events was a real possibility. Christ Church Parish between the Wando and the sea islands still remained open to the Americans. Although Clinton had tightened his grip on the city, Lincoln still had a chance to save his army. But like Clinton, Lincoln was also subject to forces beyond his control. Time would tell whether he could overcome them.

The View of Charles Town. *This 1774 painting by Thomas Leitch shows Charleston as it appeared on the eve of the American Revolution. The tall spire in the center is St. Michael's Church. Collection of the Museum of Early Southern Decorative Arts, Winston-Salem, North Carolina*

Benjamin Lincoln, by Charles Willson Peale. Independence National Historical Park, Philadelphia, Pennsylvania

General William Moultrie, by Rembrandt Peale. Courtesy of Gibbes Museum of Art/CAA, Charleston, South Carolina

Sir Henry Clinton, by Thomas Day. Courtesy of the R. W. Norton Art Gallery, Shreveport, Louisiana

Admiral Marriot Arbuthnot, by John Rising. Private Collection

Commodore Abraham Whipple, by Edward Savage. Courtesy of the U.S. Naval Academy Museum, Annapolis, Maryland

Lachlan McIntosh, by Charles Willson Peale. Independence National Historical Park, Philadelphia, Pennsylvania

John Laurens, by Charles Willson Peale. Courtesy of Gibbes Museum of Art/CAA, Charleston, South Carolina

Charles Cornwallis, 1st Marquess Cornwallis, by Thomas Gainsborough. By courtesy of the National Portrait Gallery, London

Colonel Banastre Tarleton, by Sir Joshua Reynolds. National Gallery, London

Jaeger Corps. This 1786 painting of Hessian jaegers shows the type of uniform that the unit wore and the weapons they used. The Hessian jaegers were critical to the British army's success at Charleston. Anne S. K. Brown Military Collection, Brown University Library, Providence, Rhode Island

Siege of Charleston. Other than the dress of the Highland soldier in the foreground, this nineteenth century engraving from an Alonzo Chappel painting gives a reasonably accurate representation of the siege of Charleston. Anne S. K. Brown Military Collection, Brown University Library, Providence, Rhode Island

Chapter Eleven

The Noose Tightens on Charleston Neck

In the days after their newly constructed batteries opened upon Charleston, British engineers edged their siege apparatus ever closer to the city. Lincoln and his officers, meanwhile, made what efforts they could to thwart the enemy advance. But with the British taking steps to cut off the garrison east of the Cooper, Lincoln recognized that they might soon completely invest Charleston. The American commander was faced with a series of difficult decisions that would affect not only the fate of his army and the inhabitants of the capital, but the whole of South Carolina. Lincoln was not the only one facing adversity. As the siege continued, the junior officers and enlisted men of the two armies confronted the dangers and drudgeries of siege warfare. They bore the burden of their commanders' designs.

Before they even completed their batteries in the first parallel, British engineers, under Major Moncrief's direction, pushed an approach trench toward Charleston. After a thorough examination of the ground and marshes before the city and of the American defenses, Moncrief determined that they should burrow forward from the left of the first parallel toward the American right. On the night of 9 April, British working parties constructed a battery 150 yards in front of Number Five, connected with the first parallel by a trench. On the night of 13 April, they then advanced an approach, or sap, from the front of the new battery to within 750 feet of the canal. At this point, they "commenced a Second Parallel at the Head of the Sap."[1] To begin the parallel, the men dug trenches perpendicular to the end of the sap.[2]

Interestingly, British working parties dug the approach in a relatively straight line from the first parallel to the second parallel rather than using the zigzag method recommended by Vauban. The running of a direct approach, which exposed men to enemy fire down the length of the trench, was representative of Moncrief's contempt for the rebels' military prowess. When Captain Ewald asked him why he had not constructed a communication trench from the supply depot in the British rear to the first parallel to protect men as they came forward, Moncrief responded that "the rebels do not deserve this." While Moncrief was contemptuous of their fighting ability, British soldiers who labored in and manned the trenches soon found that there was little reason for such lack of respect for their enemy's martial skills.[3]

Noting the threat to their right wing, the Americans took steps to impede the British on that flank. On 15 April, Lieutenant Colonel John Grimké directed artillerymen to move mortars on the left of the American line to the right so that they could harass the British in the approach trench. Grimké was to ensure that the mortars and a howitzer already in place on the right fired throughout the night on the British working parties. Meanwhile, General Moultrie ordered the advanced battery on the American left to fire solid shot *en recochet* on "the Enemy's new Works," meaning that shot would go bounding down the British trench tearing asunder anything in its path. In addition, Moultrie requested that a twelve pounder and three four pounders in the redoubt on the Cooper River pepper the ground between the canal and the second parallel. The Americans also "advanced a Breast Work" in front of this redoubt "for Riflemen, to annoy the Enemy in their Approach."[4]

American countermeasures profoundly hindered British progress. Captain Peebles noted on 15 April that American firing forced the working parties to "retire for a while," and Captain Ewald recorded that American enfilading shots sent cannonballs careening down the entire length of the communication trench. Captain Hinrichs counted nineteen eighteen pound balls from the American left redoubt and thirteen shells from the American right redoubt that fell into the second parallel. According to Hinrichs, "They threw their shells in a masterly manner" and all the men in his section of the trench were "covered with earth." The American barrage was so intense on the night of 14 April that he believed the rebels were attacking the second parallel. British

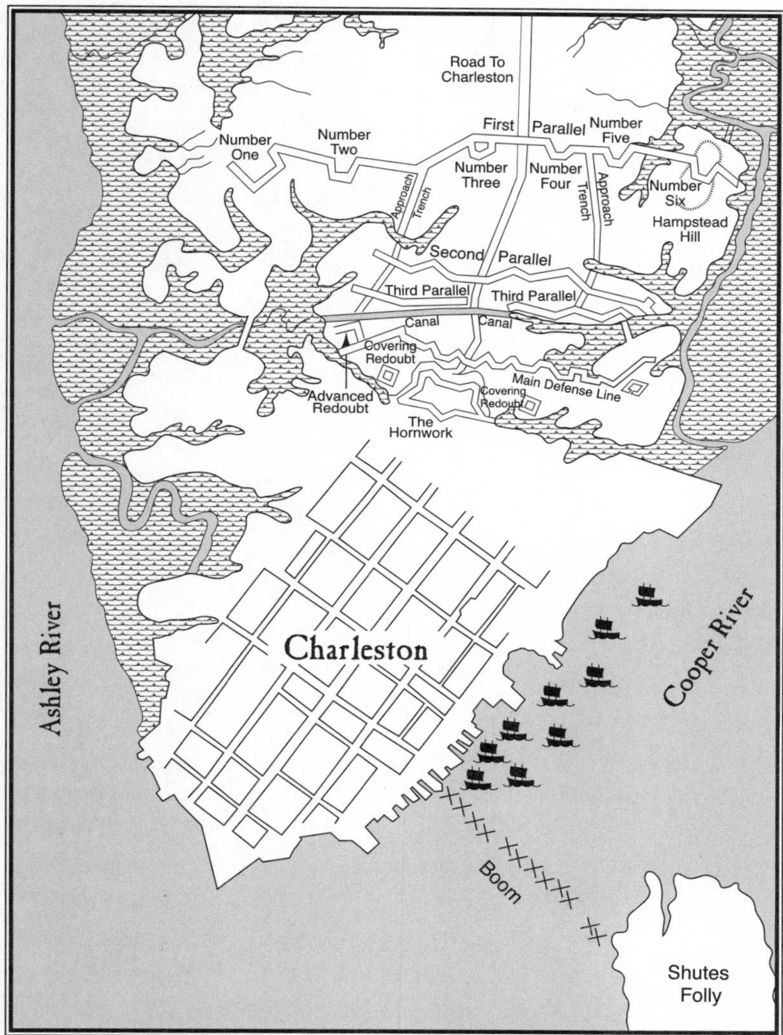

British Parallels and Approaches

and Hessian soldiers, meanwhile, found it difficult to defend against American fire as their approaches moved closer to Charleston. Major Traille of the artillery complained that the work on the American right "flanked" their advance and his men could not bring their guns to bear against it.[5]

On 16 April, Moncrief informed Clinton that continuing the approach on the Cooper River side "exposed [them] to a great fire from the Enemy's left," and in response he instructed the men to halt their digging in that area. Clinton concurred with Moncrief's assessment that they start a new approach trench on the right of the British first parallel between Numbers Two and Three. That night working parties constructed another direct sap from the first parallel toward the American left. They excavated it quickly, covering 300 yards before dawn. At the head of the sap, the laborers began a new section of the second parallel, and the following night they connected the two separate sections.[6] While there were no completed batteries in the new parallel, the British had successfully completed two of their siege parallels and would soon press ahead toward a third.[7]

Since 13 April, British troops on the neck had been able to respond to the harassing American artillery fire, and the forward progress of their approach trenches allowed them to move cannon closer to the Charleston lines. A howitzer battery and a mortar battery in their left approach soon played upon the garrison. On 14 April, General McIntosh asserted that the British kept up "an Incessant fire from their small Arms, Cannon, and Morters," while the following day Samuel Baldwin noted that "a number of bombs and some carcasses have been thrown into town." A newly established British battery at Stiles Point on James Island also cannonaded them. As with the battery at Fenwick's Point, the James Island battery was more effective against the city than against the American lines, spreading terror among the civilians. Soldiers on the lines had the benefit of fortifications designed to protect them from cannon fire—not so for civilians. Many inhabitants sought shelter in cellars and other low-lying places, but for others, life went on as usual. Lieutenant Colonel Grimké noted that during one bombardment "an Inhabitant of the Town [was] killed & a Woman wounded in Bed together."[8]

On 16 April, a cannon ball fired from the James Island battery shot off the right arm of the statue of William Pitt, which rested at the intersection of Broad and Meeting streets. The South Carolina Assembly erected the statue prior to the Revolution in commemoration of Pitt's defense of American rights during the Stamp Act crisis. The

British-inflicted damage to the statue, occurring in the midst of a siege of one of colonial America's great cities, epitomized how drastically events had turned since the colonists' first displeasure at taxation from the mother country.[9]

As the British works edged closer to the American lines, small arms took on an increasingly prominent role both for besieger and besieged. Typically, a British "Brown Bess" or French Charleville musket of the period had a range of approximately 300 yards, but could be fired accurately only up to about 80 yards. Rifles, on the other hand, were accurate up to 300 yards and had a range of almost 500 yards. In spite of its longer range, the rifle did not supplant the musket as the primary infantry weapon of eighteenth-century warfare because it could not mount a bayonet and was much slower to load and fire than the musket. In an era when a well-disciplined bayonet charge often carried the day on the battlefield, soldiers armed with rifles were at a serious disadvantage. In siege warfare, however, where soldiers protected by works had time to load their weapons, the rifle became a more effective weapon than the musket.

The Hessian jaegers had been in the vanguard of Clinton's army since the landing in February, and they now took on an even more crucial role in the siege of the city. Parties of jaegers occupied the advance works each day "to gall" American riflemen and artillerymen "with their short rifles." Meanwhile, in addition to countering the British approaches with cannon, the Americans employed rifles of their own against enemy personnel in the trenches. Riflemen posted in the breastwork that the Americans constructed on their right harassed British working parties and dueled with the jaegers. These riflemen must have contributed to Moncrief's decision to direct his new sap against the American left. On 15 April, Captain Robertson of the British artillery noted that "Musketry continues pretty briskly" on the Cooper River side of the second parallel. Casualties mounted with the addition of rifles into the mix. Small arms fire wounded two British soldiers on 15 April, and a British light infantryman who apparently peered over the wall of the trench was killed by an American rifleman on 16 April, shot through the eye. Meanwhile, rifle fire from the jaegers claimed the lives of five men of the Charleston garrison on 18 April.[10]

Besides rifles, the two armies also made use of other what would be referred to today as antipersonnel weapons. British and Hessian troops fired coehorns, or small hand mortars, at the American works. "Showers of small" shells from these weapons, General McIntosh related, "prove very mischievous, especially on our right where one Man was killed & two wounded" among the North Carolina brigade. When British saps came within 400 yards of the American line, Lincoln ordered some of the batteries to employ grapeshot against the enemy. On 17 April, Captain Ewald recorded that the Americans "fired continuously with grapeshot and musketry." On 20 April, grapeshot fired from American batteries killed two men and wounded four others in the British trenches. For both sides, the trenches were becoming increasingly precarious places to be.[11]

Despite the casualties, British working parties pressed on. After strengthening and widening the second parallel, they constructed batteries along its length and prepared to move heavy guns into them. Before Moncrief halted work on the approach on the American right, engineers had extended it beyond the second parallel toward a third. The British now pushed this sap forward once again. Amid harassing fire from the Americans, Clinton's army on the neck moved inexorably toward its objective.[12]

From the Charleston lines, Lincoln could plainly see the progress that the British were making before the town, and he was becoming increasingly pessimistic that they could hold out against them. American commissaries and quartermasters still brought stores into the city, albeit more slowly and precariously with British troops east of the Cooper, but as for reinforcements, no appreciable bodies of men were on the march to Charleston. Woodford's Virginia brigade gave a welcome boost to his army, but Lincoln was disappointed that Scott's brigade had not been in a condition to come to their assistance. The low turnout of the South Carolina militia also frustrated him. Meanwhile, Lincoln asked the state of North Carolina for 2,000 militia and 500 volunteers to replace the North Carolinians who had departed the city in March, but in April word reached Charleston that only 300 North Carolinians were coming to join them. By mid-April, Lincoln had only 4,200 men present and fit for duty in Charleston, at Fort

Moultrie, and at Lampriers Point.[13] Arrayed against him, Clinton, with the reinforcement which arrived on 18 April, could count approximately 8,300 men under his command.[14]

Lincoln also encountered problems with the city's defenses. Unaware of Arbuthnot's lethargy with regard to sending ships into the Cooper River, Lincoln anticipated that the Royal Navy would soon attempt to force their way past the line of obstructions between the Exchange and Shutes Folly. On 18 April, he asked Commodore Whipple to summon his officers to provide an opinion as to whether "the obstructions now thrown across the river . . . [are] sufficient to prevent the enemys ships from passing up the Cooper." Whipple and his captains, who seemed reluctant to take responsibility for anything, responded that "whether the obstructions . . . will answer the desired purpose, is out of our favor to determine, untill the ships come up against it." In other words, they would not know until British ships actually tested it. Charleston harbor's tricky currents, which bedeviled both American and British mariners alike, had already destroyed part of the barrier, thus increasing the likelihood that the British would succeed. Meanwhile, Lincoln's engineers were apprehensive about the ability of the land fortifications to hold out much longer. They informed Lincoln that "there was no reason to conclude the enemy could be prevented entering our Works by approach in seven days at farthest." Moreover, American commissaries determined that by 20 April they had provisions on hand for only eight to ten days.[15]

In the context of these forbidding circumstances, Lincoln summoned a council of war to discuss the situation of the garrison. After their 13 April meeting, the officers tried on several occasions to meet, but as General McIntosh noted, the gatherings were "as often interrupted so much, that we could come to no determination, or do any business." They finally gained an adequate opportunity on the morning of 20 April. The council consisted of Lincoln, Brigadier Generals Moultrie, McIntosh, Woodford, Scott, and Hogun, and Colonels Laumoy, Barnard Beekman, and Maurice Simons. After rendering an account of "the strength of the Garrison, the state of the provisions, the situation of the enemy, the information he had received relative to reinforcements, and the state of the Obstructions" in the Cooper, Lincoln "requested the opinion of the Council what measures the interest and safety of the Country called us to pursue under our present circumstances." Given the dire state of affairs, the officers really had only two choices: attempt an evacuation or propose a capitulation to the British under terms favorable to the garrison. Neither option guaranteed the safety of Charleston itself.[16]

Although the British had pushed a substantial force over the Cooper River, escape in that direction remained a viable alternative. The defensive work at Lampriers Point kept open to the Americans the road through Christ Church Parish. If they settled on an evacuation, the troops could cross the Cooper in boats under cover of darkness, land under the guns of Lampriers Point, and march to the Santee through Christ Church. Once beyond the Santee, the army would be free to elude the British forces in the South Carolina countryside and would serve as a rallying point for the state's militia. Lincoln possessed sufficient watercraft to make the attempt. In addition to the remaining warships, he had ordered General Huger in early April "to appoint parties to collect and bring to town all the boats you can find on Cooper river."[17]

General McIntosh recorded that at the 20 April council of war "some Gentlemen seem'd still inclined to an evacuation notwithstanding the difficulty appeared much greater now than when formerly Mentioned." During the 13 April meeting Lincoln had put forth the idea of evacuation, but the presence of Webster's force east of the Cooper accounted for "the difficulty" being "much greater now." Still, McIntosh strongly favored this course of action, and he suggested that the militia could act as "Guards" while the Continental troops vacated the city. Although other officers supported McIntosh's recommendation, Colonel Laumoy's arguments soon prevailed. Laumoy, an engineer who had no confidence in the strength of the Charleston fortifications, advocated offering honorable terms of capitulation to the British. He apparently assumed that Clinton would grant favorable terms in light of the garrison's gallant stand to date.[18]

In the midst of the discussion, Lieutenant Governor Gadsden, now the chief civilian official in the city in the wake of Rutledge's departure, came into the meeting and Lincoln invited him to "Sit as one of the Council." McIntosh related that after Gadsden listened to the discourse "he appeared surprised & displeased that we had entertained a thought of a Capitulation or evacuating the Garrison." The lieutenant governor insisted on consulting the remaining members of the Privy Council on the matter. He assured the officers that he would assist them with the articles of capitulation respecting the citizens of Charleston if they still deemed capitulation necessary. The meeting then adjourned till the evening.[19]

When they reconvened at Lincoln's quarters that evening, Colonel Laumoy again represented as reasons for offering terms of capitulation the insufficiency of their fortifications, the improbability of the army's holding out much longer, and the impracticability of making a successful retreat. Shortly thereafter, Gadsden, accompanied this time by four members of the Privy Council, Thomas Ferguson, Richard Hutson, Benjamin Cattell, and David Ramsay, strongly denounced the proceedings of the council of war and, as General McIntosh maintained, treated the officers "very Rudely." Gadsden declared emphatically that "the Militia were willing to Live upon Rice alone rather than give up the Town upon any Terms." He then commented acidly that "even the old Women were so accustomed to the Enemys Shot now that they traveled the Streets without fear or dread." Despite his harsh words, the lieutenant governor again consented to a capitulation if Lincoln and the officers were determined to pursue such a course. But if any of the officers were still considering evacuation, the remarks of Thomas Ferguson gave them cause to rethink their position. According to McIntosh, Ferguson pointed out that for several days the citizens of Charleston had observed with great interest that boats were being collected ostensibly for the purpose of carrying off the Continental troops. Ferguson then asserted that they "would keep a good Watch upon us," and if the Continentals attempted to withdraw from the town "he would be among the first who would open the Gates for the Enemy and assist them in attacking us before we got aboard." For Ferguson, it was defend Charleston to the last extremity or nothing. Unity of interest among the defenders was fizzling as quickly as the fuses of the mortar shells which now fell upon the city.[20]

Lincoln's letter to the Continental Congress on the subject lends support to McIntosh's assertions as they relate to the words and actions of Gadsden and the Privy Council. In explaining to Congress why he and his officers ruled out an evacuation, Lincoln recounted that "the Civil Authority were utterly averse to it, and intimated in Council if it was attempted they would counteract the measure." Lincoln was somewhat more subtle than McIntosh in his representation of the affair, but it is apparent that Gadsden and Ferguson had bullied them.[21] David Ramsay later acknowledged to Lincoln that the members of the Privy Council had not wished to "interfere" in the discussion of "military questions," but only wanted "to obtain the best terms for the citizens." In his history of the Revolution in South Carolina, however, Ramsay seemed to uphold his colleagues' posture when he asserted that "to withdraw the regular army clandestinely from the town, and leave the citizens to the mercy of an enraged enemy, without giving them the offer of joining in the intended retreat, would have been ungenerous." In threatening to prevent the escape of the army and in browbeating Lincoln to fight on, the members of the Privy Council were willing to sacrifice the security of the rest of the state, and possibly of the entire south, for the security of Charleston. Loyalty to the new union of states could only go so far.[22]

To add insult to injury, after Gadsden and the other civilian officials departed, Colonel Charles Cotesworth Pinckney abruptly came in. McIntosh related that upon entering the chamber Pinckney forgot his "usual Politeness" and "addressed Gen[era]l Lincoln in great warmth & [in] much the same Strain as the L[ieutenan]t Governor had done." He ranted that he came to prevent them from offering terms or attempting an evacuation and then accused Colonel Laumoy of indecorously fostering such proposals. As an officer of the Continental army, not only did Pinckney's conduct border on insubordination, but he had fallen into the same shortsighted trap of his fellow Charlestonians.[23]

McIntosh found himself "much hurt by the repeated Insults given to the Commanding Officer in so public a Manner, & obliquely to us all through him." To save face for his commander, McIntosh, one of the chief proponents of evacuation, now declared that such an attempt was impractical and that they should hold out "to the last extremity." All officers present concurred, with the exception of Colonel Laumoy, who insisted that they had "already come to the last extremity." After the officers adjourned for the evening, General McIntosh met privately with General Moultrie. McIntosh wanted to destroy a letter that he and Moultrie had signed just three days before. The two men had apparently drafted a memorandum on evacuating the town. Seeing little hope of successfully withdrawing the troops, Moultrie agreed that they should destroy it. Together, Generals Moultrie and McIntosh quite literally watched their proposals for the evacuation of the garrison go up in smoke.[24]

The following day, 21 April, General Lincoln again convened the council of war. Colonel Laumoy once more forcibly argued that they should offer honorable terms of capitulation to General Clinton. He suggested that if Clinton did not accept their terms the garrison might attempt a retreat. Having for all intents and purposes ruled out an evacuation the previous evening, the officers unanimously determined to treat with the British before "Affairs become more critical." For Moultrie and McIntosh, concurrence must have been difficult indeed, but they joined their comrades in signing the minutes of the council of war, which documented the decision to propose terms.[25]

Lincoln and Lieutenant Colonel John Ternant drew up proposed terms of capitulation to send to Clinton. The concessions that Lincoln sought from Clinton would, if granted, be very generous. First and foremost, he desired terms that "would admit of the Armys withdrawing, and afford security to the persons and property of the Inhabitants." Lincoln proposed that once the two sides agreed on and signed the articles of capitulation, "the town, forts and fortifications belonging to them, shall be surrendered to the commander in chief of the British forces." Subsequently, the British would allow all Continental troops, North and South Carolina militia, and American and French naval personnel thirty-six hours to withdraw from Charleston—the land forces to Lampriers Point and the naval forces to sea. The troops would keep their arms, field artillery, ammunition, and all stores that they were able to transport. After the American troops retired to Lampriers, Clinton was to give them ten days "to march wherever General Lincoln may think proper, to the eastward of Cooper's river, without any movement being made by the British troops" against them. With regard to shipping, the Royal Navy was to permit *Providence, Boston, Ranger,* and *L'Aventure* to "go unmolested" to sea. As for the citizens of

Charleston, they were to be "protected in their persons and property." The British were to grant those that remained twelve months "to dispose of their effects . . . without any molestation whatever" and allow them to remove themselves and their families from the town. Benjamin Lincoln knew that Sir Henry Clinton was no fool. He was offering an empty shell of a town and its fortifications in exchange for the entire military force extant in the southern half of the continent. But in asking for all that he possibly could, Lincoln hoped that the British general might accept some of the proposals.[26]

Lincoln sent a letter under a flag of truce to Clinton which informed him that he was "willing to enter into the Consideration of Terms of Capitulation if such can be obtained as are honorable for the Army and Safe for the Inhabitants." He suggested a cessation of hostilities for six hours "for the purpose of digesting such Articles." Lincoln addressed only Clinton in the letter, and Clinton awkwardly responded that he and Admiral Arbuthnot should have been addressed jointly. He consented to the six hour truce, but requested permission to send an officer to the ships in the harbor to notify Arbuthnot.[27]

When Arbuthnot came ashore that afternoon he argued that they should hold the rebels to the original terms they had offered them in the summons of 10 April. Lord Cornwallis agreed, while General Leslie gave no opinion. The officers waited to hear again from Lincoln.[28]

When an American officer delivered Lincoln's proposed articles of capitulation, Clinton found them such as "could not be listened to," and "so much beyond what we thought he had a right to expect that we immediately rejected them." Lincoln presented twelve separate articles, but it was the third article, which called for the garrison to safely remove themselves from the town, that prevented Clinton and Arbuthnot from heeding any of the others. Clinton could never assent to allowing the rebels to march out with arms and stores only to be able to fight another day. Captain Russell of his staff could scarcely believe "the Insolence" of the Americans in making such a bold request. The British commanders informed Lincoln that "we have in answer to your third article (for we cannot proceed further) to refer you to our former offer, as terms, which, although you cannot claim, yet we consent to grant." In pointing out that he had no right to "claim" the terms previously offered, Clinton and Arbuthnot essentially notified Lincoln that he was fortunate to be granted even that much. They declared that their terms "must be accepted immediately," and they expected an answer by ten that evening.[29]

Clinton and Arbuthnot had clearly rejected their proposals, but Lincoln and his officers were determined to fight on rather than submit to British terms. Although the enemy approaches progressed steadily toward them, they were still weeks away from being in position to carry the American works. Those weeks of continued resistance would afford reinforcements time to materialize. Moreover, Lincoln pointed out that even if the city fell, the delays that an extended siege imposed upon the British "would give the people in the neighboring States an Opportunity to rouse and embody." In holding out, the soldiers of the garrison bought time for their southern brethren.[30]

Lincoln sent an officer to Clinton and Arbuthnot to inform them that he "could not accept the terms offered" and that they "might begin firing again when they pleased." At 10:30 that night, the British again commenced firing on Charleston. Suspecting that the Americans might attempt an evacuation from the city, Clinton ordered the batteries to direct their fire toward the banks of the Cooper River to impede an escape. No such attempt was forthcoming, however. Major William Croghan asserted that the British cannonaded them during the night "with greater virulence & fury than ever" and "continued it without intermission till daylight." Throughout the night and into the next day, British batteries on the neck fired 489 rounds of solid shot and 340 shells at Charleston and its defenses. Croghan remarked that the Americans "returned [the] complement with equal ardor." He noted that "both the American & British lines seemed in a constant blaze[,] which, with the throwing & bursting of shells [and] the unremitting roar of heavy cannon . . . made an awful yet pleasing appearance."[31]

Morale remained strong among the enlisted men in spite of their circumstances. The Marquis de Bretigny, who commanded the city's French-speaking militiamen, vowed to John Lewis Gervais that talk of capitulation "had occasioned great discontent as well among the regulars as militia, who wish to defend the place to the last extremity." The

Marquis found the soldiers "in high Spirit, & so resolved as to offer to receive only half a ration a day if necessary." The state of the soldiers' morale was of great consequence since their duty would become even more dangerous and onerous as British siege lines pressed ever closer.[32]

While senior American officers probably viewed the decision to fight on as honorable and noble, continuation of hostilities meant that junior officers and enlisted men on both sides would keep on with their hard duty in the trenches. Their experience was not dissimilar to that of men who served in the trenches of the First World War. It was certainly a far cry from the typical battlefield experience of the eighteenth-century soldier. Most eighteenth-century battles were over in one day—surely true in the American Revolution—but siege warfare was more "modern" in that it lasted for several weeks. Already, British and American soldiers had withstood this "trench warfare" for over three weeks, and they had little reason to believe that the siege would end quickly. These soldiers faced an unenviable task.[33]

The almost constant artillery barrage and small arms fire between the two armies exposed soldiers, who were manning batteries, repairing damage to the lines, digging approach trenches, carrying up supplies, or simply serving as covering parties, to the threat of death or horrible disfigurement. Although crude and inaccurate by modern standards, weapons of the period could inflict horrific wounds. Solid shot fired from cannon simply sheared off arms, legs, and heads, while mortar and howitzer shells could blow a man to pieces. Captain Peebles noted that a soldier of the British light infantry "had his backside shot away" by a cannonball, while a servant of one of Peebles's fellow officers was "blown all to pieces with a shell." On the American side, General Moultrie's aide-de-camp, Philip Neyle, was killed by a cannonball, "which took away a part of his head." As the distance between the two armies lessened, rifle fire became increasingly potent. By 23 April, Captain Ewald observed that their approach trenches were so close that "one could easily throw a stone" into the American canal or advanced ditch. At this range, rifle fire took its toll on both sides. On 24 April, Colonel Richard Parker of the Virginia Continentals was killed by a rifle shot as he looked over the parapet, while American "Musquetry" took the lives of several British soldiers in the approach trenches. Even general officers were not immune to the danger. General Moultrie recounted that on one occasion, when he attempted to get into the American advanced battery, he looked up to "see the heads of twelve or fifteen men firing upon me" and "an uncommon number of bullets whistled about me." The officer commanding the advance battery exclaimed to Moultrie that it was "a thousand to one" that he was not killed. General Moultrie was obviously much luckier than many.[34]

On the lines, danger came not only from the enemy, but also from one's own weapons. Several artillerymen on both sides were killed or wounded during the siege when improperly sponged cannon went off during the loading process. In other instances, artillery pieces, which had been fired continuously, simply burst due to the intense heat of the weapon. On 18 April, a twelve pounder in the hornwork burst, severely wounding two American soldiers. The handling of ammunition was equally hazardous. The Americans lost Captain John Gilbank of the artillery on 12 April when one of their shells accidentally went off near him. Other soldiers had the misfortune to get in the way of their own fire. With men stationed in advanced works in front of the lines and with the inherently inaccurate nature of artillery pieces of the day, casualties from what today would be called friendly fire were bound to occur. Lieutenant Colonel Grimké recorded that on 18 April "a Sentinel at the abbatis near the advanced redoubt, had his arm shot off by one of our own Cannon."[35]

In addition to being physically dangerous, conditions in the trenches were extremely unpleasant for the men. Anyone who has lived in or visited the South Carolina lowcountry in the springtime knows that the region can have the most delightful weather of any place on earth at that time of year. It can also be hot, as well as stormy. On warm days, soldiers toiled away with pick and shovel with little shade from the hot sun. When it rained, the trenches filled with water and men had little cover from heavy downpours. When dry, dusty sand blew in the mouths and eyes of soldiers while thousands of insects swarmed about them. Captain Ewald summed it up best when he wrote that it "really was the unanimous wish of the besieger" that their "disagreeable task might come to an end." Ewald asserted that "the dangers and difficult work were the least of the annoyance: the intolerable heat, the lack of good water, and the billions of sandflies and mosquitoes made up the worst nuisance."[36] He noted that since the British approaches were constructed in "white, sandy soil," one could hardly open his eyes when the wind blew and "could not put a bite of bread into his mouth which was not covered with sand." The soldiers of both armies would have experienced such adverse conditions in the trenches, and their duty was by no means easy. An examination of their plight makes it easy to understand why many soldiers deserted, but it also gives one a greater appreciation for the courage and dedication of those who remained. Under these circumstances, the siege continued.[37]

On the night of 15 April, British working parties began to sap toward a third parallel, extending the left approach trench approximately 20 yards from the front of the second parallel. Clinton lamented that they were unable to proceed with "the rapidity we usually do" because of the increasing proximity to the Charleston lines. Still, on the night of 19 April his men "lengthened the direct Sap on the left for about 100 y[ar]ds," and two nights later they commenced construction of a third parallel "at the Head of the Sap." Another working party dug a 100 yard section of the new parallel on the right, connecting it to the second parallel with a direct sap. Over the next several nights, the British refined the two separate sections of the third parallel, but unlike the second, they did not join them.[38] Working parties extended the left section toward the dam on the American right, which controlled the depth of water in the canal, to give them the opportunity to drain off the water in the canal. The completed sections of the third parallel were less than 800 feet from the main American defense line.[39]

Incessant American artillery fire, and later small arms fire, slowed British progress before Charleston but did not stop it. In just over three weeks of digging, British working parties managed to construct three parallels, advancing over 2,000 feet in the process. Typically in eighteenth-century siege warfare, the besieged, in addition to bombarding the besieging army with cannon, would also sally forth from the works to attack the enemy in the trenches with fixed bayonets. In these sorties, which usually occurred under cover of darkness, the besieged sought to interrupt the progress of the besieging army's works, buy time for the garrison, or even drive off the besieger. Sallying soldiers might also "spike" the cannon of the besieging army by driving an iron spike, which was very difficult to extract, into the touch holes of the cannon to prevent them from being fired again. The prospect of sorties also had a psychological effect on the besieger in that men assigned to night duty had to be constantly aware that at any moment an enemy soldier could come charging out of the darkness with a bayonet fixed to his musket ready to stab him to death, a nightmarish thought.[40]

The Americans planned to assault the British battery on Hampstead Hill early in the siege, but the shortage of troops prevented Lincoln from ordering further attempts. The failure of Lincoln to send out sorties perplexed the British, who had firmly expected them. Clinton anticipated sorties against the Hampstead battery and against the working parties as they sapped toward the second parallel. Meanwhile, Major Peter Traille of the Royal Artillery furnished "all the heavy guns on the different Battery's" in the first parallel with case shot to defend against an enemy attack. Covering parties continued to accompany the working parties to the trenches each night. Still, the enemy had yet to sally forth. The inactivity may have lulled the British into a false sense of security.[41]

On the night of 23 April, General Moultrie instructed the officers in batteries along the lines to "keep up a fire on the Enemy's Works as usual this night." At 3:30 in the morning, however, they were to cease firing and reload their weapons with grapeshot. Meanwhile, 200 handpicked South Carolina and Virginia Continentals under the command of Lieutenant Colonel William Henderson assembled in the advanced work on the left of the American line in preparation for an assault on the British third parallel. Henderson ordered the men to fix bayonets; they were not to fire their muskets, but were to rely only on their bayonets. Moultrie's artillerymen would employ grapeshot against the British if they threatened Henderson's men on their way back to the American lines.[42]

Shortly before daybreak on 24 April, Henderson and his men crossed a temporary bridge over the canal and charged into the section of the third parallel on the British right. The British working party had just finished the night's work and were preparing to return to the rear when Henderson's men flung themselves into the trench. The attackers caught the British and Hessian troops completely by surprise, sending them into a panic. According to Captain Ewald, the British light infantry immediately fled to the second parallel, leaving the jaegers to fend for themselves against the onrushing Americans. Some of the Continentals pursued the fleeing British back toward the second parallel while the rest thrust bayonets at those men who had not escaped from the trench. Men screamed in terror and agony as steel plunged into flesh. Posted in the left section of the third parallel, Captain Hinrichs "heard a loud yelling" coming from the other section and realized that many of the Americans had already penetrated fifty paces behind them. As men in the second parallel realized what was happening they opened fire, which prompted Lieutenant Colonel Henderson to order a withdrawal to the safety of their lines. Upon their return, American batteries opened with the grapeshot to deter the British from following.[43]

As the Americans fell back, Captain Thomas Moultrie, brother of General Moultrie, was killed and two privates were wounded. Still, the sortie was a success. According to General McIntosh, the attack "was done in a few Minutes without our partys firing a Single Gun, & in the greatest order." Captain Hinrichs noted that the Americans killed and wounded at least eight British light infantrymen and Hessian jaegers, while capturing a number of others. Henderson returned to the lines with twelve prisoners, seven of whom were wounded. Moreover, General Leslie reported to Clinton that the sortie had interrupted work in that section of the parallel. The real fruits of the sally would appear the following night.[44]

Of the sortie, Captain Russell suggested that British troops posted in the third parallel "were asleep or not so attentive as they ought," while Lieutenant Christian Friedrich Bartholomai of the jaegers maintained that "the English . . . had not been especially alert, they were not aware of the rebels until they sprang over the breastwork." General Leslie could not disagree with the assessments of these officers, submitting sheepishly to Clinton that "we were a little off our guard."[45]

The following night, officers and soldiers on duty in the third parallel anxiously expected another sortie from the garrison. As the men worked, they must have restively inspected the night air for signs of any stir from the garrison. With the third parallel less than 1,000 feet from the American line, the two sides could easily hear the sounds that the other was making. American pickets posted in front of the Charleston defenses were even closer to the British. Around 1:00 in the morning, American soldiers assigned to one of these pickets grew nervous at noises coming from across the canal. Believing "the enemy were advancing in force," they fired their muskets into the night. In the main defense line, men interpreted the firing as the alarm announcing a British attack. At once, muskets, rifles, and cannons erupted along the entire American line. Captain Russell asserted that "a most tremendous Fire of Cannon[,] Shells and Musquetry commenced from . . . the Rebel Works." British and Hessian soldiers in the third parallel panicked, presuming another American sortie was underway. They quickly abandoned their posts and ran back toward the second parallel. Having witnessed the sudden burst of fire coming from the American lines and now observing men charging toward them, the troops in the first and second parallels assumed that the rebels were attacking them. They immediately opened fire with cannon and small arms on the forms pressing upon them in the darkness. Some time passed before British officers realized that it was not the rebels coming at them but their own troops retreating from the third parallel. Before the chaos subsided, the firing from the first and second parallel killed and wounded a number of British and Hessian soldiers.[46]

Oddly enough, belief on both sides that an attack was taking place had produced the mass confusion. The nervous excitement that manifested itself among men posted in the American and British works increased exponentially as darkness enveloped the armies. To an anxious soldier scanning the night for sights and sounds, shadows became enemy troops advancing in the darkness, the clank of a shovel or pick became a bayonet being fixed, voices in the distance became orders to attack. The false alarm cost the British dearly. Captain Russell noted that one officer was killed and another wounded, while among the rank and file three were killed and fifteen wounded. Other officers suggested even higher casualties. Captain Peebles represented that they suffered between twenty and thirty killed and wounded, while Ensign Hartung of the Hessians put the number at over thirty. Whatever the final number, the British sustained at least twenty casualties on the night of 25 April, most from their own fire. In two nights, they lost over forty men killed, wounded, or captured. To put the British casualties in perspective, on 27 April General Moultrie asserted that the Americans had lost only ten killed and forty wounded since the onset of the siege.[47]

The false alarm greatly annoyed Clinton. He steadfastly believed that men defending the parallels should rely on their bayonets alone for defense and that they should not even load their muskets. The incident had also unnerved Lincoln. Although deserters informed the Americans of the British casualties several days later, Lincoln was concerned that the enemy would soon make an assault on their works. To prevent a surprise night attack, he ordered men to place barrels filled with turpentine in front of the lines each night and set them ablaze to illuminate the area before the American lines. On the night of 27 April, the deputy quartermaster general delivered seventeen such barrels for this purpose. The light emitted by these incendiaries enabled American sentries to detect the approach of enemy troops, but with this measure Lincoln essentially conceded to the British that there would be no more sorties. The same burning turpentine barrels that would expose a British attack would also illuminate an American sally.[48]

Despite the disruptions of the sortie and subsequent false alarm, British working parties continued to sap toward the dam of the canal on the American right. The laborers were subject to "a deep flank fire" as they dug toward the dam, but once in possession of it, engineers could drain the canal. An assault on the American works would then be a much easier endeavor. "The Siege is so forward that things cannot hold any longer without Extremity," Clinton wrote Webster on 23 April. By extremity, Clinton referred to an assault on the American fortifications.[49]

The situation was indeed grim for Lincoln and the garrison of Charleston. They would soon discover just how grim. In late March, the Continental Congress ordered Brigadier General Louis Lebeque Duportail, chief engineer of the Continental army, "to repair, with all possible dispatch, to the southern army, and put himself under General Lincoln." Duportail rushed on to Charleston, arriving in less than a month's time on 25 April. Colonels Laumoy and Cambray had already given Lincoln a rather dour assessment of the defenses, but Duportail's words must have further dampened his hopes. Upon viewing the works, Duportail immediately asserted that they were untenable. Arguing that "the fall of the Town was unavoidable unless an Army [came] to her assistance," the French officer strongly recommended evacuation. Having missed the councils of war of a few days earlier, he was not aware of the "impracticability" of such a measure. Based on Duportail's assessment and possibly for his benefit, Lincoln assembled another council of war to reconsider it.[50]

The council of war convened at Lincoln's quarters on 26 April and consisted of Lincoln, Brigadier Generals Moultrie, McIntosh, Woodford, Scott, Duportail, Hogan, Colonels Simons and Beekman, and Commodore Whipple. Lincoln once more asked the officers "whether in their Opinion the evacuation of this garrison was an expedient and practicable measure." Unanimously, they deemed it "impracticable" to retreat from the town because of the strong British presence across the Cooper and because the move was "in opposition to the Opinion and Wishes of the Civil Authority." According to Moultrie, unnamed civilian officials had again expressed their disapproval at a withdrawal by the army. While Lincoln described it as "opposition" by the "Civil Authority," Moultrie later maintained that some citizens threatened to "cut up" their boats and "open the gates to the enemy." With a hostile enemy without and a potentially hostile populace within, evacuation of the army from the city would indeed be difficult.[51]

Recognizing that an evacuation was unlikely, and having little confidence in Charleston's ability to hold out, Brigadier General Duportail requested that Lincoln let him leave the garrison. This Lincoln refused on the grounds that it would dispirit the garrison. If they were going to sustain the defense, the officers had to keep up the morale of the troops. Meanwhile, Lincoln continued to hope that if they resisted long enough and preserved the communication over the Cooper, relief might yet arrive. The fate of Charleston's precious communication was soon to be decided east of the Cooper.[52]

Chapter Twelve

INVESTITURE

During the 20 April council of war, Lincoln informed his officers that the garrison had provisions on hand for only eight to ten days. The scarcity of provision became even more evident on 22 April, when Lincoln ordered the commissaries to reduce the daily ration of one pound of beef per man to three-fourths of a pound per man. Two days later, commissaries were able to bring enough beef into town so that Lincoln restored the full ration. The receipt of fresh provisions demonstrated that the passage over the Cooper River was still very much open to the garrison. Although evacuation was an increasingly remote possibility, uninterrupted communication over the Cooper allowed them to obtain provisions and thus carry on the defense of the city. It also provided an avenue of entry for potential reinforcements, and the longer the garrison held out, the greater the possibility that reinforcements might reach them. The passageway over the Cooper presented a ray of hope to Lincoln and his army and a point of frustration for Sir Henry Clinton, who fretted unceasingly over Arbuthnot's reluctance to push ships into the river. The fate of Charleston now hung on the Americans' ability to keep open this communication.[1]

For Lincoln, the post at Lampriers Point was the key to maintaining the communication over the Cooper. While the battery at Mount Pleasant threatened the Royal Navy's entrance into the Hog Island channel, the fortification at Lampriers kept open the Cooper and Wando Rivers to the Americans exclusively. Lincoln affirmed that no enemy ships could safely lie between Lampriers Point and the city, since any ships that passed Charleston's guns would then confront cannon fire from Lampriers as they moved up the Cooper River. In addition, the post secured the land route through Christ Church Parish. From Lampriers, a road ran northeast through Christ Church

Parish and onto the Santee River and Georgetown, providing an avenue by which supplies and reinforcements could reach the city.[2]

While Lincoln relinquished his plan to establish a string of posts along the Cooper and Wando Rivers, he recognized that Lampriers represented too important a position to abandon. He impressed upon Colonel Malmedy its significance, writing him on 18 April: "I need not remind you that your post is critical and that the greatest precaution is necessary." In addition to transferring cannon from Fort Moultrie to Lampriers, Lincoln ordered Colonel Pinckney to send slaves over to assist Malmedy in the construction of works. Moreover, on 18 April he detached 300 men from the Charleston garrison, including Lieutenant Colonel Laurens with the light infantry, to Lampriers to assist in its defense. As long as Malmedy and his men held out, hope remained for the city.[3]

Malmedy and the African American slaves under his charge had constructed a strong defensive post. When Lord Cornwallis reconnoitered Lampriers he found a "tolerable" redoubt surrounded by a "good ditch." He noted that he could not mount an attack during the day due to the presence nearby of American ships, which could bombard troops assailing the fort. Meanwhile, he observed that the approach to the American position was "difficult & intricate" making a night attack too risky. In sum, Cornwallis asserted that "the works as they appeared to me, assisted by their shipping & galleys, would subject an attempt to storm them to considerable loss."[4]

Lincoln selected the correct location for keeping open the communication, and with the assistance of the shipping, Malmedy appeared to possess requisite strength to defend it. Mounting British pressure on the neck forced Lincoln to recall Laurens and the light infantry to town, however. To replace them, he sent Malmedy seventy-five North Carolina militia—hardly an equal exchange. But Lincoln thought the light troops' presence in Charleston of greater consequence, especially if the British resorted to an assault on the works.[5]

Sir Henry Clinton knew well the value of Lampriers Point to the Americans. Although siege operations on Charleston neck had proceeded to his satisfaction, he feared that Lincoln's army might "pass in force to Lamprieres & try to escape." While Clinton anticipated that

Cornwallis could intercept the retreating American army, he still clung to the hope that Arbuthnot would push ships into the Cooper River. "I was still very desirous of having an armed force in those waters," he later explained, "to remove every possibility" of an escape. Accordingly, he continued to encourage his naval counterpart to make the attempt.[6]

Unaware of what had transpired in American councils of war, Clinton's concerns about a possible escape of the garrison were perfectly valid. Although he outnumbered Lincoln in total men, Clinton's army was split into detachments separated by two major rivers. While Lincoln's troops were consolidated primarily in Charleston, the British were spread out on James Island, west of the Ashley, on Charleston neck, and east of the Cooper. If the garrison attempted to go off east of the Cooper, they would be at least as strong as Cornwallis, and, depending on how many militia joined them, might outnumber him altogether. In Washington, Clinton had faced a commander who kept his army mobile and had not allowed it to be trapped in one place. It seemed logical that the Southern Department commander would undertake a similar strategy. So far, Lincoln had not emulated the commander in chief in his actions, but he and his men had shown that they still had plenty of fight left in them.

East of the Cooper, Lord Cornwallis sought a position to most effectively prevent an American escape. After taking pains "to procure every necessary information relative to the situation of the country & the state of provisions," he concluded it best to send "the most considerable part of my Corps" across Wappetaw Bridge to the south side of Wappetaw Creek, the lower branch of the Wando River. From here, Cornwallis could intercept an American withdrawal either up the Wando or by land through Christ Church Parish. A smaller British detachment moved to Miller's Bridge on the north branch of the Wando. In addition, Cornwallis established "posts of intelligence" toward the Cooper River to detect any movement by the enemy. The earl entrusted the area north and west of the Wando to the Cooper River to Tarleton and the Legion, instructing Tarleton to be especially mindful of landing places on the west side of the Wando and on Daniel Island. Cornwallis must have heard of the barbarous crime committed against Mrs. Fayssoux, for in issuing these orders he reminded the young cavalry officer "to use your utmost endeavors to prevent the troops under your command from committing irregularities." He did authorize Tarleton to destroy stores that they could not carry away, and Tarleton complied efficiently with this order. On 28 April, he drove off all the cattle on Daniel Island to keep them from American commissaries. Meanwhile, Lieutenant Colonel Laurens found that British troops had "squandered a vast quantity of forage & provision" on Wando neck and had "scarcely left any thing at Mrs. Pinckneys plantation." Despite Cornwallis's admonitions, British troops continued to commit "irregularities" against civilians east of the Cooper as they had throughout operations in the lowcountry.[7]

Cornwallis also endeavored to obtain information on the rebel posts at Lampriers and Mount Pleasant. The earl threw himself into his duties. When he wrote Clinton on the night of 26 April, he apologized for the "incorrectness" of his letter. "I am really greatly fatigued, having hardly closed my eyes since I saw you," he explained. He had left Clinton three days earlier. Finding Lampriers too strongly fortified to assail, Cornwallis moved a small force toward Mount Pleasant. Clinton was optimistic that Cornwallis and Lieutenant Colonel Webster would "effectually shut their principal communication with Santee river" and make investiture "most compleat." His lieutenants made more progress east of the Cooper than Clinton made with Arbuthnot.[8]

While Cornwallis arranged affairs east of the Cooper, Clinton continued to battle with Arbuthnot over naval operations *in* the Cooper. With regard to sending vessels into the river, Clinton later related that he "made use of every argument [he] could think of to impress the Admiral with conviction of its importance." Arbuthnot's obsession with Mount Pleasant remained an obstacle to the move. On 22 April, he complained that presence of the American battery there prevented him from making the attempt without support from Clinton. The following day, he reiterated that the "Rebel" post at Mount Pleasant "prevents me from sending the armed Vessels I intended through the Hog Island Channel."[9]

To prod Arbuthnot into action, Clinton suggested to him that the corps east of the Cooper provided an opportunity to detach troops toward Mount Pleasant. He informed Arbuthnot on 23 April that he was sending an officer to consult with Lieutenant Colonel Webster to determine if anything could be done to "dislodge the Enemy" from Mount Pleasant. The following day, Clinton asserted to the admiral that the British force on the other side of the river could ultimately direct its movements "to the Points which you wished could be held as a Cover for the Shipping."[10]

In the wake of Clinton's observations, Arbuthnot again pledged to push ships into the Cooper, suggesting that he would do so on 24 or 25 April. He proposed to Clinton that batteries on the neck assist the passage by firing on the wharves of the city when his ships got under way. Accordingly, Clinton instructed his chief of artillery, Major Peter Traille, to issue orders for "all the Batteries . . . to direct their fire on the Wharfes in Cooper River" in the event British vessels tried to enter the river. The artillerymen were to do "any thing to draw the Enemys attention from the Ships." Clinton's orders were for naught however. Arbuthnot still did not budge.[11]

Clinton's stratagem of extolling the success of his troops east of the Cooper as a means of inspiring Arbuthnot to action ultimately backfired, and his expositions of the army's achievements provided further excuses for the admiral. In the same letter in which he informed Arbuthnot that he was sending an officer to Webster to discuss the American position at Mount Pleasant, Clinton asserted that with the reinforcement the detachment east of the Cooper "will be in sufficient force effectually to shut all their doors." On 24 April, he remarked to Arbuthnot that British troops had "taken such a Position as effectually commanded the Enemy's Communications by Land from the Cooper to the inland Navigation by Sullivan's Island." He then affirmed that once Arbuthnot sent a naval force into Spencer's Inlet and Sewee Bay, it was "the opinion of Colonel Webster, and the other Gentlemen with him, that the Enemy cannot escape, except in very small Parties." In another letter written later that day, Clinton indicated that with the success of Webster's corps, "going into Cooper lose[s] a great degree of its Import." These words were all Arbuthnot needed to hear. He congratulated Sir Henry on "having so securely shut the door to prevent the escape of the Enemy." He also willingly complied with Clinton's wish that he dispatch ships to Spencer's Inlet and

Sewee Bay. Doing so presented little risk since there were no American land or naval forces in that vicinity to threaten them. Having done his part to cut off an American retreat, Arbuthnot then threw Clinton a curve. He wrote the British general on 26 April that since "the avenue of escape are effectually blocked off by Lord Cornwallis, which was the purpose of sending the ships into the Cooper river, I cannot think myself justified in undertaking so hazardous a measure as passing the Enemy's boom, when the object for which they were intended to be sent is so considerably absent." Clinton had so convinced him that the army could cut off the rebels that Arbuthnot argued that there was now no reason for ships to enter the Cooper. Any positive consequences from such a move would not outweigh the risks involved. Ironically, in so vigorously lauding his commanding position east of the Cooper, Clinton gave Arbuthnot a rationale for not making the attempt.[12]

Arbuthnot had presented Lincoln and the Charleston garrison a tremendous gift. His refusal to enter the Cooper River essentially guaranteed that communication with the backcountry via the Cooper and Lampriers Point would stay open. Moreover, the Americans would continue to control the Cooper from the Wando down to Shutes Folly. Meanwhile, Cornwallis determined that the post at Lampriers was too strongly fortified for his troops to risk an assault against, and on Charleston neck Clinton had dispatched all the troops he could to the other side of the river. Further detachments would slow progress of the siege. As long as Lampriers Point remained in American hands, the communication would be secure. The fate of this post and of Charleston itself now lay in the hands of Colonel Malmedy and his garrison of 100 Continentals and 200 North Carolina militia.[13]

Farther down the Cooper lay the small work at Haddrell's Point on Mount Pleasant, which had caused Arbuthnot so much consternation. Within the earthworks there, Colonel Charles Cotesworth Pinckney's men erected a three gun battery directed against the mouth of the Hog Island channel. Though not originally designed as such, the work at Mount Pleasant had become the sister and supporting fortification to Lampriers Point, keeping British vessels from the Hog Island channel, and hence from the Cooper. Together, Lampriers Point and Haddrell's

Point were the last two American positions on the east bank of the Cooper.[14]

Acting upon Clinton's suggestion, Lord Cornwallis shifted his attention to the American post at Mount Pleasant. At two o'clock in the morning of 26 April, he set out from Wappetaw Bridge with a detachment from his corps, reaching Haddrell's Point that afternoon. American troops at Haddrell's Point, upon hearing of the approach of the British, hastily evacuated the position and retreated to Fort Moultrie. When Cornwallis arrived he "found no resistance" there.[15]

Shortly after the Americans retreated, Admiral Arbuthnot came ashore to consult with Cornwallis. He was disappointed to learn that the British general did not intend to fortify Mount Pleasant, but Cornwallis explained that he had only come to reconnoiter the area and drive off the rebels if the opportunity presented itself. He noted that Clinton had only authorized him to operate on the forks of the Wando and had instructed him to avoid any undertaking that might keep him at a fixed location for an extended period of time. His men would require at least two days to erect a proper work at Mount Pleasant. Although Cornwallis demonstrated that they could drive off the Americans at Haddrell's Point with relative ease, Arbuthnot still viewed the post as a threat to his shipping. His desire for a presence at Mount Pleasant was somewhat justified. When the British galley *Comet* ran aground on 29 April in the entrance to the Hog Island channel, a detachment from Fort Moultrie moved a cannon back to the work at Haddrell's Point and sunk the vessel with their fire.[16]

While Cornwallis forced the Americans to at least temporarily abandon Mount Pleasant, he could do little about Lampriers Point. The post at Lampriers and the communication across the Cooper seemed secure, but the campaign to date had been a continuum of misperceptions. Lincoln had misjudged the reaction of the South Carolina militia to the threat to Charleston, while Clinton had misperceived Lincoln's intention to evacuate the city. Both officers had seriously miscalculated Arbuthnot's willingness to enter the Cooper River. Colonel Malmedy, in command of a strong defensive position, now misjudged the danger to that position.

Malmedy had no way of knowing that Cornwallis was limited in the scope of operations that he could undertake or that the British general viewed the American works at Lampriers as too strong for his troops to storm. Malmedy conjectured that Cornwallis would direct his next thrust against his post. On 27 April, he received word that the British were approaching him in force. Cornwallis was making no such attempt; Malmedy's informant most likely encountered one of the patrols that Cornwallis had been sending toward the Cooper and mistook it for an advancing column. Despairing of his ability to repel an attack, Malmedy, in a panic, determined to evacuate Lampriers Point. That night, the garrison withdrew from the fort in a hasty and disorderly manner. General McIntosh recorded that they "retreated in great confusion across the River." The hastiness and disorderliness of the evacuation was evidenced by the fact that Malmedy's soldiers left behind four eighteen pounders and several smaller cannon, while one boat carrying three officers and eighty men accidentally sailed into the Hog Island channel where a British ship captured it and the men onboard.[17]

More serious than the loss of men and guns was the loss of the key to Charleston's communication with the backcountry. The following day, Captain Charles Hudson of the Royal Navy occupied the fort. In Charleston, the garrison could clearly see the British Union flag flying above the works. With the loss of Lampriers Point, Lincoln no longer held a major fortified position on the east bank of the Cooper, while British troops ranged throughout St. Thomas and Christ Church parishes. Under these circumstances, it would be very difficult for sizeable bodies of troops to get into or out of the city. Likewise, American commissaries and quartermasters would be unable to sufficiently supply the garrison.[18]

Again one of Lincoln's subordinates seriously disappointed him. Like Commodore Whipple in the defense of the harbor and General Huger in the debacle at Biggin's Bridge, Malmedy failed the Southern Department commander. But much of the blame for the loss of Lampriers Point lies with Lincoln. Given the post's significance, Lincoln certainly erred both in his selection of the officer who commanded Lampriers and in assigning the men that he did to its garrison. An officer of superior rank such as General Charles Scott or General Lachlan McIntosh would have been a more appropriate choice to command such an important post. Both officers had seen extensive action throughout the war, and having been involved in the recent councils of war, each had a thorough understanding of the strategic situation of Charleston. Lincoln could easily have spared Scott, who had come to Charleston without troops, or McIntosh, who commanded the militia on the less active south side of the city. Even a more junior officer would have been a better alternative. A few days before the evacuation, Lincoln ordered back from Lampriers Lieutenant Colonel John Laurens, a man who eagerly sought the glory of battle and who spoiled for a fight. Even if Laurens remained in the fort as Malmedy's second in command, it seems unlikely that he would have let Malmedy abandon Lampriers, even if it meant risking insubordination. As to the men defending the works at Lampriers, along with Laurens Lincoln withdrew arguably the best troops in his army, the light infantry. With their departure, the majority of the Lampriers garrison consisted of militia rather than Continentals. Although Lincoln did lack men in Charleston, the judicious course of action still would have been to send a strong contingent of veteran troops to Lampriers under the command of a competent and reliable officer. Instead, Lincoln's poor decision making contributed to the loss of the post, which now posed a severe threat to the security of Charleston.

Arriving in Charleston with the rest of the retreating garrison, Malmedy found himself persona non grata. The day after the evacuation Lincoln published in general orders that "Col[onel] Malmedy will send to the Orderly Office before this Evening a written report of the Evacuation of Hobcaw." Malmedy apparently conveyed to Lincoln that he abandoned the position due to the British moving toward him in force, which was the reason Lincoln gave in his report to Congress. While Lincoln may have accepted this explanation, others in the Charleston garrison did not. Word spread rapidly that he had left the fort "in a very unmilitary manner." One officer noted that Colonel Malmedy became "somewhat disagreable to the Garrison in Consequence of the affair at Lampriers." He related that Malmedy "was advised to quit the town while there was a probability of a passage." In conjecturing on the "probability of a passage," it is unclear whether the officer was speculating on Malmedy's safety with regard to the British or the garrison of Charleston.[19]

In any case, Malmedy did leave the garrison accompanied by Edward Rutledge, signer of the Declaration of Independence and brother to Governor Rutledge, and a few other officers. After they reached the east bank of the Cooper, a British cavalry patrol fell upon them, capturing Rutledge and two officers. Malmedy was able to make his escape. Ostensibly to prevent him from sending word of the situation of the garrison to the backcountry, Cornwallis ordered cavalry and infantry patrols to search for him. For several days they combed the area, seeking out the French officer. On 5 May, Cornwallis reported to Clinton that "Malmedy has certainly been these three days in the woods near us, but we have not been able to catch him, altho' he must be in great distress." Ostracized and exiled by his comrades and hunted by his enemies, Malmedy's condition was indeed deplorable. With great difficulty he ultimately made his way to safety.[20] The capture of Edward Rutledge and the two officers coupled with the experience of Malmedy in trying to get away demonstrated that it was difficult enough for small groups of men to escape the city. For large bodies of men it would be near impossible.[21]

Still, Sir Henry Clinton was not satisfied. Without the navy's vessels in the Cooper, he continued to fear that the Charleston garrison would escape. The possibility of a move by Arbuthnot's ships into the river was surely remote. Even the seizure of the American work at Haddrell's Point by a detachment under Major Patrick Ferguson did not persuade the admiral. Clinton did not help his case when he informed Arbuthnot that a retreat by the Americans via Mount Pleasant was unlikely "when every path from it to the Country was occupied by British Troops." Such remarks further convinced Arbuthnot that entering the Cooper was unnecessary. On 29 April, he teased Clinton by suggesting that he would "push a Force into Cooper river," but he then asserted that "equal good consequences would ensue" if Clinton armed vessels that his men had captured along the Cooper and Wando. A few days later, Captain Elphinstone notified Clinton that he did not believe that Arbuthnot had "any Idea of sending a Force into Cooper." By 6 May, Clinton seems to have finally accepted that the Royal Navy was not going into the river. "As there are now no Hopes of any Naval Force being sent into Cooper," he asserted to Cornwallis, "we must do the best we can with such as we have." The army was on its own with regard to completing the investiture of Charleston.[22]

To increase the likelihood of catching Lincoln's army if they evacuated Charleston, Cornwallis set his troops in motion to find the best position to block an American retreat. A camp on "Wando Neck" between the upper branches of that river permitted Cornwallis to respond to any attempt at retreat by water up the Wando or overland through Christ Church Parish. Clinton generally concurred with the earl's plan, pointing out that a position on or near the forks of the Wando would effectively "shut all the avenues leading from Christ Church parish to the Santee when Awendaw Bridge was destroyed." Awendaw Bridge lay across Awendaw Creek on the main road to Georgetown through Christ Church Parish.[23] Clinton also suggested to Cornwallis that he send troops back toward the Cooper to prevent a retreat in that area.[24]

With the exception of a detachment at Lampriers Point and his cavalry patrols, Cornwallis kept the bulk of his troops together so that he would be strong enough to face any American force which marched through the area. He changed his position periodically, generally staying within striking distance of the forks of the Wando, but also moving closer to the Cooper as Clinton recommended. On 6 May, he camped at Manigault's between Quinby Bridge and Huger's Bridge. Located between the east branch of the Cooper and the west branch of the Wando, Cornwallis thought this position "as good as any" for the purpose of "Blockading Charlestown, or catching the garrison." From Manigault's, he could intercept the Americans if they retreated east or west of the Wando or he could strike a blow at reinforcements coming from the Santee. Cornwallis cautioned Clinton that if a considerable body of the rebels escaped from Charleston "our taking them must be uncertain as the Country is very extensive, woody, & every where practicable to infantry unencumbered with Canon & Baggage." Although confident in his ability to prevent the Americans from getting by him, he could not guarantee success. Such reports from Cornwallis could only have contributed to Clinton's uneasiness.[25]

As to reinforcements for the Charleston garrison, Cornwallis had little to fear. Colonel Abraham Buford had recently brought a Virginia Continental detachment into South Carolina, but Governor Rutledge had little success raising the militia. One officer reported that the men "are Exceeding backward in Turning out." Few collected at the designated rendezvous point at Wrights Bluff on the north side of the Santee. The American cavalry was making its presence felt again however. After the disaster at Biggin's Bridge, they retreated north of the Santee to regroup and refit. Colonel Anthony Walton White arrived from the north with a few dragoons and he now took command of all the cavalry.[26]

On 5 May, White crossed the Santee with one hundred dragoons and advanced toward Awendaw Bridge. At Ball's plantation, four miles north of the bridge, his dragoons captured a British officer and seventeen men who were foraging there. After securing their prisoners, they started back toward the Santee, expecting to cross at Lenud's, or Lenew's, Ferry. At the ferry, White decided to feed and rest half of his horses. As a result many of the American dragoon horses were unbridled, unsaddled, and totally unprepared for action. By coincidence, Lieutenant Colonel Tarleton with 150 cavalry of his own was making a foray toward Lenud's that same afternoon. Informed by a loyalist, Elias Ball, of the presence of the American dragoons and the capture of the British troops, Tarleton pushed his men forward "with the greatest expedition." As he had at Biggin's Bridge, on approaching Lenud's Ferry Tarleton quickly formed his troopers and charged upon the unsuspecting Americans, who were taken completely by surprise. After driving off the picket guard, the British cavalrymen rushed in among the main body hacking away with their sabers. They cut down between twenty and thirty officers and men in the attack. Some American cavalrymen, including Colonel White, Lieutenant Colonel Washington, and Major Jameson, jumped into the river and swam to safety, but most were not so lucky. Tarleton reported the capture of sixty-seven officers and men along with one hundred horses and all their arms. He lost only two officers and four horses. Further underscoring the disaster, in the midst of the attack the British prisoners, whom the Americans were ferrying across the river, pushed their guards overboard and made their way to safety.[27]

Tarleton had again soundly defeated the American cavalry, but this time there was little left to regroup. Cornwallis correctly asserted to Clinton that "this stroke will have totally demolished their Cavalry."

Moreover, the victory at Lenud's Ferry demonstrated the dominance that the British had obtained between the Cooper and the Santee. Clinton and Cornwallis had for all intents and purposes cut off the Americans north and east of the Cooper. For Lincoln and the garrison of Charleston, time was running out.[28]

When Edward Rutledge was captured on 3 May, British patrols also intercepted a number of letters from several gentlemen of the garrison to their wives in the country. "The letters to the Ladies are not very sanguine," Cornwallis reported to Clinton. One typifies the depths to which the garrison's morale had plunged after the loss of Lampriers Point. The letter was written by Benjamin Smith, a militia officer serving in the city, to his wife. "The enemy have turned the siege into a blockade, which, in a short time, must have the desired effect; and the most sanguine do not now entertain the smallest hope of the town being saved," Smith informed his beloved. "Our affairs," he continued, "are daily declining, and not a ray of hope remains to assure us of success." The British had cut off their communication with the country, preventing them from escaping or from being resupplied or reinforced. Smith himself had "really almost sunk under the load." He expected that "a short time will plant the British standard on our ramparts," while "the thirteen stripes will be levelled in the dust, and I [will] owe my life to the clemency of a conqueror." Despite the despondency of Smith and others, the garrison of Charleston fought on bravely. The last act had yet to play out.[29]

Chapter Thirteen

A Gallant Defense

At the 26 April council of war, Lincoln and his officers vowed to fight on, but as the siege progressed, continued resistance became increasingly difficult. With British ships in control of the harbor, Clinton's main army upon Charleston neck, detachments of British troops on James Island, west of the Ashley at Lining's Landing, and ranging throughout the Cooper-Wando basin, the city was now completely surrounded. Moreover, the British force on Charleston neck pushed their approaches and siegecraft methodically and inexorably toward the American works. The siege was consuming the very apparatus required for sustaining the defense. Stores of ammunition and provision dwindled, and loss of the communication east of the Cooper made resupply uncertain. Some like Benjamin Smith lost hope and waited the end. Still others expressed that hopelessness by deserting to the enemy. Most did not give up, however. One officer noted that despite "the many inconveniences and fatigue they Suffered" the soldiers were "in high Spirits." The British now faced the disagreeable prospect of subduing the determined defenders of Charleston, who were ready to throw back the besieging army at their own parapet if necessary.[1]

Although the British had effectively surrounded the city, they too confronted difficulties as they attempted to complete the reduction of Charleston. In addition to the garrison's resolve, shortages of ammunition and of men to conduct siege operations plagued Clinton. With the rebels refusing to yield, he became increasingly concerned that they would have to assault their works, which he was loath to do. He was well aware of the perils of attacking a well-entrenched enemy. The siege had proceeded as Clinton expected, but matters would soon reach extremity, which in the context of eighteenth-century siege warfare meant either forcing a surrender or making an assault on the American fortifications. The final weeks of the siege promised to be forbidding for both armies.

Clinton had acted with discretion since the outset of the campaign and he had no intention of changing his tack. He remarked to Sir Andrew Hamond that "the place [is] exceeding strong & we must proceed with caution." He overwhelmingly agreed with Major Moncrief "that we had better proceed as we began" by sapping toward the American fortifications. And so British working parties pressed on. Once they passed the canal, laborers would clear the abatis between the canal and the American main line, then dig forward until they made a lodgment in the American counterscarp, the outer wall of the ditch in front of their parapet. Only a few yards would separate the two armies at that point. If no surrender were forthcoming, an assault would become necessary.[2]

On the night of 25 April, British workmen commenced a direct sap from the left of the third parallel toward the *battard'eau,* or dam, on the American right. Once in control of the dam, engineers would cut a drainage trench into the canal to draw off the water in it. On the night of 1 May, working parties "opened the Sap into the Enemy's Wet Ditch," and the draining of the canal was underway. Digging the approach toward the dam was dangerous work for the British. At a range of less than 500 feet, American riflemen singled out enemy laborers while artillerymen employed grapeshot against them. On the night they cut into the canal, grapeshot from American artillery killed and wounded six British soldiers. Still, the working parties had reached their objective. Although water in the canal would take several days to drain off, the British had begun the reduction of the first major component of the Americans' defense in depth.[3]

While some British fatigue men sapped toward the dam, others concentrated on the completion of the third parallel. These men widened the trench that comprised the parallel, built up and strengthened the parapet, excavated magazines, constructed batteries, and brought cannon into them. They erected the main battery of the third parallel near the town gate on the main road leading into Charleston. From this position, their artillerymen would direct fire against the hornwork.[4]

Work continued amid tremendous cannon and small arms fire. The Americans employed muskets, rifles, and artillery against the British working parties and parallels. General Moultrie ordered that firing from the American batteries "from whence the Guns bear on the Enemy's Works do commence immediately after dark, to be continued every Night till Countermanded." As a result of American cannonades, British fatigue men constantly made repairs to damaged trenches. This activity was done in turn under more fire from enemy batteries. On 26 April, Captain Ewald noted that men toiled "the whole day under the heaviest cannon and small arms fire," while Lieutenant Wilson of the engineers recorded that they "repaired" the third parallel over the next several nights. American gunnery took its toll on the British. On 3 May, Captain Robertson asserted that seven or eight men had been "hurt" by the firing "every 24 hours for 8 or 10 Days past."[5]

Meanwhile, British cannon and small arms were by no means tranquil. The besiegers returned fire with equal virulence. The Hessian jaegers were especially effective in this duel. They directed their fire at the embrasures of American batteries, keeping American artillerists at bay during daylight hours. When Captain Hinrichs's company occupied the third parallel, Hinrichs ordered men "to stand at all times with cocked and leveled arms" and to fire "upon the slightest movement about the enemy's guns." According to General McIntosh, rifle fire was kept up continuously "Night & Day upon us." Although the Americans returned the favor (Captain Ewald related that on one occasion "the enemy riflemen used all their power to silence the fire of the jaegers"), the German marksmen inflicted severe casualties on American troops posted in the batteries. So deadly was their aim that Charles Stedman asserted that "numbers of the besieged were killed at their guns, and scarcely any escaped who ventured to show themselves over the lines." Clinton avowed that the jaegers "shot down every head the instant any appeared above the works." Colonel Richard Parker of the Virginians met just such a fate when he peered over the parapet on 24 April. With the third parallel in such close proximity to their lines, General Moultrie had American soldiers place sand bags "upon the top of our lines, for the riflemen to fire through." According to Moultrie, the openings between the sand bags were only three to four inches wide. Still, he contended, many men were killed through these holes. On 30 April, Major William Croghan observed "the number of privates killed & wounded exceedingly increased[,] so much so that they cannot readily be ascertained at present."[6]

To repair embrasures damaged by British cannon fire, the Americans resorted to working during the night when they could not be seen as easily by the jaegers. The besieged "inlisted" gangs of African American slaves into the artillery corps to assist them in this duty. These men enlisted in name only, since general orders called for detachments to proceed to town for the purpose of "pressing Negroes" to perform labor for the army. General McIntosh related that the African Americans had "to be pressed daily, & kept under guard, as the masters as well as the Slaves, were unwilling [that] they should work." When darkness fell, the African Americans set to work on the embrasures. These unfortunate men risked their lives to British rifle fire and cannon shot to keep American batteries in operation.[7]

Duty on the lines presented a dreadful spectacle for any man, black or white, free or slave. Musket, rifle, and cannon balls constantly whizzed overhead or slammed into the parapet showering men with dust and sand. Their own artillery fire boomed deafeningly and literally shook the ground. During the day, one dared not show his head above the parapet for fear of being shot down, while behind the works men dodged cannon balls and shells that bounced through the trenches or along the ground, the fuses of the shells spitting out sparks as they danced along. Occasionally, the cries of those not fortunate enough to get out of the way pierced the air. Meanwhile, the work continued. Officers shouted orders as men covered in dirt and sweat grunted, struggling to move heavy field pieces into position to be loaded or fired. Nights must have been especially trying. Darkness obscured the enemy but the flash of a cannon or rifle being fired demonstrated that he was still there. Cannon fire exploded in the night, spewing forth yellow-orange flame and hundreds of embers as the charges threw dangerous projectiles into the blackness. Between the lines, burning turpentine barrels emitted an eerie glow in the darkness. Brave men were needed on both sides to withstand the harrowing ordeal of siege warfare.

Given the conditions to which they were daily exposed, it is not surprising that men deserted. Desertions occurred with relative frequency throughout the various stages of the siege, increasing as the siege wore on. On 27 April, General McIntosh noted that five men from a James Island militia company deserted from the town in a boat, while Captain John Peebles recorded that three soldiers from the British 63rd regiment deserted on 30 April. Clinton acknowledged that two Hessians had stolen away on the night of 29 April, but he contended that many rebels were coming into the British lines from Charleston. If a soldier went over to the enemy, as opposed to running away altogether, he often disclosed to them damaging information about his former comrades. Lieutenant Colonel Grimké noted that a British deserter informed them of the British intention to pass the canal and furnished them details of the casualties the besieging army suffered in the false alarm on 25 April. Some deserters provided more information than others. Captain Peebles related the case of one man from the Charleston garrison who gave a detailed description of the American works and provisions, but Peebles also conceded that these individuals generally "know very little about the matter." Deserters at times actively assisted the enemy. Major Traille of the Royal Artillery convinced two American deserters to help them direct their fire. Traille reported to headquarters that he "sent the most intelligent of the two to the centre Mortar Battery . . . in order to point out certain marks on the Enemys works for the direction of the fire to the most advantage." Still, men who switched sides often found conditions no better with the enemy. On 2 May, Clinton asserted that among the many deserters coming in was one from the British 7th regiment "who left us 3 days since."[8]

The return of the deserter from the 7th regiment, who chose to risk the wrath of rigid British army discipline rather than remain in Charleston, gives an indication how critical conditions had become for the garrison. Convinced that the British would at length storm their works, Lincoln and his officers prepared for such an event. Brigadier General Duportail recommended that they convert the hornwork into a completely enclosed work, or citadel, and that they erect two covering redoubts, one on each side of the hornwork. By 28 April, American fatigue parties were "employed in closing the Horn Work." Detachments went into the city to collect boards and posts for construction of a palisade around the new works. On 29 April, Lincoln informed his officers "that he intended the Horn Work as [a] place of retreat for the whole Army" in the event a British assault drove them from the main line. He assigned Lieutenant Colonel Laurens and the light infantry the crucial "port guard," or picket, directly in front of the fortification to cover any retreat into it and the adjoining redoubts.[9]

Although American soldiers had a strong position to which to repair in the event of a successful British assault, Lincoln and his officers could do little about dwindling supplies. By the beginning of May, the garrison was running seriously short of provisions and of shot and shell for the artillery, the very articles they needed to continue the defense of the city. As to the latter, American gunners resorted to throwing from their cannon any piece of metal they could find. British captain Peter Russell noted that the rebels "frequently fire" ragged pieces of iron, broken bottles, old axes, and gun barrels. Similarly, Captain Ewald recorded that "the besieged threw any stuff which could be loaded from their mortars." Indeed, Lieutenant Colonel Grimké had even directed "pebbles or stones to be fired from the 10 Inch Mortar on the left of the Lines." These metal and stone projectiles must have inflicted dreadful wounds on British soldiers who were unlucky enough to be hit by them.[10]

Shortage of provisions was by far the more serious obstacle to continued operations. At the beginning of May, American stores contained enough rice to supply the garrison for approximately seven weeks.[11] In an effort to taunt American soldiers, British artillerymen fired a number of shells into Charleston charged not with gunpowder and lead, but with "Rice & Sugar." Lieutenant Colonel Grimké remarked wryly that "they are misinformed if they suppose us in want of those articles." Meat, however, was another story.[12]

The lowcountry abounded with cattle, which the Americans previously procured with ease; but with the communication east of the Cooper cut off, supplies were no longer readily available. What little beef Colonel Malmedy evacuated from Lampriers Point turned out to be spoiled and unfit to distribute to the soldiers. When Christopher Gadsden and the remaining members of the Privy Council permitted

Lincoln's officers to search citizens' houses for foodstuffs, Lincoln recounted that "scarce a sufficiency for the supply of private families was discovered." The inability of Lincoln's commissaries to obtain adequate quantities of meat soon affected the troops. On 4 May, Lieutenant Colonel Grimké noted that the meat ration was reduced to six ounces per man, less than half the normal allowance. This diminution did not preserve the garrison's stores however. On 8 May, Grimké recorded in his journal: "no more Meat Served out." Three days later, a subaltern expressed the effects of the lack of meat when he wrote simply: "Hungry guts in the Garrison." While Christopher Gadsden asserted that the soldiers were willing to subsist on rice alone, Lincoln and his officers better understood the daily needs of their men. They would be unable to resist much longer without this necessary article.[13]

The shortage of provisions also tormented the garrison's civilians. Lincoln voiced concern about the army's ability to furnish food to civilians before the British even began the siege. At the end of March, he informed Governor Rutledge that "a number of women, inhabitants of the Town," had made application to him "for rations, founded, they say, on absolute want, and a total inability to provide for themselves." These women could not feed themselves or their families, and Lincoln and his officers asked Rutledge to take measures to remove them from the garrison. Although many Charlestonians had evacuated the city before the British cut off escape routes on the neck and east of the Cooper, a number of noncombatants, perhaps a few thousand, remained behind. The want of provisions also gnawed at their bellies.[14]

Civilians who stayed also endured other privations. According to David Ramsay, British cannon fire killed twenty inhabitants during the siege and burned down thirty houses. Still, many of the hardships citizens suffered were not inflicted by British bullets, but by the actions of American troops. Soldiers searched Charlestonians' homes for food while fatigue parties impressed their slaves into service and pulled apart their fences in search of palisades. Military necessity justified such exploits and army officers or civilian officials had sanctioned them, but soldiers acting without orders also harassed the city's residents. In general orders of 29 April, Lincoln asserted that he had heard "with Concern that many Excesses have been lately committed in the

Town by Soldiers & patrols of Non-Com[missione]d Officers under a variety of pretenses." He threatened "severe punishment" to those "who plunder[ed] the houses during fire or other confusion among the inhabitants." Lincoln exhorted his officers to keep the men in camp during this period of extreme emergency and "prevent any future Complaints from the Citizens." It is interesting to note that American soldiers could free themselves from onerous duty on the lines to torment the people of Charleston. The problem was serious enough to oblige Lincoln to put forth an effort to stop it in the midst of his other concerns. Whether plundered by British troops in the countryside or harassed by American troops in Charleston itself, lowcountry civilians continued to feel the pinch of warfare. They were as much casualties of the British campaign against the city as the soldiers who manned the siege lines.[15]

Had they been fully aware of the situation of the British army on the neck, soldiers and civilians in the garrison might have found solace in the difficulties that were hindering the besiegers. Early in the siege, British artillerymen confronted a severe shortage of twenty-four pound shot, which would be crucial to battering down Charleston's defensive works. Of forty-nine British artillery pieces in place on 24 April, seventeen, or over a third, were twenty-four pounders. More than half of the shot and shell fired by British artillerists came from these guns.[16] Two months after they landed on the South Carolina coast, Clinton's army still felt the losses sustained on the voyage southward. The British had still not fully rectified the deficiency by the end of April, when Clinton ordered his officers to complete the batteries to 100 rounds of shot per gun. By 2 May, Major Traille of the artillery confessed that his men had still not completed the batteries to 100 rounds per gun, but he promised that they would do so within two days. The Americans were fortunate in that the British shortage of twenty-four pound shot prevented them from bombarding the town even more heavily than they already had.[17]

A lack of men also troubled Sir Henry. Even after reinforcements from New York arrived on 18 April, Clinton contended that he had too few soldiers to successfully conduct siege operations on Charleston neck. The necessity of maintaining a line of communication with posts west of the Ashley and of keeping a force east of the Cooper limited the number of troops that Clinton could employ in the siege. He later asserted that these obligations "reduced the troops immediately before the place to such a handful that, notwithstanding the very liberal reinforcement sent me . . . from the northward, we had scarcely a relief for the indispensable duties of the trenches." Major Traille complained to John André that "from the increasing extent of the Works there are not even now a sufficient number of Artillery soldiers for a single relief." To remedy the situation, Clinton requested Lieutenant Colonel Alured Clarke, who was posted near Moncks Corner with the 23rd regiment, to send a detachment to serve with the artillery, and he later ordered Cornwallis to return the 64th regiment to Charleston neck to assist them in draining the canal.[18]

While Clinton worried about shortages of men and shot and the inevitable American retreat, his troops encountered difficulty in draining the canal. On the evening of 1 May, Clinton noted that "the canal runs off apace," but two days later, he recorded that "the canal goes off slow." On 4 May, the elements again smiled on the garrison as "a very heavy rain [fell] during the day & night," which refilled the wet ditch. These setbacks prevented the British from pushing their approaches closer to Charleston. In the meantime, working parties endeavored to complete batteries in the third parallel.[19]

Meanwhile, the Americans continued to put up a spirited defense. Firing their cannon primarily during the night to avoid the deadly salvos of the jaegers, American artillerymen were quite effective against the British trenches and batteries. Major Traille reported to headquarters on 27 April that a twelve pounder had been "disabled by a shot from the Enemy, and . . . the Batteries are considerably damaged." Captain Hinrichs asserted that the besieged "completely shot to pieces" Battery Number Seven in the first parallel. The Hessian officer also related that on one occasion as the jaeger detachment was marching to the third parallel an American cannonball tore off one man's leg, wounded another in the thigh, and injured five others with wood splinters when the ball struck a tree. American gunners directed their fire particularly against the British advance battery in the third parallel, which the besiegers constructed to harass the hornwork. According to

Joseph Johnson, whose father served in the hornwork during the siege, American artillery fire demolished this battery. When the British rebuilt it, American cannon again left it in ruins. This exchange continued to the end of the siege. Captain Hinrichs's account confirms that this position was a focal point for American fire. He noted that "the enemy endeavored to raze our advanced batteries," leaving "much to be repaired" after each night's bombardment.[20]

With the advance stalled until the canal drained off completely, Sir Henry nervously conjectured whether the Americans would continue to stubbornly hold out. On 6 May, he wrote Cornwallis with regard to the obstinate American resistance: "I begin to think these people will be Blockheads enough to wait the assault." Clinton began making preparations for an attack, which some among the besieging army eagerly anticipated. Captain Ewald maintained that a storm of the American defenses "was the unanimous wish of the besieger," so that the "disagreeable" work of manning the trenches might come to an end. East of the Cooper, Cornwallis beseeched Clinton that if they were to assault the works, he would "take it as a favour if you will let me be of the party." He asserted that he would "be happy to attend my old friends the grenadiers & L[igh]t Infantry" once again. Clinton was not as enthusiastic as these officers and he worriedly confided to his journal that "the success of a Storm is uncertain."[21]

In considering whether to assault the Charleston defenses, Clinton again found himself frustrated by his naval counterpart. Recognizing that Lincoln would employ every available man to oppose the attacking British troops, Clinton hoped that Arbuthnot would direct his ships in the harbor to fire on American batteries defending the harbor-side of the town to prevent soldiers manning those batteries from rushing to the lines. The two British commanders had previously discussed the navy's role in the event of a storm. On 23 April, Arbuthnot asserted to Clinton that if the army were to "make a general assault against the Enemy's works," he would send "every ship" he had against the Americans. Clinton allowed that "the Ships may in that Moment be of infinite Service." As the time for the impending attack drew nearer, he reminded Arbuthnot that "should the Rebels then wait the Assault[,] The Manner in which your Excellency could best cooperate with us would be by laying ships against the Town either in Cooper or Ashley

River." He asserted that "the impression of their fire and their preventing Succours coming from the lower parts of the Town to the Lines would favour our Attack very much." Arbuthnot's letter of 2 May fully persuaded Clinton of the admiral's "desire to lend the most effectual Assistance of the Fleet to the important Attack which is now at hand." Again, Clinton expected far too much from the naval chief.[22]

After weeks of imploring Arbuthnot to force his way into the Cooper River to no avail, Clinton should not have been surprised when the admiral disappointed him again. On 4 May, Arbuthnot wrote him: "I confess it would be against my judgment to place the Ships against the Enemy's Batteries circumstanced as they are merely for a diversion." He did agree to order vessels "by their movements [to] indicate such a design to the Enemy." Clinton must have been aghast when he read the admiral's letter. He was considering risking valuable troops in an assault on a well-entrenched and well-armed enemy while Arbuthnot refused to even fire his guns. He lectured Arbuthnot in his response, arguing that "the meer Indication of a design of coming up to the Town will not I fear answer the purposes of effectual Cooperation." Only "a Solid Operation of the Fleet" as Arbuthnot proposed in his letter of 23 April would suffice. He suggested that they meet "for further deliberation on this Subject." Clinton still hoped that he could press the admiral to take "a solid part in the intended assault."[23]

Arbuthnot, however, was now involved in another operation, one in which he would unwittingly assist Clinton and the army on Charleston neck. On 27 April, Arbuthnot sent ashore a detachment of 500 seamen and marines under Captain Charles Hudson to take post in the environs of Haddrell's Point on Mount Pleasant. It was this force that first occupied Lampriers after the American evacuation. When Major Patrick Ferguson and the American Volunteers relieved them, Hudson and his men returned to Mount Pleasant, where several deserters informed Hudson of the weakened state of Fort Moultrie. Lincoln had recalled Colonel Pinckney and the bulk of the 1st South Carolina regiment to Charleston, leaving Lieutenant Colonel William Scott in command of the fort with 118 Continentals and 100 militia.[24]

When Arbuthnot received the account of the reduced state of Fort Moultrie's garrison, he ordered Captain Hudson to make an attempt on the fort. As in 1776, the south and east faces of Fort Moultrie were solidly constructed, while the west face and northwest bastion were less so, providing the British an opportunity to strike those areas with success. In the early morning hours of 4 May, Hudson landed 150 men on the northeast end of Sullivan's Island to surprise a redoubt covering the northern approaches to the fort. Shortly after coming ashore, Hudson discovered that the Americans had evacuated the redoubt and his troops immediately took possession of it.[25]

Reinforced by 200 men under Captain John Orde, Hudson summoned the garrison of Fort Moultrie on the morning of 6 May. Lieutenant Colonel Scott responded that he would defend his post to the last extremity. According to Lieutenant Allaire, who was serving with Patrick Ferguson's corps, Hudson then informed Scott that "if the fort was not given up, he would immediately storm it, and put all the garrison to the sword." After further negotiation, the American commander agreed to capitulate if Hudson allowed his troops to march out with the honors of war, the officers to wear their side arms, and the militia to return home as prisoners on parole until exchanged. Hudson consented, and on 7 May the garrison of Fort Moultrie marched out through its gates and piled their arms outside the works. The fort, which had withstood the British attack so courageously in 1776, was now, four years later, in the hands of the British.[26]

Militarily, the loss of Fort Moultrie was of little consequence to Lincoln and his army. The fort's strategic importance had lessened substantially when the Royal Navy sailed past it on 8 April. Lincoln even suggested to Rutledge shortly thereafter that they abandon it altogether. After failing to stop British ships from entering the harbor, Fort Moultrie could do little to protect the city. When British galleys moved into the cove between the town and Sullivan's Island on 26 April, they effectively cut off communication between the two positions. By that point, the significance of Fort Moultrie rested only in its past glory.[27]

In terms of morale, the loss of Fort Moultrie was of great consequence, for the news of its fall represented a severe psychological blow to the people of Charleston. Colonel Malmedy had earlier stressed to Lincoln that the possibility of the fort's demise "does alarm all the country." On 7 May, soldiers and civilians in the Charleston garrison could plainly see the British flag flying over the ramparts. According to an officer in Lincoln's army, loss of the fort dampened "the Spirits of the Citizens," who had reckoned it "impregnable." The officer noted that the inhabitants now viewed themselves as completely cut off. If Fort Moultrie could succumb to the British forces, Charleston must surely follow.[28]

The capture of Fort Moultrie was an important acquisition for the Royal Navy, since the fort could defend British ships in the harbor from any French or Spanish fleet that might appear off Charleston. The fall of the fort also held advantages for the army. Without meaning to, Admiral Arbuthnot handed General Clinton a gift of sorts. The psychological blow that the loss of Fort Moultrie dealt the garrison of Charleston, along with news of the defeat of the American cavalry at Lenud's Ferry, gave Clinton the opportunity to once again remind Lincoln of the futility of further resistance. Having received accounts of these successes and information from deserters that the garrison was running low on provisions, Clinton recognized that they might avert an assault on the town after all.

Early in the morning of 8 May, Clinton again summoned the garrison to surrender. The summons read:

> Circumstanced as I now am with respect to the place invested[,] Humanity only can induce me to lay within your reach the Terms I determined should never again be proffered.
>
> The fall of Fort Sullivan[,] The destruction on the 6th Instant of what remained of your Cavalry, the critical period to which our Approaches against the Town have brought us mark this as the term of your hopes of Succour (could you have framed any) and an hour beyond which resistance is temerity.
>
> By this last Summons therefore I throw to your Charges whatever vindictive Severity exasperated Soldiers may inflict on the unhappy people whom you devote by persevering in a fruitless defence.
>
> I shall expect your Answer untill 8 o'clock when hostilities will again commence unless the Town shall be surrendered.[29]

As with the first summons of 10 April, Clinton used the standard language of eighteenth-century siege warfare. In emphasizing recent

American defeats, Clinton pointed out to Lincoln the futility of continuing the defense, and reminded him that he was being extremely generous by again offering them the chance to surrender. Finally, he placed on Lincoln's shoulders the responsibility for any outrages which might befall the soldiers and civilians of the garrison if the British stormed the works and town.

When he received the summons, Lincoln objected that the time allotted for consideration was insufficient for him to confer with the Continental army officers, militia officers, naval captains, and civilian authorities. He sent a letter to Clinton, asserting that "there are so many different interests to be consulted that I have to propose that hostilities do not commence again till twelve." Clinton consented to this extension. In the meantime, Lincoln called a council of war "of all the General and field Officers in Garrison, and Captains of the Continental Ships."[30]

Lincoln and his officers ultimately consumed so much time discussing the situation of the garrison and drawing up proposed articles of capitulation that the American commander asked Clinton for another extension to which he consented. When Lincoln sent him the proposed articles of capitulation, Clinton suggested that in order to give them "due consideration . . . the cessation of hostilities" should remain in effect until eight o'clock in the morning of 9 May. He reminded Lincoln that if he agreed, he should make no effort to strengthen the defenses or evacuate men and supplies from the town. Clinton was still wary that the garrison might attempt to break out. He instructed Cornwallis to be on his guard, noting that if negotiations broke off, "the Continentals may try to escape your Lordship's vigilance."[31]

The twenty-four hour truce came as a welcome respite to soldiers and sailors manning the lines. They were temporarily safe from lethal cannon and small arms fire, while the stipulation that the works remain as they were relieved them from the toil of repairing fortifications. Ensign Hartung of the Hessians presumed that the Americans were badly in need of the lull in the siege. He noted that American sentries posted at the front of the works "looked very ragged, and still they have probably not put their worst there." General Moultrie would have agreed. He later recalled that fatigue among soldiers in the advanced redoubt "was so great, for want of sleep, that many faces were so swelled they could scarcely see out of their eyes."[32]

The length of the truce gave Gabriel Manigault, who was serving in the militia, "an expectation of the siege being concluded." Moultrie asserted that the militia as a whole "looked upon all the business as settled, and without orders, took up their baggage and walked into town, leaving the lines quite defenceless." British and Hessian soldiers also anticipated that the siege would end soon, although they did not wander from their posts. Ensign Hartung related that "the English laid a good many wagers" on the surrender of the town. The outcome of the siege now hung upon the negotiations of Lincoln and the British commanders, and Sir Henry was not ready to yield so easily to American demands.[33]

Upon convening the council of war in the hornwork on 8 May, Lincoln laid before the council the state of their provisions, the strength of the garrison as compiled by the adjutant general, and the prospect of reinforcements reaching them. After the officers mulled over these issues for some time, Lincoln requested that they give their opinions as to "which was the best line of conduct to be pursued in the present posture of affairs." After they adjourned for an hour, Lincoln asked the council "whether a further opposition ought to be made under our present circumstances, or terms of Capitulation proposed?" The great majority of officers favored offering terms to the British. Of sixty-one Continental, militia, and naval officers at the council of war, only twelve opposed offering terms of capitulation. The twelve dissenters included Colonel Charles Cotesworth Pinckney, Colonel Barnard Beekman, Lieutenant Colonel William Henderson, Lieutenant Colonel Laurens, and four of the Continental naval officers. These men wished to fight on. It should not be surprising that Pinckney, Beekman, Laurens, and Henderson, as native South Carolinians, wished to defend their capital to the last extremity.[34]

Although most officers agreed that they should offer terms to the British commanders, they did differ as to the nature of those terms. The council finally resolved that only the general officers would draft the proposals to be sent to the British. Brigadier General Duportail declared that they should seek honorable terms. The French officer maintained that they might even avoid giving up the Continental troops, but he was "of a contrary opinion" to the other general officers, who were ready "to propose that the Continental Troops Should be prisoners of War." Duportail argued strongly against this course of action, explaining to the Continental Congress that he "opposed that measure with all [his] might." He asserted that if they were going to surrender the regulars so easily, they might as well "hold out in order to justify Such unfavorable Conditions by a longer resistance and more distressing Situation." But he related that his "representations had not the desired effect." The proposed articles of capitulation would include a provision for the surrender of the Continental troops as prisoners of war.[35]

Lincoln and his officers submitted twelve articles to Sir Henry Clinton. The first article suggested a cessation of hostilities until the two sides agreed to terms. In addition to offering the Continental troops and sailors as prisoners of war (Article Three), Lincoln and his generals put forth that "the town and fortifications shall be surrendered to the commander in chief of the British forces, such as they now stand" (Article Two). The proposed articles also requested that the British permit the militia "to return to their respective homes" (Article Four), that they properly care for the garrison's sick and wounded (Article Five), and that they allow American officers to "keep their horses, swords, pistols, and baggage . . . and retain their servants" (Article Six). In recognition of their stout defense of the city, the American commander petitioned that at the hour of surrender the garrison would "march out with shouldered arms, drums beating, and colors flying, to a place to be agreed on, where they will pile their arms" (Article Seven). In making this request, Lincoln appealed to the British commanders to grant them the honors of war, by which the besieging army acknowledged the tenacity of the defense. Traditionally, when granted the honors of war, the surrendering army filed out of their works as if on parade while their drummers and fifers played a march of their enemy in salute of his comportment during the siege. The capitulating soldiers then proceeded to a designated place to lay down their arms. The final request related to military matters was that the British permit a vessel to carry General Lincoln's dispatches to Philadelphia (Article Twelve).[36]

As to civilian matters, Lincoln conferred with Lieutenant Governor Gadsden and the members of the Privy Council. The civilian officials offered several proposals, the substance of which Lincoln included in the articles. Gadsden and the council asked that the French consul and French or Spanish subjects residing in the town "be protected and untouched" (Articles Eight and Eleven). The French consul was to retire to a place designated by the British commander in chief, while the British were to allow French and Spanish citizens twelve months to leave the state. Regarding the citizens of Charleston, Gadsden and the council first and foremost requested that they "shall be protected in their persons and property" (Article Nine). As to their future treatment, the councilors submitted that "Twelve months time be allowed all such as do not choose to continue under the British government to dispose of their Effects real & personal in the State without any molestation whatever[,] or to remove such part thereof as they choose as well as themselves & Families" (Article Ten). Furthermore, during this twelve month period, the British would permit them to reside by their own choice "in Town or Country." In consulting Gadsden and the Privy Council, Lincoln attempted to assuage the fears of South Carolina leaders who wished to obtain some modicum of security for the people of the lowcountry. Yet by inserting this provision in the articles of capitulation, Lincoln and the South Carolinians were forcing Sir Henry to admit that some citizens would never reconcile themselves to King George. Moreover, he had to give those individuals time—and a year at that—to leave the area. Attempting to subdue a rebellion, Sir Henry was ill-prepared to make such a concession.[37]

Clinton consented outright to four of the articles. As General Duportail expected, he gave no argument to the notion of the Continental troops surrendering as prisoners of war. He also concurred that hostilities cease until they agreed upon or rejected the articles of capitulation, that British surgeons would properly care for the American sick and wounded, and that they would allow clear passage for a vessel to carry Lincoln's dispatches to Philadelphia.[38]

The other articles Clinton was unwilling to accept as drafted. The British general stipulated that the Americans surrender not only the town and fortifications, but also the shipping, artillery, and all public stores. He would permit the militia to return to their homes, but insisted they do so "as prisoners upon parole, which so long as they observe it, shall secure them from being molested in their property by the British troops." As to Lincoln's request that "the citizens shall be protected in their lives and properties," Clinton responded that "all civil officers, & the Citizens, who have borne Arms during the Siege, must be prisoners on parole; and with respect to their property in the City, shall have the same Terms as are granted to the militia." He would consider other persons in Charleston, the French consul, and French and Spanish citizens as prisoners on parole. Clinton also allowed that officers could retain their property, with the exception of their horses, which they had to dispose of before they left the town.[39]

Clinton rejected two articles altogether. With respect to Lincoln's appeal for the honors of war for the garrison, he asserted that when the garrison came forward to deliver up their arms, "the drums are not to beat a British march, or colors be uncased." He did not find the rebel army deserving of such a distinction. As to Lincoln's proposition that citizens be given twelve months to remove themselves and their property from the state, Clinton declared that "the discussion of this Article, of Course, cannot possibly be entered into at present."[40]

Clinton heretofore acted alone in negotiating with Lincoln, Arbuthnot having earlier informed him that he approved of everything Sir Henry did "respecting treaty" with the Americans, but with matters becoming more serious, Arbuthnot came ashore to consult with Clinton. On the morning of 9 May, the two officers sent Lincoln their answer to the proposed articles. The alterations they submitted greatly displeased Lincoln. He contended that articles they did not reject altogether were entirely "mutilated." Maintaining that their defensive works could continue to keep the British at bay, Lincoln adhered to his initial convictions. He was determined to protect the citizens of Charleston and their property.[41]

Lincoln wrote Clinton that the articles as proposed by he and Arbuthnot were "inadmissable," and he sent along his own "Remarks" on their changes. Lincoln insisted that "the Militia now in garrison shall be permitted to return, with their baggage, to their respective homes unmolested, and *not* be considered as Prisoners of War" (emphasis mine). He reiterated that "the Citizens of this Town, and all other Persons now in it, Inhabitants of this state, shall be secured in their persons and properties, both in Town and Country." As with the militia, the citizens were not to be considered as prisoners of war. He also declared that Article Ten stand as first proposed, although he offered that "the Persons who may claim this priviledge therein expressed" (i.e., twelve months time to dispose of their effects and evacuate to another part of the country unmolested) would give their paroles "that they will not act against the British government untill they are exchanged." At the time of surrender, Lincoln agreed that they would give up the town, fortifications, public stores, and shipping at the wharves, but they would not turn over shipping and stores deemed private property. With regard to the honors of war, Lincoln asserted that this article "stand as at first proposed," but he allowed that American drums would not beat a British march. Not only was Lincoln trying to attain extensive concessions for the militia and Charleston's civilians, he also wanted the British to acknowledge that the garrison had staged a heroic defense.[42]

Upon receiving and reviewing Lincoln's remarks late in the afternoon of 9 May, Clinton and Arbuthnot would have no part of them. They responded that only "forbearance and compassion" had induced them "to renew offers of terms you certainly had no claim to," and they declared that "the alterations you propose, are all utterly inadmissable." Hostilities would commence once more at eight o'clock that night, they asserted. The truce had come to an end. For soldiers on the lines, the respite was over.[43]

General Moultrie recounted that after the receipt of Clinton and Arbuthnot's letter, batteries on both sides "remained near an hour silent, all calm and ready, each waiting for the other to begin." Soldiers in the trenches enjoyed their last few minutes of peace. Finally, around nine P.M., portfires and linstocks descended upon the touchholes of American guns and they erupted into the night. One Continental officer remarked that the cannonade "opened with three Cheers" from the American soldiers. Captain Robertson observed that "the Rebels began with huzaaing [*sic*] and a violent Cannonade from every Gun they could fire[,] seemingly at Random as if in a drunken Frensy." British batteries promptly returned fire, and as Lieutenant Colonel Grimké asserted, the two armies engaged in "a most furious cannonade & bombardment which continued throughout the night." Lieutenant Bartholomai of the jaegers affirmed that "the sky was filled with fire and it seemed to us as if the earth shook." The noise from the guns was so great that John Lewis Gervais reported hearing the "prodigious Cannonade" as far away as the Santee River. General Moultrie provided a vivid description of this "tremendous" artillery duel. He related that both sides "threw out an immense number of shells," which appeared as "meteors crossing each other" in the night sky. When shells burst in the air, it seemed to Moultrie "as if the stars were tumbling down." Meanwhile, he professed, cannonballs whizzed past the soldiers in the trenches and batteries, and shells hissed continually among them. Ammunition chests and temporary magazines blew up while wounded men groaned all along the lines. Moultrie resolutely declared that "it was a dreadful night!"[44]

The cannonade, which continued into the following day, caused great carnage on both sides. According to Moultrie, the Americans fired off between 180 and 200 pieces of heavy cannon at the start of the bombardment. Meanwhile, British batteries in the third parallel blazed away at Charleston from a range of one hundred yards or less. Artillery in the first and second parallels also pounded the American defenses. From the outset of the firing on 9 May until the evening of 10 May, British batteries fired 469 rounds of solid shot and 345 shells at the American lines, the single largest total of any twenty-four hour period during the siege. The volume of shot and shells fired must have prompted Dr. Ramsay's remark that this British bombardment "did more execution than had taken place in the same length of time since the commencement of the siege." Gabriel Manigault agreed with General Moultrie that the action "was really dreadful," noting that within the American lines British shots "did great execution." Lieutenant Colonel Grimké related that many embrasures were "much injured" while British fire "rendered useless" two cannon in a battery near the center of the line. Charleston's noncombatants were not spared the distress. British gunners hurled carcasses (incendiary projectiles used to set fire to ships or buildings) into Charleston, and, according to Dr. Ramsay, several houses were burned while "many more were with difficulty saved."[45]

Although the garrison's soldiers and civilians suffered severely in the bombardment, American artillery fire was equally effective against British batteries and works. Captain Peebles described the "great violence" of the cannonade, noting that fire from American batteries killed or wounded twelve to fifteen officers and men. Major Traille of the Royal Artillery related that "a rebel Shot" literally split the muzzle of a British twelve pounder while another shot disabled a six pounder. According to Lieutenant Wilson, British working parties devoted a significant amount of time on 10 May to repairing the third parallel and the embrasures of batteries damaged by American fire. Well within range of rifles and subject to the tremendous firepower of heavy cannon at close range, men occupying the forward trenches now confronted more dangerous conditions than ever.[46]

American defiance presented a conundrum for Clinton. In a letter to Arbuthnot, he asserted that the refusal of offered terms implied "no good tidings" for them. They must either bombard the city into submission or make a general assault on the works. On 10 May, Clinton informed Major Moncrief that "we shall proceed as we began[,] cautiously and by sap." That night, a British working party extended the right section of the third parallel toward the center of the American works. They pushed the trench across the now-drained canal and into the abatis behind it, finally making a lodgment, as Captain Ewald noted, about "thirty paces from the main fortifications." Another working party sapped toward the advanced redoubt on the American left. American gunners and riflemen inflicted "the most terrible fire" on them, but the British were now almost to the very walls of Charleston. From his position on the lines, Lieutenant Colonel Grimké could see that the British had arrived at the abatis and were now within twenty-five yards of the parapet.[47]

Despite the decision to hold out and the vehemence of their cannon fire on 9 and 10 May, the will to resist among many in the garrison was beginning to wane. General Moultrie declared that after the tremendous cannonade "our military ardor was much abated." Soldiers manning the fortifications were near exhaustion, having been subjected to a bombardment of twenty-four hours and returning the favor themselves during that span. Lincoln observed that "the Troops on the line [were] worn down by fatigue having for a number of days been obliged to lay upon the Banquette" (the firing step inside the parapet). By 10 May, many of the militia, some of whom had left their positions during the negotiations of the preceding days, now refused to do their duty entirely. One of the junior Continental officers noted that the "Militia abandon the lines and cannot be prevail'd upon to Join," while Lincoln contended that they had literally "thrown down their Arms." General Duportail insisted that they should bring the militia "to their duty by every possible Means, by acts of authority, and if necessary by exemplary punishments," but again his fellow officers overruled him. They would not force the militia to act. Ironically, the very people that Lincoln tried to protect in his negotiations with the British were now refusing to serve him.[48]

Nor can one argue that the militia were unaware of Lincoln's efforts. Word spread quickly among the garrison as to the reasons why negotiations with the British commanders broke down. Many of the militia and civilians, it seemed, were not so unhappy after all about being considered as prisoners of war on parole. On 10 May, Lincoln received two petitions, one from the Charleston militia signed by 333 militiamen and another from the "Country militia" signed by 236. The petitions outlined their understanding that a dispute between Lincoln and Clinton over the manner in which the militia and citizens were to be classified had caused difficulties in their negotiations. The petitioners declared that "it is an indisputable proposition, that they can derive no advantage from a perseverance in resistance, with every thing that is dear to them at stake." Under these circumstances, they found it "their indispensable duty in this perilous situation of affairs to request your Honour will send out a flag, in the name of the People, intimating their acquiescence in the Terms proposed." Just the day before, Lincoln insisted to Clinton that he would not consent to the treatment of the militia and citizens as prisoners of war on parole; the militia now notified him that such a classification was perfectly acceptable. This was clearly a slap in the face to Lincoln who had done everything he could in the attempt to defend Charleston only to be abandoned by those he tried to protect. Lincoln risked much in seeking more propitious terms for the militia, the lives of the Continentals, the lives of the civilians of Charleston, and his own honor. Yet the militia now alleged that terms previously offered by the British were perfectly agreeable to them. The following day, Lincoln received two more petitions, girded in similar terms and signed by 24 of the Charleston militia and 111 of the country militia. The militia having lost the will to continue, Lincoln could do little but accept the inevitable.[49]

The American commander convened a council of war of the general officers on the morning of 11 May. Before they met, Lincoln received a letter from Lieutenant Governor Gadsden that contained sentiments similar to those invoked in the militia petitions. Gadsden asserted that it was his opinion, as well as that of the Privy Council, that "no time should be lost in renewing the negociation with Sir Henry Clinton on the Subject of Articles of Capitulation." Like the militia, the civilian authorities had lost the will to continue the fight. Even if they had not, further resistance bordered on the absurd. In addition to evaluating the militia petitions and Gadsden's letter, Lincoln and his officers thoroughly considered the state of the Continental troops, the quantity of provisions on hand, the condition of their works, the hopes of reinforcement, and the practicability of a retreat. The results of this examination yielded little hope. As Lincoln related to Washington, the militia had "thrown down their Arms," their provisions were almost exhausted, "many of our Cannon dismounted and others silenced from the want of Shot," and "the Citizens in general [were] discontented." Meanwhile, the Royal Navy blockaded the harbor and "the flower of the British Army" had pressed their approach trenches "within twenty yards of our Lines" in preparation for "a general Assault by Sea and Land." As to escape, Lincoln and his officers repeatedly deliberated upon the prospect of evacuation, and on each occasion a majority of officers found it impracticable. Moreover, little chance existed of a timely reinforcement arriving to relieve them. Under these circumstances, the council of officers advised "that proposals of Capitulation be again made to General Clinton, & the best obtained in our power." Only General Duportail refused to accede to the council's decision, and he expressed his displeasure by failing to sign the record of their proceedings. With or without Duportail's blessing, the garrison was ready to capitulate to the British forces. Charleston was lost.[50]

At two o'clock on the afternoon of 11 May, Captain Ewald and his jaegers, posted in an approach trench, heard the sound of a drum and soon after they spied an American officer on the parapet waving a white flag. Ewald ordered his men to cease firing and the officer came forward carrying a letter from Lincoln to Clinton. After directing a soldier to bring the letter to the British commander in chief, Ewald and the officer sat down in the lodgment and shared a drink of wine while they waited for Sir Henry's reply. Ewald's men had fired the last shots of the siege of Charleston. Silence fell again upon the neck, this time once and for all. Taking advantage of the stillness, many inhabitants of Charleston flocked to the lines to view the conquering army while American officers came forward to converse with British officers.[51]

As for Lincoln's letter, having two days before defied the British commanders, Lincoln now humbly addressed the following to General Clinton:

> The same motives of humanity, which inclined you to propose Articles of Capitulation to this Garrison, induced me to offer those I had the honor of sending you on the 8th instant[.] They then appeared to me such as I might offer, and you receive with honor to both parties[.] Your exception to them, as they principally concerned the militia and Citizens, I then conceived were such as could not be concurred with; but a recent application from those People, wherein they express a willingness to comply with them[,] and a wish on my part to lessen as much as may be the distresses of war to Individuals, lead me now to offer you my acceptance of them.[52]

Clinton, who had offered the garrison of Charleston two opportunities to capitulate, one on 10 April and the other on 8 May, could have rejected Lincoln's overture and demanded any terms he wanted. However tempted he was to treat the surrendering army more harshly, he determined not to do so. Of this decision, Clinton wrote home to Germain that "whatever severe Justice might dictate[,] We resolved not to press to unconditional Submission a reduced army whom we hoped Clemency might yet reconcile to us." Having soundly defeated the rebel army, to humiliate them made little sense if he was going to bring them back as subjects loyal to the King. He opted to grant the same terms he had suggested two days before. Mildly chastising Lincoln, Clinton wrote the American commander "when you rejected the favourable terms which were dictated by an earnest desire to prevent the effusion of blood and interposed Articles that were wholly inadmissible, both the Admiral and myself were of Opinion that the surrender of the Town at Discretion, was the only condition that should afterwards be attended to." In other words, the Americans were eligible for no favorable terms whatsoever. Still, Clinton continued, "as the motives which then induced them are still prevalent, I now inform you that the Terms then offered will still be granted." He informed Lincoln that he would have a copy of the articles sent out for his "ratification." The final articles of capitulation as agreed to by Clinton, Arbuthnot, and Lincoln read essentially as Clinton and Arbuthnot had revised them (see Appendix A). All that remained was for the Americans to formally surrender the town.[53]

During the late morning and early afternoon of 12 May, the junior and non-commissioned officers of all the Continental regiments mustered their men. A strong breeze blew from the eastward, but per the articles of capitulation the regimental colors, which had proudly snapped in the wind at the sites of the respective encampments along the lines, were ordered to be cased. The Continentals formed into ranks, then into column, and prepared to march out of the gate in front of the hornwork. At two o'clock, two companies of grenadiers, one British and one Hessian, took possession of the hornwork and gate. The remainder of the victorious army lined the canal and second parallel to observe the surrender ceremony. At the entrance to Charleston, General Lincoln mounted on his horse and General Moultrie on foot received the British commanders when they came forward.[54]

Once the British grenadiers established themselves in the hornwork, the defeated Americans began marching out. The brigade of artillery led the procession. Next came the South Carolina Continental regiments, followed by the North Carolinians, and then the Virginians. The Marquis de Bretigny's small battalion of French and Spanish volunteers succeeded the Continentals. Regimental drummers beat the very solemn Turk's March as they proceeded, Clinton having denied them the honor of playing a British tune. A detachment of forty British light infantry and Hessian jaegers directed the Americans to the place for laying down their arms and colors, midway between the hornwork and the canal and in between the two lines of abatis.[55] When the defeated soldiers finished piling their arms, the grenadiers in the hornwork hoisted the British flag into the sky above the formerly American fortifications, subsequent to which the Royal Artillery fired a twenty-one gun salute. Immediately thereafter, the British 7th and 63rd regiments paraded into town with colors flying and their musicians filling the air with a triumphant march. Charleston, the capital of South Carolina and the most important city in the southern states, was now officially in the hands of the British.[56]

For the Continentals, their colors cased, their drums beating the somber step, and the victorious enemy arrayed before them, the surrender must have been particularly painful. According to Lieutenant Bartholomai of the jaegers, "chagrin and anger . . . were to be seen in all their faces." The Continentals bore the brunt of the hardships in the defense of the city, but were now defeated. The Virginia brigade and most of the North Carolina troops marched hundreds of miles to reinforce Charleston, while the North and South Carolina Continentals labored in the defensive works literally for months. All regiments had undergone a solid month of British cannonades and rifle fire. The Continentals looked as if they had just withstood a siege of six weeks. The men were dirty, their faces wore the countenance of exhaustion, and their clothing was ragged. According to Ensign Hartung of the Hessians, "the rebels were in the most miserable condition, very few of them wore shoes, and the coats that most of them were wearing were all torn." Captain Ewald agreed that the American soldiers' "apparel was extremely ragged, and on the whole the people looked greatly starved."[57]

Despite their criticism of the rebels' visage, some British officers found their opponents deserving of praise. Captain Peebles maintained that the soldiers of the garrison were a "ragged dirty looking set of People as usual," but he admitted that they exhibited "more appearance of discipline than what we have seen formerly & some of their officers [are] decent looking men." Other officers of the victorious army offered a grudging respect for the American will to resist. Ensign Hartung asserted it "admirable that these people still fight for the chimerical freedom of America with such ardor." It was difficult for British and Hessian officers to understand why they would fight for such a cause.[58]

It was not difficult, however, for these officers to acknowledge the stoutness of the American defense. Ensign Hartung found the fortifications "as fine and as well constructed as they can possibly be." He conjectured that only "the want of provisions" in the garrison allowed them to capture the city under such favorable terms. General Moultrie noted that only 1,500 to 1,600 Continental troops marched out of the garrison, pointing out that a number of sick and wounded remained behind in the hospital.[59] British officers who observed the procession of Continentals asked American officers where the second division was and were astonished to find that there was not one. Impressed by the staunch American resistance with so few regulars, one British officer exclaimed to Moultrie that the garrison "had made a gallant defense."[60]

The British ordered the militia to parade separately from the regulars, and the militiamen lay down their arms "within the Works." British officers were disappointed to find that only 500 militia gave themselves up on the day of the surrender, and they suspected that the rebels were concealing their true strength. An American officer wrote that "the Enemy [are] very much surprised at the smallness of our Numbers." General Leslie, whom Clinton appointed to take command in Charleston, insisted that the militia turn out again on 15 May. He demanded that all the militia parade at Lynch's pasture in Charleston and "bring all their arms with them, guns, swords [and] pistols." According to General Moultrie, Leslie threatened that if they failed to comply he would turn the grenadiers in among them.[61]

In coercing the militia to present themselves, Leslie more than likely caused the British to obtain an incorrect accounting of men under arms in Charleston and thus to overstate the number captured. Moultrie asserted that Leslie's threat "brought out the aged, the timid, the disaffected, and the infirm, many of them who had never appeared during the whole siege." He estimated that forcing these individuals to turn out "swelled the number of militia prisoners to, at least, three times the number of men we ever had upon duty." Moultrie obviously exaggerated somewhat. Still, in a return of prisoners that Clinton sent to Lord George Germain, Clinton showed almost 300 more men in the brigade of North and South Carolina militia under General McIntosh than McIntosh himself reported on his monthly return compiled only a week before the siege ended. Clinton also informed Germain that they had taken "near a thousand sailors," but he provided no more precise accounting of these men. The British tally of Continental prisoners taken is fairly consistent with brigade returns logged by American officers in the days before the siege ended. Officially, Clinton reported to Germain that he captured "exclusive of near a thousand Sailors in arms . . . 5,618 Men," but the actual number that Lincoln had under arms at any one time was closer to 6,000.[62]

Whereas Clinton could include as captured all men in the garrison, during the siege Lincoln could only count on those who were capable of performing duty. Of the Continentals and militia in the garrison, a large proportion were either sick or wounded or lacked proper clothing and arms, and as such were unfit for duty. For instance, Lincoln's effective strength at the end of April was probably at most only 4,000 men under arms.[63]

In addition to the men captured, the soldiers of the garrison suffered 89 killed, most of whom were Continental troops; 138 men had been wounded. These figures to be sure do not include American casualties suffered at Biggin's Bridge and Lenud's Ferry. The civilian populace shared in the horrors of war throughout British operations in the lowcountry, and they certainly did so during the siege of the city, where British fire killed approximately twenty civilians. Altogether, the campaign against Charleston took the lives of some 150 Americans. Official returns for the British army showed 76 men killed and 189 wounded, while losses among the navy were 23 killed and 28 wounded, for a total of 99 killed and 217 wounded among British forces. It was a relatively small price to pay for their victory.[64] Not only had they captured the largest and most important city in the southern states, but they had taken an entire army as well. They also took possession of 400 pieces of cannon, over 5,000 muskets, and large quantities of ammunition. Meanwhile, the Royal Navy commandeered three Continental warships, *Providence, Boston,* and *Ranger,* and the South Carolina navy's *L'Aventure,* plus assorted smaller vessels. The Continental navy could ill afford the loss of three frigates while the South Carolina state navy came near to going completely out of existence.[65]

By all accounts, losses sustained in the fall of Charleston were disastrous for the American cause, not only in the south but throughout all the states. Most costly was the loss of 3,465 officers and enlisted men of the Continental regiments, which all but eliminated the Continental lines of three states, Virginia, North Carolina, and South Carolina.[66] These disciplined veterans would not be easily replaced. As the war dragged on, states found it harder to recruit men for their Continental regiments, and any new men they obtained lacked the experience and training of those lost to the enemy. In April, while the siege raged in Charleston, Washington detached two Maryland brigades to the south. With Lincoln's Continentals captives of the British, these men would provide the nucleus for a new army in the Southern Department.

Clinton hoped to exchange the Continental prisoners taken at Charleston for British troops of Burgoyne's army still being held by the Americans in Virginia. Unfortunately, over a year passed before the two sides arranged a general exchange of enlisted men. In the meantime, the British ordered the prisoners confined first in the barracks in Charleston and later onboard prison ships in the harbor, where many died in the filthy and unhealthy holds. British officers induced many others to join the King's army. Whether dying onboard a prison ship or joining the British army to avoid such a fate, the story of the Continental soldiers who fought so bravely to defend Charleston was the last tragic episode in the fall of the city. Of 2,700 enlisted men who surrendered on 12 May, General Moultrie noted that only about 1,400 remained available for exchange at the beginning of 1781. The young men who hailed from Virginia, North Carolina, and South Carolina, many of whom would never see their homes again, truly sacrificed themselves for the common good.[67]

Upon reaching Philadelphia in June, Benjamin Lincoln requested that Congress convene a formal court of inquiry into his conduct in the defense of Charleston. Members of Congress arranged for the court of inquiry, but more pressing business ultimately engaged their attention and they never summoned it. In the wake of the loss of Charleston, most delegates still held a positive opinion of Lincoln, and many defended him for his management of affairs in the Southern Department. Washington also continued to hold his subordinate in high esteem. His only criticism of operations during the siege was that the Bar was not defended as it should have been, a circumstance that Lincoln had been unable to control. In October 1780, Lincoln was exchanged for British Generals Phillips and Riedesel and thereafter returned to active duty in Washington's army.[68]

The reaction of prominent South Carolinians to Lincoln's conduct in attempting to defend their capital was mixed. David Ramsay later asserted that "much censure was undeservedly cast on General Lincoln for risking his army within the lines." Ramsay himself told Lincoln that "Carolina" owed him "much" and assured him that "it was greatly meritorious" that he was able "to keep things together" as long as he had. Governor Rutledge was among Lincoln's detractors. Rutledge wrote the South Carolina delegates in Congress an angry letter over the denouement of the campaign, asserting that "the Terms of the Capitulation are truly mortifying." He requested that the delegates send him a copy of the articles and complained that Lincoln "did not, it seems, think it at all material to inform me of it." In addition, he demanded to know why Lincoln "did not evacuate the Town, & save his Troops." Rutledge's denunciations of Lincoln may not have been so strong had he been present at the councils of war in which his fellow South Carolinians had argued so strenuously against an evacuation.[69]

Still, Rutledge's commentary begs the historian to also make inquiry into Lincoln's conduct and decision-making in the British campaign against Charleston. How much responsibility should Lincoln bear for the loss of Charleston and the loss of his army? Certainly it is easier for the historian to address this question than it was for Benjamin Lincoln to make the daily decisions that affected the outcome of the campaign. Historians began to debate this issue soon after the Revolution ended. Their assessments of Lincoln's generalship range from "great praise" due to him to "injudicious" decision-making to "indecisive and weak" to "cautious and indecisive."[70]

Historians tend to agree in two respects on Lincoln's handling of the campaign: that he yielded to civilian authorities against his better judgment in deciding to defend Charleston, and that he did not evacuate his army before the British fully invested the city. In a letter he wrote Washington in July 1780, Lincoln tried to explain to the commander in chief the reasons for his actions during the campaign. He asserted that although he had not received "an express order" from the Continental Congress to hold Charleston, the proceedings of that body conveyed their intention that he do so. In 1776, they "recommended that a vigorous defense [of Charleston] should be made," and in 1779 when it was feared the British would threaten the city again they dispatched an engineer, Lieutenant Colonel Cambray, to South Carolina "for the express purpose of fortifying the Town." Moreover, in November 1779 they sent three Continental frigates to Charleston to protect the harbor. Yet Lincoln was uncomfortable with the prospect of bottling up his army within the confines of the city. In February, with the British army advancing toward him, he declared to Governor Rutledge that he found himself "in a peculiar and very critical situation from the novelty of having Contin[enta]l troops shut up in a besieged Town." Going against his strategic sense, Lincoln remained in Charleston because he believed Congress wanted him to. Washington himself was familiar with his subordinate's dilemma. The desires of the Continental Congress and the New York Provincial Congress greatly influenced his decision to hold New York City in the summer and fall of 1776. The ensuing campaign was a disaster for Washington and the fledgling American army.[71]

While the desires of Congress were Lincoln's principal public justification for holding the city, other factors also influenced him. Lincoln understood that the success of the Revolution depended upon the support of the people. Stung by criticism of his decision to leave Charleston essentially unguarded in the spring campaign of 1779, Lincoln was wary of abandoning the South Carolina capital again. In his letter to Washington, Lincoln argued that previous to the defeat of the American cavalry at Biggin's Bridge his army could not "have retreated with honor." Later in the letter, he reiterated that the city could not, "with propriety, have been abandoned" prior to that event. These phrases suggest that Lincoln conducted operations with the views of the people in mind. He was obviously concerned with calming the fears of the civilian populace of South Carolina and securing their loyalties. In abandoning their capital, he risked losing their faith in him as a commander and their support for the cause of independence.[72]

Although Gadsden and members of the Privy Council pressured Lincoln to remain in Charleston, other South Carolina leaders urged withdrawal. In the course of the siege, Henry Laurens wrote Lincoln:

"I pray God to give you victory or open a door for an honorable retreat." If they could not save the city, Laurens was all in favor of saving the army. Governor Rutledge was obviously disappointed that Lincoln did not evacuate the army, but it is unclear at what point Rutledge decided that they should withdraw. Unfortunately, there is little extant correspondence between Lincoln and Rutledge that gives an indication that the governor wished Lincoln to evacuate. The final decision to stay, however, rested with Lincoln. Based on the views of Congress, the wishes of many South Carolinians, and his own principles, Lincoln determined to hold Charleston.[73]

Surrounded by two major rivers, mud flats, and marsh, and with a treacherous sand bar running in front of its harbor, Charleston was certainly strategically defensible with the appropriate resources and proper utilization being made of them. In the Civil War, the Confederate army withstood a siege of two-and-a-half years against what seemed like overwhelming Union forces. Lincoln, however, was not adequately supported. He had only enough troops to hold Charleston itself, and he could not attack the British west of the Ashley or fortify positions east of the Cooper as he had hoped. Washington and the Continental Congress dispatched all the troops that they could. South Carolina could have provided greater assistance. Low turnout from the backcountry militia because of fears of a smallpox outbreak in Charleston and a perceived need to defend their home districts limited Lincoln's operational opportunities. Meanwhile, the South Carolina Assembly's refusal to arm African Americans deprived him of a readily available body of men. Henry Laurens lamented that "Thousands of Muskets" lay "useless in Charles Town which might have been shouldered in our defence."[74]

Still, additional troops may not have offset some of the decisions and actions of Lincoln's subordinates. The critical point was the defense of the Bar and harbor. The burden of responsibility must fall here on Lincoln's naval commander. Had a more enterprising and daring naval officer than Commodore Abraham Whipple managed the operation, American ships may very well have kept the Royal Navy from the harbor. Given Arbuthnot's later reluctance to push ships into the Cooper River, it seems unlikely that he would have persisted in his efforts to cross the Bar had he encountered stiff resistance in trying to get over it. Without strict land and naval cooperation, the British attempt on the city must have failed. As such, Whipple and his captains fell back first from the Bar, then from Fort Moultrie, then into the Cooper River, where they were effectively useless in the defense of Charleston. With the Royal Navy inside the harbor and the British army besieging the town from the landside, Charleston indeed became a very difficult place to defend. Without reinforcements and with supplies failing, it became near impossible.

Lincoln had little choice in the selection of Whipple as his chief naval officer, the Continental Congress having appointed him to the command. The same cannot be said for some of Lincoln's other subordinates whom he assigned critical responsibilities and whose performance was equally as disappointing as Whipple's. The errors of two officers in particular, Brigadier General Isaac Huger and Colonel François Malmedy, contributed greatly to the loss of the open communication east of the Cooper River. As he relied on the naval forces to defend the Bar, Lincoln depended on Huger and the cavalry to prevent the British from making inroads east of the river. Since superiority in the cavalry arm was one of the few advantages that Lincoln possessed over Clinton, the preservation of that force was crucial to keeping the British army from detaching bodies of troops across the Cooper. While much credit must be given to Lieutenant Colonels Webster and Tarleton for planning and executing the audacious attack against the Americans at Biggin's Bridge, General Huger and his own subordinates, Lieutenant Colonel William Washington, Major Paul Vernier, and Major John Jameson, should have been on their guard against such a maneuver. The resulting disaster not only gained the British a superiority in cavalry, but also provided them an open door to the country east of the Cooper. As for Malmedy, his absurd evacuation of the post at Lampriers Point yielded up to the enemy the Americans' last significant fortified position on that side of the river, thus cementing the British hold on the region. With the fall of Lampriers, the army could not get out nor could they be reinforced or resupplied.

Lincoln's decision to hold Charleston was an honorable one, but the execution of it at its most critical point, securing the Bar, had been flawed. Once the British brought overwhelming force against Charleston, further lapses by other officers precluded the Americans from holding out longer. In summing up the operations of the siege, Lieutenant Colonel Laurens exclaimed that "besides the force of the Enemy without, we had to struggle at home against incapacity in some very important persons." His father concurred, asserting that "we shall all agree that some Men deserve to be hanged for Rascality & others merit the severest censure for inattention." The elder and younger Laurens could clearly see that Lincoln's subordinates hampered his efforts to defend the city and preserve his army. In the end, however, the loss of an army is placed upon the commander of that army, and in spite of the failures of some his subordinates, Major General Benjamin Lincoln bore the burden of the loss of Charleston upon his own shoulders.[75]

Chapter Fourteen

Appearances in This Province Are Certainly Very Favourable

News of Charleston's fall reached Philadelphia by the end of May and incited great alarm among the patriots. The capture of Charleston and of Lincoln's entire army provided the British a geographical and psychological springboard from which to launch an offensive against the Carolinas and possibly even Virginia. British commanders hoped, and rebellious Americans feared, that the victory would embolden southern loyalists and enable the British to use them to assist in the subjugation of the rebellion. Sir Henry Clinton, Lord Cornwallis, and the ministry would soon find out whether the south was truly dominated by a preponderance of loyalists who were simply waiting for a conquering British army to help them overthrow the rebels.

In the days immediately following Charleston's surrender, the captured city bustled with activity as the British employed themselves in securing the prisoners, stores, and shipping that they had taken. Officers compiled returns of prisoners while commissaries sought ways in which to feed them; quartermasters collected and inventoried weapons and stores, and naval officers prepared captured vessels for sea.[1] As for the prisoners, the British ordered the enlisted men of the Continental regiments to the barracks in Charleston while their officers went over to Haddrell's Point. Upon hearing of this disposition, Governor Rutledge suspected that the British did it so that their recruiting sergeants could convince the Continentals to "enter into the British Service, which some have done already, & many with[ou]t doubt will." By 20 May, most of the militia had given their paroles and had begun returning to their homes as agreed upon in the articles of capitulation. Captain Ewald, ever vigilant, conjectured that the British chose to parole the militia only to avoid feeding them. "This economy will cost the English dear," he wrote, "because I am convinced that most of these people will have guns in their hands again within a short time."[2]

Sir Henry Clinton would not have agreed. He too was busy in the days following the surrender compiling his official report on the capture of the city to Lord George Germain and writing to friends of his success. Clinton was glowingly optimistic about British prospects for restoring royal government to South Carolina and, more than likely, North Carolina as well. In a letter to his cousin, the Duke of Newcastle, Clinton declared: "I hope I am not too Sanguine when I say that both the Carolinas are conquered in Charles Town." He repeated this comment to General William Phillips, adding only that they should have made the attempt against South Carolina three years earlier. Clinton's optimism concerning the subjugation of the Carolinas grew in the weeks following the surrender as multitudes came in to the British forces at Charleston to declare their peaceful intentions.[3]

Before the siege concluded, Clinton began to explore the sentiment of the people of South Carolina, and he assigned James Simpson, a former crown official, the task of determining "the present disposition" of lowcountry inhabitants and the prospects of gaining "their concurrence in establishing the King's authority." In undertaking this mission, Simpson "conversed with some of the people of the first families in the province." He classified these affluent and influential South Carolinians into four distinct categories. The first consisted of those who recognized their "Error" in following along in rebellion against their King and who were ready "to head back [on] the Path by which they have been lead to their destruction." The next category included men who had kept up "the Flames of Rebellion," but who now realized that "their inevitable Ruin will ensue unless [Royal] government[,] which they all acknowledge was preferable to any they can ever hope to establish[,] is restored." Still another category comprised those who believed that "their cause was founded in Virtue," but now conceded that it was "impossible to maintain it any longer." Simpson found that men in these three categories were ready to return to their allegiance, but the fourth category consisted of individuals who asserted that the cause "ought never to be relinquished but by the general Consent of

America." Simpson noted that inhabitants who saw the error in their ways far exceeded those who viewed their cause a virtuous one and those who refused to relinquish it. He ascertained this only from conjecture, however, as he admitted to Clinton: "I have thought it proper to avoid a conversation or Encounter" with persons in the latter two categories. Simpson asserted that those willing to return to their allegiance far exceeded the number that did not wish to, yet he had not even approached the rebellious. By its nature, his assessment was skewed toward a sentiment of loyalism among South Carolinians. Simpson reported back to Clinton on 15 May and he confessed that "the shortness of the Time" of his mission and "the present Agitation" rendered his report "as circumstantial."[4]

Still, the experience of the ensuing weeks seemed to give weight to Simpson's suppositions. In the aftermath of the capitulation, men streamed into Charleston from the lowcountry and beyond to pledge allegiance to the British government or to take up arms with British troops. In Charleston itself, 200 citizens presented an address to Clinton and Arbuthnot congratulating them on their victory. At the beginning of June, Clinton gleefully reported to Germain that hundreds of South Carolinians were coming in to accept the King's protection. He asserted to his chief "that the Inhabitants from every Quarter repair to the Detachments of the Army and to this Garrison to declare their allegiance to the King and to offer their Services in Arms in Support of his government." On 25 May, Clinton noted that over "1,500 have already been here with their arms, desiring to join us." He was especially encouraged that wealthy and influential South Carolinians were proclaiming their allegiance. To William Eden, he asserted that all the men of property in South Carolina, with the exception of inveterate rebels such as John Rutledge, "have most heartily joined us with their arms." Clinton discovered surprisingly that these men openly admitted to "have been always in arms against us." He noted that since they now discerned that "the Congress can no longer protect them, they most cheerfully . . . submit." As for the common people of South Carolina, they would, as Simpson supposed, "submit quietly to the government that supports itself." The acquiescence of the commoners would make conquest of the province that much easier.[5]

The manner in which the British applied overwhelming force to subdue Charleston awed many into accepting their protection. Men such as Archibald Brown "believed that the Country was irrecoverably lost." Others accepted protection out of sheer necessity. Rawlins Lowndes, who served a term as South Carolina's governor between Rutledge's two terms, was apparently one of these men. During the month of May, British soldiers attempted to plunder his Goose Creek plantation on at least two occasions. Lowndes, confined in Charleston, complained to James Simpson of "the outrageous & indecent behaviour offered to my Wife and Family" by two soldiers on one of these raids. He lamented that the men took away one of their slaves, a mulatto girl who was a favorite of the family, and "carried off . . . all the poultry my Family had to subsist on." Meanwhile, he cried, Colonel John Simcoe and his men seized "every horse I owned in the World." "Consider one moment Sir," Lowndes continued, "the feelings of a man in this Condition, used hitherto to all the Comforts and Conveniences of Life, and now divested, in the most necessary Exigency even of the use of a Horse." For men like Rawlins Lowndes, who were being stripped of all their worldly possessions and life as they had known it, there was little left to do but submit to the British.[6]

Nor was Lowndes the only prominent South Carolinian to take the oath of allegiance. So many did that Clinton remarked to his friend William Eden that "all the rebel grandees are come in." The list included some of the most important civilian and military officials. Among the former were Charles Pinckney, previously member of the Privy Council and cousin to Charles Cotesworth and Thomas Pinckney, as well as Henry Middleton, who earlier served as president of the Continental Congress. The latter included Maurice Simons, commandant of the Charleston militia during the siege, and Daniel Horry, one of Lincoln's principal cavalry commanders. While the actions of these men, like the captured Continental soldiers who enlisted in the British service, might seem traitorous, one must examine the extreme circumstances that men like Rawlins Lowndes were subjected to before making such a judgment. As George Smith McCowen has pointed out, "desperation, fear, and weakness of human nature . . . underlay the seemingly calculated duplicity of those who changed their allegiance during the confusing days of the occupation."[7]

To inspire others to return to their allegiance, Clinton distributed a number of handbills and proclamations among the people in the wake of Charleston's surrender. He directed one of them, dated 22 May, to those "wicked and desperate Men" who were "still endeavoring to support the Flame of Rebellion" and who wished to obstruct others from seeking British protection. In the broadside, he warned that any person who attempted "to prevent the Establishment of his Majesty's Government" or who hindered or intimidated "the King's faithful and loyal Subjects, from joining his Forces, or otherwise performing those Duties their Allegiance requires; such Person or Persons so offending, shall be treated with that Severity, so hardened and criminal an Obstinacy will deserve, and his or their Estates, will be immediately seized, in order to be confiscated." Clinton assured "the King's faithful and peaceable Subjects" that British forces would support and protect them in the meantime. In another proclamation issued on 1 June by Clinton and Arbuthnot jointly, the British commanders declared that those who had rebelled would "still be received with Mercy and forgiveness, if they immediately return to their allegiance." To mollify loyalists, the officers excepted from this clemency "those who are polluted with the Blood of their Fellow Citizens, most wantonly and inhumanly shed under the mock forms of Justice, because they [the loyalists] refused submission to an usurpation which they abhorred, and would not oppose that Government with which they deemed themselves inseparably connected." They again pledged that "His Majesty's faithful and well affected Subjects . . . shall have effectual Countenance, Protection and Support" and that the "Province" would "soon be reinstated in its former prosperity[,] security and Peace."[8]

By the end of May, Clinton expressed little concern that wayward individuals would interfere with those who wished to come in to them. He asserted to Lord Cornwallis that "all the country in general, from Peedee to Savannah . . . have either come themselves or sent to accept the offers" of protection. Their acceptance of protection meant that they also agreed to take up arms. Clinton informed William Eden that inhabitants in that same Peedee to Savannah region were all "in arms to support His Majesty's government." Meanwhile, he affirmed to William Phillips that with the exception of "a few scattering militia" at Camden, there was not "a man in arms against us." He had even received a report that "friends" in North Carolina were gathering to support them.[9]

The British commander and his officers had every reason to be optimistic about the future course of operations in South Carolina. "From every Information I receive, & the Numbers of the most violent Rebels hourly coming in to offer their Services," Clinton asserted to Cornwallis, "I have the strongest Reason to believe the general Disposition of the People to be not only friendly to Government, but forward to take up Arms in its Support." The presupposition that the southern provinces were dominated by loyalists had induced them to shift their strategic focus to the south and the hypothesis seemed now to be holding true. The arrival of numbers of South Carolinians seeking to renew their allegiance to Great Britain convinced Clinton, Cornwallis, and their subordinates that southerners, by and large, were loyal to the King, or could be easily persuaded to return their loyalties to His Majesty. Moreover, British officers could arm these individuals and use them to maintain order in South Carolina. The British needed only to strengthen and extend their presence in South Carolina to completely subjugate the province. As Clinton later maintained, in the wake of Charleston's capture "nothing appeared to be wanting toward the entire suppression of rebellion but [. . .] occupying a few strong posts in the upper country, and [. . .] putting arms into the hands of the King's friends for their defense against the straggling parties of rebels who might be still lurking amongst them." Southern loyalists were now to maintain the fruits of the victory at Charleston.[10]

With the exception of provincial regiments serving with the British army, loyalists were notably absent in Clinton's operations against Charleston. There were a few minor exceptions. Lieutenant Colonel Nisbet Balfour commended Mr. Fraser of Strawberry Ferry, Elias Nicoll, and Theodore Galliard for being "extremely useful to the King's Service." For the most part, however, loyalists played a limited role in the capture of the city. Clinton explained to Germain that he had not called upon loyalists to come forward "until the Operations of the Siege were well advanced, least any unexpected Reverse . . . might expose the King's Friends to the Resentment of the Rebels." In a circular, Clinton reassured "the Loyal Inhabitants" that during the course of operations against Charleston he "avoided as much as possible every Measure" that might induce them "to rise in Favour of Government, and thus bring Danger and Trouble upon themselves" before his forces could support them.[11] Now that the British army was entrenched in South Carolina, he was ready to invite their assistance.[12]

The first step in that process was to organize a "loyal" militia. In a broadside, Clinton declared that "the Time is come, when it is equally the Interest and Duty of every good Man to be in Readiness to join the King's Troops, and assist them in establishing Justice and Liberty, and in restoring and securing their own Property." Those with families, Clinton announced, could "form a Militia to remain at Home," which would assemble only occasionally in their own district when exigency required. "Those who have no Families," the proclamation read, "it is hoped will chearfully assist his Majesty's Troops in driving their Rebel Oppressors and all the Miseries of War far from the Province." The men were to serve with the militia "for any six Months of the ensuing twelve" and were to receive pay, ammunition, and provisions in the same manner as British regulars. In addition, Clinton promised that their commanders would not march them beyond North Carolina or Georgia. Given the numbers that came in to the British by the end of May, many loyalists seem to have heeded his call.[13]

Clinton appointed a capable officer, the fiery Scot Major Patrick Ferguson, as Inspector of Militia for Georgia and the Carolinas to oversee the organization and formation of the militia. Clinton also took steps to ensure their allegiance. He insisted that known "loyal officers" lead individual militia battalions. Meanwhile, he was at first reluctant to allow Charlestonians, whom he had just taken several months to subdue, to participate in the militia. Once organized, the loyalist militia would march into the interior of the country with British regulars to complete the conquest of South Carolina.[14]

Despite their previous differences, Clinton and Cornwallis were substantially in agreement with regard to the importance of subjugating the South Carolina backcountry. Cornwallis wrote Clinton on 18 May that the presence of a British force in that region was "of the most important nature," and he contended that "without some success in the Back Country, our success at Charlestown would but little promote the real interests of Great Britain." On 15 May, just three days after the surrender, Cornwallis marched a detachment inland, as Clinton related to William Eden, "to meet, arm, and protect our friends there." Clinton concurred unequivocally with Cornwallis's assertions concerning the rest of South Carolina. On 20 May, he replied that the "advantageous manner" in which they had taken Charleston ensured the reduction of South Carolina as well as North Carolina "if the temper of our friends in those districts [i.e. the backcountry] is such as it has always been represented to us." Reports from lowcountry South Carolinians about the temper of inhabitants in the backcountry districts surely encouraged Clinton. He informed William Eden that "the rebel grandees" professed "their dread of the back-country people" who they claimed were all eager to join the British forces. Information such as this fueled Sir Henry's optimism on the eve of the next phase of operations in South Carolina.[15]

Ironically, after overseeing the victory at Charleston, Clinton was departing South Carolina and returning to New York. He appointed Lord Cornwallis to take command of all British forces in the southern provinces, leaving him with a substantial number of battle-hardened soldiers. Cornwallis's troops included six British regiments, three Hessian regiments, and six provincial regiments of loyalists, totaling 6,369 rank and file.[16] The two British generals anticipated that numerous loyalist militia would further augment their strength. Clinton asserted that he was leaving Cornwallis in South Carolina "in sufficient force to keep it against the world." Meanwhile, Cornwallis dutifully informed him that "you may depend on my utmost attention & exertions to draw the most usefull consequences from the great and important success of his Majesty's Arms in this Province." The conquest of the remainder of South Carolina was set to begin.[17]

British troops had already spread out across the rebellious province. Cornwallis marched with a detachment up the Santee River toward Camden while Lieutenant Colonel Balfour moved with another corps toward Ninety Six. Still another column advanced up the north side of the Savannah River. Cornwallis's objective was the last organized rebel resistance in South Carolina, consisting of Colonel Abraham Buford's battalion of Virginia Continentals, the remains of the cavalry, and a few militia. After Charleston capitulated, Buford retreated toward North Carolina. Tarleton and the Legion caught up with him on 29 May at the Waxhaws, near the North Carolina-South Carolina border. Buford formed his line well, but his infantry held their fire until Tarleton's cavalry were nearly upon them and the British horsemen overwhelmed the Americans. The defeat soon turned into a massacre, as British cavalrymen cut down many American soldiers when they attempted to surrender. Even Tarleton admitted that the soldiers were "stimulated . . . to a vindictive asperity not easily restrained." The Americans lost 113 men killed and 203 wounded or captured, while the British suffered only 4 killed and 13 wounded. Tarleton reported that 150 of the enemy were so badly wounded that they could not move them and so had to leave them behind on parole, demonstrating the viciousness with which British dragoons hacked away at their opponent. The British victory at the Waxhaws solidified Tarleton's reputation as a brutal and ruthless cavalry commander among southern patriots. More significantly, it destroyed the last organized American military force in South Carolina.[18]

On the heels of Tarleton's victory, Cornwallis wrote Clinton "appearances in this province are certainly very favourable & the important success of L[ieutenan]t Col[onel] Tarleton at this critical juncture will be of the greatest service." Matters certainly did appear favorable on the eve of Sir Henry's departure from South Carolina. His Majesty's forces, with acceptable casualties, captured the largest and most important city in the southern colonies, thousands of South Carolinians were taking the oath of allegiance and flocking to the King's standard, British troops had all but eliminated organized resistance in South Carolina, and they were now successfully establishing themselves across the province.[19]

By 8 June, Clinton and Arbuthnot were ready to sail. Before departing, Clinton had one final proclamation to issue. This proclamation, dated 3 June, may have been one too many for Sir Henry, however. In it, Clinton demanded that all South Carolinians assist in the cause of their King and he insisted that no one remain neutral. He asserted that "it is fit and proper that all persons should take an active part in Settling and Securing his Majesty's government and delivering the

Country from that anarchy which for some time past hath prevailed." In consequence, he excused all prisoners on parole, who had not participated in the defense of Charleston, from their parole as of 20 June. This group included men who turned themselves in to the British but who did not take the oath of allegiance. Clinton now expected them to actively assist in subduing the rebellion. He closed the broadside by declaring that those "who shall afterwards neglect to return to their allegiance and to His Majesty's government will be considered as Enemies and Rebels to the same and treated accordingly." In putting forth this pronouncement, Clinton allowed no one to sit on the fence. In Sir Henry's view, failing to pledge one's loyalty was tantamount to a state of rebellion. After taking steps to organize a loyal militia, he wanted to ensure that there would be men to fill those militia battalions.[20]

Clinton erred seriously in issuing this proclamation.[21] Charles Stedman, a loyalist officer, complained that the act "blended indiscriminately together" the "inhabitants who were really loyal, and those who were nominally so." Stedman claimed that "loyalists murmured because notorious rebels, by taking the oath of allegiance, and putting on a shew of attachment, became entitled to the same privileges with themselves." Meanwhile, prisoners of war on parole who were "enjoying a kind of neutrality" believed the proclamation "abrogated the paroles that had been granted, and, in one instant, converted them either into loyal subjects or rebels." As John Pancake has pointed out, the proclamation certainly induced many to take the oath of allegiance to the King, but it also pushed others, who had been content to remain on their farms and wait out the end of the war, back into rebellion. Clinton patently recognized that many rebels who had come in were reluctant to take up arms against their countrymen. He noted to Cornwallis that they "have some scruples about carrying arms against the Congress." It was one thing to peacefully submit to the British forces, but to actively assist them in running down their former comrades was quite another. Clinton was forcing them to make just such a choice. Strategically, the proclamation turned out to be a poor decision on Sir Henry's part.[22]

Since the proclamation would not go into effect until 20 June, Clinton would not be present to observe its effects personally. As his ship pulled away from the city, the conquest of which represented his greatest personal accomplishment and the largest British victory of the war, then moved past Fort Moultrie where the British forces had been humiliated in 1776 but which was now in their possession, and down along the mighty Bar that was slated to be such a deterrent to the Royal Navy, Clinton could only feel confident that the success at Charleston might well lead to the complete subjugation of the south. A few days before he sailed, he wrote Germain: "I may venture to assert that there are few men in South Carolina who are not either our Prisoners or in Arms with us." Cornwallis and the other British officers and soldiers who remained in South Carolina would discover very soon just how wrong Sir Henry had been.[23]

Just five weeks after Sir Henry Clinton's departure, a party of rebels under Colonel William Bratton routed a detachment of loyalists under Captain Christian Huck at Williamson's plantation in northwestern South Carolina, killing Huck and thirty-five of his men. Meanwhile, other bodies of patriots were forming under such commanders as Elijah Clarke, Thomas Sumter, and Francis Marion, whose injured ankle was now healed and he ready to take the field. Operating in small parties of fifty or less or at other times with several hundred men, these partisan leaders continually harassed British outposts or attacked vulnerable detachments of British regulars and loyalist militia along their routes of march.[24]

Not even the overwhelming defeat of a second American army in August could keep rebellious South Carolinians from the field. The Continental Congress appointed the hero of Saratoga, Major General Horatio Gates, to replace Lincoln as commander of the Southern Department. Gates marched his army, consisting of the two Maryland brigades sent by Washington, a brigade of Virginia militia, and a brigade of North Carolina militia into South Carolina, and attempted to threaten the British post at Camden. On 16 August at Camden Cornwallis's army completely shattered Gates's army. British troops easily forced the American militia from the field and inflicted severe casualties on the Continentals. With the loss of over 1,000 men killed, wounded, and captured, Camden was the worst battlefield defeat of the war for the Americans.

Occurring just three months after the fall of Charleston, it stood to reason that the disaster at Camden would have broken the back of the rebellion in the south, but as the British soon discovered, inhabitants throughout the backcountry of South Carolina and Georgia vociferously resisted them. Cornwallis's second in command, Lord Francis Rawdon, reported to Clinton that the appearance of Gates's army in South Carolina "unveiled to us a fund of Disaffection in this Province of which we could have formed no Idea[,] And even the dispersion of that Force [at Camden] did not extinguish the Ferment which the hope of its support had raised."[25]

After the victory at Camden Cornwallis planned a move into North Carolina. He hoped that this measure would "prevent Insurrections" on the frontier of South Carolina which he noted "is very disaffected." Cornwallis ultimately postponed the operation against North Carolina due, as he informed Clinton, to "the great sickness of the Army, the intense Heat, and the necessity of totally subduing the Rebel Country between the Santee and Pedee." The British were able to make little headway against the incursions of Francis Marion in that region. By the end of October, Lord Rawdon was still reporting that "the Majority of the Inhabitants of that Tract between the Pedee and the Santee are in Arms against us." Meanwhile, on 19 September Colonel John Harris Cruger, posted at Augusta with his New York Volunteers, informed Cornwallis that he had put down a "most dangerous and daring insurrection" led by Elijah Clarke. Cruger concluded that if it had succeeded "the Inhabitants of the Country on both sides [of] the [Savannah] River[,] being yet amazingly disaffected[,] would have been in Arms and like a Torrent bore down [on] the friends of Government." Cruger was well aware that rebellious elements of the populace were out there and ready to embody at a moment's notice, hanging like a sword of Damocles over those who declared allegiance to the King.[26]

While the rebels of South Carolina and Georgia resisted, the loyalists failed to materialize in sufficient numbers or with sufficient determination to be of much assistance to the British. In August, Cornwallis complained that the "Experience" of Major Patrick Ferguson and other officers in attempting to raise loyalists had been "totally against" them. Loyalists that did organize and arm in South Carolina disappointed Cornwallis. "I have found the Militia fail so totally when put to the Trial in this Province," he later noted to Clinton. A segment of the population in South Carolina was to be sure loyal to Britain, as the brutal civil war that was emerging in the state would prove, but loyalists did not exist in the numbers that the British command anticipated. Even James Simpson acknowledged in his report to Clinton "the Loyalists . . . are not so numerous as I expected."[27]

How had British commanders made such an egregious miscalculation of loyalty to the Crown of the people of South Carolina? While many South Carolinians accepted the King's peace in the wake of the fall of Charleston, Clinton was under the impression that their sentiments represented the general sentiment of inhabitants throughout the province. As he asserted to Cornwallis: "I have the strongest Reason to believe the general Disposition of the People to be not only friendly to [Royal] Government, but forward to take up Arms in its support." Why did Clinton make such an assessment? This question can be best addressed by examining those who did come in to the British lines in the weeks following the surrender. Loyalists would obviously have been the first to seek British protection, and they alone swelled the numbers coming in. They had suffered patiently and quietly under the rebel government and were now eager to welcome their liberators. Thomas Harvy and Moses Eastan of Four Holes on the upper Edisto typified the long-suffering loyalists. In mid-March they wrote Clinton of "the Distresses" of the inhabitants of South Carolina who were "willing and Ready to Ade and assist" the British. In Clinton's mind, the presence in South Carolina of a multitude of these tormented "friends" of the King was confirmed in the weeks after the surrender as hundreds streamed into Charleston.[28]

Clinton also maintained that many rebels sought British protection. These men were primarily from the lowcountry however, which also skewed his estimate of the numbers in South Carolina willing to accept Royal government. Clinton had heard that backcountry inhabitants were predominantly loyal, but he had no hard evidence to support those reports. Here, the rumors of the smallpox outbreak in Charleston, which had deterred so many South Carolina militiamen from flying to Lincoln's army, were ironically providential. The fact that few of the state's militia joined Lincoln, thus reducing the number that the British army captured, left Clinton and his officers in the dark about the real strength of the rebel militia in South Carolina. By not turning out, rebellious South Carolinians freed themselves to fight another day and resist the inevitable British drive into the back-country.

Besides rebels and loyalists, another segment of the population was a factor in South Carolina: those who might have remained neutral had Clinton permitted them to. This group included men who had supported the cause of independence, but who were now sufficiently impressed by British strength to opt to remain on the sidelines. As General Moultrie pointed out, these men accepted British offers "in hopes they would have been suffered to remain peaceably and quietly at home with their families, and to have gone on with their business undisturbed." But Clinton's 3 June proclamation, which threatened to treat "as Enemies and Rebels" all those who neglected "to return to their allegiance," forced them to make a choice. The choice was not a difficult one for any who had heard of British depredations against the civilian populace throughout the lowcountry. British foraging parties plundered farms and plantations, abused women remaining at home, carried off livestock and slaves, and left many families with little or nothing. Moreover, rumors abounded that the British intended to use southerners' freed slaves against them. These stories, as well as accounts of the brutality of Tarleton's men at the Waxhaws, filtered among the people quickly. As they spread by word of mouth throughout the countryside the details of British cruelty became greatly exaggerated, further inciting the inhabitants' anger. To men who had to choose between allegiance to the King or rebellion, the answer was unambiguous. The British army appeared to them as an invading and plundering army, one which they had to resist. Men and women of the backcountry would side with their countrymen in rebellion.[29]

Ironically, Sir Henry Clinton and other British officers starkly opposed the mistreatment of civilians, but the nature of their operations, attempting to subjugate a rebellion among a primarily hostile populace, ultimately led to incidents against the inhabitants. These incidents occurred with greater frequency when British foraging expeditions ranged throughout the countryside. While the British high command was generally averse to plundering, they could do little to supervise enlisted men in foraging parties as they visited farms and plantations. Meanwhile, many British officers, whom Stephen Conway has labeled hard-liners, believed that the army should take a more harsh approach in subduing the rebellion, and their actions at the local level often contradicted the ideas of Clinton and other conciliatory officers. Whether British commanders sanctioned such activity or not, when word of soldiers' depredations spread among the people, they interpreted it as official British policy. Southerners' perceptions that the British were actively pursuing a policy of plundering certainly brought many to arms against them. As Rachel Klein has pointed out, by participating in plundering raids, the British failed to make peace with those who would have otherwise accepted their offers of protection.[30]

The British relationship with and attitude toward South Carolina's civilians emerged quite clearly in the campaign against Charleston. Clinton himself set the tone with his orders issued to the commissaries of captures to seize cattle, horses, forage, rice, and other articles useful to the army from abandoned "Habitations and Plantations" of rebels. Meanwhile, foraging soldiers frequently harassed and abused civilians they encountered, both male and female. Their victims extended to every corner of the lowcountry. The widow Keir of James Island, Ann Fayssoux of St. Thomas Parish, Lady Colleton of Fair Lawn, William Giekie of Charleston neck, Edward Ellington of Goose Creek, and others like them had all suffered at the hands of British and Hessian soldiers in the course of the campaign. Even loyal inhabitants such as William Carson of Wadmalaw Island complained that hardly a day passed in which "the Cattle [were not] killed, the women insulted, & even the negroes plundered." Unsanctioned by their officers these irregularities may have been, but they were part of a cycle that would continue as the King's troops moved throughout South Carolina. The already rebellious sentiment of South Carolinians, which British actions and patriots' perceptions of those actions stoked to a flaming hatred, precluded the British forces from ever being able to reclaim South Carolina for the Crown.[31]

The capture of Charleston provided the British a spectacular victory, but it was also the first step that led them toward Yorktown. Cornwallis and his officers realized over the course of the summer of 1780 that the conquest of Charleston did not ensure the conquest of South Carolina, as Sir Henry Clinton had predicted. The British experience after Charleston differed little from their experience in the north earlier in the war. The British demonstrated at Charleston, as they had previously at New York and Newport, Rhode Island, that with combined sea and land forces they could easily capture the coastal cities of North America. The Royal Navy's transports transferred armies from point to point with relative ease and then supplied them with food and other essentials once they went ashore. This mode of warfare was a definite advantage along the coast, but when the army moved inland and away from the navy's support they had to proceed primarily on foot and at the same rate as their rebel opponents. Meanwhile, the farther they removed themselves from their provision-laden storeships, the more difficult it became for the army to acquire foodstuffs. British officers had to obtain supplies from loyal inhabitants or by means of foraging expeditions, and as we have seen, the consequent evils of foraging only antagonized an already hostile populace.

The British could capture coastal cities such as Charleston, but they were unable to control the hinterlands. Cornwallis and the British army established a chain of defensive posts and forts across South Carolina, but they failed to preserve order throughout the province. Outside their defenses, they and the loyalists were vulnerable to raids by parties under Sumter, Marion, Pickens, Elijah Clarke, and William Harden. Determined resistance in the South Carolina backcountry demonstrated that South Carolinians were as rebellious as their northern counterparts. But the loss of two armies, at Charleston and at Camden, made their continued resistance even more difficult and even more remarkable. Historians tend to agree that victory in the Carolinas could not have been won without the Continental army led by Nathanael Greene, but it can also be argued that Greene could not have succeeded if not for the patriotic ardor of the Carolinians.

As for Cornwallis, after losing two large detachments of his own at Kings Mountain in October and at Cowpens in January 1781, he finally set out on his long-anticipated invasion of North Carolina, which he hoped would contribute to the pacification of South Carolina. After chasing Greene's army across North Carolina, Cornwallis enticed the American general into a battle at Guilford Court House in March 1781. The British drove Greene's army from the field, but only after Cornwallis lost a quarter of his men killed and wounded. Among the mortally wounded was Lieutenant Colonel James Webster, who had opened the door for investiture of Charleston. Recognizing that he had fared little better in North Carolina than he had in South Carolina, Cornwallis withdrew to the coast shortly after the battle. From there, he moved into Virginia. Ordered by Clinton to establish a defensive position in Virginia accessible to the Royal Navy, Cornwallis chose a small town on the York River known as Yorktown.

Just seventeen months after the British forces had left Benjamin Lincoln no choice but to surrender his army and Charleston to them, Lord Cornwallis found himself in a similar predicament, besieged by the combined American and French armies under Washington and Rochambeau. In the course of negotiations over the proposed articles of capitulation for the surrender of the British garrison at Yorktown, Cornwallis requested the honors of war for his troops as they marched out to deliver up their arms. Washington, however, agreed to grant only those that Clinton had given to the garrison of Charleston the year before. Cornwallis could do little else but accept. On 19 October 1781 the British soldiers filed out of their trenches at Yorktown and paraded between the lines of American and French troops drawn up on either side of the road. Cornwallis, claiming illness, did not ride out at the head of his troops, but instead sent his second in command, Brigadier General Charles O'Hara. When O'Hara approached Washington to formally surrender the garrison, Washington directed him to his own second in command, Major General Benjamin Lincoln, who accepted the surrender. He and the Americans had come a long way in the previous seventeen months. The loss at Charleston had been avenged.

Appendix A

ARTICLES OF CAPITULATION AS PROPOSED BY BENJAMIN LINCOLN AND AS FINALIZED BY SIR HENRY CLINTON AND MARRIOT ARBUTHNOT

Articles as proposed by General Lincoln	*Final Articles of Capitulation as granted by Clinton and Arbuthnot*
Article 1. That all acts of hostility and works shall cease between the besiegers and besieged until the Articles of Capitulation shall be agreed on, signed and executed, or collectively rejected.	Article 1. All acts of hostility and work shall cease, until the Articles of Capitulation are finally agreed to or rejected.
Article 2. The town and fortifications shall be surrendered to the commander in chief of the British forces, such as they now stand.	Article 2. The town and fortifications with the shipping at the wharves, artillery, and all public stores whatsoever shall be surrendered in their present state to the commanders of the investing forces. Proper officers shall attend from the respective departments to receive them.
Article 3. The Continental troops and sailors with their baggage shall be conducted to a place to be agreed on, where they will remain prisoners of war until exchanged. While prisoners, they shall be supplied with good and wholesome provisions in such quantity as is served out to the troops of His Brittanic Majesty.	Article 3. Granted.

Article 4. The militia now in garrison shall be permitted to return to their respective homes and be secured in their persons and property.	Article 4. The militia now in garrison shall be permitted to return to their respective homes as prisoners on parole, which parole as long as they observe, shall secure them from being molested in their property by the British troops.
Article 5. The sick and wounded shall be continued under the care of their own surgeons, and be supplied with medicines and such necessaries as are allowed to the British hospitals.	Article 5. Granted
Article 6. The officers of the army and navy shall keep their horses, swords, pistols and baggage which shall not be searched and retain their servants.	Article 6. Granted, except with respect to the horses, which will not be allowed to go out of town, but may be disposed of by a person left from each corps for that purpose.
Article 7. The garrison shall at an hour appointed, march out with shouldered arms, drums beating and colors flying to a place to be agreed on, where they will pile their arms.	Article 7. The whole garrison shall at an hour to be appointed, march out of the town to the ground between the works of the place and the canal where they will deposit their arms. The drums are not to beat a British march, or colors to be uncased.

Article 8. That the French Consul, his house papers, and other moveable property shall be protected and untouched, and a proper time granted to him for retiring to any place that may afterwards be agreed upon between him and the commander in chief of the British forces.	Article 8. Agreed with this restriction, that he is to consider himself as a prisoner of war on parole.
Article 9. That the citizens shall be protected in their persons and properties.	Article 9. All civil officers and the citizens who have borne arms during the siege must be prisoners upon parole and with respect to their property in the city shall have the same terms as are granted to the militia and all other persons now in the town, not described in this or other article, are notwithstanding understood to be prisoners on parole.
Article 10. That a twelve months time be allowed all such as do not choose to continue under the British government to dispose of their effects, real and personal in the State without any molestation whatever, or to remove such part thereof as they choose, as well as themselves and families, and that during that time, they or any of them, may have it at their option to reside occasionally in town or country.	Article 10. The discussion of this article of course cannot possibly be entered into at present.

Article 11. That the same protection to their persons and properties, and the same time for the removal of their effects be given to the subjects of France and Spain as required for the citizens in the previous articles.	Article 11. The subjects of France and Spain shall have the same terms as are granted to the French Consul.
Article 12. That a vessel be permitted to go to Philadelphia with the General's dispatches which are not to be opened.	Article 12. Granted, and a proper vessel with a flag will be provided for that purpose.

Source: Papers of Sir Henry Clinton, William L. Clements Library

Appendix B

BRITISH AND AMERICAN FORCES IN THE SIEGE OF CHARLESTON AS OF 30 APRIL 1780

British Forces under the Command of Lieutenant General Sir Henry Clinton

Charleston Neck (Major General Alexander Leslie):

1st Battalion of British Light Infantry

2nd Battalion of British Light Infantry

1st Battalion of British Grenadiers

2nd Battalion of British Grenadiers

7th Regiment of Foot (Royal Fusiliers)

42nd Regiment of Foot

63rd Regiment of Foot

71st Regiment of Foot

Detachment of the Royal Artillery

Hessian Jaegers

Grenadier Battalion von Graff

Grenadier Battalion von Lengerke

Grenadier Battalion von Linsing

Grenadier Battalion von Minnigerode

West of the Ashley (Major General Johann Christoph von Huyn):

Regiment von Dittfurth

Regiment von Huyn

Prince of Wales American Regiment (Brown's Corps)

East of the Cooper (Lieutenant General Charles Earl Cornwallis):

23rd Regiment of Foot (Royal Welch Fusiliers)

33rd Regiment of Foot

64th Regiment of Foot

American Volunteers (Ferguson's Corps)

British Legion

New York Volunteers

North Carolina Volunteers

Queen's Rangers

South Carolina Royalists

Volunteers of Ireland

American Forces under the Command of Major General Benjamin Lincoln

Charleston Neck:

Battalion of Light Infantry (Lieutenant Colonel John Laurens)

Scott's Brigade (Brigadier General Charles Scott):

–Heth's Virginia Detachment

–Parker's Virginia Detachment

–2nd South Carolina Regiment

–3rd South Carolina Regiment

Woodford's Brigade (Brigadier General William Woodford):

–1st Virginia Regiment

–2nd Virginia Regiment

–3rd Virginia Regiment

Hogun's Brigade (Brigadier General James Hogun):

–1st North Carolina Regiment

–2nd North Carolina Regiment

–3rd North Carolina Regiment

Brigade of South Carolina Artillery (Colonel Barnard Beekman):

–1st South Carolina Regiment (less three companies serving at Fort Moultrie)

–4th South Carolina Regiment (South Carolina Artillery Regiment)

–Continental Independent Company (North Carolina Artillery)

–Charleston Battalion of Artillery

Batteries on South Bay:

Charleston Militia Brigade (Colonel Maurice Simons):

–1st Battalion of Charleston Militia

–2nd Battalion of Charleston Militia

–The Marquis de Bretigny's Corps

–Spanish Corps

Brigade of Country Militia (Brigadier General Lachlan McIntosh):

–North Carolina Militia

–South Carolina Militia

Fort Moultrie (Lieutenant Colonel William Scott):

Three Companies of 1st South Carolina Regiment

South Carolina Militia

Notes

Chapter 1

1. Don Higginbotham, *The War of American Independence: Military Attitudes, Policies, and Practice, 1763–1789* (New York: Macmillan, 1971), 151; Piers Mackesy, *The War for America, 1775–1783* (Lincoln: University of Nebraska Press, 1964), 61–62.

2. Higginbotham, *The War of American Independence,* 176–77; John S. Pancake, *1777: The Year of the Hangman* (Tuscaloosa: University of Alabama Press, 1977), 87–88.

3. Jonathan R. Dull, *A Diplomatic History of the American Revolution* (New Haven: Yale University Press, 1985), 55, 58–63, 92–96; Higginbotham, *The War of American Independence,* 226–27, 230–34.

4. Mackesy, *War for America,* 181–86; Henry Clinton, *The American Rebellion: Sir Henry Clinton's Narrative of His Campaigns, 1775–1782, with an Appendix of Original Documents,* ed. William B. Willcox (New Haven: Yale University Press, 1954), 87.

5. John A. Tilley, *The British Navy and the American Revolution* (Columbia: University of South Carolina Press, 1987), 119–20, 139; John Shy, "British Strategy for Pacifying the Southern Colonies, 1778–1781," in *The Southern Experience in the American Revolution,* ed. Jeffrey J. Crow and Larry E. Tise (Chapel Hill: University of North Carolina Press, 1978), 160.

6. John S. Pancake, *This Destructive War: The British Campaign in the Carolinas, 1780–1782* (Tuscaloosa: University of Alabama Press, 1985), 25–27; Ira D. Gruber, "Britain's Southern Strategy," in *The Revolutionary War in the South: Power, Conflict, and Leadership,* ed. W. Robert Higgins (Durham, N.C.: Duke University Press, 1979), 218–20.

7. Paul H. Smith, *Loyalists and Redcoats: A Study in British Revolutionary Policy* (Chapel Hill: University of North Carolina Press, 1964), 10, 18–21, 89; Pancake, *This Destructive War,* 12–13.

8. Germain to Clinton, 21 March 1778, quoted in Smith, *Loyalists and Redcoats,* 84; Shy, "British Strategy," 160, 162–63.

9. Smith, *Loyalists and Redcoats,* 89–90; Clinton, *The American Rebellion,* 11, 423.

10. Smith, *Loyalists and Redcoats,* 25–26.

11. Although Charles Town did not officially become Charleston until its incorporation in 1783, I have elected to use Charleston throughout the text.

12. Pancake, *This Destructive War,* 23–24.

13. Ibid.

14. Smith, *Loyalists and Redcoats,* 30, 170.

15. Clinton, *The American Rebellion,* 106.

16. Pancake, *This Destructive War,* 32.

17. Campbell's efforts in the Georgia backcountry are covered in Clyde R. Ferguson, "Carolina and Georgia Patriot and Loyalist Militia in Action, 1778–1783," in *The Southern Experience in the American Revolution,* 174–79.

18. See Robert K. Wright Jr., *The Continental Army* (Washington, D.C.: Center of Military History, United States Army, 1983), 82–84, 431. Early in the war, the Continental Congress established separate geographic departments to simplify the command structure in the great expanse of the North American continent. The departments they ultimately created were the Eastern Department (New England), Northern (New York), Canadian, Middle, Highlands, Western, and Southern Departments. Department commanders acted independently, making all necessary decisions as they related to the situation in their geographic commands, but they were still responsible to the Continental Congress and to Washington as commander in chief. The vast distances between the various departments and Philadelphia, especially the Southern Department, made it necessary for them to exercise substantial autonomy in their theaters of operation. Each department commander had to be capable enough to make strategic decisions on his own without waiting for word from his superiors.

19. David B. Mattern, *Benjamin Lincoln and the American Revolution* (Columbia: University of South Carolina Press, 1995), 15, 22, 32, 40, 49; John Carroll Cavanagh, "The Military Career of Major General Benjamin Lincoln in the War of the American Revolution" (Ph.D. diss., Duke University, 1969), 58, 97, 125, 133.

20. Cavanagh, "The Military Career of Benjamin Lincoln," 132–33; Mattern, *Benjamin Lincoln,* 4, 56–57.

21. William Moultrie, *Memoirs of the American Revolution, So Far As It Related to the States of North and South Carolina, and Georgia* (New York, 1802), 1:261–62, 269–70.

22. Ibid., 1:367, 374–75, 377–78, 387.

23. Ibid., 1:387–88, 398, 408–10.

24. Ibid., 1:362–63, 405–12.

25. Ibid., 1:424–27.

26. See Don Higginbotham, *The War of American Independence,* 197. In 1777, General Gates granted favorable terms to Burgoyne's army because he feared that General Clinton was going to force his way up the Hudson to relieve Burgoyne. Gates agreed to let the British troops return to England on parole, but the Continental Congress later negated the terms of this "convention" which kept the prisoners of Saratoga in America.

27. Moultrie, *Memoirs of the American Revolution,* 1:427–33; Christopher Gadsden, Thomas Ferguson, and John Edwards were the members of the Privy Council opposed to the measure as pointed out by E. Stanly Godbold Jr. and Robert H. Woody, *Christopher Gadsden and the American Revolution* (Knoxville: University of Tennessee Press, 1982), 194.

28. Moultrie, *Memoirs of the American Revolution,* 1:433–35.

29. Ibid., 1:435, 437.

30. See Edward McCrady, *The History of South Carolina in the Revolution, 1775–1780* (New York: Russel & Russel, 1901), 364–70, and James Haw, *John and Edward Rutledge of South Carolina* (Athens: University of Georgia Press, 1997), 121–23, 126–27. Edward McCrady, who in 1901 published the most thorough account of South Carolina's participation in the Revolution, a work which has yet to be surpassed in detail, argued against the notion that Rutledge and the Privy Council were acting selfishly or perfidiously. McCrady first questioned Moultrie's estimate of the number of men available to defend Charleston, arguing that the troops available were probably closer to Rutledge's figure of 2,500 than Moultrie's 3,100. He also claimed that Rutledge honestly believed that the British had 7,000 to 8,000 men. Given such odds, they had no choice but to parley, McCrady maintained. McCrady then laid his case on a different text of the message sent to Prevost concerning the neutrality of the state. According to McCrady, this version of the message, most likely provided by Lieutenant Colonel John Laurens, offered that "the State and Harbour should be considered as neutral during the war," but at the war's conclusion, South Carolina would be granted the same concessions as the other states. McCrady asserted that Rutledge and the Privy Council, although they were offering the state's

neutrality, were still considering their sister states in the process. In examining McCrady's assertions, it must be remembered that in spite of his thorough research and attention to detail, McCrady was writing his history of South Carolina in the Revolution as a South Carolinian. Writing in the aftermath of the Civil War, McCrady was influenced by the sectionalism of the age. More recently, in his biography of John and Edward Rutledge, James Haw argues that Governor Rutledge knew exactly what he was doing when he made his offer of neutrality. Haw maintains that Rutledge and other South Carolina leaders believed that the northern states and Continental Congress had ignored the plight of the south and essentially abandoned them. Since the other states had failed to support South Carolina, she was absolved from "further obligation to the United States." Thus, the South Carolinians could make the offer of neutrality with clear consciences; Moultrie, *Memoirs of the American Revolution,* 1:435; "Rivington's Royal Gazette, New York, June 19," *The Gazette of the State of South Carolina,* 4 August 1779.

31. Moultrie, *Memoirs of the American Revolution,* 1:476–77; David Ramsay to Benjamin Rush, 31 August 1779, *David Ramsay, 1749–1815: Selections from His Writings,* ed. Robert L. Brunhouse, in *Transactions of the American Philosophical Society Held at Philadelphia for Promoting Useful Knowledge,* vol. 55, part 4 (Philadelphia: The American Philosophical Society, 1965), 64; Cavanagh, "The Military Career of Benjamin Lincoln," 157.

Chapter 2

1. Clinton, *The American Rebellion,* 116, 118–20, 134, 151, 423; Smith, *Loyalists and Redcoats,* 107.

2. William B. Willcox, *Portrait of a General: Sir Henry Clinton in the War of Independence* (New York: Alfred A. Knopf, 1964), 3, 5, 9, 17–19, 24, 29.

3. Willcox, Introduction to Clinton, *The American Rebellion,* xvi–xvii, xxi, xlv, xlix; Willcox, *Portrait of a General,* 66–68, 104–5, 500, 505–7.

4. Willcox, *Portait of a General,* 211–12, 222–25.

5. Clinton, *The American Rebellion,* 105–6, 136, 143–44, 151.

6. Ibid., 143, 151, 418–19.

7. Walter J. Fraser Jr., *Charleston! Charleston! The History of a Southern City* (Columbia: University of South Carolina Press, 1989), 127–28, 135; George C. Rogers Jr., *Charleston in the Age of the Pinckneys* (Norman: University of Oklahoma Press, 1969; Columbia: University of South Carolina Press, 1980), 3–4.

8. Robert M. Weir, *Colonial South Carolina: A History* (Millwood, N.Y.: KTO Press, 1983), 141, 160; Weir, *"A Most Important Epocha": The Coming of the Revolution in South Carolina* (Columbia: University of South Carolina Press, 1970), 4; Walter Edgar, *South Carolina: A History* (Columbia: University of South Carolina Press, 1998), 150–51.

9. Fraser, *Charleston! Charleston!*, 112; Rogers, *Charleston*, 10–12; Jerome J. Nadelhaft, *The Disorders of War: The Revolution in South Carolina* (Orono: University of Maine at Orono Press, 1981), 19–24; Edgar, *South Carolina*, 123.

10. "A Frenchman Visits Charleston in 1777," trans. Elmer Douglas Johnson, *The South Carolina Historical and Genealogical Magazine* 52, no. 2 (1951): 91; "Charleston in 1774 as Described by an English Traveler," ed. John Bennett, *The South Carolina Historical and Genealogical Magazine* 47, no. 3 (1946): 180; Platte Grenadier Battalion Journal which sailed to America as the Koehler Grenadier Battalion, was later called the Graf Grenadier Battalion, and finally the Platte Grenadier Battalion, 4 June 1780, Lidgerwood Hessian Transcripts (Morristown National Historical Park, Morristown, N.J.), English translation by Bruce E. Burgoyne on microfiche 1.

11. "A Frenchman Visits Charleston," 91; Platte Grenadier Battalion Journal, 4 June 1780, Lidgerwood Hessian Transcripts; "Charleston Described by English Traveler," 179.

12. Clinton, *The American Rebellion*, 140, 145–46, 149; William T. Bulger, "The British Expedition to Charleston, 1779–1780" (Ph.D. diss., University of Michigan, 1957), 57–59.

13. Clinton, *The American Rebellion*, 144, 149–51; Moultrie, *Memoirs of the American Revolution*, 2:33.

14. The French and Americans suffered over eight hundred casualties. Among the killed were Brigadier General Kasimir Pulaski and Sergeant William Jasper, who at the battle of Sullivan's Island in 1776 leaped upon the parapet in the face of British cannon fire and planted the South Carolina flag on the ramparts.

15. Christopher Ward, *The War of the Revolution* (New York: Macmillan, 1952), 2:688–94; Moultrie, *Memoirs of the American Revolution,* 2:33, 36–37, 40–42.

16. Clinton, *The American Rebellion,* 149; Willcox, *Portrait of a General,* 91, 505–7.

17. Henry Clinton, Journal of the Siege of Charleston (1780), 24 May 1780, Sir Henry Clinton Papers, William L. Clements Library, University of Michigan, Ann Arbor, Mich. (hereafter cited as Clinton Siege Journal); Tilley, *The British Navy,* 163–65.

18. Willcox, *Portrait of a General,* 285.

19. Tilley, *The British Navy,* 173; R. Arthur Bowler, *Logistics and the Failure of the British Army in America, 1775–1783* (Princeton: Princeton University Press, 1975), 19.

20. The number of troops embarked on the expedition is taken from an embarkation list prepared by Major Carl Baurmeister in Bernard Uhlendorf, trans. and ed., *The Siege of Charleston with an Account of the Province of South Carolina: Diaries and Letters of Hessian Officers from the von Jungkenn Papers in the William L. Clements Library,* vol. XII, University of Michigan Publications on History and Political Science, (Ann Arbor: University of Michigan Press, 1938), 108–9; Clinton, *The American Rebellion,* 158.

21. By the time of the American Revolution, the British infantry regiment was comprised of ten companies. Of these ten, one was designated a light infantry company and another a grenadier company. Together they were referred to as the flank companies. Generally, the best and fittest men in the regiment served in these companies. The flank companies of all the regiments of an army or division were often taken from their regiments and consolidated into separate battalions of light infantry and grenadiers to perform specialized service with the army. Light infantry battalions were used for scouting, protecting the flanks of the army when it was marching, skirmishing with the enemy, and other duties requiring a quick mobile force. Grenadier battalions were used as shock troops in the line of battle. See H. C. B. Rogers, *The British Army of the Eighteenth Century* (New York: Hippocrene Books, Inc., 1977), 42–43, 75, and Edward E. Curtis, *The Organization of the British Army in the American Revolution* (1926; reprint, New York: AMS Press, 1969), 4.

22. Johann Ewald, *Diary of the American War: A Hessian Journal,* trans. and ed. Joseph P. Tustin (New Haven: Yale University Press, 1979), 190; Embarkation return of Baurmeister in Uhlendorf, *The Siege of Charleston,* 108–9.

23. Ewald, *Diary of the American War,* 190–91; Uhlendorf, *The Siege of Charleston,* 369; Henry Clinton to Marriot Arbuthnot, 26 December 1779, Sir Henry Clinton Papers, William L. Clements Library, University of Michigan, Ann Arbor, Mich. (hereafter cited as Clinton Papers); Ward, *War of the Revolution,* 2:612.

24. Clinton, *The American Rebellion,* 123–24, 153; Clinton to Arbuthnot, 26 December 1779, Clinton Papers; Clinton Siege Journal, 4 April 1780, ibid.

25. Ewald, *Diary of the American War,* 192–94; Clinton, *The American Rebellion,* 154; Uhlendorf, *The Siege of Charleston,* 119, 141.

26. Ewald, *Diary of the American War,* 193; Clinton, *The American Rebellion,* 159–60; John Grant to Henry Clinton, 5 February 1780, Clinton Papers.

27. Clinton, *The American Rebellion,* 159–60; Henry Clinton to Marriot Arbuthnot, 4 March 1780, Clinton Papers.

28. Thomas Tonken to John André, 4 February 1780, Clinton Papers; Clinton, *The American Rebellion,* 159; Charles Stedman, *The History of the Origin, Progress, and Termination of the American War* (1794; reprint, New York: New York Times and Arno Press, 1969), 2:177; Return of men and women on board of the undermentioned transports and the number of days the following species of provisions will serve them, off Tybee Island, 5 February 1780, Clinton Papers; Journal of George Philip Hooke, 20 January 1780, Orderly Book Collection, William L. Clements Library.

29. Uhlendorf, *The Siege of Charleston,* 23; Clinton, *The American Rebellion,* 159.

30. The unit originally commanded by Lord Cathcart was also referred to as the British Legion or simply the Legion. Lieutenant Colonel Banastre Tarleton commanded the Legion throughout its service in the southern states. See Mark Mayo Boatner, *Encyclopedia of the American Revolution* (New York: David McKay Company, 1966), 114–15.

31. Peter Russell, "The Siege of Charleston: Journal of Captain Peter Russell, December 25, 1779 to May 2, 1780," *The American Historical*

Review 4, no. 3 (1899), 481; Clinton, *The American Rebellion,* 160; Banastre Tarleton, *A History of the Campaigns of 1780 and 1781, in the Southern Provinces of North America* (London: T. Cadell, 1787), 8; Bulger, "British Expedition to Charleston," 82.

32. Undated Clinton memorandum containing intelligence report on Charleston, filed at the end of December 1779, Clinton Papers; Clinton, *The American Rebellion,* 160–61.

33. Clinton Siege Journal, 4 April 1780, Clinton Papers; Return of men and women on board of the undermentioned transports and the number of days the following species of provisions will serve them, off Tybee Island, 5 February 1780, ibid.; Clinton, *The American Rebellion,* 160.

34. Clinton, *The American Rebellion,* 161; Clinton to Arbuthnot, 29 January 1780, Clinton Papers.

35. Russell, "Journal of Peter Russell," 483; Ewald, *Diary of the American War,* 195.

36. Ewald, *Diary of the American War,* 195–96.

37. Russell, "Journal of Peter Russell," 483–84; Uhlendorf, *The Siege of Charleston,* 181; Ewald, *Diary of the American War,* 196.

38. The route on which the British marched ran along the present day route of Bohicket Road on Johns Island.

39. Uhlendorf, *The Siege of Charleston,* 181; Ewald, *Diary of the American War,* 196.

40. Uhlendorf, *The Siege of Charleston,* 181–83; Ewald, *Diary of the American War,* 196; Diary kept by Ensign Hartung of the vacant Huyne Regiment, 11 February 1780, Lidgerwood Hessian Transcripts (Morristown National Historical Park, Morristown, N.J.), English translation on microfiche 333 (hereafter cited as Hartung Diary).

Chapter 3

1. Benjamin Lincoln to Council, 11 February 1780, Benjamin Lincoln Papers, November 1779–July 1780, Massachusetts Historical Society, Boston, Mass. (hereafter cited as Lincoln Papers).

2. Benjamin Lincoln to John Mathews, 24 January 1780, Benjamin Lincoln Letterbook, Boston Public Library, Rare Books Department, Courtesy of the Trustees, Boston, Mass.; Lincoln to Abraham Whipple, 17

January 1780, ibid.; Lincoln to Richard Caswell, 29 January 1780, ibid.; Lincoln to the Committee of Correspondence, 24 January 1780, ibid.

3. When Clinton called for the force under General Paterson to join his own before Charleston, it took Paterson's troops twelve days to march from Savannah to the Ashley River. See Clinton to Germain, 13 May 1780, Clinton Papers.

4. Lincoln to Daniel Horry, 1 February 1780, Benjamin Lincoln Letterbook; Lincoln to Francis Marion, 31 January 1780, ibid.; Horry to Lincoln, 6 February 1780, Lincoln Papers.

5. Lincoln to the Continental Congress, 11 February 1780, The Papers of the Continental Congress, 1774–1789 (National Archives, Washington, D.C.) National Archives Microfilm Publication M247, roll 177, item 158, RG 360, (hereafter cited as PCC); Lachlan McIntosh, "Journal of the Siege of Charlestown, 1780," in *University of Georgia Libraries Miscellanea Publications, No. 7,* ed. Lilla Mills Hawes (Athens: University of Georgia Press, 1968), 96; Extracts from the Journal of Mrs. Gabriel (Ann Ashby) Manigault, 1754–1781, 13, 15, 16 February 1780, Manigault Family Papers, 1685–1971, South Carolina Historical Society, Charleston, S.C.; David Ramsay, *History of the Revolution in South Carolina, from a British Province to an Independent State* (Trenton, N.J.: 1785), 2:46; Gabriel Manigault Journal, 1774–1784, 10 February 1780, South Carolina Historical Society, Charleston, S.C.

6. *Journals of the Continental Congress, 1774–1789,* ed. Worthington C. Ford et al. (Washington, D.C., 1904–37), 15:1253–1254, 1314–1315 (hereafter cited as *JCC*); John Rutledge to the French Commodore, 10 January 1780, Lincoln Papers; *The South-Carolina and American General Gazette,* 4 February 1780; *The Gazette of the State of South Carolina,* 9 February 1780; Henry Laurens to Nathaniel Peabody, 5 February 1780, *The Papers of Henry Laurens, Volume 15: December 11, 1778–August 31, 1782,* ed. David R. Chestnutt and C. James Taylor (Columbia: University of South Carolina Press, 2000), 234.

7. See E. Wayne Carp, *To Starve the Army at Pleasure: Continental Army Administration and American Political Culture, 1775–1783* (Chapel Hill: University of North Carolina Press, 1984) for an excellent discussion of how the states both assisted and hindered the war effort during the Revolution.

8. *JCC* 15 (1779): 1256, 1314–1315.

9. *JCC* 15 (1779): 1253–1254, 1257; William M. Fowler Jr., *Rebels under Sail: The American Navy during the Revolution* (New York: Charles Scribner's Sons, 1976), 110, 215; Invoice of Sundry Stores Received from Colonel John Mitchell Deputy Quarter Master General on Board the Schooner Dove Captain Edward Ledger Commander, 25 November 1779, Lincoln Papers.

10. Tilley, *The British Navy,* 102–4; Memorandum on Route intended to send the Arms to South Carolina and from thence to join General Lincoln under the Conduct of Captain Edward Leger, filed at the end of November 1779, Lincoln Papers.

11. *JCC* 15 (1779): 1256; Washington to James Hogun, 19 November 1779, *The Writings of George Washington from the Original Manuscript Sources, 1745–1799,* ed. John C. Fitzpatrick (Washington, D.C.: United States Government Printing Office, 1931–44), 17:133; Wright Jr., *The Continental Army,* 299–303; Washington to Jonathan Trumbull, 20 November 1779, *Writings of George Washington,* 17:147; Washington to the President of Congress, 20 November 1779, ibid., 17:151.

12. Washington to the President of Congress, 29 November 1779, *Writings of George Washington,* 17:206; Washington to the President of Congress, 2 December 1779, ibid., 17:212–13; Washington to Benjamin Lincoln, 12 December 1779, ibid., 17:247–48.

13. Washington to the President of Congress, 29 November 1779, *Writings of George Washington,* 17:206; Washington to Benjamin Lincoln, 12 December 1779, ibid., 17:248; Washington to the President of Congress, 2 December 1779, ibid., 17:213; Strength returns of the Virginia Continental regiments and the main army serving with Washington are from Charles H. Lesser, ed., *The Sinews of Independence: Monthly Strength Reports of the Continental Army* (Chicago: The University of Chicago Press, 1976), 140–41.

14. Washington to the President of Congress, 29 November 1779, *Writings of George Washington,* 17:207–8; Washington to the Board of War, 23 November 1779, ibid., 17:175; McIntosh, "Journal of Siege of Charlestown," 98; Washington to Benjamin Lincoln, 12 December 1779, *Writings of George Washington,* 17:248; Journal of Peter Timothy, 7 April 1780, South Carolina Historical Society, Charleston.

15. Erna Risch, *Supplying Washington's Army* (Washington, D.C.: Center of Military History, United States Army, 1986), 20–23; For Washington's

response to soldiers destroying fences, see General Orders, 3 December 1779, *Writings of George Washington,* 17:214–15 and General Orders, 29 December 1779, ibid., 17:331–32.

16. Benjamin Lincoln to the Committee of Correspondence, 31 January 1780, Thomas Addis Emmet Collection, New York Public Library (hereafter cited as Emmet Collection); Daniel Horry to Lincoln, 11 February 1780, Lincoln Papers; John Jameson to Lincoln, 11 February 1780, ibid.

17. Ramsay, *Revolution in South Carolina,* 2:46; Lincoln to Washington, 22 February 1780, Benjamin Lincoln Letterbook; Moultrie, *Memoirs of the American Revolution,* 1:262, 265, 274, 285; *Journals of the General Assembly and House of Representatives, 1776–1780,* ed. William Edwin Hemphill, Wylma Anne Wates and R. Nicholas Olsberg (Columbia: University of South Carolina Press, 1970), 242; John Faucheraud Grimké, Orderly Book, 11, 18 February 1780, Continental Army Southern Department Records, 1778–1790, South Carolina Historical Society, Charleston (hereafter cited as Grimké Orderly Book); Wright Jr., *The Continental Army,* 305–9.

18. Lincoln to Caswell, 15 December 1779, 3 January 1780, Benjamin Lincoln Letterbook; Lincoln to Jefferson, 4 January 1780, ibid.

19. Lincoln to Andrew Williamson, 16 January 1780, Benjamin Lincoln Letterbook; Lincoln to Richard Parker and John Jameson, 28 January 1780, ibid.; Lesser, *Sinews of Independence,* 161.

20. See Grimké Orderly Book, 12 February 1780, South Carolina Historical Society. Interestingly, there were so many "Frenchmen" in Charleston "who from their want of Knowledge in the English Language are incapable of rendering equal services by being incorporated with Americans" that Lincoln ordered them to form a separate militia company which served under the Marquis de Bretigny.

21. Monthly Return of Charlestown Brigade of Militia, 29 February 1780, Lincoln Papers; Lesser, *Sinews of Independence,* 154; Lincoln to the Committee of Correspondence, 19 December 1779, Benjamin Lincoln Letterbook; Horry to Lincoln, 11 February 1780, Lincoln Papers; Hugh F. Rankin, *The North Carolina Continentals* (Chapel Hill: University of North Carolina Press, 1971), 218.

22. Cavanagh, "The Military Career of Benjamin Lincoln," 188; Mattern, *Benjamin Lincoln,* 92; Lincoln to Rutledge, 30 January 1780, Benjamin Lincoln Letterbook; John Laurens to Henry Laurens, 27 January

1780, *Papers of Henry Laurens,* 15:232–33; Lincoln to Washington, 17 July 1780, Lincoln Papers; *Journals of the General Assembly,* 251, 255, 262, 276; Clinton, *The American Rebellion,* 162.

23. Lincoln to Washington, 17 July 1780, Lincoln Papers; Moultrie, *Memoirs of the American Revolution,* 1:476–77.

24. Rogers, *Charleston,* 58–59; Moultrie, *Memoirs of the American Revolution,* 1:362–63, 406, 431; McCrady, *South Carolina in the Revolution,* 451–52.

25. Lincoln to the Committee of Correspondence, 19 December 1779, Benjamin Lincoln Letterbook; Lincoln to Washington, 11 February 1780, ibid.

26. Laumoy to Lincoln, 4 March 1780, Emmet Collection.

27. *Journals of the General Assembly,* 251, 262–64; Lincoln to Rutledge, 26 February, 15 March 1780, Benjamin Lincoln Letterbook.

28. Edwin C. Bearss, "The First Two Fort Moultries: A Structural History" (Washington, D.C.: U.S. Department of the Interior, National Park Service, 1968), 2, 8, 10–11, 17.

29. Account of Stores at Fort Moultrie, 12 February 1780, Lincoln Papers; Lincoln to the Committee of Correspondence, 8 January 1780, ibid.; Bearss, "The First Two Fort Moultries," 1.

30. Lincoln to Washington, 17 July 1780, Lincoln Papers; [Louis-Antoine Magallan de la Morliere], "A French Account of the Siege of Charleston," ed. Richard K. Murdoch, *The South Carolina Historical Magazine* 67, no. 3 (1966), 141; Tilley, *The British Navy,* 176–77; *Journals of the General Assembly,* 255; Bearss, "The First Two Fort Moultries," 2; Uhlendorf, *The Siege of Charleston,* 325; Stedman, *History of the American War,* 2:178.

31. Lincoln to the Committee of Correspondence, 19 December 1779, Benjamin Lincoln Letterbook; Ramsay, *Revolution in South Carolina,* 2:50–51; Tarleton, *Campaigns of 1780 and 1781,* 52–53; Lincoln to Washington, 27 January 1780, Benjamin Lincoln Letterbook.

32. Lincoln to the Committee of Correspondence, 19 December 1779, Benjamin Lincoln Letterbook; Lincoln to Washington, 17 July 1780, Lincoln Papers; Tilley, *The British Navy,* 122.

33. Ramsay, *Revolution in South Carolina,* 2:47–48; Lincoln to Rutledge, 14 February 1780, Benjamin Lincoln Letterbook; Orders of Governor Rutledge, 11 February 1780, Lincoln Papers.

34. *The Orderly Book of Captain Benjamin Taliaferro, 2nd Virginia Detachment, Charleston, South Carolina, 1780,* ed. Lee A. Wallace (Richmond: Virginia State Library, 1980), 54–56, 63, 66.

35. Whipple to Rutledge, 13 February 1780, Abraham Whipple Letterbook, Manuscripts Collection, Rhode Island Historical Society, Providence, R.I.; Warrant of John Rutledge, 18 February 1780, ibid.; Rutledge to Lincoln, 18 February 1780, ibid.

36. Grimké Orderly Book, 13 February 1780, South Carolina Historical Society; Lincoln to Rutledge, 28 January 1780, Benjamin Lincoln Letterbook.

37. Lincoln to the Committee of Correspondence, 8 January 1780, Lincoln Papers.

Chapter 4

1. Clinton, *The American Rebellion,* 161; Thomas Tonken to John André, 13 February 1780, Clinton Papers; Gregory Townsend to André, 17 February 1780, ibid.; George Keith Elphinstone to Clinton, 18 February 1780, ibid.

2. The young boy's "poor dialect" was most likely Gullah, a mixture of English and African speech patterns still recognizable in the South Carolina lowcountry even today. Given that their native tongue was German, the jaegers' inability to comprehend the "dialect" is understandable.

3. Ewald, *Diary of the American War,* 197–98; Uhlendorf, *The Siege of Charleston,* 185.

4. Horry to Lincoln, 16 February 1780, Lincoln Papers.

5. Uhlendorf, *The Siege of Charleston,* 185–87; Ewald, *Diary of the American War,* 197, 199; Lincoln to Washington, 22 February 1780, Benjamin Lincoln Letterbook.

6. Uhlendorf, *The Siege of Charleston,* 187; Ewald, *Diary of the American War,* 199; Thomas Tonken to John André, 26 February 1780, Clinton Papers.

7. Uhlendorf, *The Siege of Charleston,* 187–89; Undated Clinton memorandum, filed at the end of March 1780, Clinton Papers.

8. Gregory Townsend to John André, 17 February 1780, Clinton Papers; Uhlendorf, *The Siege of Charleston,* 189–91; Clinton to Elphinstone, 15 February 1780, Clinton Papers; Elphinstone to Clinton, 18 February 1780,

ibid.; Peter Traille to John André, 19 February 1780, ibid.; Ewald, *Diary of the American War,* 202.

9. From Colonel Barnard Beekman's Notes in McIntosh, "Journal of Siege of Charlestown," 112; Lincoln to Washington, 23 January, 22 February 1780, Benjamin Lincoln Letterbook; Ramsay, *Revolution in South Carolina,* 2:50.

10. Lincoln to Malmedy, 12 February 1780, Benjamin Lincoln Letterbook; Peter Timothy to Lincoln, 13, 14, 17 February 1780, Lincoln Papers; Lincoln to Daniel Horry, 15 February 1780, Benjamin Lincoln Letterbook.

11. Lincoln to Horry, 15 February 1780, Benjamin Lincoln Letterbook; Moultrie, *Memoirs of the American Revolution,* 2:45–46; Lincoln to the Continental Congress, 22 February 1780, PCC (National Archives Microfilm Publication M247, roll 177); From Colonel Barnard Beekman's Notes in McIntosh, "Journal of Siege of Charlestown," 112.

12. Moultrie, *Memoirs of the American Revolution,* 2:50; Clinton, *The American Rebellion,* 165; Tarleton, *Campaigns of 1780 and 1781,* 5, 8; Uhlendorf, *The Siege of Charleston,* 189.

13. Daniel Horry to Lincoln, 18 February 1780, Lincoln Papers; Lincoln to the Continental Congress, 29 February 1780, PCC (National Archives Microfilm Publication M247, roll 177).

14. Daniel Horry to Lincoln, 18 February 1780, Lincoln Papers; Moultrie to Lincoln, 23 February 1780, ibid.; Uhlendorf, *The Siege of Charleston,* 193, 195; Ewald, *Diary of the American War,* 202–3; Marion to Isaac Harleston, 29 February 1780, Emmet Collection.

15. John Jameson to Lincoln, 11 February 1780, Lincoln Papers; Moultrie to Lincoln, 26 February 1780, ibid.

16. Lincoln to the Committee of Correspondence, 8 January 1780, Lincoln Papers; Lincoln to Washington, 17 July 1780, ibid.

17. Lincoln to Caswell, 3 March 1780, Benjamin Lincoln Letterbook; Horry to Lincoln, 18, 20 February 1780, Lincoln Papers; Moultrie, *Memoirs of the American Revolution,* 2:43–44; Lincoln to the Continental Congress, 2 December 1779, PCC (National Archives Microfilm Publication M247, roll 177); Platte Grenadier Battalion Journal, 4 May 1780, Lidgerwood Hessian Transcripts; Ramsay, *Revolution in South Carolina,* 2:46, 48.

18. Moultrie, *Memoirs of the American Revolution,* 2:55–56; Grimké Orderly Book, 1 March 1780, South Carolina Historical Society; R. W.

Gibbes, ed., *Documentary History of the American Revolution: Chiefly in South Carolina, 1764–1782* (1853–57; reprint, Spartanburg, S.C.: The Reprint Co., 1972), 2:129; Ramsay, *Revolution in South Carolina,* 2:48, 52; Lincoln to Caswell, 3 March 1780, Benjamin Lincoln Letterbook.

19. Lincoln to Caswell, 3 March 1780, Benjamin Lincoln Letterbook; William Skirving to William Moultrie, 26 February 1780, Collections of the Charleston Museum, Charleston, S.C.

20. Clinton to George Hay, 13[?] February 1780, Clinton Papers; Clinton to James Moncrief, 13 February 1780, ibid.; The Hay instructions are undated but are filed in 13 February 1780 correspondence in the Clinton Papers and were probably issued at the same time as that of Moncrief; See also Bowler, *Logistics and the Failure of the British Army,* 42–49, 86.

21. Stephen Conway, "To Subdue America: British Army Officers and the Conduct of the Revolutionary War," *The William and Mary Quarterly* 43, no. 3 (1986): 382, 385–86; André memorandum on "Proposed Regulations in '79 and Orders Issued in Consequence," filed at the end of December 1779, Clinton Papers.

22. Clinton to George Hay, 13[?] February 1780, Clinton Papers; Clinton to James Moncrief, 13 February 1780, ibid.

23. Ewald, *Diary of the American War,* 199, 202.

24. Memo of Marriot Arbuthnot, 5 February 1780, *The Keith Papers: Selected from the Letters and Papers of Admiral Viscount Keith,* ed. W. G. Perrin, Publications of the Navy Records Society, vol. 62 (London: Navy Records Society, 1927), 1:145–46; Peter Russell to John André, 18 February 1780, Clinton Papers; William Carson to James Simpson, 1 May 1780, ibid.; Russell, "Journal of Peter Russell," 485–86.

25. Undated Clinton memorandum, filed at the end of February 1780, Clinton Papers; Tarleton, *Campaigns of 1780 and 1781,* 5.

26. Clinton to Arbuthnot, 20, 24 February 1780, Clinton Papers; Thomas Tonken to John André, 23 February 1780, ibid.; Peter Russell to John André, 24 February 1780, ibid.; Arbuthnot to Clinton, 27 February 1780, ibid.; Moultrie to Lincoln, 22 February 1780, Lincoln Papers.

27. Clinton, *The American Rebellion,* 159; Clinton Siege Journal, 4 April 1780, Clinton Papers.

28. Clinton, *The American Rebellion,* 160; Clinton to Arbuthnot, 4 March 1780, Clinton Papers; Arbuthnot to Clinton, 1, 5 March 1780, ibid.; Memorandum of Peter Russell containing "Minutes of such Parts of the

Commander in Chiefs Letters to the Admiral as have not been answered," filed at the end of April 1780, ibid.; John Wilson, Journal of the Siege of Charlestown, 3 March 1780, Charleston Library Society, Charleston, S.C. (hereafter cited as Wilson Journal).

29. This is the present day site of Dill Wildlife Sanctuary.

30. Clinton to Arbuthnot, 20, 24 February 1780, Clinton Papers; Russell, "Journal of Peter Russell," 487; Ewald, *Diary of the American War,* 202; Clinton to Lord George Germain, 9 March 1780, Clinton Papers; Clinton, *The American Rebellion,* 161; Clinton to Elphinstone, 18 February 1780, *Keith Papers,* 1:149.

31. Archibald Robertson, *Archibald Robertson, Lieutenant-General Royal Engineers: His Diaries and Sketches in America, 1762–1780,* ed. Harry Miller Lydenberg (1930; reprint, New York: New York Public Library and Arno Press, 1971), 214; Russell, "Journal of Peter Russell," 488; Uhlendorf, *The Siege of Charleston,* 193.

32. Whipple to Samuel Tucker and Thomas Simpson, 15 February 1780, Abraham Whipple Letterbook; Lincoln to Whipple, 28 February 1780, ibid.; Whipple to Captain Corinet, 28 February 1780, ibid.; Robertson, *Archibald Robertson: His Diaries and Sketches in America,* 215; Ewald, *Diary of the American War,* 203; Hartung Diary, 28 February 1780, Lidgerwood Hessian Transcripts.

33. Ewald, *Diary of the American War,* 203–4; Russell, "Journal of Peter Russell," 488.

34. Clinton to Arbuthnot, 4 March 1780, Clinton Papers; Clinton, *The American Rebellion,* 161; Ewald, *Diary of the American War,* 205.

35. Uhlendorf, *The Siege of Charleston,* 205; Ewald, *Diary of the American War,* 205; Hartung Diary, 11 March 1780, Lidgerwood Hessian Transcripts; Wilson Journal, 11, 12, 13 March 1780, Charleston Library Society.

36. Peter Timothy to Henry Laurens, 13 March 1780, Henry W. Kendall Collection of the Papers of Henry Laurens, South Caroliniana Library, University of South Carolina, Columbia (hereafter cited as Laurens Papers); Uhlendorf, *The Siege of Charleston,* 205; Gabriel Manigault Journal, 12 March 1780, South Carolina Historical Society; John Laurens to Henry Laurens, 14 March 1780, *Papers of Henry Laurens,* 15:251; Christopher Duffy, *Fire and Stone: The Science of Fortress Warfare 1660–1860* (Newton Abbot: David & Charles, 1975), 156.

37. Wilson Journal, 14, 16, 17 March 1780, Charleston Library Society; Russell, "Journal of Peter Russell," 490; Lincoln to the Continental Congress, 14 March 1780, PCC (National Archives Microfilm Publication M247, roll 177).

38. Extracts from the Journal of Mrs. Gabriel Manigault, 26 February 1780, South Carolina Historical Society; Uhlendorf, *The Siege of Charleston,* 211; Clinton Siege Journal, 14 April 1780, Clinton Papers.

39. Weekly Return of the Brigade of Foot Commanded by Colonel Richard Parker, 18 March 1780, Lincoln Papers; Lincoln to the Committee of Correspondence, 8 January 1780, ibid.; Rankin, *The North Carolina Continentals,* 219; Lincoln to Washington, 4 March 1780, Benjamin Lincoln Letterbook; Moultrie, *Memoirs of the American Revolution,* 2:50; Lesser, *Sinews of Independence,* 154–55; Marion to Lincoln, 5 March 1780, Lincoln Papers.

40. Commissary records for the British army, which listed the number of men drawing rations in each regiment, show a total of 6,839 men receiving rations in the British and Hessian regiments at the beginning of March 1780. Of the men who drew rations, approximately eight men per regiment or battalion were staff personnel, who would not be considered as fit for action, so Clinton's effectives would have numbered approximately 6,700. Even if this figure is reduced by twenty-five percent to account for those unfit for duty and women drawing rations, Clinton's effectives would have numbered just over 5,000, still in excess of Lincoln's total number of troops.

41. Abstract of Fresh Meat and Rice Issued to His Majesty's Troops, by the Commissaries of Captures, between 24th February and 16th March, 1780, Clinton Papers; Wright Jr., *The Continental Army,* 48–49.

42. Francis Marion to Lincoln, 5 March 1780, Lincoln Papers; Philip Neyle to Lincoln, 7 March 1780, ibid.; Moultrie to Lincoln, 26 February 1780, ibid.; Risch, *Supplying Washington's Army,* 189–91; Isaac Huger to Lincoln, 9 March 1780, Lincoln Papers; John Jameson to Lincoln, 15 March 1780, ibid.; Russell, "Journal of Peter Russell," 491.

43. Clinton, *The American Rebellion,* 161; Peter Timothy to Lincoln, 13 February 1780, Lincoln Papers; Tilley, *The British Navy,* 173, 178; Arbuthnot to Clinton, 17 February, 5 March 1780, Clinton Papers; Elphinstone to Clinton, 17 February 1780, ibid.

44. Clinton, *The American Rebellion,* 161; Clinton Siege Journal, 4 April 1780, Clinton Papers; Clinton to Elphinstone, 16 March 1780, ibid.

45. Clinton, *The American Rebellion,* 162; Clinton Siege Journal, 4 April 1780, Clinton Papers; Clinton to Germain, 9 March 1780, ibid.

Chapter 5

1. P. C. Coker III, *Charleston's Maritime Heritage, 1670–1865* (Charleston, S.C.: CokerCraft Press, 1987), 104, 106; Fowler, *Rebels under Sail,* 108, 110, 150–52; Whipple to the Marine Board, 13 February 1780, Abraham Whipple Letterbook.

2. Lincoln to John Rutledge, 18 January 1780, Benjamin Lincoln Letterbook; Lincoln to Whipple, 30 January 1780, ibid.

3. Lincoln to Washington, 17 July 1780, Lincoln Papers; Hoysted Hacker and others to Lincoln, 1 February 1780, Emmet Collection.

4. Lincoln to Whipple, 13, 20 February 1780, Abraham Whipple Letterbook.

5. Whipple to Tucker and Simpson, 20 February 1780, Abraham Whipple Letterbook; Whipple to Hacker, 24 February 1780, ibid.; Lincoln to Washington, 17 July 1780, Lincoln Papers; Lincoln to Whipple, 26 February 1780, Abraham Whipple Letterbook.

6. Lincoln to Whipple, 26 February 1780, Abraham Whipple Letterbook; Whipple to Lincoln, 27 February 1780, ibid.; Whipple to Samuel Tucker, 20 February 1780, ibid.

7. Lincoln to Whipple, 26 February 1780, Abraham Whipple Letterbook; *JCC* 15 (1779): 1253.

8. See Fowler, *Rebels under Sail,* 110, 245–46, and Nathan Miller, *Sea of Glory: A Naval History of the American Revolution* (Annapolis: Naval Institute Press, 1974), 528–29. The other five were *Trumbull, Alliance, Confederacy, Deane,* and *Pallas.*

9. It is interesting to note that one of the pilots was illiterate. Rather than signing, Jonathan Whitaker made his mark.

10. Whipple to Lincoln, 27 February 1780, Abraham Whipple Letterbook.

11. Peter Timothy to Lincoln, 14, 17 February 1780, Lincoln Papers; Peter Timothy, Report from the Observatory, 18 February 1780, ibid.; John Laurens to Henry Laurens, 10 March 1780, *Papers of Henry Laurens,* 15:249.

12. Whipple to Rutledge, 13 February 1780, Abraham Whipple Letterbook; Rutledge to Whipple, 13 February 1780, ibid.; Russell, "Journal of Peter Russell," 485; John Lewis Gervais to Henry Laurens, 22 March 1780, Laurens Papers; Lincoln to Whipple, 28 February 1780, Abraham Whipple Letterbook; Whipple to Hoysted Hacker, 29 February, 9 March 1780, ibid.; Whipple to Samuel Tucker, 10 March 1780, ibid.

13. Russell, "Journal of Peter Russell," 489, 491; Clinton, *The American Rebellion,* 162; Whipple to Lincoln, 9 March 1780, Abraham Whipple Letterbook; John Laurens to Henry Laurens, 10 March 1780, *Papers of Henry Laurens,* 15:249.

14. Arbuthnot to Clinton, 19 February, 3, 16 March 1780, Clinton Papers.

15. Tilley, *The British Navy,* 178–79; Arbuthnot to Clinton, 16 March 1780, Clinton Papers.

16. Tilley, *The British Navy,* 179; Uhlendorf, *The Siege of Charleston,* 377; Lincoln to Whipple, 9 March 1780, Abraham Whipple Letterbook; Ewald, *Diary of the American War,* 210; Arbuthnot to Clinton, 16 March 1780, Clinton Papers.

17. Moultrie, *Memoirs of the American Revolution,* 2:60; Whipple to Lincoln, 27 February 1780, Abraham Whipple Letterbook; Lincoln to Washington, 25 March 1780, Benjamin Lincoln Letterbook.

18. Lincoln to Washington, 17 July 1780, Lincoln Papers; Whipple and Captains to Rutledge and Lincoln, 11 March 1780, Abraham Whipple Letterbook; Lincoln to Whipple, 16 March 1780, Lincoln Papers.

19. Lincoln to Whipple, 16 March 1780, Lincoln Papers; Whipple to Lincoln, 17 March 1780, Abraham Whipple Letterbook; Simpson to Whipple, 12 March 1780, ibid.; Whipple to Lockwood and Pyne, 15 March 1780, ibid.; Lincoln to Washington, 17 July 1780, Lincoln Papers; John Laurens to Henry Laurens, 25 March 1780, *Papers of Henry Laurens,* 15:255; Whipple to Hoysted Hacker, 19 March 1780, Abraham Whipple Letterbook; Moultrie, *Memoirs of the American Revolution,* 2:58.

20. McIntosh, "Journal of Siege of Charlestown," 99; Russell, "Journal of Peter Russell," 491; Tarleton, *Campaigns of 1780 and 1781,* 48; A Journal of the Proceedings of His Majesty's Ship Roebuck. Sir Andrew Snape Hamond Commander, and kept by George Palmer Lieutenant of the Said Ship—from the 13 May 1779 to the 6 June 1780, 20, 21 March 1780, Trustees of the National Maritime Museum, London, ADM L/R 160.

21. The captains who voted against the attempt were Samuel Tucker of *Boston,* Thomas Simpson of *Ranger,* J. Courannat of *L'Aventure,* James Pyne of *Truite,* Marshall Boetis of the galley *Lee* and George Farragut of the galley *Revenge.* Tucker and Simpson were captains of the Continental navy while the other captains belonged to the South Carolina state navy.

22. Whipple memorandum of application made by Captain Crawley along with opinions of captains, 20 March 1780, Abraham Whipple Letterbook.

23. These figures consist of *Renown* (50), *Roebuck* (44), *Romulus* (44), four frigates with thirty-two guns each, and one sloop of war with twenty guns for a British total of 286. For the Americans, *Bricole* (44), *Providence* (32), *Boston* (32), *Queen of France* (28), *Truite* (26), *L'Aventure* (26), *Ranger* (20), and forty guns of Fort Moultrie for a total of 248. Account of Stores at Fort Moultrie, 12 February 1780, Lincoln Papers.

24. Lincoln to Washington, 17 July 1780, Lincoln Papers; Whipple and Captains to Lincoln, 20 March 1780, ibid.; John Laurens to Henry Laurens, 25 March 1780, *Papers of Henry Laurens,* 15:255.

25. Lincoln to Washington, 17 July 1780, Lincoln Papers; Whipple and Captains to Lincoln, 20 March 1780, Abraham Whipple Letterbook.

26. Lincoln to Washington, 17 July 1780, Lincoln Papers; Whipple and Captains to Lincoln, 20 March 1780, Abraham Whipple Letterbook; Gervais to Henry Laurens, 22 March 1780, Laurens Papers; John Laurens to Henry Laurens, 25 March 1780, *Papers of Henry Laurens,* 15:255.

27. Lincoln to Whipple, 20 March 1780, Lincoln Papers; Gabriel Manigault Journal, 21 March 1780, South Carolina Historical Society; Moultrie, *Memoirs of the American Revolution,* 2:60.

28. John Lewis Gervais to Henry Laurens, 22 March 1780, Laurens Papers.

29. Clinton to Arbuthnot, 20 March 1780, Clinton Papers; Clinton Siege Journal, 4 April 1780, ibid.; Clinton to William, 1st Baron Auckland, 20 March 1780, ibid.

Chapter 6

1. Tarleton, *Campaigns of 1780 and 1781,* 5.

2. Grimké Orderly Book, 13 February 1780, South Carolina Historical Society; *Orderly Book of Benjamin Taliaferro,* 66, 74.

3. Grimké Orderly Book, 28 February, 9 March 1780, South Carolina Historical Society; *Orderly Book of Benjamin Taliaferro,* 82, 89; Rutledge to Lincoln, 1 March 1780, Lincoln Papers.

4. Grimké Orderly Book, 26 February, 2 March 1780, South Carolina Historical Society; John Laurens to Henry Laurens, 14 March 1780, *Papers of Henry Laurens,* 15:251.

5. Grimké Orderly Book, 2, 21 February 1780, South Carolina Historical Society; General Benjamin Lincoln's Order Book, 1779–1780, 15 February 1780, University of Georgia Libraries, Athens (microfilm, South Carolina Department of Archives and History), (hereafter cited as Lincoln Order Book).

6. Declaration of Archibald Gamble, 30 June 1780, Emmet Collection; James Cannon to Lincoln, filed at the end of July 1780, Lincoln Papers; Declaration of James Cannon, 28 June 1780, Emmet Collection.

7. Alexander S. Salley, ed., *Documents Relating to the History of South Carolina during the Revolutionary War* (Columbia: Historical Commission of South Carolina, 1908), 22–41; Muster Roll of Captain Baker's Company in the 2nd Regiment Commanded by Colonel Francis Marion, 29 March 1780, Richard Bohun Baker Papers, 1780–1783, South Carolina Historical Society; Alexander S. Salley, comp., *Records of the Regiments of the South Carolina Line in the Revolutionary War,* edited by Alida Moe (Baltimore: Genealogical Publishing Co., 1977), 14–27; Walter J. Fraser, "Reflections of 'Democracy' in Revolutionary South Carolina?: The Composition of Military Organizations and the Attitudes and Relationships of the Officers and Men, 1775–1780," *South Carolina Historical Magazine* 78, no. 3 (1977): 208–9; *Orderly Book of Benjamin Taliaferro,* 69, 77, 134.

8. Edward C. Papenfuse and Gregory A. Stiverson, "General Smallwood's Recruits: The Peacetime Career of the Revolutionary War Private," *The William and Mary Quarterly* 30, no. 1 (1973): 117–32; John R. Sellers, "The Common Soldier in the American Revolution," in *Military History of the American Revolution: The Proceedings of the Sixth Military History Symposium, USAF Academy,* ed. Stanley J. Underdal (Washington, D.C.: United States Air Force, 1976), 151–61; James Kirby Martin and Mark Edward Lender, *A Respectable Army: The Military Origins of the Republic, 1763–1789* (Arlington Heights, Ill.: Harlan Davidson, 1982), 90–91, 94–95; Fraser, "Reflections of 'Democracy' in Revolutionary South Carolina," 211.

9. Charles Royster, *A Revolutionary People at War: The Continental Army and American Character, 1775–1783* (New York: W. W. Norton, 1979), 223, 307, 373–78; See Fred Anderson, *A People's Army: Massachusetts Soldiers and Society in the Seven Years' War* (Chapel Hill: University of North Carolina Press, 1984), 155–56. Anderson makes a similar argument for Massachusetts men who served in the Seven Years' War, maintaining that greater aspirations such as religion motivated enlisted men to fight.

10. Fraser, "Reflections of 'Democracy' in Revolutionary South Carolina," 205, 211–12; Lincoln Order Book, 19 March 1780, University of Georgia Libraries.

11. R. B. Baker to Eliza B. Baker, 29 March 1780, copy in Clinton Papers; *Orderly Book of Benjamin Taliaferro,* 54; Lincoln to Whipple, 12 February 1780, Abraham Whipple Letterbook; Grimké Orderly Book, 29 February, 3 March 1780, South Carolina Historical Society.

12. Grimké Orderly Book, 29 February 1780, South Carolina Historical Society; Lincoln Order Book, 9 March 1780, University of Georgia Libraries; *Orderly Book of Benjamin Taliaferro,* 89, 138.

13. *Orderly Book of Benjamin Taliaferro,* 110.

14. Lincoln Order Book, 16 February 1780, University of Georgia Libraries; Grimké Orderly Book, 16 February, 3 March 1780, South Carolina Historical Society; *Orderly Book of Benjamin Taliaferro,* 110.

15. William Gilmore Simms, *South Carolina in the Revolutionary War: Being a Reply to Certain Misrepresentations and Mistakes of Recent Writers, in Relation to the Course and Conduct of this State* (Charleston, S.C.: Walker and James, 1853), 88, 177; Russell, "Journal of Peter Russell," 490; John Peebles, *John Peebles' American War: The Diary of a Scottish Grenadier, 1776–1782,* ed. Ira D. Gruber (Mechanicsburg, Pa.: Stackpole Books; Gloucestershire: Sutton Publishing, 1998), 349–50 (quotes from *John Peebles' American War: The Diary of a Scottish Grenadier, 1776–1782* are reproduced with kind permission from Sutton Publishing Ltd.).

16. John André, Report of Intelligence, filed with 15 March 1780 correspondence, Clinton Papers.

17. Lincoln to the Continental Congress, 4 March 1780, PCC (National Archives Microfilm Publication M247, roll 177); Lincoln to Washington, 4 March 1780, Benjamin Lincoln Letterbook; Thomas Pinckney to Harriott

Pinckney, 30 March 1780, "Letters of Thomas Pinckney, 1775–1780," ed. Jack L. Cross, *South Carolina Historical Magazine* 58, no. 4 (1957): 236–37; Gibbes, *Documentary History of the American Revolution,* 2:129; R. B. Baker to Eliza B. Baker, 29 March 1780, copy in Clinton Papers; David Ramsay to Benjamin Rush, 21 March 1780, *David Ramsay: Selections from His Writings,* 65.

18. Moultrie, *Memoirs of the American Revolution,* 2:58; Lincoln to the Continental Congress, 24 March 1780, PCC (National Archives Microfilm Publication M247, roll 177); Dull, *Diplomatic History of the American Revolution,* 108–9, 112.

19. Moultrie, *Memoirs of the American Revolution,* 2:65; Grimké Orderly Book, 26 March 1780, South Carolina Historical Society; Huger to Lincoln, 18 March 1780, Lincoln Papers.

Chapter 7

1. Clinton to Elphinstone, 22 March 1780, Clinton Papers; Russell, "Journal of Peter Russell," 492; Clinton, *The American Rebellion,* 163; Clinton Siege Journal, 4 April 1780, Clinton Papers.

2. Russell, "Journal of Peter Russell," 492; Ewald, *Diary of the American War,* 215; Tarleton, *Campaigns of 1780 and 1781,* 7–8.

3. Tarleton, *Campaigns of 1780 and 1781,* 8; William Washington to Lincoln, 15 March 1780, Lincoln Papers.

4. William Sanders to Lincoln, 15 March 1780, Lincoln Papers; William Washington to Lincoln, 15 March 1780, ibid., James Ladson to Isaac Huger, 16 March 1780, ibid.; Anthony Allaire, *Diary of Lieut. Anthony Allaire* (New York: New York Times and Arno Press, 1968), 7.

5. Russell, "Journal of Peter Russell," 492; Uzal Johnson, Memorandum of Occurances during the Campaigne, 1780–1781, 26 March 1780, Princeton University Library (South Carolina Historical Society, typewritten transcription); Ewald, *Diary of the American War,* 214.

6. Ewald, *Diary of the American War,* 214; Allaire, *Diary of Lieut. Anthony Allaire,* 8.

7. Return of Captured Forage, 7 March 1780, Clinton Papers; Return of Commissarys of Captures, 10 March 1780, ibid.; Return of the Number of Horses & Draught Oxen Received into the Quarter Master General's

Department for the Service of the Government from the Commissarys of Captures from the Fourteenth of February Last to the Twenty Second of March 1780, both Days inclusive, ibid.; Return of Cattle Now in the Pen at Pinkney's Plantation, 28 March 1780, ibid.

8. Ewald, *Diary of the American War,* 202; Sarah Lowndes to Rawlins Lowdnes, 17 May 1780, Clinton Papers.

9. Richard Lorentz to John André, 4 April 1780, Clinton Papers; William Giekie to Clinton, 4 May 1780, ibid.; Russell, "Journal of Peter Russell," 486; William Carson to James Simpson, 1 May 1780, Clinton Papers.

10. Commissarys of Captures Return of Negroes Horses etc., 17 March 1780, Clinton Papers; John André to Lord Cathcart, 4 March 1780, ibid.; William Carson to James Simpson, 1 May 1780, ibid.

11. Sylvia R. Frey, *Water from the Rock: Black Resistance in a Revolutionary Age* (Princeton: Princeton University Press, 1991), 113–14, 119.

12. Cornwallis to Clinton, 11 May 1780, Clinton Papers; Clinton to Cornwallis, 20 May 1780, ibid.

13. William Carson to James Simpson, 1 May 1780, Clinton Papers; James Paterson to Clinton, 3 April 1780, ibid.; Cornwallis to Clinton, 11 May 1780, ibid.; Charles Morris and John McNamara Hays to John André, 22 March 1780, ibid.

14. Uhlendorf, *The Siege of Charleston,* 223; Peter Timothy, Journal of Observations from the 26th of March, 1780 to 26th April, 1780, 27 March 1780, South Carolina Historical Society (hereafter cited as Timothy Journal); Allaire, *Diary of Lieut. Anthony Allaire,* 9; Ewald, *Diary of the American War,* 215.

15. Uhlendorf, *The Siege of Charleston,* 219, 223, 229; Russell, "Journal of Peter Russell," 492–93.

16. This is the present day site of Old Town Creek.

17. Russell, "Journal of Peter Russell," 492–93; Timothy Journal, 27 March 1780, South Carolina Historical Society; Wilson Journal, 22 March 1780, Charleston Library Society; Lincoln to the Continental Congress, 24 March 1780, PCC (National Archives Microfilm Publication M247, roll 177).

18. Uhlendorf, *The Siege of Charleston,* 223–25; Ewald, *Diary of the American War,* 215–16.

19. Lincoln to the Continental Congress, 24 March 1780, PCC (National Archives Microfilm Publication M247, roll 177); Grimké Orderly Book, 29 March 1780, South Carolina Historical Society; Weekly Return of Colonel Laurens's Battalion Light Infantry, 7 May 1780, Lincoln Papers; John Laurens to Henry Laurens, 31 March 1780, *Papers of Henry Laurens,* 15:263.

20. The British line of march would have approximated the present day route of Dorchester Road.

21. Russell, "Journal of Peter Russell," 493; Uhlendorf, *The Siege of Charleston,* 225; Ewald, *Diary of the American War,* 218.

22. Generally, a fleche is a small V-shaped earthwork open in the rear.

23. Russell, "Journal of Peter Russell," 493–94; John Laurens to Henry Laurens, 31 March 1780, *Papers of Henry Laurens,* 15:263; Gregory D. Massey, "A Hero's Life: John Laurens and the American Revolution" (Ph.D. diss., University of South Carolina, 1992), 370; Uhlendorf, *The Siege of Charleston,* 227; Ewald, *Diary of the American War,* 218–19.

24. The jaeger's rifle shot through Hyrne's cheek gives testimony to the accuracy of the jaegers' fire. The Hessian rifleman was obviously attempting a headshot at the vulnerable American officer when he hit him in the cheek.

25. John Laurens to Henry Laurens, 31 March 1780, *Papers of Henry Laurens,* 15:263.

26. Ibid.; Ewald, *Diary of the American War,* 219; Timothy Journal, 30 March 1780, South Carolina Historical Society.

27. Ewald, *Diary of the American War,* 219; John Laurens to Henry Laurens, 31 March 1780, *Papers of Henry Laurens,* 15:263; Gabriel Manigault Journal, 30 March 1780, South Carolina Historical Society; Moultrie, *Memoirs of the American Revolution,* 1:404; Timothy Journal, 30 March 1780, South Carolina Historical Society.

28. "Original Journals of the Siege of Charleston, S.C. in 1780," *The Magnolia; or, Southern Apalachian* 1, no. 6 (1842): 366.

29. Russell, "Journal of Peter Russell," 494; From Colonel Barnard Beekman's Notes in McIntosh, "Journal of Siege of Charlestown," 113.

30. Clinton, *The American Rebellion,* 163; Wilson Journal, 30 March 1780, Charleston Library Society; Timothy Journal, 31 March 1780, South Carolina Historical Society.

31. Ewald, *Diary of the American War,* 219; William Woodford to Lincoln, 26 March 1780, Emmet Collection; Ramsay to Benjamin Rush, 31 August 1779, *David Ramsay: Selections from His Writings,* 63–64.

Chapter 8

1. This discussion of siege warfare is from Christopher Duffy, *Fire and Stone,* 10–12.

2. Duffy, *Fire and Stone,* 109–11, 124; John W. Wright, "Notes on the Siege of Yorktown in 1781 with Special Reference to the Conduct of a Siege in the Eighteenth Century," *William and Mary College Quarterly Historical Magazine* 12, no. 4 (1932): 231–33.

3. Duffy, *Fire and Stone,* 152–53; Wright, "Notes on Siege of Yorktown," 231; Moultrie, *Memoirs of the American Revolution,* 2:36–37.

4. Duffy, *Fire and Stone,* 12, 98, 112, 123.

5. Jac Weller, "Revolutionary War Artillery in the South," *Georgia Historical Quarterly* 46, no. 3 (1962): 254–56; B. P. Hughes, *British Smooth-Bore Artillery: The Muzzle Loading Artillery of the 18th and 19th Centuries* (Harrisburg, Pa.: Stackpole Books, 1969), 28–30, 37, 39; Harold L. Peterson, *Round Shot and Rammers* (Harrisburg, Pa.: Stackpole Books, 1969), 33, 66.

6. Weller, "Revolutionary War Artillery," 257–58; Pancake, *This Destructive War,* 40; Duffy, *Fire and Stone,* 118–19.

7. Duffy, *Fire and Stone,* 119; Hughes, *British Smooth-Bore Artillery,* 27–31, 37, 39; Peterson, *Round Shot and Rammers,* 68; Weller, "Revolutionary War Artillery," 259, 261.

8. Peterson, *Round Shot and Rammers,* 66; Duffy, *Fire and Stone,* 116; Weller, "Revolutionary War Artillery," 258–59.

9. Russell, "Journal of Peter Russell," 497; John Faucheraud Grimké, Journal of the Siege of Charles Town, 14 April 1780, Continental Army Southern Department Records, 1778–1790, South Carolina Historical Society (hereafter cited as Grimké Journal).

10. A small section of the curtain of the hornwork can still be seen in Marion Square today.

11. Clinton, *The American Rebellion,* 163; Natalie P. Adams, "'Now a Few Words about the Works . . . Called the Old Royal Work': Phase I Archaeological Investigations at Marion Square, Charleston, South Carolina" (Stone Mountain, Ga.: New South Associates, 1998), 4, 18, 25;

Duffy, *Fire and Stone,* 65–66; Uhlendorf, *The Siege of Charleston,* 55, 91; Ewald, *Diary of the American War,* 240–41.

12. Ewald, *Diary of the American War,* 240–41; Duffy, *Fire and Stone,* 61; Clinton, *The American Rebellion,* 163; Clinton Map 314, Clinton Papers.

13. Ewald, *Diary of the American War,* 241; Clinton, *The American Rebellion,* 163; Uhlendorf, *The Siege of Charleston,* 415.

14. Clinton, *The American Rebellion,* 163; Ewald, *Diary of the American War,* 241; McIntosh, "Journal of Siege of Charlestown," 103; Ramsay, *Revolution in South Carolina,* 2:49; John Laurens to Henry Laurens, 9 April 1780, *Papers of Henry Laurens,* 15:269.

15. Lincoln to Rutledge, 4 December 1779, Benjamin Lincoln Letterbook; Rutledge to Lincoln, 4, 6 December 1779, Lincoln Papers; Uhlendorf, *The Siege of Charleston,* 227–29.

16. Grimké Journal, 31 March 1780, South Carolina Historical Society; Grimké Orderly Book, 28 March 1780, ibid.; John Lewis Gervais to Henry Laurens, 29 March 1780, Laurens Papers.

17. Moultrie, *Memoirs of the American Revolution,* 2:62, 106–7; Grimké Orderly Book, 16 April 1780, South Carolina Historical Society; John Wells Jr. to Henry Laurens, 24 March 1780, Laurens Papers.

18. Lincoln to Washington, 17 July 1780, Lincoln Papers; Lincoln to the Continental Congress, 24 March 1780, PCC (National Archives Microfilm Publication M247, roll 177); Lincoln to Caswell, 25 March 1780, Benjamin Lincoln Letterbook.

19. Lincoln to the Continental Congress, 24 March 1780, PCC (National Archives Microfilm Publication M247, roll 177); Lincoln to Woodford, 17 March 1780, Benjamin Lincoln Letterbook.

20. McIntosh, "Journal of Siege of Charlestown," 98–99; *Orderly Book of Benjamin Taliaferro,* 68, 115; Weekly Return of the Brigade of Foot Commanded by Colonel Richard Parker, 18 March 1780, Lincoln Papers.

21. Clinton Siege Journal, 2 April 1780, Clinton Papers.

Chapter 9

1. Russell, "Journal of Peter Russell," 494; Uhlendorf, *The Siege of Charleston,* 233–35; Wilson Journal, 1 April 1780, Charleston Library

Society; Platte Grenadier Battalion Journal, 1 April 1780, Lidgerwood Hessian Transcripts; Ewald, *Diary of the American War,* 221; Clinton Siege Journal, 2 April 1780, Clinton Papers.

2. The British constructed the redoubts and subsequent parallel across the peninsula just below present day Spring Street west of King Street and between Columbus and Spring Streets east of King. In determining the locations of the British parallels, approach trenches, and fortifications, I have relied on Plan of the Siege of Charlestown in South Carolina, Clinton Map 308, Clinton Papers, A Sketch of the Operations Before Charlestown the Capital of South Carolina, copy in the Charleston Museum, Charleston, S.C., and Map of Charleston and its vicinity showing the original Settlement of 1670 at Albemarle Point, The Oyster Point Settlement of 1672, and subsequent extensions of 1783 and 1849, prepared to accompany Mayor Courtenay's Centennial Address, 13 August 1883, copy in the Charleston Museum. The last two maps show the British first parallel as being constructed further away from the Charleston defenses, in the environs of Line, Bogard, and Columbus Streets. The original Clinton map puts the first parallel much closer to Spring Street however. Redoubt Number Three, the approximate center of the first parallel, lay at the southwest corner of the intersection of King and Spring Streets.

3. Wilson Journal, 1 April 1780, Charleston Library Society; Uhlendorf, *The Siege of Charleston,* 41, 235.

4. Samuel Baldwin, "Diary of Events in Charleston, S.C., from March 20th to April 20th, 1780," *Proceedings of the New Jersey Historical Society* 2, no. 2 (1847): 81; Grimké Journal, 2 April 1780, South Carolina Historical Society; Peebles, *John Peebles' American War,* 355; Russell, "Journal of Peter Russell," 494; Timothy Journal, 2 April 1780, South Carolina Historical Society.

5. Peebles, *John Peebles' American War,* 355; Uhlendorf, *The Siege of Charleston,* 41; Timothy Journal, 31 March, 2 April 1780, South Carolina Historical Society.

6. Hampstead Hill was in the area which is today bordered by East Bay, Amherst, America, and Blake Streets in Charleston. Urban sprawl and the presence of the bridges over the Cooper River now prevent one from appreciating the elevated position of this ground vis-à-vis the surrounding area.

7. Wilson Journal, 2, 3 April 1780, Charleston Library Society; Clinton Siege Journal, 2 April 1780, Clinton Papers.

8. Major William Croghan's Journal, 9 February to 4 May 1780, 3 April 1780, MS Sparks 60, by permission of the Houghton Library, Harvard University, Boston, Mass.; Russell, "Journal of Peter Russell," 495; Peebles, *John Peebles' American War,* 355–56.

9. Wilson Journal, 3 April 1780, Charleston Library Society; Clinton to Arbuthnot, 4 April 1780, Clinton Papers; Clinton Siege Journal, 4 April 1780, ibid.; Ewald, *Diary of the American War,* 224.

10. John Wells Jr. to Henry Laurens, 9 April 1780, *Papers of Henry Laurens,* 15:275; Russell, "Journal of Peter Russell," 495; Moses Young Memorandum, 31 March to 7 April 1780, Laurens Papers; John Laurens to Henry Laurens, *Papers of Henry Laurens,* 15:270.

11. Whipple to Simpson, 3 April 1780, Abraham Whipple Letterbook; Russell, "Journal of Peter Russell," 495; Ewald, *Diary of the American War,* 224; Wilson Journal, 4 April 1780, Charleston Library Society; Moses Young Memorandum, 31 March to 7 April 1780, Laurens Papers; John Laurens to Henry Laurens, 9 April 1780, *Papers of Henry Laurens,* 15:270.

12. Wilson Journal, 5, 6, 7 April 1780, Charleston Library Society; Clinton to Arbuthnot, 4 April 1780, Clinton Papers; Clinton Siege Journal, 7 April 1780, ibid.; Timothy Journal, 5 April 1780, South Carolina Historical Society; Grimké Journal, 5 April 1780, ibid.

13. John Lewis Gervais to Henry Laurens, 7 April 1780, Laurens Papers; Platte Grenadier Battalion Journal, 5 April 1780, Lidgerwood Hessian Transcripts.

14. Ewald, *Diary of the American War,* 224–25; Clinton Siege Journal, 6 April 1780, Clinton Papers; John Lewis Gervais to Henry Laurens, 7 April 1780, Laurens Papers.

15. Timothy Journal, 6, 7 April 1780, South Carolina Historical Society; Rutledge to Lincoln, 7 April 1780, Emmet Collection; John Lewis Gervais to Henry Laurens, 7 April 1780, Laurens Papers; James Duncan to Elphinstone, 7 April 1780, *Keith Papers,* 1:161–62.

16. Russell, "Journal of Peter Russell," 495; Clinton Siege Journal, 6 April 1780, Clinton Papers; Grimké Orderly Book, 5 April 1780, South Carolina Historical Society.

17. Clinton Siege Journal, 4 April 1780, Clinton Papers.

18. See Benjamin Franklin Stevens, ed., *The Campaign in Virginia, 1781: An Exact Reprint of Six Rare Pamphlets on the Clinton-Cornwallis*

Controversy with Very Numerous Important Unpublished Manuscript Notes by Sir Henry Clinton K.B., 2 vols. (London, 1888).

19. Willcox, *Portrait of a General,* 65, 282–83, 314–15; Miscellaneous Clinton memorandum describing relations with Cornwallis, filed at the end of March 1780, Clinton Papers; Clinton to Thomas Pelham-Clinton, second duke of Newcastle, incomplete letter filed at the end of May 1780, ibid.; John André to Clinton, 3 April 1780, ibid.

20. Clinton Siege Journal, 2, 5 April 1780, Clinton Papers; Willcox, *Portrait of a General,* 315–16.

21. Clinton Siege Journal, 6 April 1780, Clinton Papers; John André, Memorandum of what passed relative to taking Duty at Charlestown, 2 April 1780, ibid.

22. Russell, "Journal of Peter Russell," 495; Baldwin, "Diary of Events," 80; André, Memorandum of what passed relative to taking Duty at Charlestown, 2 April 1780, Clinton Papers.

23. Thomas Pinckney to Harriott Pinckney, 30 March 1780, "Letters of Thomas Pinckney," 236–37; David Ramsay to Benjamin Rush, 8 April 1780, *David Ramsay: Selections from His Writings,* 66; Timothy Journal, 6 April 1780, South Carolina Historical Society; Moultrie, *Memoirs of the American Revolution,* 2:62.

24. Grimké states this occurred on 6 April while Ewald claims 8 April, but it appears to have occurred on 7 April.

25. Grimké Journal, 6 April 1780, South Carolina Historical Society; Russell, "Journal of Peter Russell," 495; Moultrie, *Memoirs of the American Revolution,* 2:63; Gabriel Manigault Journal, 7 April 1780, South Carolina Historical Society; Moses Young Memorandum, 31 March to 7 April 1780, Laurens Papers; Platte Grenadier Battalion Journal, 7 April 1780, Lidgerwood Hessian Transcripts.

26. *Orderly Book of Benjamin Taliaferro,* 127; John Wells Jr. to Henry Laurens, 9 April 1780, *Papers of Henry Laurens,* 15:273; Moses Young Memorandum, 31 March to 7 April 1780, Laurens Papers; Clinton Siege Journal, 7 April 1780, Clinton Papers.

27. Ewald, *Diary of the American War,* 226; Hartung Diary, 7 April 1780, Lidgerwood Hessian Transcripts.

28. Shutes Folly was much larger in the eighteenth century than it is today. At low tide it was virtually impassable on the side between it and Mount Pleasant.

29. Lincoln to the Continental Congress, 24 March 1780, PCC (National Archives Microfilm Publication M247, roll 177).

30. Tarleton, *Campaigns of 1780 and 1781,* 48–49; Lincoln to the Continental Congress, 24 March 1780, PCC (National Archives Microfilm Publication M247, roll 177); John Laurens to Henry Laurens, 9 April 1780, *Papers of Henry Laurens,* 15:271; John Laurens to Henry Laurens, 25 March 1780, ibid., 15:255–56; Report of Admiralty Office, 22 February 1780, Lincoln Papers; Lincoln to Washington, 17 July 1780, ibid.; John Wells Jr. to Henry Laurens, 24 March 1780, Laurens Papers.

31. Arbuthnot to Clinton, 5 April 1780, Clinton Papers.

32. Clinton Siege Journal, 4 April 1780, Clinton Papers; Clinton to Arbuthnot, 4 April 1780, ibid.; Arbuthnot to Clinton, 5 April 1780, ibid.

33. Clinton Siege Journal, 8 April 1780, Clinton Papers; Arbuthnot's report of the action is included in Tarleton, *Campaigns of 1780 and 1781,* 49; Timothy Journal, 8 April 1780, South Carolina Historical Society.

34. Moses Young Memorandum, 31 March to 7 April 1780, Laurens Papers; Timothy Journal, 8 April 1780, South Carolina Historical Society; Tarleton, *Campaigns of 1780 and 1781,* 49; Warwick Oben, A Journal of the Proceedings of His Majesty's Ship Richmond Commencing the 22d July 1779 & Ending the 22d July 1780, 9 April 1780, Trustees of the National Maritime Museum, London, ADM L/R 132; W. D. Waudby, Journal for His Majesty's Ship Raleigh, 9 October 1779 to 8 October 1780, 9 April 1780, Trustees of the National Maritime Museum, ADM L/R 385.

35. Timothy Journal, 8 April 1780, South Carolina Historical Society; Tarleton, *Campaigns of 1780 and 1781,* 49; Gabriel Manigault Journal, 8 April 1780, South Carolina Historical Society.

36. Platte Grenadier Battalion Journal, 8 April 1780, Lidgerwood Hessian Transcripts; Hartung Diary, 8 April 1780, ibid.; John Laurens to Henry Laurens, 9 April 1780, *Papers of Henry Laurens,* 15:271; Ewald, *Diary of the American War,* 226.

37. Ewald, *Diary of the American War,* 227; Uhlendorf, *The Siege of Charleston,* 243; Timothy Journal, 8 April 1780, South Carolina Historical Society; Platte Grenadier Battalion Journal, 8 April 1780, Lidgerwood Hessian Transcripts.

38. Clinton Siege Journal, 9, 10 April 1780, Clinton Papers.

39. Ibid.; Clinton to Arbuthnot, 8, 13 April 1780, ibid.

40. Clinton Siege Journal, 9, 10 April 1780, Clinton Papers; Ewald, *Diary of the American War,* 225; John Laurens to Henry Laurens, 9 April 1780, *Papers of Henry Laurens,* 15:269.

41. Clinton Siege Journal, 10 April 1780, Clinton Papers.

42. K. B. referred to Clinton's title of Knight of the Bath.

43. The summons is included in Lincoln to Washington, 17 July 1780, Lincoln Papers.

44. Franklin Benjamin Hough, ed., *The Siege of Savannah by the Combined American and French Forces under the Command of Gen. Lincoln and the Count D'Estaing in the Autumn of 1779* (1866; reprint, New York: Da Capo Press, 1974), 89–90; Otho Holland Williams to John Harris Cruger, 3 June 1781, *The Papers of General Nathanael Greene, Volume VIII: 30 March–10 July 1781,* ed. Dennis M. Conrad (Chapel Hill: University of North Carolina Press, 1995), 339; Geoffrey Parker, ed., *The Thirty Years War* (London: Routledge, 1984), 112.

45. Lincoln to Washington, 17 July 1780, Lincoln Papers; Hartung Diary, 10 April 1780, Lidgerwood Hessian Transcripts.

46. Russell's assessment obviously does not include naval casualties.

47. Clinton Siege Journal, 10 April 1780, Clinton Papers; Ewald, *Diary of the American War,* 228; Russell, "Journal of Peter Russell," 497; Robertson, *Archibald Robertson: Diaries and Sketches in America,* 222; Peebles, *John Peebles' American War,* 359–60.

48. McIntosh, "Journal of Siege of Charlestown," 100–101.

49. Croghan Journal, 13 April 1780, MS Sparks 60.

50. Grimké Journal, 13 April 1780, South Carolina Historical Society; Uhlendorf, *The Siege of Charleston,* 249; Ewald, *Diary of the American War,* 228; Clinton Siege Journal, 14 April 1780, Clinton Papers.

51. Grimké Journal, 13 April 1780, South Carolina Historical Society; McIntosh, "Journal of Siege of Charlestown," 100.

52. Uhlendorf, *The Siege of Charleston,* 249; Russell, "Journal of Peter Russell," 497; Joseph Johnson, *Traditions and Reminiscences Chiefly of the American Revolution in the South: Including Biographical Sketches, Incidents and Anecdotes, Few of Which Have Been Published, Particularly of Residents in the Upper Country* (Charleston, S.C.: Walker and James, 1851), 248; Gervais to Henry Laurens, 17 April 1780, *Papers of Henry Laurens,* 15:278.

53. Gadsden had only recently become Lieutenant Governor. The South Carolina constitution of 1778 provided that in the lieutenant governor's absence, the governor could empower any member of the Privy Council to act in his place. Since Lieutenant Governor Bee was in Philadelphia, Rutledge assigned Gadsden to take his place. See McCrady, *South Carolina in the Revolution,* 464–65; Lincoln to Rutledge, 8 April 1780, Benjamin Lincoln Letterbook; Lincoln to Washington, 17 July 1780, Lincoln Papers; John Lewis Gervais to Henry Laurens, 17 April 1780, *Papers of Henry Laurens,* 15:277.

54. Hugh F. Rankin, *Francis Marion: The Swamp Fox* (New York: Thomas Y. Crowell Company, 1973), 44–45.

55. Gervais to Henry Laurens, 17 April 1780, *Papers of Henry Laurens,* 15:277.

Chapter 10

1. Lampriers is variously called Lempriere's, Lempriers, and Lamprier's by many of the participants. Both Lincoln and Clinton referred to it as Lampriers which is the spelling I have used throughout this work.

2. Lincoln to Isaac Huger, 8 April 1780, Lincoln Papers; Lincoln to Washington, 17 July 1780, ibid.; John Laurens to Henry Laurens, 9 April 1780, *Papers of Henry Laurens,* 15:269; Lincoln to Malmedy, 11 April 1780, Lincoln Papers.

3. Malmedy to Lincoln, 8 April 1780, Lincoln Papers; Lincoln to Rutledge, 8 April 1780, Benjamin Lincoln Letterbook; Lincoln to Samuel Huntington, 9 April 1780, ibid.

4. Malmedy to Lincoln, 8 April 1780, Lincoln Papers; Lincoln to Whipple, 9 April 1780, Abraham Whipple Letterbook; Lincoln to Malmedy, 11 April 1780, Lincoln Papers.

5. Lincoln to Charles Cotesworth Pinckney, 11 April 1780, Benjamin Lincoln Letterbook; Lincoln to Samuel Huntington, 9 April 1780, ibid.; Malmedy to Lincoln, 12 April 1780, Lincoln Papers.

6. Lincoln to Washington, 17 July 1780, Lincoln Papers; Tarleton, *Campaigns of 1780 and 1781,* 14.

7. Clinton Siege Journal, 13 April 1780, Clinton Papers; Clinton, *The American Rebellion,* 164–65; Tarleton, *Campaigns of 1780 and 1781,* 15;

Russell, "Journal of Peter Russell," 497; Instructions for Lieutenant Colonel Webster, 12 April 1780, Clinton Papers.

8. Clinton Siege Journal, 10, 13 April 1780, Clinton Papers; Instructions for Lieutenant Colonel Webster, 12 April 1780, Clinton Papers.

9. Allaire, *Diary of Lieut. Anthony Allaire,* 11; Clinton, *The American Rebellion,* 165.

10. Biggin's Bridge and Church were located just south of the current Highway 52 bridge over the Tail Race Canal in Moncks Corner. The ruins of Biggin's Church are still visible today.

11. Allaire, *Diary of Lieut. Anthony Allaire,* 11; Huger to Lincoln, 13 April 1780, copy in Clinton Papers; Tarleton, *Campaigns of 1780 and 1781,* 16; Huger to Thomas Rutledge, 12 April 1780, Lincoln Papers.

12. Tarleton, *Campaigns of 1780 and 1781,* 15–16.

13. Ibid., 16–17; Tarleton to Clinton, 15 April 1780, Clinton Papers; Stedman, *History of the American War,* 2:183.

14. Stedman, *History of the American War,* 2:183; Tarleton to Clinton, 15 April 1780, Clinton Papers; Clinton, *The American Rebellion,* 166.

15. John Lewis Gervais to Henry Laurens, 28 April 1780, *Papers of Henry Laurens,* 15:287.

16. Benjamin Lincoln, Journal from the 10th of April to the 12th of May inclusive, 16, 20 April 1780, enclosed in Lincoln to the Continental Congress, 24 May 1780, PCC (National Archives Microfilm Publication M247, roll 177).

17. Tarleton, *Campaigns of 1780 and 1781,* 16–17; John Lewis Gervais to Henry Laurens, 28 April 1780, *Papers of Henry Laurens,* 15:287; John Laurens to Henry Laurens, 9 April 1780, ibid., 15:271; Allaire, *Diary of Lieut. Anthony Allaire,* 11.

18. Instructions for Lieutenant Colonel Webster, 12 April 1780, Clinton Papers; Gervais to Laurens, 28 April 1780, *Papers of Henry Laurens,* 15:288; Gervais to Laurens, 13 May 1780, ibid., 15:292; James Custer to Laurens, 4 March 1780, ibid., 15:239n. 2; John André memorandum on "Proposed Regulations in '79 and Orders Issued in Consequence," filed at the end of December 1779, Clinton Papers.

19. Probably Mary Middleton Butler, the wife of Major Pierce Butler of the South Carolina militia.

20. John Lewis Gervais to Henry Laurens, 28 April 1780, *Papers of Henry Laurens,* 15:288; Gervais to Laurens, 13 May 1780, ibid., 15:292.

21. Deposition against Henry McDonaugh signed by Banastre Tarleton and Patrick Ferguson, 15 April 1780, Clinton Papers; Tarleton to John André, Undated letter filed at the end of April 1780, ibid.; Allaire, *Diary of Lieut. Anthony Allaire,* 12.

22. Tarleton to John André, Undated letter filed at end of April 1780, Clinton Papers; Stedman, *History of the American War,* 2:183; Return of Prisoners Confined in the Provost, 21 May 1780, Clinton Papers.

23. Sarah Lowndes to Rawlins Lowndes, 17 May 1780, Clinton Papers. The fact that this letter is included in Clinton's papers indicates that he or at the very least his aides-de-camp were aware of the problem of soldiers passing themselves off as legitimate foraging parties.

24. Return of Prisoners Confined in the Provost, 21 May 1780, Clinton Papers.

25. Clinton Siege Journal, 14, 19 April 1780, Clinton Papers; Clinton to Arbuthnot, 14 April 1780, ibid.

26. Clinton Siege Journal, 10 April 1780, Clinton Papers; Arbuthnot to Clinton, 14 April 1780, ibid.; Clinton to Arbuthnot, 13 April 1780, ibid.

27. Arbuthnot to Clinton, 11, 13 April 1780, Clinton Papers; Clinton to Arbuthnot, 13, 14 April 1780, ibid.

28. Arbuthnot to Clinton, 14 April 1780, Clinton Papers; Andrew Hamond to Elphinstone, 14 April 1780, *Keith Papers,* 1:165–66.

29. Arbuthnot to Clinton, 15, 16 April 1780, Clinton Papers; Clinton to Arbuthnot, 16, 17 April 1780, ibid.; Clinton to James Webster, 18 April 1780, ibid.

30. Clinton to Arbuthnot, 18 April 1780, Clinton Papers; Clinton Siege Journal, 18 April 1780, ibid.; Clinton to Webster, 18 April 1780, ibid.; Clinton to Balfour, 18 April 1780, ibid.

31. Arbuthnot to Clinton, 19 April 1780, Clinton Papers; Clinton to William Phillips, 25 May 1780, ibid.; Clinton Siege Journal, 9, 14, 20 April 1780, ibid.; Clinton to Arbuthnot, 22 April 1780, ibid.

32. Clinton to Arbuthnot, 24 April 1780, No. 2, Clinton Papers; Clinton to Arbuthnot, 22 April 1780, ibid.

33. The battery was located in present day Old Village in Mount Pleasant. Shutes Folly was much broader in 1780 than it is today, making the passage between it and Hog Island, present day Patriot's Point, an extremely difficult one for sailing ships.

34. Hudson to Arbuthnot, 22 April 1780, Clinton Papers; Arbuthnot to Clinton, 22 April 1780, ibid.

35. Arbuthnot to Clinton, 23 April 1780, Clinton Papers.

36. Clinton, *The American Rebellion,* 167; Russell, "Journal of Peter Russell," 498–99; Clinton to Arbuthnot, 23 April 1780, No. 2, Clinton Papers; Clinton to Webster, 23 April 1780, ibid.; Patrick Ferguson to Clinton, 22 April 1780, ibid.

37. Clinton to Cornwallis, 23 April 1780, Clinton Papers; The strength of the force under Cornwallis is shown on Clinton Map 312, Clinton Papers; André to Clinton, 3 April 1780, ibid.; Clinton to Lord Lincoln, Undated letter filed at the end of May 1780, ibid.

38. Clinton, *The American Rebellion,* 167; Clinton to Cornwallis, 23 April 1780, Clinton Papers; Clinton to Webster, 23 April 1780, ibid.; Clinton to Arbuthnot, 23 April 1780, No. 2, ibid.

Chapter 11

1. The new battery in front of Number Five lay within the block created by present day Nassau, Amherst, Hanover, and Reid Streets. The approach trench then ran toward the American line between Nassau and Hanover Streets and the second parallel was begun in the environs of Mary Street.

2. Clinton Siege Journal, 4, 10 April 1780, Clinton Papers; Wilson Journal, 9, 11, 12, 13 April 1780, Charleston Library Society.

3. Ewald, *Diary of the American War,* 230.

4. Grimké Orderly Book, 15, 16 April 1780, South Carolina Historical Society; Grimké Journal, 18 April 1780, ibid.

5. Peebles, *John Peebles' American War,* 360; Ewald, *Diary of the American War,* 230; Uhlendorf, *The Siege of Charleston,* 249–51; Peter Traille to John André, 15 April 1780, Clinton Papers.

6. The right approach was begun in the environs of present day Coming and Spring Streets and ran southwest toward the second parallel. From the Ashley River side of Charleston neck, the completed second parallel ran approximately along Morris Street west of King and approximately along Mary Street east of King.

7. Clinton Siege Journal, 16 April 1780, Clinton Papers; Wilson Journal, 16, 17 April 1780, Charleston Library Society.

8. Wilson Journal, 14 April 1780, Charleston Library Society; McIntosh, "Journal of Siege of Charlestown," 101; Baldwin, "Diary of Events," 84; Johnson, *Traditions of the American Revolution,* 250, 252; Grimké Journal, 17 April 1780, South Carolina Historical Society.

9. McIntosh, "Journal of Siege of Charlestown," 102; Johnson, *Traditions of the American Revolution,* 250; Fraser, *Charleston! Charleston!,* 113.

10. Croghan Journal, 14 April 1780, MS Sparks 60; Grimké Journal, 18 April 1780, South Carolina Historical Society; Ewald, *Diary of the American War,* 230; Robertson, *Archibald Robertson: Diaries and Sketches in America,* 224; Peebles, *John Peebles' American War,* 361.

11. McIntosh, "Journal of Siege of Charlestown," 102; Grimké Orderly Book, 16 April 1780, South Carolina Historical Society; Ewald, *Diary of the American War,* 230; Clinton Siege Journal, 20 April 1780, Clinton Papers.

12. Wilson Journal, 15, 18, 19, 20 April 1780, Charleston Library Society; Clinton Siege Journal, 18 April 1780, Clinton Papers.

13. This figure consists of the estimate of Lincoln's adjutant general, Lieutenant Colonel John Ternant, compiled at the conclusion of the siege plus 1,100 sailors who came ashore from Whipple's ships.

14. Benjamin Lincoln, Journal from the 10th of April to the 12th of May inclusive, 20 April 1780, enclosed in Lincoln to the Continental Congress, 24 May 1780, PCC (National Archives Microfilm Publication M247, roll 177); John Ternant to Lincoln, 24 May 1780, Emmet Collection; John Wells Jr. to Henry Laurens, 24 March 1780, Laurens Papers; Clinton Map 312, Clinton Papers.

15. Benjamin Lincoln, Journal from the 10th of April to the 12th of May inclusive, 20 April 1780, enclosed in Lincoln to the Continental Congress, 24 May 1780, PCC (National Archives Microfilm Publication M247, roll 177); Lincoln to Whipple, 18 April 1780, Abraham Whipple Letterbook; Whipple and Captains to Lincoln, 18 April 1780, ibid.

16. McIntosh, "Journal of Siege of Charlestown," 103; At a Council of Officers held in Garrison, Charlestown April 20 and 21st 1780, No. 18 enclosed in Lincoln to the Continental Congress, 24 May 1780, PCC (National Archives Microfilm Publication M247, roll 177).

17. Lincoln to Huger, 1 April 1780, Benjamin Lincoln Letterbook.

18. McIntosh, "Journal of Siege of Charlestown," 103–4.

19. Ibid., 104.

20. Ibid.

21. See Charles E. Bennett and Donald R. Lennon, *A Quest for Glory: Major General Robert Howe and the American Revolution* (Chapel Hill: University of North Carolina Press, 1991), 56–60. Relations with South Carolina authorities could be tricky to say the least. Lincoln's predecessor in the Southern Department, Robert Howe, had actually fought a duel with Christopher Gadsden during his tenure in command.

22. At a Council of Officers held in Garrison, Charlestown April 20 and 21st 1780, No. 18 enclosed in Lincoln to the Continental Congress, 24 May 1780, PCC (National Archives Microfilm Publication M247, roll 177); Ramsay to Lincoln, 27 May 1780, *David Ramsay: Selections from His Writings,* 66–67; Ramsay, *Revolution in South Carolina,* 2:56.

23. McIntosh, "Journal of Siege of Charlestown," 104–5.

24. Ibid.

25. Ibid., 105; At a Council of Officers held in Garrison, Charlestown April 20 and 21st 1780, No. 18 enclosed in Lincoln to the Continental Congress, 24 May 1780, PCC (National Archives Microfilm Publication M247, roll 177).

26. McIntosh, "Journal of Siege of Charlestown," 106; At a Council of Officers held in Garrison, Charlestown April 20 and 21st 1780, No. 18 enclosed in Lincoln to the Continental Congress, 24 May 1780, PCC (National Archives Microfilm Publication M247, roll 177); Lincoln's proposed articles of capitulation are in Moultrie, *Memoirs of the American Revolution,* 2:74–77.

27. Lincoln to Clinton, 21 April 1780, Clinton Papers; Clinton to Lincoln, 21 April 1780, ibid.; Clinton to Arbuthnot, 21 April 1780, ibid.; Russell, "Journal of Peter Russell," 498–99.

28. Clinton Siege Journal, 21 April 1780, Clinton Papers.

29. Ibid.; Clinton, *The American Rebellion,* 168; Russell, "Journal of Peter Russell," 499; Clinton and Arbuthnot's response is in Moultrie, *Memoirs of the American Revolution,* 2:77.

30. McIntosh, "Journal of Siege of Charlestown," 106; Lincoln to Washington, 17 July 1780, Lincoln Papers.

31. Croghan Journal, 21 April 1780, MS Sparks 60; Clinton Siege Journal, 21 April 1780, Clinton Papers; Return of Ammunition Expended on

the Different Batteries from the evening of the 21st to the evening of the 22nd April 1780, ibid.

32. Gervais to Henry Laurens, 28 April 1780, *The Papers of Henry Laurens,* 15:284.

33. Duffy, *Fire and Stone,* 145.

34. Peebles, *John Peebles' American War,* 360, 363; Moultrie, *Memoirs of the American Revolution,* 2:64, 83; Ewald, *Diary of the American War,* 232; Grimké Journal, 24 April 1780, South Carolina Historical Society; Russell, "Journal of Peter Russell," 499.

35. Grimké Journal, 18 April 1780, South Carolina Historical Society; John Lewis Gervais to Henry Laurens, 17 April 1780, *Papers of Henry Laurens,* 15:278.

36. No doubt the sandflies to which Ewald refers were the notorious "no-see-ums" which make their appearance annually in Charleston in the spring and fall.

37. Ewald, *Diary of the American War,* 234.

38. The section of the third parallel on the British right ran approximately along present day Radcliffe Street. On the British left, they began the parallel in the area of the intersection of present day Elizabeth and Judith Streets. From the head of the sap, they extended the left section toward the right in an uneven line along Ann Street and toward the left along Judith Street.

39. Clinton Siege Journal, 15 April 1780, Clinton Papers; Wilson Journal, 15, 19, 21, 22, 23 April 1780, Charleston Library Society.

40. Duffy, *Fire and Stone,* 127.

41. Clinton Siege Journal, 14 April 1780, Clinton Papers; Traille to John André, 15 April 1780, ibid.

42. Grimké Orderly Book, 23 April 1780, South Carolina Historical Society; Benjamin Lincoln, Journal from the 10th of April to the 12th of May inclusive, 24 April 1780, enclosed in Lincoln to the Continental Congress, 24 May 1780, PCC (National Archives Microfilm Publication M247, roll 177); Grimké Journal, 24 April 1780, South Carolina Historical Society.

43. Peebles, *John Peebles' American War,* 365; Grimké Journal, 24 April 1780, South Carolina Historical Society; Ewald, *Diary of the American War,* 233; Uhlendorf, *The Siege of Charleston,* 261–63; Gabriel Manigault Journal, 24 April 1780, South Carolina Historical Society.

44. Gabriel Manigault Journal, 24 April 1780, South Carolina Historical Society; McIntosh, "Journal of Siege of Charlestown," 107; Uhlendorf, *The Siege of Charleston,* 263; Grimké Journal, 24 April 1780, South Carolina Historical Society; Clinton Siege Journal, 24 April 1780, Clinton Papers.

45. Russell, "Journal of Peter Russell," 499; Heinrich Carl Philipp von Feilitzsch and Christian Friedrich Bartholomai, *Diaries of two Ansbach Jaegers,* trans. and ed. Bruce E. Burgoyne (Bowie, Md.: Heritage Books, 1997), 136; Clinton Siege Journal, 24 April 1780, Clinton Papers.

46. Gabriel Manigault Journal, 25 April 1780, South Carolina Historical Society; Benjamin Lincoln, Journal from the 10th of April to the 12th of May inclusive, 25 April 1780, enclosed in Lincoln to the Continental Congress, 24 May 1780, PCC (National Archives Microfilm Publication M247, roll 177); McIntosh, "Journal of Siege of Charlestown," 108; Russell, "Journal of Peter Russell," 500; Uhlendorf, *The Siege of Charleston,* 265; Hartung Diary, 25 April 1780, Lidgerwood Hessian Transcripts.

47. Russell, "Journal of Peter Russell," 500; Peebles, *John Peebles' American War,* 365; Hartung Diary, 25 April 1780, Lidgerwood Hessian Transcripts; Moultrie, *Memoirs of the American Revolution,* 2:64.

48. Clinton Siege Journal, 25 April 1780, Clinton Papers; McIntosh, "Journal of Siege of Charlestown," 109; Grimké Orderly Book, 27, 28 April 1780, South Carolina Historical Society.

49. Wilson Journal, 25 April 1780, Charleston Library Society; Clinton Siege Journal, 26 April 1780, Clinton Papers; Clinton to Webster, 23 April 1780, ibid.

50. *JCC* 16 (1780): 316; Duportail to the Continental Congress, 17 May 1780, PCC (National Archives Microfilm Publication M247, roll 181, Item 164); Moultrie, *Memoirs of the American Revolution,* 2:80.

51. At a Council of Officers held in Garrison of Charlestown April 26th 1780, No. 19 enclosed in Lincoln to the Continental Congress, 24 May 1780, PCC (National Archives Microfilm Publication M247, roll 177); Lincoln to Washington, 17 July 1780, Lincoln Papers; Moultrie, *Memoirs of the American Revolution,* 2:80.

52. Duportail to the Continental Congress, 17 May 1780, PCC (National Archives Microfilm Publication M247, roll 181); Moultrie, *Memoirs of the American Revolution,* 2:80.

Chapter 12

1. Grimké Orderly Book, 22, 24 April 1780, South Carolina Historical Society.

2. Lincoln to Washington, 17 July 1780, Lincoln Papers.

3. Lincoln to Malmedy, 11, 18 April 1780, Lincoln Papers; John Ternant to Lincoln, 24 May 1780, Emmet Collection.

4. Cornwallis to Clinton, 26, 28 April 1780, Clinton Papers.

5. Grimké Orderly Book, 22 April 1780, South Carolina Historical Society; McIntosh, "Journal of Siege of Charlestown," 107–8; John Ternant to Lincoln, 24 May 1780, Emmet Collection.

6. Clinton to Cornwallis, 23 April 1780, Clinton Papers; Clinton to James Webster, 23 April 1780, ibid.; Clinton, *The American Rebellion,* 167.

7. Cornwallis to Clinton, 24 April 1780, Clinton Papers; Tarleton, *Campaigns of 1780 and 1781,* 37–38; Tarleton to Clinton, 28 April 1780, Clinton Papers; John Laurens to Lincoln, 20 April 1780, Collections of the Charleston Museum.

8. Cornwallis to Clinton, 24, 26 April 1780, Clinton Papers; Clinton to Cornwallis, 25 April 1780, ibid.

9. Clinton, *The American Rebellion,* 167; Clinton Siege Journal, 21 April 1780, Clinton Papers; Clinton to Arbuthnot, 22 April 1780, ibid.; Arbuthnot to Clinton, 22, 23 April 1780, ibid.

10. Clinton to Arbuthnot, 23 April 1780, No. 2, Clinton Papers; Clinton to Arbuthnot, 24 April 1780, No. 2, ibid.

11. Clinton to Cornwallis, 24 April 1780, Clinton Papers; Arbuthnot to Clinton, 25 April 1780, ibid.; Clinton to Traille, 26 April 1780, ibid.

12. Clinton to Arbuthnot, 23 April 1780, No. 2, Clinton Papers; Clinton to Arbuthnot, 24 April 1780, No. 1, ibid.; Clinton to Arbuthnot, 24 April 1780, No. 2, ibid.; Arbuthnot to Clinton, 23 April 1780, No. 2, ibid.; Arbuthnot to Clinton, 26 April 1780, ibid.

13. Lincoln to Isaac Huger, 8 April 1780, Lincoln Papers; John Ternant to Lincoln, 24 May 1780, Emmet Collection.

14. Benjamin Lincoln, Journal from the 10th of April to the 12th of May inclusive, 26 April 1780, enclosed in Lincoln to the Continental Congress, 24 May 1780, PCC (National Archives Microfilm Publication M247, roll 177); Gabriel Manigault Journal, 26 April 1780, South Carolina Historical Society.

15. Allaire, *Diary of Lieut. Anthony Allaire,* 13; Cornwallis to Clinton, 26 April 1780, Clinton Papers.

16. Arbuthnot to Clinton, 27 April 1780, Clinton Papers; Russell, "Journal of Peter Russell," 501.

17. Benjamin Lincoln, Journal from the 10th of April to the 12th of May inclusive, 27 April 1780, enclosed in Lincoln to the Continental Congress, 24 May 1780, PCC (National Archives Microfilm Publication M247, roll 177); McIntosh, "Journal of Siege of Charlestown," 109; Charles Hudson to Clinton, 28 April 1780, Clinton Papers; Arbuthnot to Clinton, 29 April 1780, ibid.

18. Charles Hudson to Clinton, 28 April 1780, Clinton Papers; McIntosh, "Journal of Siege of Charlestown," 109.

19. Grimké Orderly Book, 29 April 1780, South Carolina Historical Society; Benjamin Lincoln, Journal from the 10th of April to the 12th of May inclusive, 27 April 1780, enclosed in Lincoln to the Continental Congress, 24 May 1780, PCC (National Archives Microfilm Publication M247, roll 177); Croghan Journal, 26 April 1780, MS Sparks 60; Subaltern's Journal included in McIntosh, "Journal of Siege of Charlestown," 119.

20. See Nathanael Greene to Thomas McKean, 11 September 1781 and Greene to Alexander Martin, 25 November 1781, *The Papers of General Nathanael Greene, Volume IX: 11 July 1781–2 December 1781,* ed. Dennis M. Conrad (Chapel Hill: University of North Carolina Press, 1997), 328, 625, 626n. 1. Malmedy continued to serve in the Southern Department under both Horatio Gates and Nathanael Greene, commanding North Carolina troops in the battle of Eutaw Springs in September 1781. He died from wounds sustained in a duel later that year.

21. Cornwallis to Clinton, 3, 5 May 1780, Clinton Papers.

22. Allaire, *Diary of Lieut. Anthony Allaire,* 15; Clinton to Arbuthnot, 28 April 1780, Clinton Papers; Arbuthnot to Clinton, 29 April 1780, ibid.; Clinton to Cornwallis, 2, 6 May 1780, ibid.

23. This road ran roughly along the route of present day Highway 17. Present day Awendaw Bridge is in the same location as it was in 1780.

24. Cornwallis to Clinton, 26 April, 1 May 1780, Clinton Papers; Clinton to Cornwallis, 25 April, 1 May 1780, ibid.

25. Cornwallis to Clinton, 1, 5, 7, 11 May 1780, Clinton Papers.

26. Rutledge to unknown officer, 14 April 1780, Robert Wilson Gibbes Collection of Revolutionary War Manuscripts, South Carolina Department

of Archives and History, Columbia, S.C.; Unknown officer to Rutledge, 16 May 1780, ibid.

27. Tarleton, *Campaigns of 1780 and 1781,* 19–20; Gervais to Henry Laurens, 13 May 1780, *Papers of Henry Laurens,* 15:291–92; Cornwallis to Clinton, 6, 26 May 1780, Clinton Papers.

28. Cornwallis to Clinton, 6, 7 May 1780, Clinton Papers.

29. Cornwallis to Clinton, 3 May 1780, Clinton Papers; Benjamin Smith's letter is in Stedman, *History of the American War,* 2:181–82.

Chapter 13

1. Subaltern's Journal included in McIntosh, "Journal of Siege of Charlestown," 118.

2. Clinton Siege Journal, 20 April, 5 May 1780, Clinton Papers; Clinton to Arbuthnot, 1 May 1780, ibid.

3. Wilson Journal, 25, 27, 30 April, 1 May 1780, Charleston Library Society; Ewald, *Diary of the American War,* 234; Clinton Siege Journal, 1 May 1780, Clinton Papers.

4. Wilson Journal, 26, 27, 28, 29 April 1780, Charleston Library Society; Ewald, *Diary of the American War,* 233.

5. Grimké Orderly Book, 1 May 1780, South Carolina Historical Society; Ewald, *Diary of the American War,* 233; Wilson Journal, 27, 29, 30 April 1780, Charleston Library Society; Robertson, *Archibald Robertson: Diaries and Sketches in America,* 227.

6. Uhlendorf, *The Siege of Charleston,* 269–71; McIntosh, "Journal of Siege of Charlestown," 109; Ewald, *Diary of the American War,* 232; Stedman, *History of the American War,* 2:185; Clinton, *The American Rebellion,* 170; Moultrie, *Memoirs of the American Revolution,* 2:85; Croghan Journal, 30 April 1780, MS Sparks 60.

7. Grimké Orderly Book, 24 April, 2, 8 May 1780, South Carolina Historical Society; McIntosh, "Journal of Siege of Charlestown," 109.

8. Ibid.; Peebles, *John Peebles' American War,* 367–68; Clinton Siege Journal, 30 April, 2 May 1780, Clinton Papers; Grimké Journal, 30 April 1780, South Carolina Historical Society; Traille to John André, 27 April 1780, Clinton Papers.

9. Grimké Journal, 28, 29 April, 1 May 1780, South Carolina Historical Society; McIntosh, "Journal of Siege of Charlestown," 110; Grimké Orderly Book, 30 April, 1 May 1780, South Carolina Historical Society.

10. Russell, "Journal of Peter Russell," 501; Ewald, *Diary of the American War,* 232; Grimké Orderly Book, 25 April 1780, South Carolina Historical Society.

11. The commissary general for the Charleston garrison showed 1,604 barrels of rice on hand on 5 May, 1780. On 13 May, the British found 1,393 barrels of rice in the Continental stores, so the garrison had consumed 211 barrels in eight days. Hence, Lincoln's army at the beginning of May had enough rice to last over seven weeks. See Provisions Now in the Commissary General of Purchases Stores, 5 May 1780, Lincoln Papers and Return of Provisions & ca. Found in the Publick Stores in Charles Town South Carolina, 13th May, 1780, 15 May 1780, Clinton Papers.

12. Grimké Journal, 2 May 1780, South Carolina Historical Society.

13. Lincoln to Washington, 17 July 1780, Lincoln Papers; Provisions Now in the Commissary General of Purchases Stores, 5 May 1780, ibid.; Benjamin Lincoln, Journal from the 10th of April to the 12th of May inclusive, 20 April 1780, enclosed in Lincoln to the Continental Congress, 24 May 1780, PCC (National Archives Microfilm Publication M247, roll 177); Grimké Journal, 4, 8 May 1780, South Carolina Historical Society; Subaltern's Journal included in McIntosh, "Journal of Siege of Charlestown," 121.

14. Lincoln to Rutledge, 27 March 1780, Benjamin Lincoln Letterbook.

15. Ramsay, *Revolution in South Carolina,* 2:62; Grimké Orderly Book, 29 April 1780, South Carolina Historical Society; Croghan Journal, 15 April 1780, MS Sparks 60.

16. For instance, of 850 projectiles fired on the garrison on the night of 21 April, twenty-four pound shot comprised 489 of them.

17. Clinton Siege Journal, 14 April 1780, Clinton Papers; Disposition of the Royal Artillery under the Command of Major Traille, 24 April 1780, ibid.; Peter Traille, Return of Ammunition Expended on the Different Batteries from the evening of the 21st to the evening of the 22nd April 1780, ibid.; Traille to John André, 29 April, 2 May 1780, ibid.

18. Clinton, *The American Rebellion,* 168; Traille to John André, 24 April 1780, Clinton Papers; Sir Alured Clarke to André, 25 April 1780, ibid.; Clinton to Cornwallis, 1 May 1780, ibid.

19. Clinton Siege Journal, 1, 3, 4 May 1780, Clinton Papers; Wilson Journal, 4 May 1780, Charleston Library Society.

20. Peter Traille to John André, 27 April 1780, Clinton Papers; Uhlendorf, *The Siege of Charleston,* 271–73, 277, 279, 281; Johnson, *Traditions of the American Revolution,* 249; Peter Traille, Return of Ammunition expended on the different Batteries from the evening of the 2nd to the evening of the 3rd May 1780, Clinton Papers.

21. Clinton to Cornwallis, 6 May 1780, Clinton Papers; Clinton, *The American Rebellion,* 170; Ewald, *Diary of the American War,* 234; Cornwallis to Clinton, 7 May 1780, Clinton Papers; Clinton Siege Journal, 5 May 1780, ibid.

22. Arbuthnot to Clinton, 23 April 1780, Clinton Papers; Clinton to Arbuthnot, 24 April 1780, No. 2, ibid.; Clinton to Arbuthnot, 1, 5 May 1780, ibid.

23. Arbuthnot to Clinton, 4 May 1780, Clinton Papers; Clinton to Arbuthnot, 5 May 1780, ibid.; Clinton Siege Journal, 6 May 1780, ibid.

24. Tarleton, *Campaigns of 1780 and 1781,* 50, 55.

25. Ibid., 50–51; John Knowles to Clinton, 10 May 1780, Clinton Papers.

26. John Knowles to Clinton, 10 May 1780, Clinton Papers; Allaire, *Diary of Lieut. Anthony Allaire,* 15; Articles of Capitulation agreed on between Capt. Charles Hudson of His Brittannic Majestys Navy & Lieut. Colonel Scott Commandant of Fort Moultrie on the surrender of that Fort, 7 May 1780, Emmet Collection.

27. Lincoln to Rutledge, 8 April 1780, Benjamin Lincoln Letterbook; Benjamin Lincoln, Journal from the 10th of April to the 12th of May inclusive, 26 April 1780, enclosed in Lincoln to the Continental Congress, 24 May 1780, PCC (National Archives Microfilm Publication M247, roll 177).

28. Malmedy to Lincoln, 8 April 1780, Lincoln Papers; Moultrie, *Memoirs of the American Revolution,* 2:84–85; Subaltern's Journal included in McIntosh, "Journal of Siege of Charlestown," 118.

29. The summons is included in Lincoln to Washington, 17 July 1780, Lincoln Papers.

30. Lincoln to Clinton, 8 May 1780, Benjamin Lincoln Letterbook; Moultrie, *Memoirs of the American Revolution,* 2:87; Benjamin Lincoln, Journal from the 10th of April to the 12th of May inclusive, 8 May 1780, enclosed in Lincoln to the Continental Congress, 24 May 1780, PCC (National Archives Microfilm Publication M247, roll 177).

31. Lincoln to Clinton, 8 May 1780, Benjamin Lincoln Letterbook; Moultrie, *Memoirs of the American Revolution,* 2:90–91; Clinton to Cornwallis, 8 May 1780, Clinton Papers.

32. Hartung Diary, 8 May 1780, Lidgerwood Hessian Transcripts; Moultrie, *Memoirs of the American Revolution,* 2:83.

33. Gabriel Manigault Journal, 8 May 1780, South Carolina Historical Society; Moultrie, *Memoirs of the American Revolution,* 2:92; Hartung Diary, 9 May 1780, Lidgerwood Hessian Transcripts.

34. At a Council of General & Field Officers Held in the Garrison of Charlestown, 8 May 1780, Lincoln Papers.

35. Duportail to the Continental Congress, 17 May 1780, PCC (National Archives Microfilm Publication M247, roll 181).

36. Lincoln's proposed articles of capitulation are in Moultrie, *Memoirs of the American Revolution,* 2:87–89.

37. Christopher Gadsden, Proposals from the Lieutenant Governor and the Council of the State of South Carolina, 8 May 1780, Emmet Collection; Moultrie, *Memoirs of the American Revolution,* 2:87–89.

38. The Answer of General Clinton & Vice Admiral Arbuthnot to the Articles of Capitulation Proposed May 8 1780, No. 10 enclosed in Lincoln to the Continental Congress, 24 May 1780, PCC (National Archives Microfilm Publication M247, roll 177).

39. Ibid.

40. Ibid.

41. Clinton Siege Journal, 22 April 1780, Clinton Papers; Lincoln to Washington, 17 July 1780, Lincoln Papers.

42. Lincoln to Clinton, 9 May 1780, Benjamin Lincoln Letterbook; Lincoln, Remarks in reply to Answers on the Articles of Capitulation proposed, Emmet Collection.

43. Moultrie, *Memoirs of the American Revolution,* 2:96.

44. Ibid.; Subaltern's Journal included in McIntosh, "Journal of Siege of Charlestown," 120; Robertson, *Archibald Robertson: Diaries and Sketches in America,* 228; Grimké Journal, 9 May 1780, South Carolina Historical Society; von Feilitzsch and Bartholomai, *Diaries of two Ansbach Jaegers,* 143; John Lewis Gervais to Henry Laurens, 13 May 1780, *Papers of Henry Laurens,* 15:290.

45. Moultrie, *Memoirs of the American Revolution,* 2:96; Benjamin Lincoln, Journal from the 10th of April to the 12th of May inclusive, 9 May

1780, enclosed in Lincoln to the Continental Congress, 24 May 1780, PCC (National Archives Microfilm Publication M247, roll 177); Peter Traille, Report of Ammunition expended at the different Batteries from the evening of the 9th to the evening of the 10th May 1780, Clinton Papers; Ramsay, *Revolution in South Carolina,* 2:58; Gabriel Manigault Journal, 9 May 1780, South Carolina Historical Society; Grimké Journal, 10 May 1780, South Carolina Historical Society.

46. Peebles, *John Peebles' American War,* 371; Report of Ammunition expended at the different Batteries from the evening of the 9th to the evening of the 10th May 1780, Clinton Papers; Wilson Journal, 10 May 1780, Charleston Library Society.

47. Clinton to Arbuthnot, 11 May 1780, Clinton Papers; Clinton Siege Journal, 10 May 1780, ibid.; Wilson Journal, 10 May 1780, Charleston Library Society; Uhlendorf, *The Siege of Charleston,* 287; Ewald, *Diary of the American War,* 236; Grimké Journal, 11 May 1780, South Carolina Historical Society.

48. Moultrie, *Memoirs of the American Revolution,* 2:97; Lincoln to Washington, 17 July 1780, Lincoln Papers; Subaltern's Journal included in McIntosh, "Journal of Siege of Charlestown," 120; Duportail to the Continental Congress, 17 May 1780, PCC (National Archives Microfilm Publication M247, roll 181).

49. The Petition of Divers Inhabitants of Charles-Town in Behalf of Themselves and Others Their Fellow Citizens, 10, 11 May 1780, Lincoln Papers; The Humble Petition of the Country Militia Now in Charles-Town, 11 May 1780, ibid.; Benjamin Lincoln, Journal from the 10th of April to the 12th of May inclusive, 10, 11 May 1780, enclosed in Lincoln to the Continental Congress, 24 May 1780, PCC (National Archives Microfilm Publication M247, roll 177).

50. At a Council of War Held in Charles-Town, 11 May 1780, Lincoln Papers; Lincoln to Washington, 17 July 1780, ibid.

51. Ewald, *Diary of the American War,* 237; Gabriel Manigault Journal, 11 May 1780, South Carolina Historical Society; Subaltern's Journal included in McIntosh, "Journal of Siege of Charlestown," 121.

52. Lincoln to Clinton, 11 May 1780, Benjamin Lincoln Letterbook.

53. Clinton to Germain, 13 May 1780, Clinton Papers; Clinton to Lincoln, 11 May 1780, No. 17 enclosed in Lincoln to the Continental Congress, 24 May 1780, PCC (National Archives Microfilm Publication M247, roll 177).

54. The most detailed accounts of the surrender are by Captain Hinrichs in Uhlendorf, *The Siege of Charleston,* 289–93 and Captain Peebles in Peebles, *John Peebles' American War,* 372–73.

55. The place of surrender was in all probability on the west side of King Street between present day Vanderhorst and Warren Streets.

56. Uhlendorf, *The Siege of Charleston,* 291–93; Peebles, *John Peebles' American War,* 372–73; Hartung Diary, 12 May 1780, Lidgerwood Hessian Transcripts; Moultrie, *Memoirs of the American Revolution,* 2:108; Subaltern's Journal included in McIntosh, "Journal of Siege of Charlestown," 121.

57. von Feilitzsch and Bartholomai, *Diaries of two Ansbach Jaegers,* 145; Hartung Diary, 12 May 1780, Lidgerwood Hessian Transcripts; Ewald, *Diary of the American War,* 238.

58. Peebles, *John Peebles' American War,* 372; Hartung Diary, 12 May 1780, Lidgerwood Hessian Transcripts.

59. John Ternant noted that only 1,805 Continentals were fit for duty on 11 May. See Ternant to Lincoln, 24 May 1780, Emmet Collection.

60. Hartung Diary, 13 May 1780, Lidgerwood Hessian Transcripts; Moultrie, *Memoirs of the American Revolution,* 2:108.

61. Grimké Journal, 12 May 1780, South Carolina Historical Society; Robertson, *Archibald Robertson: Diaries and Sketches in America,* 229; Uhlendorf, *The Siege of Charleston,* 297; Subaltern's Journal included in McIntosh, "Journal of Siege of Charlestown," 121; Moultrie, *Memoirs of the American Revolution,* 2:108–9.

62. Ibid., 2:109; Return of the Rebel Forces Commanded by Major General Lincoln at the Surrender of Charles Town 12th May 1780, Now Prisoners of War, enclosed in Clinton to Germain, 4 June 1780, Clinton Papers; A Monthly Return of the Brigade of Country Militia under the Command of Brigadier General McIntosh Now at Head Quarters Charlestown, 5 May 1780, copy in Clinton Papers; Return of the North Carolina Brigade of Foot, Commanded by Brigadier General Hogun, 6 May 1780, copy in ibid.; A Weekly Return of the 1st Virginia Brigade Commanded by William Woodford Esq. Brigadier General, 1 May 1780, copy in ibid.; Clinton to Germain, 4 June 1780, Clinton Papers; Lesser, *Sinews of Independence,* 161–63.

63. These 4,000 men would have consisted of Ternant's estimate plus 1,000 sailors. That all the sailors were present and fit for duty is a very

great assumption indeed. See Ternant to Lincoln, 24 May 1780, Emmet Collection.

64. The British would suffer significantly greater casualties in single day engagements later in the war, namely the battles of Guilford Courthouse and Eutaw Springs. At Guilford, the British suffered 93 men killed and 439 wounded, and at Eutaw Springs they lost 85 men killed and 351 wounded. See Ward, *War of the Revolution,* 2:793 and Pancake, *This Destructive War,* 220.

65. Lincoln to the Continental Congress, 24 May 1780, PCC (National Archives Microfilm Publication M247, roll 177); Ramsay, *Revolution in South Carolina,* 2:62; Return of the Killed and Wounded of the Troops under the Command of His Excellency General Sir Henry Clinton, from the Debarkation in South Carolina the 11th February to the Surrender of Charles Town 12th May 1780, Clinton Papers; Arbuthnot's report on the navy's casualties and ships taken is in Tarleton, *Campaigns of 1780 and 1781,* 51–53, 67; Clinton to William Phillips, 25 May 1780, Clinton Papers; Coker, *Charleston's Maritime Heritage,* 114.

66. I am greatly indebted to the work of Charles H. Lesser, whose wonderful study of monthly strength reports of the Continental army, *The Sinews of Independence,* breaks down systematically the returns of the Continental officers and enlisted men who were captured at Charleston. At the time of Charleston's surrender, Colonel Abraham Buford's battalion of Virginia Continentals was north of the Santee River. Receiving word that Charleston had surrendered, Buford fell back toward North Carolina. Tarleton and the British Legion caught up to him at the Waxhaws, near the North Carolina–South Carolina border, and virtually cut his detachment to pieces. Thus was destroyed the last organized body of Continental troops in South Carolina.

67. Clinton to William Phillips, 25 May 1780, Clinton Papers; Moultrie, *Memoirs of the American Revolution,* 2:141, 148–49, 401–3.

68. Mattern, *Benjamin Lincoln,* 111; Cavanagh, "The Military Career of Benjamin Lincoln," 203–4.

69. Ramsay, *Revolution in South Carolina,* 2:59; Ramsay to Lincoln, 13 August 1781, *David Ramsay: Selections from His Writings,* 67; Rutledge to the delegates of South Carolina in Congress, 24 May 1780, John Rutledge Letters, 1780–1782, Charleston Library Society, Charleston, S.C.

70. David Ramsay, in his history of the American Revolution in South Carolina, claimed that "great praise" was due Lincoln "for his judicious and spirited conduct in baffling, for three months, the greatly superior force of Sir Henry Clinton and admiral Arbuthnot." Henry Lee, who had an extremely successful career as a cavalry commander in the southern theater under Nathanael Greene, gave a more deliberate assessment of Lincoln's conduct in his memoirs on the war in the south. Lee held that Lincoln's decision to preserve Charleston, "though faithful," was "injudicious." He maintained that Lincoln was too "brave and amiable" to resist the forces that pushed him into defending the city. South Carolina historian Edward McCrady was far less generous in his commentary on Lincoln. McCrady alleged that Lincoln's conduct after the first summons on 13 April "was indecisive and weak" and that "he allowed his measures to be discussed, his military councils to be interfered with and dictated to by civilians, and his authority to be slighted." McCrady also asserted that Lincoln "possessed neither the indomitable will and heroic courage of Moultrie, nor any of the great qualities of leadership which Sumter, Marion and Pickens were soon to display." More recently, biographers of Benjamin Lincoln have attempted to give a more even appraisal of Lincoln's generalship. David Mattern argues that the Continental Congress did not give Lincoln proper support in his command of the Southern Department. He contends that the Congress "failed to provide guidance, much less show interest, in the affairs of the Southern Department." But Mattern cannot deny that Lincoln made an unwise decision in holding Charleston. He agrees with McCrady that "Lincoln had sacrificed his better judgment to the threats and entreaties of South Carolina's civil authorities." John Caroll Cavanagh affirms that Lincoln "was often cautious and indecisive under pressure" and "made few important decisions" without summoning councils of war. Still Cavanagh doubts that any other commander could have dealt with the problems of the Southern Department much more effectively. He points out that the British held every strategic advantage during the campaign, while Lincoln suffered troop and supply shortages primarily due to the selfish interests of the South Carolinians. See Ramsay, *Revolution in South Carolina,* 2:60; Henry Lee, *The Revolutionary War Memoirs of General Henry Lee* (1869; reprint, New York: Da Capo Press, 1998), 150–51; McCrady, *The History of South Carolina in the*

Revolution, 444, 463; Mattern, *Benjamin Lincoln,* 76, 108; Cavanagh, "American Military Leadership in the Southern Campaign: Benjamin Lincoln," in *The Revolutionary War in the South: Power, Conflict and Leadership,* ed. W. Robert Higgins (Durham, N.C.: Duke University Press, 1979), 113, 131; Cavanagh, "The Military Career of Benjamin Lincoln," 204.

71. Lincoln to Washington, 17 July 1780, Lincoln Papers; Lincoln to Rutledge, 14 February 1780, Benjamin Lincoln Letterbook; Higginbotham, *The War of American Independence,* 152.

72. Lincoln to Washington, 17 July 1780, Lincoln Papers.

73. Laurens to Lincoln, 19 April 1780, Collections of the Charleston Museum.

74. Laurens to the South Carolina delegates in Congress, 14 May 1780, *Papers of Henry Laurens,* 15:296.

75. John Laurens to Henry Laurens, 25 May 1780, *Papers of Henry Laurens,* 15:300; Henry Laurens to the South Carolina delegates in Congress, 23 May 1780, ibid., 15:298.

Chapter 14

1. See Moultrie, *Memoirs of the American Revolution,* 2:109–111; Uhlendorf, *The Siege of Charleston,* 297–99; and Ewald, *Diary of the American War,* 239–40. It was during the task of collecting and storing captured arms and ammunition that the infamous magazine explosion occurred. While a party of British soldiers were piling seized American muskets in a storehouse used by the Americans as a powder magazine, one of the loaded muskets went off igniting the stored powder. The resulting explosion killed a number of British soldiers, many of whose body parts were literally strewn about the city.

2. Peebles, *John Peebles' American War,* 373–75; Rutledge to the South Carolina delegates in Congress, 24 May 1780, Charleston Library Society; Ewald, *Diary of the American War,* 238, 241–42.

3. Clinton to Germain, 13 May 1780, Clinton Papers; Clinton to Henry Fiennes Pelham-Clinton, second duke of Newcastle, 15 May 1780, ibid.; Clinton to William Phillips, 25 May 1780, ibid.

4. James Simpson to Clinton, 15 May 1780, Clinton Papers.

5. George Smith McCowen Jr., *The British Occupation of Charleston, 1780-82* (Columbia: University of South Carolina Press, 1972), 10; Clinton to Germain, 4 June 1780, Clinton Papers; Clinton to William Phillips, 25 May 1780, ibid.; Clinton to William Eden, 30 May 1780, ibid.; Clinton to Nisbet Balfour, 30 May 1780, ibid.; Simpson to Clinton, 15 May 1780, ibid.

6. The Petition of Mary Brown in Cynthia A. Kierner, *Southern Women in Revolution, 1776–1800: Personal and Political Narratives* (Columbia: University of South Carolina Press, 1998), 122–24; Rawlins Lowndes to James Simpson, 20 May 1780, Clinton Papers; Sarah Lowndes to Rawlins Lowndes, 17 May 1780, ibid.

7. Clinton to William Eden, 30 May 1780, Clinton Papers; McCowen, *The British Occupation of Charleston,* 52–53, 72, 78.

8. Clinton, *The American Rebellion,* 174–75; Peebles, *John Peebles' American War,* 378; Proclamation of Sir Henry Clinton, 22 May 1780, Clinton Papers; Proclamation of Henry Clinton and Marriot Arbuthnot, 1 June 1780, Emmet Collection.

9. Clinton to Cornwallis, 1 June 1780, Clinton Papers; Clinton to Eden, 30 May 1780, ibid.; Clinton to Phillips, 25 May 1780, ibid.

10. Clinton to Cornwallis, 29 May 1780, Clinton Papers; Clinton, *The American Rebellion,* 175.

11. The British most likely distributed this undated proclamation in the week after the surrender. Captain John Peebles claimed that the 22 May proclamation was not issued until 28 May, while in an entry for 22 May, he made reference to a proclamation with language similar to the undated proclamation which was "spreading about in the Country." Hence the undated proclamation was circulating some time before 22 May. Given that it would have taken several days to disseminate throughout the low-country, they must have issued it shortly after the surrender. See Peebles, *John Peebles' American War,* 376, 378.

12. Nisbet Balfour, Copy of a Paper Inclosed to Lord Cornwallis, 18 May 1780, Clinton Papers; Clinton to Germain, 14 May 1780, ibid.; Clinton, *The American Rebellion,* 124; Undated Proclamation of Henry Clinton Issued between 12 May and 4 June 1780, copy in Clinton Papers.

13. Undated Proclamation of Henry Clinton Issued between 12 May and 4 June 1780, copy in Clinton Papers.

14. Clinton to Patrick Ferguson, 22 May 1780, Clinton Papers; Clinton to William Eden, 30 May 1780, ibid.

15. Cornwallis to Clinton, 18 May 1780, Clinton Papers; Clinton to Henry Fiennes Pelham-Clinton, second duke of Newcastle, 15 May 1780, ibid.; Clinton to Eden, 30 May 1780, ibid.; Clinton to Cornwallis, 20 May 1780, ibid.

16. The units remaining with Cornwallis were the British 7th, 23rd, 33rd, 63rd, 64th, and 71st regiments, a detachment of the Royal Artillery, the Hessian regiments von Dittfurth, von Huyn, and d'Angelelli, and the provincial American Volunteers, New York Volunteers, Prince of Wales American regiment, Volunteers of Ireland, British Legion, South Carolina Royalists, and North Carolina Volunteers.

17. State of the Troops under the Command of Lieutenant General Lord Cornwallis, 15 June 1780, Clinton Papers; Clinton to William Eden, 30 May 1780, ibid.; Cornwallis to Clinton, 21 May 1780, ibid.

18. Clinton to Eden, 30 May 1780, Clinton Papers; Clinton to William Phillips, 25 May 1780, ibid.; Tarleton, *Campaigns of 1780 and 1781,* 30–31; Banastre Tarleton, Return of Rebels killed, wounded and taken in the affair at Waxsaw, 29 May 1780, Clinton Papers.

19. Cornwallis to Clinton, 2 June 1780, Clinton Papers.

20. Willcox, *Portrait of a General,* 322; Proclamation of Henry Clinton, 3 June 1780, Clinton Papers.

21. See Willcox, *Portrait of a General,* 321. Clinton biographer William B. Willcox argues that Clinton suffered a bad lapse of judgment in issuing this proclamation. According to Willcox, Clinton became too confident and simply overreached himself.

22. Stedman, *History of the American War,* 2:198–99; Pancake, *This Destructive War,* 70; Clinton to Cornwallis, 1 June 1780, Clinton Papers.

23. Willcox, *Portrait of a General,* 309; Clinton to Germain, 4 June 1780, Clinton Papers.

24. Pancake, *This Destructive War,* 83–84.

25. Extract of Rawdon to Clinton, 24 October 1780, filed after 14 May 1780 correspondence, Clinton Papers.

26. Extract of Cornwallis to Clinton, 22 September 1780, filed after 14 May 1780 correspondence, Clinton Papers; Extract of Cornwallis to Clinton, 19 September 1780, ibid.; Extract of Rawdon to Clinton, 24 October 1780, ibid.; Extract of Cruger to Cornwallis, 19 September 1780, ibid.

27. Extract of Cornwallis to Clinton, 29 August 1780, filed after 14 May 1780 correspondence, Clinton Papers; Extract of Cornwallis to Clinton, 22 September 1780, ibid.; Simpson to Clinton, 15 May 1780, ibid.

28. Clinton to Cornwallis, 29 May 1780, Clinton Papers; Thomas Harvy and Moses Eastan to Clinton, 18 March 1780, ibid.

29. Moultrie, *Memoirs of the American Revolution,* 2:210; Frey, *Water from the Rock,* 113, 141.

30. Stephen Conway, "To Subdue America," 392, 401, 406–7; Klein, "Frontier Planters and the American Revolution: The South Carolina Backcountry, 1775–1782," in Ronald Hoffman, Thad W. Tate and Peter J. Albert, ed. *An Uncivil War: The Southern Backcountry during the American Revolution* (Charlottesville, Va.: University Press of Virginia, 1985), 62.

31. Clinton to George Hay, 13[?] February 1780, Clinton Papers; William Carson to James Simpson, 1 May 1780, ibid.

Bibliography

Manuscript Sources

Baker, Richard B. Muster Roll of Captain Baker's Company in the 2nd Regiment Commanded by Colonel Francis Marion. Richard Bohun Baker Papers, 1780–1783. South Carolina Historical Society, Charleston, S.C.

Clinton, Sir Henry. Papers. William L. Clements Library, University of Michigan, Ann Arbor, Mich.

Collections of the Charleston Museum, Charleston, S.C. (Contain a number of documents relating to the siege of Charleston).

Continental Congress. Papers. Record Group 360. National Archives, Washington, D.C. (Specifically, National Archives Microfilm Publication M247, roll 177, item 158 and roll 181, item 164).

Croghan, William. Major William Croghan's Journal, 9 February–4 May 1780. MS Sparks 60. The Houghton Library, Harvard University, Cambridge, Mass.

Grimké, John Faucheraud. Journal of the Siege of Charles Town. Continental Army Southern Department Records, 1778–1790. South Carolina Historical Society, Charleston, S.C.

———. Orderly Book. Continental Army Southern Department Records, 1778–1790. South Carolina Historical Society, Charleston, S.C.

Hartung. Diary Kept by Ensign Hartung of the Vacant Huyne Regiment. Lidgerwood Hessian Transcripts. Morristown National Historical Park, Morristown, N.J.

Hooke, George Philip. Journal. Orderly Book Collection. William L. Clements Library, University of Michigan, Ann Arbor, Mich.

Laurens, Henry. Papers. Henry W. Kendall Collection. South Caroliniana Library, University of South Carolina, Columbia, S.C.

Lincoln, Benjamin. Letterbook. Boston Public Library. Rare Books Department. Courtesy of the Trustees.

Lincoln, Benjamin. Orderly Book, 1779–1780. University of Georgia Libraries, Athens, Ga.

Lincoln, Benjamin. Papers. Massachusetts Historical Society, Boston.

Lincoln, Benjamin. The Siege of Charleston—Lincoln Papers. Thomas Addis Emmet Collection. New York Public Library, New York.

Manigault, Ann Ashby. Extracts from a journal kept by Mrs. A. M., 1754–1781. Manigault Family Papers. South Carolina Historical Society, Charleston, S.C.

Manigault, Gabriel. Journal, 1774–1784. South Carolina Historical Society, Charleston, S.C.

Oben, Warwick. A Journal of the Proceedings of His Majesty's Ship Richmond Commencing the 22d July 1779 & Ending the 22d July 1780. Trustees of the National Maritime Museum, Greenwich, England.

Palmer, George. A Journal of the Proceedings of His Majesty's Ship Roebuck, Sir Andrew Snape Hamond Commander, and Kept by George Palmer Lieutenant of the Said Ship—from the 13 May 1779 to the 6 June 1780. Trustees of the National Maritime Museum, Greenwich, England.

Platte Grenadier Battalion Journal Which sailed to America as the Koehler Grenadier Battalion was Later Called the Graf Grenadier Battalion, and Finally the Platte Grenadier Battalion. Lidgerwood Hessian Transcripts. Morristown National Historical Park, Morristown, N.J.

Rutledge, John. Letter to the South Carolina delegates in Congress, 24 May 1780. John Rutledge Letters, 1780–1782. Charleston Library Society, Charleston, S.C.

———. Letter from Rutledge to unknown officer, 14 April 1780, and letter from unknown officer to Rutledge, 16 May 1780. Robert Wilson Gibbes Collection of Revolutionary War Manuscripts. South Carolina Department of Archives and History, Columbia, S.C.

Timothy, Peter. Journal of Observations from the 26th of March, 1780 to 26th April, 1780. South Carolina Historical Society, Charleston, S.C.

Waudby, W. D. Journal for His Majesty's Ship Raleigh, 9 October 1779 to 8 October 1780. Trustees of the National Maritime Museum, Greenwich, England.

Whipple, Abraham. Letterbook. Manuscripts Collection. Rhode Island Historical Society, Providence, R.I.

Wilson, John. Journal of the Siege of Charlestown by the Corps of British Engineers under the Command of Capt. Moncrief Commencing Feb. 29th and ending May 12th, 1780, When the Town Capitulated. Charleston Library Society, Charleston, S.C.

Newspapers

The Gazette of the State of South Carolina
The South-Carolina and American General Gazette

Published Primary Accounts

Allaire, Anthony. *Diary of Lieut. Anthony Allaire.* New York: New York Times and Arno Press, 1968.

Baldwin, Samuel. "Diary of Events in Charleston, S.C., from March 20th to April 20th, 1780." *Proceedings of the New Jersey Historical Society* 2, no. 2 (1847): 77–86.

"Charleston in 1774 as Described by an English Traveler." Edited by John Bennett. *The South Carolina Historical and Genealogical Magazine* 47, no. 3 (1946): 179–80.

Clinton, Henry. *The American Rebellion: Sir Henry Clinton's Narrative of His Campaigns, 1775–1782, with an Appendix of Original Documents.* Edited by William B. Willcox. New Haven: Yale University Press, 1954.

Continental Congress. *Journals of the Continental Congress, 1774–1789.* Edited by Worthington C. Ford et al. 34 vols. Washington, D.C., 1904–1937.

[de la Morliere, Louis-Antoine Magallan]. "A French Account of the Siege of Charleston." Edited by Richard K. Murdoch. *South Carolina Historical Magazine* 67, no. 3 (1966): 138–54.

Ewald, Johann. *Diary of the American War: A Hessian Journal.* Translated and edited by Joseph P. Tustin. New Haven: Yale University Press, 1979.

"A Frenchman Visits Charleston in 1777." Translated by Elmer Douglas Johnson. *The South Carolina Historical and Genealogical Magazine* 52, no. 2 (1951): 88–92.

Gibbes, R. W., ed. *Documentary History of the American Revolution: Chiefly in South Carolina, 1764–1782.* 3 vols. 1853–1857. Reprint, Spartanburg, S.C.: The Reprint Co., 1972.

Greene, Nathanael. *The Papers of General Nathanael Greene.* 11 vols. to date. Edited by Richard K. Showman and Dennis M. Conrad. Chapel Hill: University of North Carolina Press, 1976–.

Hough, Franklin B. *The Siege of Charleston by the British Fleet and Army under the Command of Admiral Arbuthnot and Sir Henry Clinton Which*

Terminated with the Surrender of the Place on the 12th of May, 1780. Albany: J. Munsell, 1867. Reprint, Spartanburg, S.C.: The Reprint Co., 1975.

———. *The Siege of Savannah By the Combined American and French Forces Under the Command of Gen. Lincoln and the Count D'Estaing in the Autumn of 1779.* 1866. Reprint, New York: Da Capo Press, 1974.

Journals of the General Assembly and House of Representatives, 1776–1780 [of South Carolina]. Edited by William Edwin Hemphill, Wylma Anne Wates, and R. Nicholas Olsberg. Columbia: University of South Carolina Press, 1970.

Keith, George Keith Elphinstone. *The Keith Papers, Selected from the Letters and Papers of Admiral Viscount Keith.* Edited by W. G. Perrin. Publications of the Navy Records Society, vol. 62. London: Navy Records Society, 1927.

Laurens, Henry. *The Papers of Henry Laurens.* 15 vols. to date. Edited by Philip M. Hamer, George C. Rogers Jr., David R. Chesnutt, and C. James Taylor. Columbia: University of South Carolina Press, 1968–.

Lee, Henry. *The Revolutionary War Memoirs of General Henry Lee.* Edited by Robert E. Lee. 1869. Reprint, New York: Da Capo Press, 1998.

McIntosh, Lachlan. "Journal of the Siege of Charlestown, 1780." In *University of Georgia Libraries Miscellanea Publications, No. 7,* edited by Lilla Mills Hawes, 96–122. Athens: University of Georgia Press, 1968.

Moultrie, William. *Memoirs of the American Revolution, So Far As It Related to the States of North and South Carolina, and Georgia.* 2 vols. New York, 1802.

"Original Journals of the Siege of Charleston, S.C. in 1780." *The Magnolia; or, Southern Apalachian* 1, no. 6 (1842): 363–74.

Peebles, John. *John Peebles' American War: The Diary of a Scottish Grenadier, 1776–1782.* Edited by Ira D. Gruber. Mechanicsburg, Pa.: Stackpole Books; Gloucestershire: Sutton Publishing, 1998.

Pinckney, Thomas. "Letters of Thomas Pinckney, 1775–1780." Edited by Jack L. Cross. *South Carolina Historical Magazine* 58, no. 4 (1957): 67–83.

Ramsay, David. *History of the Revolution in South Carolina, from a British Province to an Independent State.* 2 vols. Trenton, N.J., 1785.

———. *David Ramsay, 1749–1815: Selections from His Writings.* Edited by Robert L. Brunhouse. In *Transactions of the American Philosophical Society for Promoting Useful Knowledge,* vol. 55, part 4. Philadelphia: The American Philosophical Society, 1965.

Robertson, Archibald. *Archibald Robertson, Lieutenant-General Royal Engineers: His Diaries and Sketches in America, 1762–1780.* Edited by Harry Miller Lydenburg. New York: New York Public Library, 1930. Reprint, New York: New York Times and Arno Press, 1971.

Russell, Peter. "The Siege of Charleston: Journal of Captain Peter Russell, December 25, 1779 to May 2, 1780." *The American Historical Review* 4, no. 3 (1899): 478–501.

Salley, Alexander S., ed. *Documents Relating to the History of South Carolina during the Revolutionary War.* Columbia: Historical Commission of South Carolina, 1908.

———. *Records of the Regiments of the South Carolina Line in the Revolutionary War.* Compiled by Alexander S. Salley. Edited by Alida Moe. Baltimore: Genealogical Publishing Co., 1977.

Stedman, Charles. *The History of the Origin, Progress, and Termination of the American War.* 2 vols. 1794. Reprint, New York: New York Times and Arno Press, 1969.

Stevens, Benjamin Franklin, ed. *The Campaign in Virginia, 1781: An Exact Reprint of Six Rare Pamphlets on the Clinton-Cornwallis Controversy with Very Numerous Important Unpublished Manuscript Notes by Sir Henry Clinton K.B.* 2 vols. London, 1888.

Taliaferro, Benjamin. *The Orderly Book of Captain Benjamin Taliaferro, 2nd Virginia Detachment, Charleston, South Carolina, 1780.* Edited by Lee A. Wallace. Richmond: Virginia State Library, 1980.

Tarleton, Banastre. *A History of the Campaigns of 1780 and 1781, in the Southern Provinces of North America.* London: T. Cadell, 1787.

Uhlendorf, Bernhard A., trans. and ed. *The Siege of Charleston with an Account of the Province of South Carolina: Diaries and Letters of Hessian Officers from the von Jungkenn Papers in the William L. Clements Library.* University of Michigan Publications on History and Political Science, vol. 12. Ann Arbor: University of Michigan Press, 1938.

von Feilitzsch, Heinrich Carl Philipp and Christian Friedrich Bartholomai. *Diaries of two Ansbach Jaegers.* Translated and edited by Bruce E. Burgoyne. Bowie, Md.: Heritage Books, 1997.

Washington, George. *The Writings of George Washington from the Original Manuscript Sources, 1745–1799.* 39 vols. Edited by John C. Fitzpatrick. Washington, D.C.: United States Government Printing Office, 1931–1944.

Secondary Works

Adams, Natalie P. "'Now a Few Words about the Works . . . Called the Old Royal Work': Phase I Archaeological Investigations at Marion Square, Charleston, South Carolina." Stone Mountain, Ga.: New South Associates, 1998.

Anderson, Fred. *A People's Army: Massachusetts Soldiers and Society in the Seven Years' War.* Chapel Hill: University of North Carolina Press, 1984.

Bearss, Edwin C. "The First Two Fort Moultries: A Structural History." Washington, D.C.: U.S. Department of the Interior, National Park Service, 1968.

Bennett, Charles E., and Donald R. Lennon. *A Quest for Glory: Major General Robert Howe and the American Revolution.* Chapel Hill: University of North Carolina Press, 1991.

Boatner, Mark Mayo. *Encyclopedia of the American Revolution.* New York: David McKay Company, 1966.

Bowler, R. Arthur. *Logistics and the Failure of the British Army in America, 1775–1783.* Princeton: Princeton University Press, 1975.

Bulger, William T. "The British Expedition to Charleston, 1779–1780." Ph.D. diss., University of Michigan, 1957.

Carp, E. Wayne. *To Starve the Army at Pleasure: Continental Army Administration and American Political Culture, 1775–1783.* Chapel Hill: University of North Carolina Press, 1984.

Cavanagh, John Carroll. "American Military Leadership in the Southern Campaign: Benjamin Lincoln." In *The Revolutionary War in the South: Power, Conflict, and Leadership,* edited by W. Robert Higgins, 101–31. Durham, N.C.: Duke University Press, 1979.

———. "The Military Career of Major General Benjamin Lincoln in the War of the American Revolution." Ph.D. diss., Duke University, 1969.

Coker, P. C. *Charleston's Maritime Heritage, 1670–1865.* Charleston: Coker-Craft Press, 1987.

Conway, Stephen. "To Subdue America: British Army Officers and the Conduct of the Revolutionary War." *The William and Mary Quarterly* 43, no. 3 (1986): 381–407.

Curtis, Edward E. *The Organization of the British Army in the American Revolution.* New Haven: Yale University Press, 1926. Reprint, New York: AMS Press, 1969.

Duffy, Christopher. *Fire and Stone: The Science of Fortress Warfare, 1660–1860.* Newton Abbot: David & Charles, 1975.

Dull, Jonathan R. *A Diplomatic History of the American Revolution.* New Haven: Yale University Press, 1985.

Edgar, Walter. *South Carolina: A History.* Columbia: University of South Carolina Press, 1998.

Ferguson, Clyde R. "Carolina and Georgia Patriot and Loyalist Militia in Action, 1778–1783." In *The Southern Experience in the American Revolution,* edited by Jeffrey J. Crow and Larry E. Tise, 174–99. Chapel Hill: University of North Carolina Press, 1978.

Fowler, William M. *Rebels under Sail: The American Navy during the Revolution.* New York: Charles Scribner's Sons, 1976.

Fraser, Walter J. *Charleston! Charleston! The History of a Southern City.* Columbia: University of South Carolina Press, 1989.

———. "Reflections of 'Democracy' in Revolutionary South Carolina? The Composition of Military Organizations and the Attitudes and Relationships of the Officers and Men, 1775–1780." *South Carolina Historical Magazine* 78, no. 3 (1977): 202–12.

Frey, Sylvia. *Water from the Rock: Black Resistance in a Revolutionary Age.* Princeton: Princeton University Press, 1991.

Godbold, E. Stanly Jr., and Robert H. Woody. *Christopher Gadsden and the American Revolution.* Knoxville: University of Tennessee Press, 1982.

Gruber, Ira D. "Britain's Southern Strategy." In *The Revolutionary War in the South: Power, Conflict, and Leadership,* edited by W. Robert Higgins, 205–38. Durham, N.C.: Duke University Press, 1979.

Haw, James. *John and Edward Rutledge of South Carolina.* Athens: University of Georgia Press, 1997.

Higginbotham, Don. *The War of American Independence: Military Attitudes, Policies, and Practice, 1763–1789.* New York: Macmillan, 1971.

Hughes, B. P. *British Smooth-Bore Artillery: The Muzzle Loading Artillery of the 18th and 19th Centuries.* Harrisburg, Pa.: Stackpole Books, 1969.

Johnson, Joseph. *Traditions and Reminiscences Chiefly of the American Revolution in the South: Including Biographical Sketches, Incidents and Anecdotes, Few of Which Have Been Published, Particularly of Residents in the Upper Country.* Charleston: Walker and James, 1851.

Katcher, Philip R. N. *Encyclopedia of British, Provincial, and German Army Units, 1775–1783.* Harrisburg, Pa.: Stackpole Books, 1973.

Kierner, Cynthia A. *Southern Women in Revolution, 1776–1800: Personal and Political Narratives.* Columbia: University of South Carolina Press, 1998.

Klein, Rachel. "Frontier Planters and the American Revolution: The South Carolina Backcountry, 1775–1782." In *An Uncivil War: The Southern Backcountry during the American Revolution,* edited by Ronald Hoffman, Thad W. Tate and Peter J. Albert, 37–69. Charlottesville: University Press of Virginia, 1985.

Lesser, Charles H. *The Sinews of Independence: Monthly Strength Reports of the Continental Army.* Chicago: University of Chicago Press, 1976.

Mackesy, Piers. *The War for America, 1775–1783.* Lincoln: University of Nebraska Press, 1964.

Martin, James Kirby, and Mark Edward Lender. *A Respectable Army: The Military Origins of the Republic, 1763–1789.* Arlington Heights, Ill.: Harland Davidson, 1982.

Massey, Gregory D. *John Laurens and the American Revolution.* Columbia: University of South Carolina Press, 2000.

———. "A Hero's Life: John Laurens and the American Revolution." Ph.D. diss., University of South Carolina, 1992.

Mattern, David B. *Benjamin Lincoln and the American Revolution.* Columbia: University of South Carolina Press, 1995.

McCowen, George Smith. *The British Occupation of Charleston, 1780–82.* Columbia: University of South Carolina Press, 1972.

McCrady, Edward. *The History of South Carolina in the Revolution, 1775–1780.* New York: Macmillan, 1901.

Miller, Nathan. *Sea of Glory: A Naval History of the American Revolution.* Annapolis, Md.: Naval Institute Press, 1974.

Nadelhaft, Jerome J. *The Disorders of War: The Revolution in South Carolina.* Orono: University of Maine at Orono Press, 1981.

Pancake, John S. *1777: The Year of the Hangman.* Tuscaloosa: University of Alabama Press, 1977.

———. *This Destructive War: The British Campaign in the Carolinas, 1780–1782.* Tuscaloosa: University of Alabama Press, 1985.

Papenfuse, Edward C., and Gregory A. Stiverson. "General Smallwood's Recruits: The Peacetime Career of the Revolutionary War Private." *The William and Mary Quarterly* 30, no. 1 (1973): 117–32.

Peterson, Harold L. *Round Shot and Rammers.* Harrisburg, Pa.: Stackpole Books, 1969.

Rankin, Hugh F. *Francis Marion: The Swamp Fox.* New York: Thomas Y. Crowell Company, 1973.

———. *The North Carolina Continentals.* Chapel Hill: University of North Carolina Press, 1971.

Risch, Erna. *Supplying Washington's Army.* Washington, D.C.: Center of Military History, United States Army, 1986.

Rogers, George C. *Charleston in the Age of the Pinckneys.* Norman: University of Oklahoma Press, 1969. Reprint, Columbia: University of South Carolina Press, 1980.

Rogers, H. C. B. *The British Army of the Eighteenth Century.* New York: Hippocrene Books, 1977.

Royster, Charles. *A Revolutionary People at War: The Continental Army and American Character, 1775–1783.* New York: W. W. Norton, 1979.

Sellers, John R. "The Common Soldier in the American Revolution." In *Military History of the American Revolution: The Proceedings of the Sixth Military History Symposium, USAF Academy,* edited by Stanley J. Underdal, 151–61. Washington, D.C.: United States Air Force, 1976.

Shy, John. "British Strategy for Pacifying the Southern Colonies, 1778–1781." In *The Southern Experience in the American Revolution,* edited by Jeffrey J. Crow and Larry E. Tise, 155–73. Chapel Hill: University of North Carolina Press, 1978.

[Simms, William Gilmore]. *South-Carolina in the Revolutionary War: Being a Reply to Certain Misrepresentations and Mistakes of Recent Writers, in Relation to the Course and Conduct of This State.* Charleston: Walker and James, 1853.

Smith, Paul H. *Loyalists and Redcoats: A Study in British Revolutionary Policy.* Chapel Hill: University of North Carolina Press, 1964.

Tilley, John A. *The British Navy and the American Revolution.* Columbia: University of South Carolina Press, 1987.

Ward, Christopher. *The War of the Revolution.* 2 vols. New York: Macmillan, 1952.

Weir, Robert M. *"A Most Important Epocha": The Coming of the Revolution in South Carolina.* Columbia: University of South Carolina Press, 1970.

———. *Colonial South Carolina: A History.* Millwood, N.Y.: KTO Press, 1983.

Weller, Jac. "Revolutionary War Artillery in the South." *Georgia Historical Quarterly* 46, nos. 3 and 4 (1962): 250–73 and 377–87.

Willcox, William B. *Portrait of a General: Sir Henry Clinton in the War of Independence.* New York: Alfred A. Knopf, 1964.

Wright, John W. "Notes on the Siege of Yorktown in 1781 with Special Reference to the Conduct of a Siege in the Eighteenth Century." *William and Mary College Quarterly Historical Magazine* 12, no. 4 (1932): 229–49.

———. *Some Notes on the Continental Army.* New Windsor Cantonment Publication No. 2. Cornwallville, N.Y.: Hope Farm Press, 1963.

Wright, Robert K. *The Continental Army.* Washington, D.C.: Center of Military History, United States Army, 1983.

Index